In the name of God, the Compass

Sayyid Quṭb

❧

IN THE SHADE OF
THE QUR'ĀN

Fī Ẓilāl al-Qur'ān

VOLUME V

❧

SŪRAH 6

Al-An'ām

———— ❧ ————

Translated and Edited by
Adil Salahi

———— ❧ ————

THE ISLAMIC FOUNDATION
AND
ISLAMONLINE.NET

Published by

THE ISLAMIC FOUNDATION

Markfield Conference Centre,
Ratby Lane, Markfield, Leicestershire LE67 9SY, United Kingdom
Tel: (01530) 244944, Fax: (01530) 244946
E-mail: i.foundation@islamic-foundation.org.uk
Website: www.islamic-foundation.org.uk

Quran House, PO Box 30611, Nairobi, Kenya

PMB 3193, Kano, Nigeria

ISLAMONLINE.NET,
PO Box 22212, Doha, Qatar
E-mail: webmaster@islam-online.net
Website: www.islamonline.net

British Library Cataloguing-in-Publication Data
Qutb, Sayyid, 1903–1966
    In the shade of the Qur'an: fi zilal al-Qur'an,
    Vol. 5: Surah 6: Al-An'am. translated and edited by Adil
    Salahi
    1. Koran
    I. Title
    II. Salahi, Adil
    III. Islamic Foundation
    297.1'227

ISBN 0–86037–302–9
ISBN 0–86037–307–X pbk

Typeset by: N.A.Qaddoura
Cover design by: Imtiaze A. Manjra

Printed in Great Britain by Antony Rowe Ltd, Chippenham, Wiltshire

Contents

Transliteration Table

Consonants. Arabic

initial: unexpressed medial and final:

ء	'		د	d		ض	ḍ		ك	k
ب	b		ذ	dh		ط	ṭ		ل	l
ت	t		ر	r		ظ	ẓ		م	m
ث	th		ز	z		ع	'		ن	n
ج	j		س	s		غ	gh		هـ	h
ح	ḥ		ش	sh		ف	f		و	w
خ	kh		ص	ṣ		ق	q		ي	y

Vowels, diphthongs, etc.

Short: ﹷ a   ﹻ i   ﹹ u

long: ﹷـا ā   ﹹـو ū   ﹻـي ī

diphthongs: ﹷـوْ aw

               ﹷـىْ ay

The Author's Method of Writing

Introduction by Adil Salahi

A number of contemporary scholars well versed in the discipline of *Tafsīr*, or Qur'ānic commentary, describe *In the Shade of the Qur'ān* as a 'literary' commentary. Whether this is a description of praise or otherwise depends on the person using it. Some of us may be reluctant to move away from traditional commentary works and do not see the need for a new approach that makes the treasures of the Qur'ān accessible to the modern reader. But no scholar of merit has ever questioned the high standing this book occupies in Qur'ānic scholarship in general, not merely in the twentieth century. But how true is it to say that this book is a literary commentary; and what would the author have felt should he have heard this description?

That the author was a literary figure, there is no doubt. Early in his career, he wrote a couple of novels, literary essays, and poetry of high merit. He was also a full participant in some of the disputes that engaged the literary circles of Egypt to the full in the second quarter of the twentieth century. He was the author of a book on literary criticism considered among the best in the Arabic language to appear during that same period. Moreover, his book on Qur'ānic imagery, *al-Taṣwīr al-Fannī fī al-Qur'ān* (published 1935) provides a complete theory of Qur'ānic literary excellence, which he later developed in a book on the scenes of the Day of Resurrection portrayed in the Qur'ān, *Mashāhid al-Qiyāmah fī al-Qur'ān* (published 1945). This shows that the author's literary approach was the path he followed long before he embarked on writing his first articles that later developed into this voluminous work, as we explained in the Introduction to Volume III.

However I do not think that the author would have been flattered to read that *In the Shade of the Qur'ān* is a literary commentary on the

Divine book. At no time does the author stop to point out the literary aspects of a certain mode of expression, except where this would support the point of discussion, which is always the meaning imparted, the directive issued, the legislation enacted, the principle laid down, etc. Thus, the literary aspect is always a secondary issue which is used when helpful to the main purpose. Indeed, in some of his later writings the author decries any attempt to study the Qur'ān from any angle other than that of faith: it is a message from God, and it must be approached in that sense. This means that we must understand it in order to implement it. When we approach the Qur'ān in this way, we will find that it gives us all the intellectual, literary, scientific and other treasures it contains. This is the point he was keen to develop both in this book and in *Milestones*, his last work.

Nevertheless, no one who reads *In the Shade of the Qur'ān* fails to appreciate its literary merit. The author's style ranks among the finest in the Arabic language. But the author's literary prowess is not at issue here. A writer could be of exceptional scientific talent, but this does not make his writing scientific unless he adopts a scientific approach in his treatment of his subject matter. Hence, we can say very clearly that at no time does the author attempt to provide a literary study of the Qur'ān in his commentary. Had he chosen to do so, he would have come up with a study of great merit. But what he has given us is far more valuable, one in which the literary aspect is interwoven, but not the main focus.

Two factors combine to give *In the Shade of the Qur'ān* its distinctive position among Qur'ānic studies. The first is the author's standpoint in his approach to the Qur'ān and the themes it discusses. Other authors have written extensively about the Qur'ān, its style, literary supremacy, scientific truth, historical accounts, wide-ranging appeal, etc. Each might have made an exceptional achievement in the area chosen for study. But Sayyid Quṭb takes a different stand. He considers the Qur'ān first and foremost a message addressed to mankind, utilising every element that appeals to human nature and influences human thinking. The author of the Qur'ān, God Almighty, is fully aware of everything that may have a bearing on the human heart, mind and soul, and what influence may be brought to bear on human nature to ensure its positive response. In this light, every minute detail is of significance, and must be given its full consideration when we study the Qur'ān. Hence, we find *In the Shade of the Qur'ān* highlighting certain points which are rarely given importance in earlier commentaries. These may be, in the Qur'ānic text, supplementary to the main point under discussion, but they have, nevertheless, an important role to play in maintaining the Qur'ān's appeal to human nature. By the same token, we find them highlighted by Sayyid Quṭb to give us an insight into the Qur'ānic style we can hardly find elsewhere.

The second factor is the author's personal way of studying his subject matter. *In the Shade of the Qur'ān* appeared in Arabic in 30 volumes, each dealing with what is known as *juz'*, or part of the Qur'ān. But these parts had no more significance than markings which divided the Qur'ān into 30 parts of equal length. A person who reads one *juz'* a day will complete the Qur'ān once a month which keeps him or her familiar with the Qur'ān throughout their lives. Each such part of the Qur'ān takes about half an hour to recite.

When Sayyid Quṭb embarked on writing his commentary on a *juz'* of the Qur'ān, he did not start with the traditional research method, looking for material, reading other authors and commentators, researching any scientific aspect the Qur'ān touches upon in that particular part. He did nothing of this. He concentrated on gathering the import of the Qur'ānic address as it appeals to human nature in that particular part. Therefore, he spent a whole month reading nothing other than that particular part of the Qur'ān. He could read it two, three or four times every day, or even more, or he could concentrate on a short passage of it, a page, or even a particular verse. This was a deliberate effort to live in the atmosphere that part of the Qur'ān generates. There was no rigidity in this approach. The month devoted to this task could be a few days longer or shorter as the task required. The important thing was that the author should be satisfied that he had gathered the message of that part in its entirety and identified its points of appeal to human nature in addition to having fully grasped its subject matter.

What is important in this particular method is the fact that the Qur'ān gives us its finer touches on careful and repeated readings. Thus, we may on occasion find that a verse which we have read hundreds, if not thousands, of times suddenly giving us a meaning that had remained unnoticed by us for so many years. What brings this meaning to the front is a host of factors, such as proper concentration, clarity of mind, repeated and careful reading, as well as external elements that may not be immediately relevant to the point under study. This is why so many students of the Qur'ān have spoken about its glittering meanings, describing it as a diamond that gives a new brightness when light is directed on it from a new angle. Once you see such fresh glitter shining out of a particular verse, you will not fail to see it in future whenever you read that verse with your mind attentive to what you are reciting.

In this month of personal study of the part of the Qur'ān he was to write on, Sayyid Quṭb tried to capture all such glittering meanings. And, to a large extent, he succeeded.

When he was satisfied with his own reading of the part to be commented on, and felt that he had the necessary experience to 'live in its shade' as he preferred to call this experience, Sayyid Quṭb would read earlier commentaries on the same part. He would refer to the most reliable ones, like those of al-Ṭabarī and Ibn Kathīr, both of which were written several centuries ago, and to more recent ones as well. He would also read on any subject that may be relevant to any verse in that part. The object of his readings would be two-fold. The first to make sure that his understanding of the part under discussion encompassed all details in Islamic law that branch out of that part of the Qur'ān, and that his understanding was in line with the Prophet's statements relevant to any verse or *sūrah* under discussion. The second was to support his views with any scholarly argument, be it legal, social, scientific, or philosophical.

An example that illustrates fully Sayyid Quṭb's method is his commentary on Verse 59 in the *sūrah* discussed in this volume. The verse, which is discussed fully in Chapter 8, is translated as follows: "*With Him are the keys to what lies beyond the reach of human perception: none knows them but He. He knows all that the land and sea contain; not a leaf falls but He knows it; and neither is there a grain in the earth's deep darkness, nor anything fresh or dry but is recorded in a clear book.*" We find the author dwells at length on the major areas that are touched upon in a word or two in this verse, and paints for us a panoramic view of the great world which these touches bring before our eyes. He sees in them evidence that this book, the Qur'ān, could never have been conceived or authored by a human being, for no human being would have ever thought to support his argument in the way this verse does. The author quotes from Western scientists in different fields. His quotations are very selective. He is not after supporting evidence for the truth of God's creation, but rather he finds in their writings what confirms the magnificence of the Qur'ānic references, made more than 1300 years before any such scientific confirmation of their truth was ready to hand.

Long as his discussion of this verse is, we are captivated by the depth of his insight and the power of his presentation. Here we see a unique aspect of Sayyid Quṭb's excellence. He is more at home when commenting on the Qur'ān than in his other Islamic writings. The Qur'ān gives him the platform to cast a cosmic view on life, man and the universe. Thus, his profound faith in God's message is reflected to the full. And he is at his best when he brings his literary power and his broad knowledge into interaction with the Qur'ānic statements.

Another aspect of Sayyid Quṭb's method of preparing his commentary is the care he takes to explain the conditions, circumstances or practices to which the Qur'ān refers. Thus, when the present *surah* speaks about the practices of the Arabs in pre-Islamic days with regard to the animals they slaughtered and the offerings they made to their idols in cattle, agricultural produce or children, he relies on information provided by earlier commentators. This enables the reader to gain all the information he would have received from referring to such early commentaries, as well as the understanding of Sayyid Quṭb, based on his profound knowledge. What is more, all this is expressed in a beautiful style, which combines power with finesse, yet still remains easy to read.

This volume provides perhaps the clearest example that demonstrates the special merits of *In the Shade of the Qur'ān*. The author looks at the *surah* in totality and finds a unity of theme that permeates every page and every verse. At the same time, the *surah* deals with two major issues: faith and law. He shows most clearly how the whole *surah* in its two parts maintains its unity and brings out, by the style it adopts and the vocabulary it uses, a marked complementarity between the two, making them equally important in the life of the Muslim community and every individual Muslim.

Perhaps the method the author has adopted in preparing his subject is at the heart of the excellence of this priceless work. Had he adopted the opposite approach of finding out first what had been written on each part and then relied on his own reading, we would perhaps have had a totally different commentary. As it is, Qur'ānic scholarship is much richer for his efforts. May God reward him as He rewards His best servants.

London   **Adil Salahi**
Jumādā al-Ākhirah 1422 AH
September 2001

SŪRAH 6

Al-An 'ām
(Cattle)

Prologue

This *sūrah* belongs to the part of the Qur'ān revealed to the Prophet when he was in Makkah. Although this part of the Qur'ān was revealed to the Prophet (peace be upon him) over a period of thirteen years, it deals with only one question. The nature of this question did not change, although the manner of its presentation varied according to the style of the Qur'ān. We, therefore, see this question being constantly presented in a new light, just as if it were being raised for the first time. What is this primary and most fundamental question of this new religion? Essentially, it is the question of faith with its two main aspects, Godhead and His servants, and the relationship between them. It is addressed to every human being in that particular capacity, i.e. as a human being. In this respect, an Arab at the time of the revelation of the Qur'ān, or in any other subsequent generation, and a non-Arab of any generation, are equal.

This is the ever-present question with which man must deal; it is the question of man's existence in the universe, his ultimate goal, and his relationship with the universe and other creatures. More importantly, it is the question which deals with the relationship between man and the Creator of the universe and all creation. We say that this question does not change, because it relates to man's very being.

The part of the Qur'ān revealed in Makkah explains to man the secret of his existence and the secret of the universe surrounding him. It tells him who he is, where he has come from, for what purpose and where he will go in the end. Who brings him from non-existence into

1

being, who takes him away and to what destiny? It also informs man about the nature of the things he can touch and see and the things which he can sense and conceive without being able to see. It answers his questions concerning the Originator of this universe, which is full of mysteries: Who controls it and who brings about changes? Similarly, this part of the Qur'ān tells man how to relate to the Creator, to the physical world, and to other human beings.

This great question is the pivot around which human existence turns. It will continue to occupy this position for the rest of time. The full thirteen years of the Makkan period were devoted to explaining and expounding this fundamental question. Indeed, all other questions concerning human life may be said to stem from it.

The Qur'ān made this question its only subject without moving on to discuss any subsidiary topics concerning human life. This continued to be the case until God had decided that the fundamental issue of faith had been fully explained and correctly understood by the community chosen by Him to establish the Islamic faith in a practical human environment.

The advocates of the divine faith who work for the establishment of Islam in real life should carefully consider this most significant fact. They should reflect on the reasons for devoting thirteen full years to the expounding of the central issue of faith, without discussing any of the details of the Islamic system or the legislation to be implemented in an Islamic society.

In His infinite wisdom, God willed that the issue of faith and belief should be the one addressed by His message right from its very first day. He also willed that His Messenger (peace be upon him) should start his first advocacy steps by calling on people to believe that there is no deity other than God. He was also to devote all efforts to explaining to people who their true Lord is, so that they may submit themselves to Him alone.

From the viewpoint of man's limited understanding, this does not appear an easy way to reach the hearts of the Arabs at that time. The Arabs knew their language well and clearly understood the meaning of the term, *ilāh*, i.e. deity, and the phrase, *lā ilāh illā Allāh*, i.e. there is no deity other than God. They realized that Godhead signified sovereignty, and that when sovereignty was recognized to belong to God alone, this meant that all authority exercised by priests, tribal chiefs, and rulers would revert to God. Thus, only God's authority would prevail in people's hearts and consciences, in matters of both religious observance and practical life, such as business, the distribution of wealth and the dispensation of justice; in short, the authority over man's body and soul.

The Arabs at the time of the Prophet knew very well that the declaration that 'there is no deity other than God' was a challenge to the worldly authority that usurped the first and foremost attribute of God, namely, sovereignty. It was a rebellion against all situations established on the basis of such usurpation, a rebellion against any authority that ruled on the basis of a man-made law not sanctioned by God Almighty. The Arabs, who knew their language well, were well aware what the message based on 'there is no deity other than God' meant in relation to their traditions and the powers they exercised. Hence their hostility towards this message, and hence their war against it, determined as they were to nip it in the bud.

So why did the Islamic call begin in this manner? What was the divine wisdom behind allowing it to be faced with such brazen hostility?

A Call for Freedom?

When the Prophet Muḥammad (peace be upon him) was given his message, the most fertile and wealthiest parts of the Arab lands were not in Arab hands. Syria, in the north, was under the control of the Byzantines who appointed puppet Arab rulers to conduct its affairs. Similarly, in the south, Yemen was under the tutelage of the Persian Empire who appointed local Arab governors. The only independent Arab parts were the Ḥijāz and Najd, barren deserts with a few oases dotted about here and there.

Muḥammad (peace be upon him) was distinguished in his community for his honesty and truthfulness, and for his mature judgement. The leaders of the Quraysh, the major Arab tribe, had earlier made him the arbiter in a dispute that threatened to cause a major war, and were very pleased with his judgement. Moreover, he belonged to the leading family in the top Quraysh clan, the Hashimites. Hence, it would have been easy for him to launch an Arab nationalist movement aimed at uniting the Arabian tribes that had been weakened by long periods of feuding and disputation. He could then have directed them towards the goal of liberating their lands from the colonial rule of the Byzantines to the north and the Persians to the south. He could then have been in a position to establish a strong and united Arab state throughout the Arabian Peninsula.

It could be argued that had the Prophet (peace be upon him) directed his call in this way, all the Arabs would most probably have responded positively to him. In turn, this would have spared him thirteen years of tortuous opposition by those who wielded power in Arabia.

It may also be argued that when Arabia had thus responded to the Prophet's call and recognized his leadership, and when he had led the Arabs to such national glory, he could have used all his power and standing to convince the Arabs to accept the message entrusted to him by his Lord. He could then have preached the faith based on God's oneness. He would have made the Arabs surrender themselves to God after they had submitted to his authority.

But God who knows all did not, in His wisdom, direct his Messenger to follow this route. Instead, He directed him to declare that "there is no deity other than God", and to bear with his few Companions all the ensuing persecution.

Again why did this happen? It was not God's purpose to subject His Messenger and the believers to oppression. But God knew that replacing Byzantine or Persian tyranny with Arab tyranny was not the right way. For all tyranny is the same. The earth belongs to God and must submit purely to God. This cannot be achieved unless the banner of 'no deity other than God' is unfurled across the earth. Man is servant to God alone, and this cannot be maintained except when the banner of 'no deity other than God' is raised high. And this must be done in the way an Arab who knows his language well understands: all sovereignty belongs to God alone; there is no law other than God's law; all authority belongs to God. The only grouping of people which Islam proclaims is based on faith, in which Arabs, Byzantines, Persians and people of all races and colours are equal, flying God's banner.

And this is the way.

A Call for Social Justice?

At the time when the Prophet received the message God entrusted to him, Arabian society was in a very bad way with regard to the distribution of wealth and social justice. A handful of people monopolized all wealth and commerce. Moreover, they were able to multiply their resources through usurious transactions. The great majority of people, on the other hand, were poor and hungry. Besides, the wealthy ones also enjoyed a position of honour and distinction, while the majority were deprived of all that.

It would have been easy for Muḥammad (peace be upon him) to start a social movement, declaring war against the aristocracy, and calling for social justice through the redistribution of wealth. Had he done so, Arab society would have been split into two: the great majority would have supported him against the tyranny of wealth and nobility. This would have been better than the opposition he faced from the whole of society when he declared that 'there is no deity other than God'. For when he did so, only a few noble souls were able to rise to the sublimity of his call.

It may be said that had Muḥammad (peace be upon him) followed this route, gaining the support of the majority and defeating the minority opposing him, he could have utilized his power to establish the faith based on God's oneness which God had entrusted to him. He would, thus, have been able to make people submit to their Lord after they had submitted to his authority.

But God, in His infinite wisdom, did not direct His Messenger to follow this path. God knows that this is not the way. He knows that social justice can only be achieved fully through a comprehensive ideological concept that submits all affairs to God. With such a concept people would willingly accept whatever God rules in respect of fair distribution and mutual social solidarity. Thus, both the giver and the recipient realize that they are implementing a divine system and hope to be well rewarded for their obedience both in this life and in the life to come. Thus, such a society would be free of both greed and grudges. Things are not put into effect by strong-handed measures that strike terror into people's hearts. People do not feel desolate, and their spirits are not broken, as is the case under systems based on principles other than that of God's oneness.

Why Not Moral Reform?

The standards of morality that prevailed in Arabia at the time when the Prophet was given his message were at a very low ebb, even though some natural virtues of uncorrupted Bedouin life were still retained.

Oppression was the rule of the day. This is especially clear in the poetry of the time, such as that of Zuhayr ibn Abī Sulmā who writes: "Whoever does not defend his property with arms will find it plundered, and whoever does not oppress others will himself be oppressed." A motto that was commonly held in pre-Islamic Arabia was: "Help your brother, whether he inflicts or suffers injustice."

Drinking and gambling were recognized social traditions. Indeed, people took pride in such habits. All Arab poetry of the pre-Islamic days of ignorance reflects this very clearly. An example may be taken from a poem by Ṭarfah ibn al-'Abd:

> Had it not been for three practices a young man enjoys, I would not have cared when I meet my death.
>
> One of these is that I beat those who counsel moderation to a drink of wine which is so potent that it bubbles when it is mixed with water.
>
> Drinking, the pursuit of pleasure and spending whatever I lay my hands on have been my life.
>
> And because of that my whole clan has abandoned me, like a camel with a terrible itch.

Promiscuity in various forms was common practice in society. 'Ā'ishah, the Prophet's wife, describes in an authentic *ḥadīth*:

> Four types of matrimonial relationship were common in the days of *jāhiliyyah*.[1] The first of these was the one we have today: a man makes a proposal to marry another man's daughter or his ward, pays her dowry, and marries her. A second type was that a man would tell his wife, after she had finished a menstrual period, to call on a particular man and become pregnant by him. The husband in this case would stay away from his wife and would

---

1. *Jāhiliyyah* is the term often used in the Islamic context to refer to the situation that prevailed in Arabia before the advent of Islam. It is derived from a root that signifies 'ignorance'. Thus, when we speak of the days of *jāhiliyyah*, we mean the days of ignorance. But the term does not simply signify a period of time, rather it refers to a state or condition where people are unaware of the true nature of God and their relationship with Him. In this perspective, the term refers to any human situation that does not place belief in God's oneness as its prime concept, and which should be reflected in people's behaviour, literature, morality as well as their social, economic and political systems. – Editor's note.

not touch her until she was clearly pregnant. He would then have intercourse with her if he so wished. The husband resorted to this in order to have a son of better traits. This relationship was known as *istibḍāʿ*. Another type of relationship was that a number of men, less than 10, would have one woman and each would have sexual intercourse with her. Should she become pregnant and give birth to a child, she would send for them after a few nights to come over. None of them would be able to stay away. When they gathered at her place, she would say to them, "You know what has been going on between us, and now I have a child". She would point to one of them and say, "It is your child". She named whomever she wanted, and the child would be named as that person's child, and he could not deny this. A fourth type of relationship was that many men would associate with the one woman, who would not refuse anyone. Such women were prostitutes. They used to place a flag on their doors as a sign of what they did. Whoever wanted a prostitute was free to go to her. Should any prostitute get pregnant and give birth, they would go to her and call in an expert in recognizing resemblances. He would ascribe the child's paternity to one of them, and the child would be considered his. He would not refuse this. (Related by al-Bukhārī in the *Ṣaḥīḥ,* Book of Marriage.)

It was certainly possible for Muḥammad, (peace be upon him) to have started a movement for moral reform, aiming at purging society of immorality, helping people to purify their lives, and establishing higher moral values and standards. Like every moral reformer, he would have found a good response from people naturally inclined against moral degeneration. They would have supported such a move from the outset.

But God, in His wisdom and perfect knowledge, did not direct His Messenger to follow this route, because God knew that this was not the right way. God knows that morality must be based on a faith that establishes standards and defines values, making clear which authority sanctions these and what reward and punishment such authority can administer to those who observe these and those who violate them. Unless such a faith is well established, all values and moral standards remain unstable, without accountability, control, authority or reward.

Results in Abundance

When, after strenuous efforts, the faith was established in people's hearts and the authority behind it was properly acknowledged; when people recognized their Lord and worshipped Him alone; when people were free of the pressures of other authorities and the pressures of their own desires; when the concept of 'no deity other than God' was imprinted on people's hearts, God accomplished with it, and with those who believed in it, all that people might have suggested in the way of reform.

The land was now free of Byzantium and Persia, but their colonial rule had not been replaced by an Arab power. Instead God's authority took their place. The land was now free of all tyranny.

Society was freed of all social injustice, because the Islamic system was established to administer God's justice, according to the principles approved by God Himself. The banner of social justice was raised in God's name, but it was called the banner of Islam, on which was written, 'there is no deity other than God'.

People's morals were elevated; hearts and souls were purified; and the medium of control was people's own consciences. Hence, the mandatory and discretionary punishments prescribed by God were not needed, except in very few cases. People were eager to earn God's reward. They were ashamed to be seen by Him violating His orders, feared to incur His punishment. Such feelings took the place of any police administration and the various punishments it could impose.

In its social order, morality and life in general, humanity was raised to a summit it had never achieved before. It was not to attain that summit again except under Islam.

All this happened because those who established Islam, in its state, government system, laws and regulations, had already established it in their consciences and lives in the form of faith, morality, worship and behaviour. For their efforts in establishing this religion, they were promised only one thing which included nothing of victory and power, not even for Islam through their efforts. The promise they received had nothing to do with the life of this world. They were promised Paradise. That is their reward for all their hard striving, withstanding hard trials, unwavering advocacy of Islam, confronting the forces of *jāhiliyyah* with the message of 'no deity other than God', hateful as it certainly is to those in power at all times and places.

God put those people to trial and they proved themselves to be steadfast, caring little for any personal gain. They showed themselves not to be looking for reward in this world, no matter how valuable it may be, not even victory for Islam through their own efforts. They were devoid of pride of lineage, tribe, ethnic origin, nationality or country. When they proved all this, God knew that they could fulfil the greatest trust, should it be assigned to them. They would be true to the faith which assigns all sovereignty to God alone, including authority over hearts and consciences, behaviour and worship, body and soul, and all situations. They would fulfil the trust granted to them when they were given power to implement God's law and establish total justice. They would not use such power to serve their own interests or those of their clan, community, nation or race. They would use that power only to serve the divine faith and the divine law, because they knew that only God gave them that power.

This blessed system would not have been established to such a high standard, had the work of Islamic advocacy raised any banner other than that of 'no deity other than God'. It could not have prospered without taking this way, rough and difficult as it may appear at first glance, easy and blessed in reality. Had the Islamic message started its initial stages as a nationalist movement, or one of social or moral reform, or had it raised another banner alongside that of 'there is no deity other than God', its system would not have remained pure for the sake of God alone.

The Faith or Its Detailed Systems

We now have a clear idea of the reasons behind the fact that the parts of the Qur'ān revealed in Makkah concentrated on imprinting the fundamental principle of 'there is no deity other than God' on people's hearts and minds, even though it appeared difficult in comparison to other ways.

Moreover, it was important that the advocates of Islam should seriously reflect on the fact that these Makkan parts of the Qur'ān concentrated on the issue of faith, without discussing the details of the system to be based on it or the laws governing transactions under this system.

It is the nature of the Islamic faith that has necessitated this approach. Islam in its entirety is based on the belief in God's oneness: all its systems and laws branch out of this essential principle. A high, great

9

tree, with thick and wide branches, must establish its roots deep into the earth and spread them over a wide area, in proportion to its size. Similarly, the Islamic system extends into all aspects of life, dealing with all human affairs, large and small. It regulates human life, not only in this present world but also in the life to come, and not merely in our dealings with the world we see around us, but with the one beyond, which we sense but cannot see. Its legal provisions do not cover only material transactions, but deal also with what is kept deep at heart, as well as intentions and ideas. Thus, we see that it represents a huge institution with great and far-reaching dimensions.

This aspect of the nature of Islam defines the way it is to be founded and organized. It makes it clear that the proper establishment of the faith on solid foundations and its thorough interaction with all aspects of the human soul are a necessary prerequisite for the proper progress of the faith. It is also a guarantee of a proper relationship between the stem and branches of the tree and its roots.

When belief in 'there is no deity other than God' penetrates into the deep recesses of people's hearts, the system based on it is simultaneously well established. It is clear that it is the only system acceptable to those who believe in this faith. They will submit to this system even before its details and regulations are presented to them. Such submission is the corollary of accepting the faith. It is in the spirit of such submission that the early Muslims received Islamic laws and regulations. They expressed their satisfaction, objecting to no rule or regulation, showing no hesitation to implement them as soon as they were issued. Thus, the practices of drinking, usury and gambling, as well as other habits of the pre-Islamic days of ignorance, were abolished. Indeed, they were eradicated with no more than a few verses of the Qur'ān, or a few statements by the Prophet (peace be upon him). Compare this with the efforts of secular governments. They try hard to achieve only a small measure of such success, devoting all their legal authorities, laws and law-enforcement machinery, media and public awareness schemes to it. Yet the maximum they achieve is to detect violations done on the surface, while society continues to be plagued with illegal practices.[2]

---

2. For details of how the prohibition of intoxicants was implemented in Islamic society see *In the Shade of the Qur'ān*, Vol. IV, pp. 243–50. Refer also to Abu'l Ḥasan 'Alī Nadwī, *Islam and the World*, for a discussion of how the USA has miserably failed to do so – Author's note.

A Practical System

Another aspect of the nature of this religion is reflected by the method of action it adopts: this religion of Islam is both practical and serious, aiming to regulate and control everyday affairs. It looks at practical matters and determines whether to approve, modify or change them altogether. Therefore, its legislation applies only to existing conditions in a community that recognizes God's sovereignty in the first place.

Islam is not a theory dealing with assumptions. It is a way of life dealing with existing situations. Hence, it must be established in a Muslim community which believes that 'there is no deity other than God', and acknowledges that sovereignty belongs to God alone. It denies the authority of anyone else and refuses legitimacy of any situation that is not based on this fundamental principle.

Only when such a community comes into existence, and it begins to face its own practical problems does this religion begin to establish its systems and formulate its laws. These will be implemented by people who in principle have already submitted themselves to them and rejected all other systems and laws. It is also necessary that those who believe in the Islamic faith should have sufficient power over themselves and in their society to enable them to implement Islamic systems and laws. Only in this way can the Islamic system be respected and Islamic law appear serious. Moreover, the Muslim community will then have practical issues that need to be addressed by the enactment of laws and regulations.

The Muslims in Makkah did not have power to organize their life or the life of their community. Nor did they have an autonomous community with its own problems that needed to be addressed according to God's law. Hence, laws and regulations were not given to them in God's revelations. The revelations only gave them a faith and a code of morality derived from faith after it had established itself firmly in people's hearts and souls. But when the Muslims established their state in Madinah, one which exercised power, the laws were given to them and the system to establish them was outlined. Thus Islam began to face the practical needs of the Muslim community, because the Muslim state guaranteed respect and implementation of the law.

God Almighty did not wish to send down the details of the system and the laws and regulations when they were still in Makkah, so that they would have them in place, to be implemented as soon as they established their state in Madinah. This would have gone against the nature of the Islamic faith. Islam is far more practical and serious than this. It does not provide hypothetical solutions to hypothetical problems. It looks at the prevailing conditions and circumstances, determines what needs sorting out and interacts with it in its own unique way.

People today may suggest that Islam should provide models for a political system and legal codes and regulations, even though we do not have a single society determined to implement God's law to the exclusion of all other laws and having the wherewithal to carry this through. But these people do not understand the nature of this religion or how it operates in life as God wants it to operate. They want Islam to change its nature, mode of operation and history so that it follows the same pattern as man-made theories and methods. They try to force Islam out of its way in order to satisfy temporary desires which are the product of a defeatist mentality. They want Islam to mould itself in the form of hypotheses and abstractions, dealing with unreal assumptions. But God wants this religion to have its own character: a faith to fill people's hearts and rule over their consciences, making sure that people submit to no one other than Him, and that they derive their laws from no other source than Him. When a community that adopts this faith comes into being and enjoys practical control in society, they will have the laws and regulations that cater for their practical needs.

It must be clear to the advocates of Islam that when they call for Islamic revival, they are actually calling on people to adopt the Islamic faith, even though they may claim to be Muslims and have birth certificates to support this claim. People should be made to understand that Islam means, in the first place, to believe fully and completely that 'there is no deity other than God'. The practical import of this belief is to acknowledge that sovereignty and authority over all human affairs belongs to God alone, and a rejection of those who claim such authority for themselves. In this way the belief in God's oneness is firmly established in their hearts and manifested in their worship and daily practices.

This question must be the basis for Islamic advocacy today, just like it was when Islam was first revealed. Thirteen years of Qur'ānic revelations in Makkah were devoted to this question.

When a group of people embrace Islam in this, its true sense, they become the community well suited to implement Islam in practical life. This is because this community has already decided to conduct its life on the Islamic basis, submitting to no authority other than God's. And when such a community is actually in place, it begins to look at the fundamental concepts of the Islamic system and to use these concepts for the enactment of laws and regulations that meet its practical needs.

Some undoubtedly sincere people who do not fully understand the nature of the Islamic faith and its method of operation are in a hurry. They imagine that presenting fundamental Islamic principles, and even detailed Islamic legislation, to people will facilitate the task of Islamic advocacy and win a favourable outcome for Islam. But this is a myth born out of their haste and impatience. It is the same type of myth as that which might have been suggested to the Prophet to start his message under a nationalist, social or moral banner, so as to give Islam an easier path.

It is essential that people's hearts be totally devoted to God alone, declaring total submission to Him and accepting, in principle, only His law, even before they are told anything of the details of that law. Their driving point must be their desire to be free of any power other than that of God's. Their acceptance of Islam must not be motivated by belief that its system is superior to other systems in such and such details.

There is no doubt that God's law is intrinsically good, because it is formulated by God. Man-made laws will never be as good as God's law. But this is not the basic point in Islamic advocacy. Such advocacy must be based on the fact that accepting God's law, to the exclusion of all other laws, is Islam itself. Indeed, Islam can have no other practical meaning. Whoever wants to adopt Islam has made his choice and resolved this issue. He or she will not need to be further persuaded by the beauty and superiority of the Islamic system. All this is taken for granted.

The Qur'ānic Treatment of the Faith Issue

We need to discuss how the Qur'ān addressed the issue of faith during the thirteen years of the Makkan period. Certainly it did not present it in the form of a theory or a theological study. Nor was it presented in the form of a scholastic discourse of the type which was later to be known as *'ilm al-kalām*, which dealt mainly with the concept of God's oneness.

None of this! The Qur'ān simply addresses human nature, utilizing all the signs, indicators and pointers within man's own soul and in the universe at large. Thus it liberates human nature from all the pressures that have beclouded its receptive faculties and opens up windows to the world. Thus is human nature able to make the right and proper response. The *sūrah* we are discussing in this volume provides a perfect example of this unique method.

More specifically, the Qur'ān launched a practical campaign against the pressures disrupting the proper functioning of human nature. The field of battle was living human souls. Success could not have been achieved without a direct confrontation which aimed to rend the curtains that had fallen on people's hearts and minds and to remove the walls and psychological blocks that stood between man and the truth. Nor was intellectual argumentation, based on verbal logic, which was the hallmark of the scholastic theology of later times, appropriate for the purpose. The Qur'ān confronted a whole human environment, with all its conditions and circumstances, and addressed the whole human entity within this environment. Similarly, a purely 'theological' address was unsuitable. Although Islam is a faith, it also incorporates a code to be implemented in practical life. It does not confine itself to the narrow spheres of theological discourse.

As the Qur'ān worked to establish the faith in the hearts and consciences of the Muslim community, it also fought a hard and determined battle against the surrounding *jāhiliyyah* and against the remaining traces of *jāhiliyyah* in the new community's conscience, morals and practices. Thus, the structure of the Islamic faith was raised under these circumstances, but not in the form of a theory or intellectual discourse, but in a practical and organized social set-up represented by the Muslim community itself. The growth of the Muslim community in its understanding of its faith, and its implementation in practice, as well as its awareness and training to confront *jāhiliyyah*, mirrored the growth of the ideological structure and gave it practical manifestation. Here we see the true Islamic method that reflects its nature and spirit.

The advocates of Islam need to fully understand this dynamic method of operation so that they can realize that the stage of building the faith, which took such a long time in Makkah, was not separate from the stage of practical organization in which the Muslim community came into existence. It was not a stage of having a theory to learn and study. It was a single stage to lay the foundations of the faith, the community and its practical structure all at the same time. The same applies every time the Islamic structure is raised again.

The stage of building the faith should be long, moving gradually and steadily. No theoretical study of the faith is needed, but rather a single stage that aims to translate Islamic beliefs into practical reality, reforming people's consciences, building a community that reflects the growth of faith, and forming a dynamic movement that challenges *jāhiliyyah*. This last challenge is fought out in people's hearts and lives, so that Islam is seen to be a living faith growing steadily as the fight rages on.

An Error to Be Avoided

From the Islamic point of view, it is a great error, indeed a serious danger, that the faith should simply evolve into an abstract theory for academic study.

It is not because the Qur'ān was being revealed for the first time that it took thirteen years to build its faith. Had He so willed, God could have revealed the Qur'ān in full at the beginning and allowed the new Muslims a lengthy period to study it, until they had fully grasped the 'Islamic theory'.

In His infinite wisdom, however, God wanted something different. He wanted to put in place a unique method of operation that laid the foundation of the faith, the community and the movement all at the same time. He wanted the community and the movement to be founded on faith, and He wanted the faith to grow with the dynamic progress of the community. He wanted the practical life of that community to be a mirror of the faith. God, limitless is He in His glory, knew that the refinement of souls and the building of communities could not be achieved overnight. Hence, it was necessary that raising the structure of the faith should take the same length of time as the building of the community and the refinement of believers' souls. Thus, when faith had taken its full shape, the community reflected its maturity in practice.

This is the nature of this religion as defined in the light of the Qur'ānic revelations in Makkah. We need to understand its nature and not try to change it under the influence of an impatient, defeatist mentality, brought under pressure from man-made theories and doctrines. It is with this particular nature and with its particular qualities that Islam was able to bring the first Muslim community into existence. Similarly, it can mould the same type of community, using the same nature and qualities, whenever it needs to come into being, by God's will.

We should be aware of the error and danger involved in trying to narrow down the dynamic Islamic faith into a 'theory' for intellectual discussion, trying to show its superiority over man-made theories. The Islamic faith must take shape in living souls, be an active organization and a movement striving against the surrounding *jāhiliyyah*. Viewed in this light, the Islamic faith takes up a much larger space in people's hearts and lives, and exercises a much more profound influence on their minds, than any theory. Indeed, it produces all the benefits of a theory but does not remain confined to it.

The Islamic concept of Godhead, the universe, man and life is not only perfect and comprehensive, but also positive and practical. By nature, it dislikes being reduced to a merely intellectual concept, as this is contrary to its nature. It needs to be personified in human beings, in an active organization and in a practical situation so that it comes into its full shape, theoretically and practically, at the same time. Every theoretical progress that moves ahead of, and is not reflected in, practical progress is both erroneous and hazardous when viewed from the Islamic perspective.

God says in the Qur'ān: "*We have divided the Qur'ān into parts so that you may recite to people with deliberation. We have indeed bestowed it from on high step by step.*" (17: 106) This shows that the revelation of the Qur'ān one small part at a time is intended, just like its recitation with deliberation, so that its structure is raised as God wants it to be: a faith represented in a dynamic society, and not a mere theory.

A Divine Method

The advocates of Islam must be well aware that just as this religion is a divine revelation, its method of operation, which is harmonious with its nature, is also God-given. It is not possible to separate the truth of Islam and its method of action. They must also realize that just like Islam wants to change people's beliefs and practices, it also wants to change their intellectual and operational methods which formulate concepts of belief and bring about social change. Islam aims to build a faith at the same time as it builds a community and a nation. It also initiates its own independent mode of thinking, in the same way as it initiates its own concepts and way of life. All are parts of a complete whole.

Now that we know what method of action Islam adopts, we should also know that this method is permanent: it is not applicable to just a certain stage, environment or the special circumstances that pertained when the first Muslim community came into existence. It is a method of action which is indispensable for Islamic revival. Islam has never confined its objective to changing people's beliefs and conditions; it also aims to change their outlook and way of thinking. As a method of action, Islam is divine and fundamentally different from all human methods. We cannot achieve the type of life this divine religion wants to establish unless we adopt its divinely-ordained method, intended by God to reform human thought and practice.

When we try to give Islam the guise of a theory to be studied, we move away from the divine method of operation and thinking. We subject Islam to human modes of thinking, as though the divine method is inferior and as though we want to elevate it to that superior standard! This is extremely dangerous.

The function of the divine method is to give us, the advocates of Islam, a new way of thinking to dissociate ourselves from *jāhiliyyah*. If we were to impose on Islam a way of thinking alien to its nature, popular as it may be, we nullify its function in human life and deprive ourselves of a great opportunity to be free of the pressure of the ignorant ways of thinking which prevail in our world. Such ways of thinking will continue to have their influence on our minds and lives. Again, this is extremely dangerous.

In Islam, the way of thinking and the methods of operation are no less important than the conceptual beliefs or the practical system. In fact, these are inseparable. Important as we may think it to present Islamic beliefs and systems in a refined, expounding form, we must not forget that such presentation will not bring Islam into being as a practical reality or a dynamic movement. We must not lose sight of the fact that the only people to benefit from such a presentation are those who are already working within an Islamic movement. The maximum benefit these people will have is to interact with it at the level they have already reached while working for Islam.

To recap, Islamic belief concepts must materialize in a practical movement which, in turn, should be a true representation of its beliefs. This is the natural Islamic method of operation, which is superior, more effective and far better suited to human nature than trying to formulate theories in an intellectual manner before people are engaged in a dynamic movement of Islamic advocacy which aims to put Islam into practice.

If this is true for the fundamental concepts of belief, it is even more so in respect of the system on which the Islamic concept is founded, and its legal details.

The *jāhiliyyah* surrounding us puts some sincere advocates of Islam under pressure to hasten the Islamic system. It even tries to confound them by asking: "What are the details of the system which you are advocating? What research, details and projects have you prepared to put it into effect?" In all this, the *jāhiliyyah* tries to force the advocates of Islam off their proper course. It wants them to move beyond the stage of building the ideological structure so as to change the nature of the divine method whereby the theory takes shape through the dynamic movement, and the system develops through practice, and where detailed laws are enacted to meet practical needs and solve real problems.

It is the duty of the advocates of Islam to expose these tactics and refuse to have a system and a method of operation imposed on their religion. They must insist on adopting the method of operation Islam has chosen for itself, because it is one of the main factors of its strength. It is also the source of their strength. Hence, those who are devoid of faith must not be allowed to play tricks on them and divert their attention from their true path.

From the Islamic point of view, the method of operation emanates from the truth of Islam, and the two are inseparable. No alien method can raise the structure of Islam. Western methods may be suitable for their own man-made systems, but they are totally unsuitable for the divine system we believe in. To operate the Islamic method is just as necessary as adherence to the faith itself and the system it puts in place. This is not confined to the first Muslim community, or first Islamic movement, as some people suggest. It applies to every Islamic movement which aims at Islamic revival.

This is my final word on this subject. I hope that by expounding the nature of the Qurʾānic method of operation, as outlined in the Makkan parts of the Qurʾān, I have done my duty. I hope that the advocates of Islam may now be clear about their method, trust that it is the best and the one that leads to success. I hope that they realize that through it they will be triumphant. *"Surely this Qurʾān shows the way to that which is most upright."* (17: 9)

A Sample of Makkan Revelations

This *sūrah*, the first Makkan *sūrah* we discuss in this work, provides a complete sample of the parts of the Qurʾān revealed in Makkah. We have outlined above the nature, characteristics and method of these parts. We see all these in this *sūrah*, its main theme, the way it is approached and how it is presented. At the same time, the *sūrah* has, like every individual *sūrah* of the Qurʾān, its distinctive character which no attentive reader can fail to recognize. Indeed, every *sūrah* has its own character, features, central idea, and method of presenting its main theme. Not only so, but each *sūrah* uses its own inspiration, images, subtleties of meaning, and general ambience. These are all featured in its presentation of its subject matter. Moreover, each *sūrah* uses its own special expressions that may be repeated at intervals, even when it tackles one theme or several related themes. It is not the theme that delineates the character of a *sūrah*, but its special and distinctive features.

Nevertheless, this *sūrah* tackles its subject matter in a unique way. At every turn, in every situation or scene, it brings out in sharp relief all the awesome splendour of what is being portrayed, keeping us spellbound, breathless as we follow its scenes and hear its changing, powerful rhythm. This is certainly true! I feel it in my heart as I follow the flow of the *sūrah*, its scenes and beats. I think that no reader or listener of any degree of intelligence could fail to appreciate something of its awesome splendour.

The whole *sūrah* presents the truth of Godhead as it is reflected in life and the universe, human soul and conscience, the secrets of the world around us and the secrets of the world beyond the reach of our faculties of perception. It also presents it in the scenes of the creation of the universe, life and human creation, as well as in the destruction of past communities to allow new ones to take their place. It further presents the truth of Godhead in scenes of human nature as it faces the universe, different events, turns of fortune, blessings and trials, and in scenes of divine power over all aspects of human life, be they apparent or hidden, present or future. It finally presents the same truth in scenes of the Day of Resurrection, as creatures are brought before their Lord.

From start to finish, the *surah* discusses the theme of faith, in all its features and aspects. It takes the human soul, in its totality, by the hand, and roams over the whole universe, looking at inspirations of faith, observing light and darkness, the sun, the moon, the stars, cultivated gardens and ones growing wild, the rain that falls on them and the waters running through them. In this great round, the *surah* also shows the human soul the doom suffered by past generations and their remains. It floats with it through the darkness of land and sea, the secrets of the world beyond and those of the human soul itself. It looks at how the living comes out of the dead and the dead out of the living, the seed planted in the darkness of the soil and the sperm planted in the darkness of the uterus. Then, suddenly, the earth is full of *jinn* and humans, birds, beasts, generations of living things past and present, and angels watching over the living at night and during the day.

It is a huge panorama that overwhelms our souls and sensations. But it is presented with fine, creative touches which bring the scenes and meanings before us, full of life. Thus, we see every familiar scene and experience every familiar feeling as though we experience them for the first time, unseen and unfelt by anyone before us.

In its quick flow of imagery, inspirations, rhythms, and shades, it resembles a fast, wide river, its waves constantly breaking. As one wave reaches its breaking place, the next one follows very closely behind, almost reaching out to the one that has just gone by. The flow remains continuous, unending.

In each of these flowing and closely successive waves, the same rich splendour is there to see. And in all the scenes portrayed, we have superb harmony. Thus, we are absolutely enchanted by it all. The *surah* addresses man's heart and mind from every angle and in every possible way.

We say at the outset that with our own human description and style, we cannot make any headway in presenting the rhythm and beat of the *surah*. Instead, we must leave the *surah* itself, with its own beat, to address human hearts. What we are doing here is simply to try to provide a bridge between the Qur'ān and those who, by their own life conditions, are isolated from life in the atmosphere generated by the Qur'ān.

Such life does not mean simply to read the Qur'ān frequently and to study its different disciplines. What we mean is that one should live in conditions, movements, struggles and concerns similar to those which witnessed the revelation of the Qur'ān. This means that a person should confront the *jāhiliyyah* that has spread all over the earth, dedicating all his thoughts, feelings and actions to the revival of Islam in his own soul and life as well as in the souls and life of mankind.

Such is the atmosphere generated by the Qur'ān. When we live in this atmosphere, we are able to appreciate the Qur'ān fully, because it is in such an atmosphere that it was revealed and worked. Those who do not experience this atmosphere remain isolated from the Qur'ān, no matter how keenly they study it and how deeply they delve into its academic disciplines.

Our attempt to provide a bridge between the sincere among such people and the Qur'ān will not achieve any results unless they cross that bridge and come over to live in the atmosphere of the Qur'ān by deed and practice. Only then will they begin to experience this blessing with which God favours His servants.

To Truly Know God

This *sūrah* tackles the main issue of faith, Godhead and servitude. Its approach is to make known to people who their true Lord is, answering questions like: Who is He? What is the origin of this existence? What are the secrets beyond it? Who are these creatures? Who brings them into being; and who gives them their provisions and controls their affairs? Who turns their hearts and sights? Who controls the sequence of their days and nights? Who initiates them; and then re-initiates them? For what purpose has He created them? What term has He appointed for them? To what destiny does He deliver them? And then, as regards this life springing up here and there: who initiates it in such a lifeless environment? What about the pouring rain, the opening buds, the tightly piled grain, the piercing star, the breaking dawn, the darkness of the night as it covers all, and the cosmos beyond: who controls all this? What secrets do they hide and what news do they bring? Then again, all these generations that come and go, prosper and perish: who gives them power on earth and who takes it away and leaves them to perish? Why are they placed in control of the world, and why are they left to be ruined? And what remains beyond death of reckoning and reward?

The *surah* takes our hearts and minds over such endless horizons and into such depths. There is no attempt to provide a theory of faith, or start a theological argument. The *surah* simply aims to make known to people who their true Lord is, so that they may submit themselves to Him alone, surrendering their consciences, souls, efforts, traditions, worship and all their lives to the Almighty, the only deity in the universe.

The whole drift of the *surah*, from start to finish, follows this direction: God is the Creator, the provider, the owner, the almighty who knows all that is concealed. He turns hearts and sights as He turns nights into days. As such, God should be the one who rules over human life to the exclusion of all others. No one else can legislate or judge, permitting certain things and prohibiting others. Such authority belongs to God and may not be exercised by anyone else. For none other than God can create, provide, give life, cause death, cause benefit or harm, give or deprive, or exercise any control over oneself or others in this life or in the life to come. The *surah* provides numerous proofs in the scenes and situations it discusses with its unique style, bringing in a multitude of effects and inspirations of every sort and type.

The great issue the *surah* addresses is that of Godhead and submission in the heavens and on earth, and in its broadest spectrum. However, the immediate occasion that brings up this issue and emphasizes the need for its implementation is that of food and animal slaughter. The *jāhiliyyah* society exercised the authority to make certain things lawful and others forbidden, and established certain rituals concerning offerings, agricultural produce and offspring. It is these details that are discussed towards the end of the *surah*. (See verses 118–21 and 136–40.)

Permissible or Forbidden

A host of statements and influences are brought together as the *surah* confronts the unbelievers with this issue of animal slaughter and offerings, as an example of a question requiring legislation. It links this issue to the main theme of faith, Godhead and submission, making it one of belief or disbelief, submission to God or rejection of Him.

This impresses on our minds an essential element in the nature of Islam: that is, that every single detail in human life is subject to God's absolute authority embodied in His law. To reject God's authority over a matter of detail represents rebellion against His sovereignty and a rejection of Islam altogether.

Providing such a host of influences is indicative of the importance Islam attaches to purging all aspects of human life of any trace of authority exercised by human beings over any matter, no matter how trivial it may be. All matters of human life must be related to the fundamental Islamic concept of God's absolute sovereignty and authority, acknowledging His Godhead on earth as it is acknowledged in the universe.

The *sūrah* comments on the *jāhiliyyah* rituals concerning animal and agricultural produce and the offerings made of these. Some of its comments are direct, showing the absurdity and contradiction in these rituals, while other comments seek to link the exercise by human beings of the authority to prohibit and make permissible with the major issue of faith. They make it clear that to follow God's directives in these matters is to follow His straight path. Whoever turns away from this path abandons the Islamic faith altogether. (Verses 141–53)

We see in these verses that this detailed matter of permissibility and prohibition in connection with animal slaughter and offspring, animal and agricultural offerings, as used to be practised in *jāhiliyyah*, is linked to much greater issues. These include guidance or error, following God's law or Satan's footsteps, God's grace or punishment, testifying to God's oneness or making other people equal to Him, etc. The same expressions used when discussing the overall issue of faith are also used here. Additionally, the *sūrah* introduces at this particular point a host of inspirations and influences such as the scene of creation and life in cultivated and wild-growing gardens, the picture of date trees, olives and pomegranates with their myriad colours and fruits, the scene of testimony and that of the painful punishment of unbelievers. These are the same scenes portrayed earlier in the *sūrah* when it discusses the main issue of faith, in its totality. All this carries an unmistakable pointer to the nature of the Islamic faith and its outlook in the matter of sovereignty and legislation on matters of great or little importance.

As we are explaining the *sūrah*'s thematic approach in tackling the total issue of faith, we might have gone ahead of the *sūrah* to speak about a matter of detail under the issue of legislation and sovereignty.

We do not say that this matter of detail has required all this host of statements and inspirations, or necessitated the splendid exposition of the truth of Godhead in its broader area. What we rather say is that this matter of detail has been linked in the *sūrah* to all these. This linkage shows the nature of this religion of Islam and how it looks at the question of legislation and sovereignty in all matters, large and small.

Let us now proceed to give a brief outline of the *sūrah* and its special features before we begin to discuss it in detail.

The *Sūrah*'s Revelation

Several reports by Ibn 'Abbās, Asmā' bint Yazīd, Jābir, Anas ibn Mālik and 'Abdullāh ibn Mas'ūd confirm that this *sūrah* was revealed in Makkah on one occasion.

Nothing in these reports or in the subject matter of the *sūrah* indicates the particular time of its revelation in the Makkan period. According to the most likely chronological order of revelation, this *sūrah* comes after *Sūrah* 15, *Al-Ḥijr*, which gives it number 55 in that order. But as we said in the Prologue to *Sūrah* 2 (Vol. I), we cannot, on the basis of this information, make any definitive judgement as to the time of revelation of different *sūrahs*. The reports we have on this particular point speak mainly of the revelation of the beginning, not the whole, of any particular *sūrah*. It may be that some later parts of an earlier *sūrah* are revealed after parts of a later *sūrah*. The *sūrah* we are discussing in this volume was revealed in its entirety at one go, but we cannot define the exact date of its revelation, although we feel it likely that it was after the early years of the Islamic message, maybe in the fifth or sixth year. In stating this probability we rely only on its number in the order of revelation and the wide variety of subjects it tackles at length. All this suggests a long ongoing argument with the unbelievers, who persisted in their rejection of the Prophet's message. This is, perhaps, what requires a detailed discussion of issues on the lines we have here, and necessitates comforting God's Messenger so as to remove the effects of long and determined opposition to his message.

Another report by Ibn 'Abbās and Qatādah suggests that the entire *sūrah* was revealed in Makkah, with the exception of two of its verses which were revealed later in Madinah. The first of these is Verse 91, which states: "*No true understanding of God have they when they say:*

'God has never revealed anything to any human being.' Say: Who, then, revealed the Book which Moses brought to people as a light and a guidance? You transcribe it on sheets to show around, while you suppress much. You have been taught [by it] what neither you nor your forefathers had ever known. Say: God, and leave them to their play and foolish chatter." The report suggests that it refers to two Jewish men, Mālik ibn al-Ṣayf and Ka'b ibn al-Ashraf. The second verse in question is the one stating: "It is He who has brought into being gardens – both of the cultivated type and those growing wild – and the date-palm, and fields bearing different produce, and the olive tree, and the pomegranates, all resembling one another and yet so different. Eat of their fruit when they come to fruition, and give (to the poor) what is due to them on harvest day. But do not waste, for He does not love the wasteful." (Verse 141) This verse is reported to refer to Thābit ibn Qays al-Anṣārī, although Ibn Jurayj and al-Māwardī suggest that it refers to Mu'ādh ibn Jabal.

In so far as the report goes concerning Verse 91, it is possible, considering that it mentions the Torah, the book Moses brought as a light and guidance, and that it addresses the Jews directly. However, different reports by Mujāhid and Ibn 'Abbās suggest that the reference to those who denied God's revelation to anyone were the idolaters in Makkah and hence the verse is a Makkan revelation. A different reading of the verse gives it in the third person, saying, 'They transcribe it on sheets to show around, and they suppress much.' According to this reading, which is admissible and favoured by al-Ṭabarī, this statement gives information about the Jews and does not address them. Thus, the entire verse is concerned with the unbelievers.

As for the second verse, it cannot be a Madinan revelation, because it comes in between verses revealed in Makkah and if it was to be left out until later, the flow of discourse would be interrupted. Thus, the verses before it would be cut off from those after it, while the topic discussed does not allow such interruption.

What has caused some scholars to consider Verse 141 a Madinan revelation is that they consider the order included in it, 'Eat of their fruit when they come to fruition, and give (to the poor) what is due to them on harvest day', to refer to zakāt. Details of zakāt legislation concerning agricultural produce were given in Madinah. But this is not imperative in understanding this statement. We have other authentic reports stating that it refers to charity in general, not to zakāt in particular, or that it means that Muslims are required to feed those who pass by their farms on harvest day or on the day when fruits are picked. These reports state that *zakāt* on agricultural produce was later specified at the rate of 10 per cent in certain situations and 5 per cent in others. This means that this verse is also a Makkan revelation.

Al-Tha'labī states that this *sūrah* was revealed in Makkah with the exception of verses 91–3 and 151–3. As for the first three, we have shown that the first of these could only have been revealed in Makkah. The same applies to the other two. As for the second group, to the best of my knowledge, there is not a single report attributed to any of the Prophet's Companions or their successors suggesting that they are Madinan revelations. Their subject matter does not indicate that either. They speak about certain concepts and practices of the days of ignorance. These are closely related to the theme of permissibility and prohibition in respect of slaughtered animals and offerings to which we have already referred. Therefore, we are inclined to consider these verses as Makkan revelations.

In the Amīrī edition of the Qur'ān it is suggested that verses 20, 23, 91–2, 114, 141 and 151–3 were revealed in Madinah. We have discussed most of these. The others, 20, 23 and 114 do not include anything that suggests their revelation in Madinah except that the people of earlier revelations are mentioned in them. But this is not clear evidence, because we have other references to the people of earlier revelations in other Makkan verses.

In the light of the foregoing, we are more inclined to take the reports stating that the entire *sūrah* was revealed in Makkah on the same night. These reports are given by two of the Prophet's Companions, 'Abdullāh ibn 'Abbās and Asmā' bint Yazīd. The report by Asmā' mentions a particular incident in which she was present. She says: "The *sūrah* entitled *al-An'ām,* or Cattle, was bestowed from on high in full to the Prophet when I was holding the rein of the Prophet's she-camel. Its weight almost broke the she-camel's bones". (Related by Sufyān al-Thawrī through Layth and Shahr ibn Ḥawshab.)

Al-Ṭabarānī relates the other report by Ibn 'Abbās: "The *sūrah al-An'ām* was revealed at night in full in Makkah, with seventy thousand angels around, raising their voices with glorification of God."

These two reports are more reliable than those which suggest that some of its verses were revealed in Madinah. Our objective analysis supports this. In fact, the whole body of the *sūrah* and its flow makes it a complete unit, and suggests that it is like a flowing river, or a rushing flood, without barriers or impediments. Its construction confirms or at least markedly strengthens these reports.

The Main Theme

We have referred briefly to the main theme and overall characteristics of the *sūrah*. We need to add here a brief word on them.

Anas ibn Mālik quotes the Prophet as saying: "The *sūrah al-An'ām* was bestowed from on high, with a great many angels in attendance, blocking the horizon, raising their voices with God's glorification, and the earth shaking under them." God's Messenger was repeating: "Limitless in His glory is God Almighty."

This great procession of angels and this shaking of the earth impart a clear impression to the *sūrah*. Indeed, the *sūrah* itself may be described as a procession which makes our hearts and the whole universe shake. It provides multitudes of situations, scenes, inspirations and rhythms, which flow like waves one after another. As one wave reaches its breaking place, the next one follows very closely on its heels, almost reaching out to the one that precedes it. The flow remains continuous, unending.

Its central theme is seen as a whole. It is not possible to break the *sūrah* into sections, each dealing with a particular aspect of the main theme. What we have is a succession of waves, or rounds, each picking up where the previous one left off and complementing it. Hence, we are not going to discuss in these introductory remarks the topics the *sūrah* touches on. We will only give samples of its successive waves.

The *sūrah* starts with a confrontation with the idolaters who associate partners with God, while the indicators of God's oneness stare them in the face, presenting themselves everywhere, both in the great universe and within their own souls. It puts to them the truth of Godhead, presented in panoramic touches depicting the whole universe as also their own existence. All this in three quick verses showing universal existence at its widest and deepest: "*All praise is due to God, who has created the heavens and the earth, and brought into being darkness and light; yet those who disbelieve regard other beings as equal to their Lord. It is He who has created you out of clay, and then has decreed a term (for you), and there is another term known only to Him. Yet you are still in doubt. He alone is God in the heavens and on earth. He has full knowledge of all that you keep secret and all that you do openly.*

He knows what you earn." (Verses 1–3) Three short verses the first comprises the whole universe and its existence, the second speaks of the human world in its entirety, and the third shows how Godhead encompasses both types of existence. How splendid! How comprehensive!

Against such a universal view testifying to the Creator's oneness, idolatry and doubt sound extremely singular. They have no place in the universal system or in human nature, or in people's hearts and minds.

At this very moment the second wave begins by presenting the attitude of those who deny all the signs and indicators they see in the world around them and within themselves. As this singular attitude is shown, it is immediately followed with a warning, coupled with a reminder of the destruction of earlier communities. God's overwhelming power is, thus, seen in full view. The stubborn attitude of those rejecting the truth in the face of such manifest truth appears to be strange indeed. We realize that it is not proofs that they lack but rather sincerity and an open mind. (Verses 4–11)

Immediately after that another wave begins, defining the truth of Godhead as it is clearly reflected in God's ownership of everything in the heavens and earth, and what takes its rest at night or day. It is also seen in the fact that God is the only one who provides for all creation, the one who feeds them and is fed by none. Hence, He is the only guardian and the only protector, to whom all creatures must submit themselves. It is He who punishes the disobedient ones in the life to come, who can bring benefit and cause harm, and who has power over all things. (Verses 12–19)

A fourth wave speaks of the fact that the people of earlier revelations are aware of this newly revealed book, i.e. the Qur'ān, which is rejected by the idolaters. It describes idolatry as the worst type of wrongdoing. It also shows the idolaters as they are gathered on the Day of Judgement. They are asked about the partners they used to associate with God, and their surprising answer is to deny having done so. In this round, the idolaters are shown with unfunctioning faculties of reception: they cannot pick up any inspiration to accept the faith, and their hearts cannot appreciate the signs calling on them to believe. Hence they describe the Qur'ān as 'fables of the ancients'. They are told here that they only ruin themselves when they counsel others not to respond to divine guidance. They are shown as they are brought before the Fire on the Day of Judgement. In their predicament, they wish that they could be returned to this life so that they would not deny God's revelations, but join the believers instead. This round then takes us back to this life to see the unbelievers denying resurrection and life after death. By way of comment, they are shown standing before their Lord on the Day of Resurrection, carrying their burdens on their backs, and being asked about their denial. It concludes with an unequivocal statement that those who deny the meeting with their Lord on the Day of Judgement are certainly the losers, and that this present life is too trivial in comparison to what the God-fearing receive in the hereafter. (Verses 20–32)

The fifth wave addresses the Prophet to comfort him and dispel his grief at the denial he receives from the unbelievers. He is told that he has a good example in the cases of earlier messengers sent by God. They were denied and received hostile opposition, but they remained steadfast until God gave them victory. It states that the laws God has set in operation will not be changed, but they cannot be hastened either. If the Prophet cannot withstand their rejection, then he may try to bring them a miracle by his own human endeavour. Had God so willed, He would have brought them all to His guidance. But His will has so determined that those whose natural receptive faculties are not switched off will respond to divine guidance, while those who are dead will not make such a response. He will resurrect them and they will all return to Him. (Verses 33–6)

The *sūrah* goes on, wave after wave, along the same lines as the examples we have just given. Some of the later waves are even higher than the ones we have cited. In dealing with some aspects its rhythm is of an even stronger beat and higher cadence.

Unique Subject Treatment

We have already said that this *sūrah* deals with its subject matter in a very unique way. At every turn, in every situation or scene, it brings out in sharp relief all the awesome splendour of what is being portrayed, keeping us spellbound, breathless as we follow it. Now we will refer to particular verses confirming this, and the reader needs to carefully consider these for full appreciation. No matter how hard we try to describe this effect, we cannot give more than a vague feeling of it.

The central theme of the *sūrah* is to state the truth of Godhead and to give human beings sufficient knowledge about their true Lord so that they submit themselves to Him alone. Thus, it has much to say about providing proper witnesses and demarcating the lines that separate the believers from the unbelievers. Thus, this truth becomes clear in a believer's mind and he is able to declare it with power and firmness in the face of those who take the opposite attitude. (Verses 14–19)

On warnings, the *sūrah* shows how God's power encompasses all. When confronted with God's power, human nature is freed of all stifling pressures and turns to its true Lord, forgetting the false deities people associate with Him. (Verses 40–7)

The *sūrah* has much to say about God's knowledge of all that is secret or concealed, and the time appointed for the death of every living thing. He has full power over everything on land and sea, day and night, in this life and in the life to come. (Verses 59–62)

Human nature will undoubtedly turn towards God once it opens up to receive the inspiring guidance seen clearly in the world around us. Numerous are the pointers that address human nature appealing to its innate purity. (Verses 74–82)

The *sūrah* paints several scenes of life opening up. Thus we see images of the break of day, the approach of night, the bright stars, the darkness on land and sea, the pouring rain, growing vegetation, ripening fruits. In all this the unity of God, the only Creator and Originator is seen in perfect clarity. To ascribe partners or children to God sounds most absurd indeed. (Verses 95–103)

Finally on addressing our prayers to God alone, offering our worship, life and death purely to Him, denouncing any attempt to seek a Lord other than Him, and acknowledging His authority over this life and the designation of man's role in it, and over the hereafter and the question of reckoning and reward, the *sūrah* ends with a humble prayer. (Verses 161–5)

These are only six examples of the breathtaking splendour the *sūrah* employs at every turn and in every scene. We should also refer here to the exceptional harmony the *sūrah* provides in drawing its different scenes. We will, however, give but three examples, leaving the full explanation to our detailed commentary.

The *sūrah* is full of different scenes and situations, but they all share one aspect in common. In each, the *sūrah* practically brings the listener to the scene to look at it carefully and to reflect on the situation described. This is done through words that almost show us the movement physically. Thus, the scenes painted include people whom the listener sees with his own eyes. Consider in this respect verses 27, 30, 93–4 and also 22–4.

When the *sūrah* warns the unbelievers against God's punishment and His overwhelming power, they are physically brought before such punishment, as though they see how it is inflicted. Consider here verses 40–1 and 46–7.

In describing the situation of sinking into error after one has recognized the truth through divine guidance, the *sūrah* shows us a moving scene which we stop to look at very carefully, even though the text does not include any order or suggestion that we should do so. This is given in verses 71–3.

Similarly the *sūrah* brings the listener before the picture of ripening fruit in gardens where we see life springing up and manifesting in the colours and fruits that could only be produced by God's hand. All this is seen at its best in Verse 99. Indeed, such perfect harmony is the common feature of all the scenes and situations described in the *sūrah*.

Another aspect of such perfect harmony, which is not unrelated to what we have already said, are the scenes bringing in or calling for witnesses. The scenes of the Day of Resurrection are portrayed as though they are providing witnesses for what the unbelievers do in this life, or scenes denouncing the unbelievers and drawing attention to them. Examples of these have been given, and they all start with "If you could but see…". Closely related to these are the scenes calling for witnesses to testify to the faith itself, and then to testify to divine law. Both are treated in the same way. At the beginning of the *sūrah* witnesses are called to testify to the truth of faith in its entirety, as we see in Verse 19. Then when a special occasion arises, concerning the question of prohibition and permissibility, the *sūrah* paints a new scene and calls for witnesses on this particular issue, in the same way as witnesses are called for the faith. This implies that the two are the same and ensures perfect harmony which is characteristic of the Qur'ānic style. This call for witnesses occurs in Verse 150.

Another type of harmony is that of expression, which is seen in repeating certain words and phrases in different contexts to indicate that they refer to the same point in different ways. Thus, in the first verse of the *sūrah*, the unbelievers are said to regard certain beings as equal to their Lord in order to indicate that they associate partners

31

with Him. Then in Verse 150, those who formulate legislation for themselves are also described as regarding others as equal to their Lord. Thus, the same description is given to associating partners with God and to the exercise of the authority to legislate. This is especially significant both in the idea it expresses and in the way it is expressed.

The term 'God's way' is used to refer to the Islamic faith in general (Verse 126) and in speaking about legislation with regard to permissibility and the prohibition of slaughtered animals and agricultural produce. (Verse 153) This indicates that the issue of legislation is the same as the issue of faith. To accept God's legislation is to follow His way, and to reject it is to deviate from His way. Thus, it is shown as a question of faith or unfaith, *jāhiliyyah* or Islam.

We move on now to look at the *sūrah* in more detail. However, instead of dividing it into chapters as we have done with other *sūrahs*, we will, in this instance, follow the natural pattern of this particular *sūrah*, as it moves through one wave after another.

I

The Origin of Life

Al-An 'ām (Cattle)

*In the Name of God, the Merciful,
the Beneficent*

All praise is due to God, who
has created the heavens and the
earth, and brought into being
darkness and light; yet those
who disbelieve regard other
beings as equal to their Lord. (1)

It is He who has created you
out of clay, and then has
decreed a term (for you), and
there is another term known
only to Him. Yet you are still
in doubt. (2)

He alone is God in the heavens
and on earth. He has full
knowledge of all that you keep
secret and all that you do openly.
He knows what you earn. (3)

A Framework Is Set

These three opening verses strike the basic notes as they lay the foundation for the subject matter of the *sūrah*, namely, faith. "*All praise is due to God, who has created the heavens and the earth, and brought into being darkness and light; yet those who disbelieve regard other beings as equal to their Lord.*" (Verse 1)

The *sūrah* starts with praising God and glorifying Him as only He, the Creator and Originator of all things, deserves to be praised and glorified. Thus, the initial touches stress the foremost quality of Godhead, namely, creation. To start with, it refers to creation in the two widest expanses of existence, the heavens and earth. It then adds the two greatest phenomena that result from the creation of the heavens and the earth according to a deliberate plan, namely, darkness and light. This initial touch, then, takes into view the magnificent stars and planets which we see in the universe, the unimaginable distances separating them and the numerous phenomena which result from their orbital movements. It then wonders at those people who behold this awesome existence, itself a great testimony to the infinite ability of the Supreme Creator and His faultless planning, but who still refuse to believe in God, acknowledge His oneness or praise Him. Instead, they associate partners with Him whom they allege to be His equals: "*Yet those who disbelieve regard other beings as equal to their Lord.*" All this clear evidence in the universe thus loses its effect on the human mind and soul. The irony is of the same magnitude as the stars and the planets, the endless distances separating them and the all-enveloping phenomena that result from their creation. It is indeed greater.

The picture continues to unfold with its reference to human existence which follows the existence of the universe and the two phenomena of darkness and light. This is a remarkable Qur'ānic touch taking us from the darkness of clay to the light of active life. We perceive here the full artistic harmony at work, with the reference to darkness and light made at the outset. Another closely intertwined subtlety prepares us for a first term appointed for death and a second term appointed for resurrection known only to God. We, thus, have two contrasting notions to contemplate, namely idleness and movement and a dull clay contrasted with life created by God. The gap between these opposites both in time and nature, is wide indeed. All this should inspire every human heart with the certainty that it is all part of God's scheme and that we will all be gathered to Him. Yet those who are addressed by this *surah* continue to have doubts: *"Yet you are still in doubt."* (Verse 2)

A third touch in these short verses combines the two previous ones within the same framework, making it clear that God is the only deity in the whole universe, including the human world: *"He alone is God in the heavens and on earth. He has full knowledge of all that you keep secret and all that you do openly. He knows what you earn."* (Verse 3)

The One who has created the heavens and the earth is the only God in them. All attributes and qualities of Godhead belong to Him alone and both the heavens and the earth acknowledge them without hesitation. This acknowledgement is reflected in their submission to the laws God has set in operation in them and in their willing fulfilment of His commandments. The same should apply to human life. God is the Creator of man, the heavens and earth alike. In man's original making is the clay of this earth. All his qualities which combine to make of him a human being have been given to him by God. His physical entity is subject to the laws of nature God has set in operation. Man has no say in all this. He is created and given his existence by God's will, not by his parents' design. They may have intercourse, but they cannot effect conception by their own will. Man is born according to the laws God has established for the term of pregnancy and the conditions of childbirth. Man uses for breathing the air God has placed over the earth in the quantities and ratios He has willed. His breathing conforms to the quantity and method God has chosen for him. He feels pain, hunger, thirst, happiness, or in short, he lives in accordance with God's law; he has no say in any of it. In all this he is in the same position as the heavens and the earth.

Moreover, God knows what man keeps secret and what he does in the open. He knows what he does and what he earns, be it done in public or in private. It is, then, more befitting for man to follow God's laws in that area of his life over which he has been given full control. This includes his chosen faith, values and practices. If he does, he achieves harmony between his natural life which is subject to God's law and his free-will in those areas where he exercises his free choice. Thus, he precludes internal conflict and saves himself from being pulled in opposite directions by two unequal laws: one set by God and one made by man. The two cannot be placed on the same level.

This powerful opening to the *surah* addresses man's heart and mind, pointing out the evidence derived from creation and from life, for man is able to see such evidence in the world around him and within himself. It is an address which moves away from theology and philosophy in order to awaken human nature as it portrays the movement of creation according to a deliberate scheme and in a manner that states facts without indulging in argumentation. The creation of the heavens and the earth, their organization according to a clear system, and the creation of life – the most important aspect of which is human life – and its movement along its definite course, put human nature face to face with the truth and strongly reassure it of God's oneness. God's oneness is the core topic of the whole *surah*. It is what the entire Qur'ān aims to establish. The question is not confined to God's existence, as such. Throughout human history, the basic problem was not that of accepting the existence of a deity, but rather the inability of recognizing that true deity and giving Him His true attributes.

The pagan Arabs addressed initially by this *surah* did not deny God's existence altogether. Indeed, they acknowledged His existence and that He was the Creator who provided sustenance to His creation, and who owned the universe and caused life and death. They acknowledged many of His attributes as the Qur'ān states. The reason then for classifying them as pagans was their unwillingness to come to the logical conclusion of God's actual existence, in other words, that God must be given authority over their whole lives, without their associating any partners with Him in that. Nor did they acknowledge their duty to implement God's law as the only acceptable law in human life. It was not enough for them to acknowledge God's existence and to give Him those attributes which would make them believers. Here at the beginning of this *surah,* the fact that God is the Creator of both man and the universe, and that He governs the life of both and has full knowledge of men's secret thoughts and their public actions and what they hide and reveal are stated as an introduction which leads to the inevitable conclusion that all sovereignty belongs to God alone.

Both sets of evidence concerning creation and life represented the most perfect evidence put to the unbelievers so that they may acknowledge the major concept of God's oneness and sovereignty and act on it in their practical life. Furthermore, both concepts represented perfect refutations of all new concepts denying God's existence, hollow or sophisticated as they might be.

In point of truth, it is exceedingly doubtful that those atheists actually believed themselves. Most probably, the whole concept of atheism started as a manoeuvre to confront the Church. Zionism then exploited it for its own ends, because it tries to demolish the basic foundation of human life, so that no human community other than its own can take it as a basis for its code of living. This they state in the Protocols of the Elders of Zion. The result they aim to achieve is the collapse of humanity so that they can exercise control over it, since they preserve for themselves the source of true power, namely faith.

When Evil Schemes Seem to Triumph

No matter how much they scheme, the Zionists cannot overpower human nature which, deep at heart, knows that there is a Lord who has created this universe. Human nature, however, may not be able to recognise the right attributes of the true Lord of the universe and it may deviate through giving authority to others beside Him. When such deviation occurs in human nature, it becomes unbeliever or idolater.

Some individuals, however, may have a corrupt nature that leads to the malfunctioning of their natural faculties and responses. It is such individuals who may succumb to wicked designs aiming to make them deny God's existence altogether. Such individuals will remain only a small minority. Indeed, the real atheists today do not number more than a few millions in Russia and China, compared to the hundreds of millions who suffer under the tyranny of those atheists. All the efforts which have gone on unabated for over forty years to utilise the means of education and information to spread atheism could not achieve more than this.[1]

The Zionists' wicked designs have sought to reduce religion to a set of rituals, thus seeking to minimise its influence on practical life. In this way, they are able to persuade people that they remain believers while acknowledging that other lords legislate for them and regulate their practical activities. Hence, the Zionists undermine humanity altogether, even though people maintain the delusion that they are believers.

Their ultimate aim has always been to destroy Islam, because they know from their own history that they can never overcome it as long

---

1. These comments were written in the early 1960s. – Editor's note.

as it continues to be implemented in practice. They also know that they can overcome Muslims only when they do not truly implement Islam, regardless of the fact that they may consider themselves Muslim. Presenting the notion that religion is properly followed when it actually has little or no influence on people's life is necessary for the Zionist plot to succeed.

I feel, although God knows best, that the Zionist Jews and the Christian neo-Crusaders have reached the point of despair in their attempts to uproot Islam from its strongholds in Africa, Asia and Europe as well. They have lost all hope that they can make Muslim populations adopt atheism through materialistic creeds, and they no longer entertain any hope of being able to convert Muslims to other religions through missionary work or direct colonialism. This is due to the fact that atheism is repugnant to human nature. It is even rejected by pagans, let alone by Muslims. For their part, other religions do not even hope or attempt to replace Islam in the mind of any Muslim.

Perhaps it is because of this despair that Zionist Jews and Christian neo-Crusaders have changed their tactics. They no longer try to confront Islam openly through Communism or missionary work. They have adopted more subtle and wicked designs. They now try to establish systems and regimes which give themselves a superficial Islamic colour and which pay lip-service to Islam. Once they have donned this mask, such regimes start to carry out all the projects and plans recommended by missionary conventions and Zionist protocols, which could not be implemented in a direct and open manner.

These regimes may profess to be Muslim, or at least declare that they respect religion, but at the same time, they suspend God's law altogether and replace it with a man-made one that makes lawful what God has declared unlawful. They advocate concepts of life and moral values that undermine Islamic ones, using in the process all methods and media that influence public opinion against religious views and beliefs. In strict adherence to the conclusions of missionary conventions and Zionist protocols, they force Muslim women out of their homes, pleading the cause of progress, civilisation and the interests of development, work and productivity. This they do when millions remain unemployed, living below the poverty line. They promote permissiveness among both sexes while claiming to respect faith and to adhere to it. Despite all this, people continue to think that they live as true Muslims in a Muslim society. Is it not true, they ask, that the good among them continue to offer their prayers and observe their fasting? The central question of whether sovereignty belongs to God alone or to a diversity of deities no longer concerns them since they have been tricked into thinking that it has nothing to do with religion and that they can continue to be Muslims while conducting their lives on the basis of values and laws that are not derived from Islam.

In order to ensure the success of their trickery and to hide their involvement, world Zionism and neo-Crusaders stir up superficial conflicts and hostilities which show these regimes to be opposed to them. This they do at the same time as providing them with material and moral support, protecting them both discreetly and openly, and using their own intelligence services to ensure their survival. In this way, they remove all suspicion from their puppets who fulfil for them what they have been unable to fulfil for themselves after more than three centuries of effort to destroy the faith and moral values of the Muslims. Thus, these regimes do the work of the Zionists and Christian missionaries and deprive the Muslims of their first source of power, namely, conducting their lives on the basis of their faith.

A minority of people in the vast area of the Muslim world, nevertheless, remain undeluded and cannot be brought round to accept unfaith as an image of Islam. They reject the deception that paints transgression and permissiveness as progress and civilisation. All sorts of false accusations are levelled at this minority. It is subjected to a war of extermination while international news agencies and the mass media remain deaf, dumb and blind. Even simple, well-meaning Muslims may think that it is only a clash of personalities or a sectarian battle that has nothing to do with the unabating fight against the religion of Islam. Those of them who are perturbed to see the weakening of religious and moral values are naïvely preoccupied with trying to correct some minor offences, thinking that they fulfil their task by speaking up against them. They are fully preoccupied with side issues when the foundations of this faith are being destroyed, God's authority is being usurped and human life is governed by false gods that they have been ordered to reject.

The Zionist Jews and Christian neo-Crusaders are pleased with themselves for having pulled off this trick. They had long despaired of managing to undermine Islam by spreading atheism or converting Muslims through missionary work.

We have, however, unlimited hope that God will render their efforts futile. Our trust in the power of this religion of Islam knows no limit. They will continue to scheme, but God will foil their schemes. It is He who says: *"They devised their plots, but their plots are all within God's grasp, even though their plots are so powerful as to move mountains. Never think that God may ever fail to fulfil the promise which He has given to His messengers. Indeed God is Almighty, able to exact retribution."* (14: 46–7)

At the beginning of the *sūrah*, the evidence of creation and life is placed in a powerful confrontation with atheism. When it is put to atheists, they find themselves driven to false and devious arguments.

When we consider the existence of this universe and the system that governs it, we are bound to conclude that, naturally and logically, it is the work of a Creator who has devised its elaborate system. It is impossible for us to perceive that something comes into existence out of nothing, unless we acknowledge the existence of a deity who creates, originates and brings into existence. By contrast, atheists try to mend the flaws in their argument by saying that it is not necessary to suppose that non-existence preceded existence. One of them even became known as the philosopher of spiritualism, as he defends it against materialism. Some naïve Muslims may speak highly of him and quote him in support of their faith as if they want to support the faith God has revealed by a statement of one of His servants. This philosopher was a Jew named Bergson who claimed that the existence of the universe was not preceded by non-existence.

What basis does he provide for his claims? Does he rely on human intellect? Certainly not. He himself admits that the human mind can only perceive of existence coming after non-existence. Does he rely on inspiration from God? He makes no such claim, although he says that by intuition, mystics have always come to the conclusion of the existence of a deity. Hence, we must accept this intuition, which has been so consistent. [The deity Bergson talks about is not God, as we conceive of Him. The deity, to him, is life.] Upon what other source does he rely, then, to prove his theory? We simply do not know.

We must always come back to acknowledging the existence of a creator who has made this universe and brought it into existence. We simply cannot explain the existence of the universe without resorting to this concept. The point, however, is not merely that the universe exists, but rather that it operates according to laws and measures which never fail. Every possibility is calculated accurately in devising these laws. After long contemplation, the human mind can still only comprehend a small portion of them.

The same applies to life. We cannot explain how the gulf between life and matter – whatever definition we give to matter, including radioactivity – is crossed unless we admit it to be the work of a deity who creates according to a deliberate and elaborate scheme. He has created the universe in a condition which allows the emergence and sustainability of life. With all the remarkable characteristics distinguishing human life, it has to be classified as higher than animal life. However, man has been created of clay, which means that he is made of the same material as this earth. There must then have been a will that gave him life as well as his human characteristics according to a definite purpose.

All attempts by atheists to explain the emergence of life have failed, even by the standards of the human mind itself. The latest I have read in this field was an attempt by the American philosopher Durant who tries to draw some sort of analogy between the type of movement within the nucleus, which he calls a degree of life, and the type of life which we know. He, indeed, makes a great effort to bridge the gap between dull matter and active life, only to be in a position of denying the concept of the creator who gives life to what is lifeless.

His tireless efforts have not availed him or other materialists of anything. If we were to presume that life is an innate quality within matter, and that there is no other power endowed with a will to originate life, we have to explain why life, which is within matter, manifests itself in several degrees, some of which are higher and more sophisticated than others. Why does life manifest itself in a mechanical, unintelligent movement in the nucleus, while it appears in an organic form in plants and in a more sophisticated organic form in other living things? If all matters have an innate quality of life, how is it that some matters take of this quality more than others, in the absence of a will and elaborate planning? How is it that life has several degrees? We can only understand this gradation if it is the work of a conscious will which plans and chooses. If it is left to matter, assuming that it has life, to do according to its own designs, our human intellect cannot understand or explain this gradation.

The Islamic view of the origin of life in its different grades is the only acceptable explanation of this phenomenon which cannot be explained by the materialists no matter how hard they try. In this commentary, we do not move away from the Qur'ānic method. Hence, we confine ourselves to confronting the fallacies of atheism by the evidence of creation, life and deliberate planning. The Qur'ān does not consider the question of God's existence as its main question because God knows that human nature rejects the premises of atheism. The real question is that of God's oneness and the establishment of His authority on human life. This is the basic question elaborated in this *sūrah,* as we have seen in its opening verses.

2

Stubborn Rejection

Whenever a revelation comes to them from their Lord, they [who are unbelievers] turn their back upon it. (4)

وَمَا تَأْتِيهِم مِّنْ ءَايَةٍ مِّنْ ءَايَتِ رَبِّهِمْ إِلَّا كَانُوا عَنْهَا مُعْرِضِينَ ٤

Thus they have denied the truth now that it has come to them. In time, they shall have full information about that which they used to deride. (5)

فَقَدْ كَذَّبُوا بِالْحَقِّ لَمَّا جَاءَهُمْ فَسَوْفَ يَأْتِيهِمْ أَنۢبَٰٓؤُا۟ مَا كَانُوا بِهِ يَسْتَهْزِءُونَ ٥

Do they not see how many a generation We have destroyed before them – people whom We had made more powerful in the land than We have made you, and for whom We sent down abundant water from the sky, and made rivers flow at their feet? Yet We destroyed them for their sins, and raised up another generation in their place. (6)

أَلَمْ يَرَوْا كَمْ أَهْلَكْنَا مِن قَبْلِهِم مِّن قَرْنٍ مَّكَّنَّٰهُمْ فِى ٱلْأَرْضِ مَا لَمْ نُمَكِّن لَّكُمْ وَأَرْسَلْنَا ٱلسَّمَاءَ عَلَيْهِم مِّدْرَارًا وَجَعَلْنَا ٱلْأَنْهَٰرَ تَجْرِى مِن تَحْتِهِمْ فَأَهْلَكْنَٰهُم بِذُنُوبِهِمْ وَأَنشَأْنَا مِنۢ بَعْدِهِمْ قَرْنًا ءَاخَرِينَ ٦

Even if We had sent down to you a book written on paper, and they had touched it with their own hands, surely the unbelievers would still say: "This is nothing but plain sorcery". (7)

وَلَوْ نَزَّلْنَا عَلَيْكَ كِتَٰبًا فِى قِرْطَاسٍ فَلَمَسُوهُ بِأَيْدِيهِمْ لَقَالَ ٱلَّذِينَ كَفَرُوا إِنْ هَٰذَا إِلَّا سِحْرٌ مُّبِينٌ ٧

They say: "Why has not an angel been sent down to him?" If We had sent down an angel, all would have been decided, and they would have been allowed no further respite. (8)

وَقَالُواْ لَوۡلَآ أُنزِلَ عَلَيۡهِ مَلَكٌ وَلَوۡ أَنزَلۡنَا مَلَكًا لَّقُضِيَ ٱلۡأَمۡرُ ثُمَّ لَا يُنظَرُونَ ۝

And even if We had appointed an angel as Our messenger, We would certainly have made him [appear as] a man, and thus We would have confused them just as they are now confusing themselves. (9)

وَلَوۡ جَعَلۡنَٰهُ مَلَكًا لَّجَعَلۡنَٰهُ رَجُلًا وَلَلَبَسۡنَا عَلَيۡهِم مَّا يَلۡبِسُونَ ۝

Indeed other messengers have been derided before your time, but those who scoffed at them were eventually overwhelmed by the very thing they have derided. (10)

وَلَقَدِ ٱسۡتُهۡزِئَ بِرُسُلٍ مِّن قَبۡلِكَ فَحَاقَ بِٱلَّذِينَ سَخِرُواْ مِنۡهُم مَّا كَانُواْ بِهِۦ يَسۡتَهۡزِءُونَ ۝

Say: Go all over the earth and see what was the fate of those who denied the truth. (11)

قُلۡ سِيرُواْ فِي ٱلۡأَرۡضِ ثُمَّ ٱنظُرُواْ كَيۡفَ كَانَ عَٰقِبَةُ ٱلۡمُكَذِّبِينَ ۝

Overview

This is the second opening passage of the *sūrah*, following the first that spoke of the truth of God's existence as it is reflected in the creation of the heavens and the earth and the origination of darkness and light. It is further reflected in the creation of man from the very substance of this earth, determining the term of his first life that ends in death while keeping secret another time fixed for resurrection, and in God's full knowledge of what people may do and have done both in public and in private.

This existence of the Divine Being is unique, unlike any other existence, because there is no creator other than God. It is so clear and overpowering that to deny it, in spite of all the great signs testifying to it, is an unjustifiable enormity.

When the *sūrah* portrays the attitude of the unbelievers who oppose the Islamic message in the face of such undeniable and overpowering existence, their attitude appears singularly insupportable. Thus, the Qur'ān wins this first round, scoring its win in the depth of people's nature, despite their apparent and stubborn rejection.

This passage of the *sūrah* portrays this unreasonable stubbornness, issuing on the one hand a stern warning and on the other a reminder of the fate of earlier rejecters. The admonition is stacked with various but highly effective touches that follow the initial jolt that shakes people's hearts at the outset of the *sūrah*.

Social Attitudes and the Decline of Nations

> *Whenever a revelation comes to them from their Lord, they [who are unbelievers] turn their back upon it. Thus they have denied the truth now that it has come to them. In time, they shall have full information about that which they used to deride. Do they not see how many a generation We have destroyed before them – people whom We had made more powerful in the land than We have made you, and for whom We sent down abundant water from the sky, and made rivers flow at their feet? Yet We destroyed them for their sins, and raised up another generation in their place.* (Verses 4–6)

It is clear that turning away from the truth is an obstinate position taken by the unbelievers, and this in the face of all the evidence pointing to its error. They do not lack signs and pointers which guide people to faith, nor do they lack evidence to prove the truth of the message and the genuine honesty of the Messenger conveying it, nor do they lack evidence of Godhead. These are the basic concepts they are called upon to accept. All they lack is the will to respond to clear evidence, overcome irrational stubbornness and reflect on the truth presented to them: "*Whenever a revelation comes to them from their Lord, they [who are unbelievers] turn their back upon it.*" (Verse 4) Such deliberate obstinacy against all evidence and clear signs needs the threat of severe punishment to jolt them out of their attitude, remove the barriers of their conceit and reawaken their natural responses: "*Thus they have denied the truth now that it has come to them. In time, they shall have full information about that which they used to deride.*" (Verse 5)

The truth has come to them from the Creator of the heavens and the earth, who has brought into being darkness and light and created man out of clay. It is He alone who is God in the heavens and on earth, and who has full knowledge of all that people keep secret or do openly, as well as all that they earn. What has come to them from Him is the truth, and they have rejected it, insisting on describing it as false, turning away from Divine revelations and deriding the call to faith. Hence, they are told to watch for the true information which is certain to come to them concerning that which they used to scorn. This is a general threat given without any details of its nature or timing. Thus, they are kept in suspense, waiting, expecting at every moment to receive what they are threatened with of unspecified suffering.

Their attentions and minds are drawn to the calamities that befell past nations which, like them, rejected the truth. They even had some knowledge of those nations and what happened to them in the remains of the people of 'Ād of al-Aḥqāf and Thamūd of al-Ḥijr. The Arabs of Makkah used to pass by these remains when they went on their winter and summer journeys to Yemen and Syria respectively. They also passed by the destroyed towns of the Prophet Lot's people, Sodom and Gomorrah, and were aware of the tales that were in circulation concerning what happened to those people. They should, therefore, reflect on these peoples' fate: "*Do they not see how many a generation We have destroyed before them – people whom We had made more powerful in the land than We have made you, and for whom We sent down abundant water from the sky, and made rivers flow at their feet? Yet We destroyed them for their sins, and raised up another generation in their place.*" (Verse 6)

Those earlier generations were well established in the land and given power which was much greater than that enjoyed by the Quraysh, the first people addressed by the Qur'ān. God also sent them rain which brought into their lives fertility, growth and abundance. But they disobeyed their Lord and were subsequently destroyed by Him. God then raised up another generation to take over and wield power. No matter how powerful a community may be, God can easily inflict severe punishment on them. When those people were destroyed, the earth did not feel their absence since another generation was raised in their place. Life continued as if nothing had happened.

People tend to overlook this fact when they are prosperous. They forget that it is God who gives them power in order to test them to determine how faithful they are to their pledges to worship Him alone and to follow His guidance. Will they honour their covenant with the One who has placed them in charge of His earth, or will they create false deities for themselves which usurp the rights and attributes of Godhead and treat what has been entrusted to their charge as their own property?

Very often people tend to overlook this fact, and consequently deviate from the terms of their covenant with God that has placed them in charge of the earth. They, therefore, abandon the way of living God has laid down for them, unaware initially of the consequences to which they expose themselves. Corruption gradually creeps into their lives and they move further away from divine guidance. This continues until they reach such a stage that the threats outlined by God are inevitably put into effect. Doom may take different processes: God may eliminate some people altogether, inflicting on them suffering that engulfs them from above or springs from beneath their feet. At other times, God may punish them with famine, a heavy death toll and poor harvests. Both types of punishment were inflicted on different nations. God may, alternatively, cause some of them to endure the might of others until trust can no longer exist between them, and they are considerably weakened. God may give power over them to some of His servants, who may or may not abide by God's code, this to weaken their forces and uproot them from the land in which they exercised their power. Life continues in this cycle. It is a happy person who realises that it is a manifestation of God's laws in operation and that it is all a test. He is then true to his part of his covenant with God. By contrast, it is a miserable person who overlooks this fact and deludes himself with thoughts that he has been able to acquire strength and prosperity by his own knowledge or methods, or by mere coincidence.

People are often deceived when they see a despotic ruler, a corrupt or atheist person enjoying power on earth, able to escape punishment. But people are hasty. They see only the beginning or the middle of the route but not its end to which such person arrives at the appropriate time. We can see examples of it in how ancient generations who defied God and His messengers were destroyed. In the Qur'ān, our attention is drawn to their fates so that we realise that the end is not what we see at a particular point in time. The statement, *'We destroyed them for their sins'*, is often repeated in the Qur'ān in a variety of ways. Such repetition aims to establish a certain fact and to clarify a part of the Islamic interpretation of historical events. It shows that sins do destroy sinners and that it is God who brings about their destruction. This is a law which remains in operation although an individual or a generation may not see it within their own limited life span. It simply engulfs nations when they allow sins to become an essential part of their lifestyle.

As we have said, this statement gives us a glimpse of the Islamic interpretation of history, because the destruction of past nations and their replacement with new generations are due in part to the effect of sin on the constitution of nations. They create a condition which inevitably leads to destruction, either through a sudden calamity that God causes to befall them as used to happen in ancient history, or through natural, progressive decline which weakens nations as they wander aimlessly in a sinful maze.

In relatively recent history, we have enough examples of the effects on nations of uncontrolled indulgences, permissiveness, promiscuity and treating women as little more than sexual objects. The collapse of the Greek and Roman Empires provide such examples, but we can also discern the beginning of the decline of nations that still seem to enjoy power and affluence such as France and Britain.

A materialistic interpretation of history gives this aspect no room whatsoever, because it does not recognise the moral aspect of life or the religious foundations on which it is based. It is, thus, forced into accepting some laughable justifications of events in human history which have their very foundations in the religious and moral aspects of human life.

On the other hand, comprehensive, serious and realistic as it is, the Islamic interpretation of history gives the material aspect its due importance while recognising other influential factors that are denied by others who stubbornly refuse to acknowledge all the facts of life. With the Islamic interpretation, we visualise God's will operating behind all that takes place in the universe. We see how consciousness, feelings, beliefs and concepts do change within man and do influence human behaviour. This interpretation does not overlook any single factor of God's law which regulates life in general.

Stubborn Rejection of Evident Facts

The *sūrah* goes on to describe the nature of obstinate rejection, delineating for us a very strange type of people whom we meet in every age and every community. These are people who deny what is so clear and undeniable. The Qur'ān depicts this type of people in its own inimitable style, using only a few words to bring it to life in front of our eyes: *"Even if We had sent down to you a book written on paper, and they had touched it with their own hands, surely the unbelievers would still say: 'This is nothing but plain sorcery'."* (Verse 7)

What causes them to turn away from God's revelations is not the lack of strong and clear evidence of their truthfulness. They are only being unreasonably stubborn. Their denial is firmly held as though it was a matter of principle. Such an attitude allows no consideration of any evidence or proof. Had God chosen to send down the Qur'ān to His Messenger by means other than revelation, which they cannot see, and put it on paper which they can feel and see, and had they touched this paper with their own hands, they would still reject the evidence of their own hands and eyes. They would emphatically claim: *"This is nothing but plain sorcery."* (Verse 7)

This is an image of a singularly contemptible nature, one which invites strong hostility. With such a nature there is no room for argument or scholarly discussion. Yet we meet such people in all communities and across all generations. Depicting their nature in this way serves more than one purpose: it delineates to the rejecters themselves their spiteful attitude in its true colours, just like one who lifts the mirror in front of a person with an ugly face so that he can see himself and put a stop to his overbearing behaviour. It also gives the believers an added incentive to adhere strongly to the truth, uninfluenced by the general atmosphere of denial and rejection they see around them. They are, thus, more resilient in the face of oppression and persecution.

It also tells us how compassionate and forbearing God is, as He gives those rejecters a chance to mend their ways and does not smite them immediately for their stubbornness. All these elements were part of the weaponry available to the Muslim community in their fight against the unbelievers.

The *sūrah* then gives us an example of the suggestions made by the unbelievers, and this reveals both their hardened stubbornness and their ignorance. They suggest that an angel could have accompanied the Prophet in conveying his message to give proof that he was truly God's Messenger. The reply shows how ignorant they were of the angels' nature and why God sent them to do the tasks He assigned to them. It is only because of His mercy that God does not act on their suggestion: "*They say: 'Why has not an angel been sent down to him?' If We had sent down an angel, all would have been decided, and they would have been allowed no further respite. And even if We had appointed an angel as Our messenger, We would certainly have made him [appear as] a man, and thus We would have confused them just as they are now confusing themselves.*" (Verses 8–9)

This was not a new suggestion made by the Quraysh unbelievers. Many communities before them had muted the same as we are told in the Qur'ān. The suggestion and the Qur'ānic reply to it at this point raise a number of issues, as we will presently see.

Firstly, the pagan Arabs did not deny God altogether, but they wanted proof that the Prophet Muḥammad (peace be upon him) was truly His Messenger and that the book he recited to them was truly revealed to him by God. They wanted a particular proof, namely, that an angel be sent to him to confirm his claim. This was just one of the numerous suggestions reported in the Qur'ān. A number of these are mentioned in *Sūrah* 17, The Night Journey: "*They say: 'We shall not believe in you till you cause a spring to gush forth for us from the earth, or [till] you have a garden of date trees and vines, and you cause running waters to flow through it, or till you cause the sky to fall upon us in pieces, as you have threatened, or till you bring God and the angels face to face before us, or till you have a house of gold, or you ascend to heaven. Indeed we shall not believe in your ascent to heaven until you bring a book for us to read.' Say, 'All glory belongs to my Lord. Surely I am only a man and a Messenger.' Nothing has ever prevented people from believing [in God] whenever guidance has come to them except for their saying: 'Can it be that God has sent a human being as His Messenger?' Say, 'Had there been angels walking about on earth as their natural abode, We would have sent them an angel messenger from heaven.'*" (17: 90–5)

Such suggestions betray both obstinacy and ignorance. They had known God's Messenger for a long time and their long experience told them much about his honesty and truthfulness to the extent that they gave him the title *Al-Amīn*, which means 'the trustworthy'. They continued to deposit their valuables with him for safekeeping, even when they were fiercely opposed to him. When he left for Madinah, he entrusted his cousin 'Alī with the task of returning to the Quraysh the valuables they had kept with him. He even did this at the time when they were plotting to assassinate him in his own home.

They were as certain of his truthfulness as they were of his honesty. When, in compliance with God's command, he stood on top of the hill of al-Ṣafā to call on them, as a community, to believe in his message, he started by asking them whether they would believe him if he were to tell them a piece of news of which they were totally unaware. They all replied in the affirmative, relying on their experience of him as a man who always told the truth. Had they truly wanted to know whether he was telling the truth when he said that he was God's Messenger, his past would have been more than sufficient as proof.

Later in the *sūrah*, God tells His Messenger that those rejecters do not actually reject his message as false: "*We know too well that what they say grieves you. Yet it is not you that they charge with falsehood; but it is God's revelations that the wrongdoers deny.*" (Verse 33) It is, then, just their persistent attitude of rejection, motivated only by a stubborn turning away from the truth. They never doubted the truthfulness of the Prophet Muḥammad (peace be upon him).

Moreover, they had in the Qur'ān itself a proof which was more telling than the material proofs they demanded. In itself, and in its inimitable style, the Qur'ān tells that it has been revealed by God whose existence they did not deny. Most assuredly, they realised this and knew it for certain. They possessed a fine literary and artistic sense which must have made it clear to them that, in its excellence, the Qur'ān greatly surpassed the farthest limits of human ability. A person who has the gift of artistic expression is better able to recognise and appreciate this than one who has not. Anyone with this gift will tell us clearly that the Qur'ān surpasses all that human literary excellence can produce. No one denies this except a person who deliberately tries to suppress what he knows.

Moreover, the contents of the Qur'ān, i.e. the concepts of faith and the method it utilises to drive these concepts home to people, as also its touches and influences, were all totally new to human minds. They were unknown in human artistic expression. The Arabs were not unaware of all these facts. They recognised them within themselves. Their statements and attitudes showed that they did not doubt that the Qur'ān was revealed by God.

All this makes it clear that, in point of fact, their suggestions were not made to seek a proof. They were simply born out of an unyielding stubbornness. Their position was truly as God describes in the preceding verse: *"Even if We had sent down to you a book written on paper, and they had touched it with their own hands, surely the unbelievers would still say: 'This is nothing but plain sorcery'."* (Verse 7)

A World of Creation Beyond Human Senses

The second issue was that the Arabs knew about the angels and requested that God should send down an angel to support His Messenger and confirm the truth of his message. They knew nothing, however, of the nature of this type of creation, i.e. the angels, which is known only to God. Hence, they formulated their own arbitrary conceptions of these creatures and the sort of relationship which existed between them and their Lord on the one hand, and with the earth and its inhabitants on the other. The Qur'ān refers to the Arabian misconceptions about the angels and the legends of pagan nations. It points out their errors so that anyone who is guided to accept the Islamic faith will revise their concepts about the universe and its creatures. As such, Islam provides a method to set man's reason, feelings, heart and conscience on the right course and to rectify both situations and practices. One of the Arabs' ill-conceived concepts, identified in the Qur'ān as having been formulated in their pre-Islamic days, was their belief that the angels were God's daughters. Limitless is He in His glory and sublimely exalted above anything that people may ascribe to Him! As such, they believed angels were able to intercede with God and their intercession was never refused. It is thought that some of the more important idols were symbols of angels.

The Qur'ān refutes on several occasions the first erroneous concept the Arabs held. For example, in *Sūrah* 53, The Star, we read: *"Have you ever considered al-Lāt and al-'Uzzā as well as Manāt, the third of this tirade? Why for yourselves would you choose only male offspring, whereas to Him you assign female: that is indeed an unfair division! These [idols] are nothing but empty names which you have invented, you and your forefathers, for which God has bestowed no warrant from on high. They who worship them follow nothing but surmise and their own wishful thinking, although right guidance has indeed come to them from their Lord. Does man imagine that it is his due to have all that he might wish for, despite the fact that both the life to come and this present life belong to God alone? For, however many angels there be in the heavens, their intercession can be of no avail to anyone, except after God has given leave [to intercede] for whomever He wills and with whom He is well-pleased. It is only such as do not really believe in the life to come that regard the angels as female beings; and since they have no knowledge of that at all, they follow nothing but surmise: yet never can surmise take the place of truth."* (53: 19–28)

The Qur'ān also provides the true facts, correcting the Arab unbelievers' erroneous concept about the angels' nature. This is provided in these two verses in this *sūrah* as it is given elsewhere in the Qur'ān: *"They say: 'Why has not an angel been sent down to him?' If We had sent down an angel, all would have been decided, and they would have been allowed no further respite."* (Verse 8)

This is part of the information provided in the Qur'ān on the nature of the angels created by God. The unbelievers proposed that an angel should be sent down, but it has been part of God's law that He sends down angels to this planet only to destroy a particular community for having rejected their messenger. Had God responded to the Arab unbelievers' suggestion and sent down an angel, then the whole issue would have been resolved and they would have been destroyed without allowing them any further time to consider their position. Was this the alternative they wished for? Would it not be better for them to realize how limitless God's grace is when He does not respond to their suggestion, because it would have brought about their own destruction? They are, thus, made to see the facts with their own eyes, so that they may realise how ignorant they are about their own interests and about the process of sending down angels. It is their ignorance which has brought them to the edge of ruin and which causes them to reject proper guidance and divine mercy. Hence, they persistently demand evidence and proof.

The other part of the definition of the angels as God's own servants is provided by the second verse: *"And even if We had appointed an angel as Our messenger, We would certainly have made him [appear as] a man, and thus We would have confused them just as they are now confusing themselves."* (Verse 9)

What they demand is that God sends an angel to confirm the Prophet's message. As creatures, angels are different from human beings. They have their own nature which is known only to God. Since we know nothing about them other than what we are told by God who has created them, we know that they cannot walk on earth in their own form of creation, because they do not live on this planet. However, they have the ability to take human form when they undertake a task relevant to human life, such as conveying God's message or destroying those unbelievers whom God wishes to destroy, or giving support to believers or fighting against their enemies. The Qur'ān tells us of other duties they may be commanded to fulfil, and they do not disobey God in whatever He bids them to do. They simply do what they are bid.

Therefore, if God wanted to send an angel to confirm His Prophet's message, that angel would have appeared to mankind in the form of a man, not in his own angelic form. This would have made the confusion persist, especially when Muḥammad (peace be upon him) would sometimes say to them, "I am Muḥammad whom you have known very well. God has sent me as a messenger to warn you and give you happy news". How much greater would their confusion be if an angel came to them in the form of a man whom they did not know and said, "I am an angel sent by God to confirm the message preached by His Messenger"? To them, that angel would only appear as a man like them. They were confusing simple facts. If God were to send an angel, He would have given it human form and would have confused the very thing the unbelievers were themselves confusing. They would not have been able to see right guidance.

Thus, God points out their ignorance about the nature of His creation and His law. Additionally, their stubborn rejection, which has neither justification nor supporting evidence, is also exposed.

Angels: Their Life and Role

The third issue raised in these verses is that of the nature of Islamic philosophy, particularly with regard to the world we see all around us and the worlds which lay beyond our perception. Islam teaches its followers to formulate a particular understanding of these worlds and a proper approach to them. One of these is the world of angels in whom we believe. Believing in the angels is an essential component of Islamic faith which requires every Muslim to believe in God, His angels, books, messengers, the Last Day and destiny.

To believe in an imperceptible world represents a great departure in man's life, helping him to break out of his limited and narrow physical existence and to perceive the existence of a world beyond. Thus, man is not limited to the narrow world of physical perception. Indeed, to impose such a limitation is to force human perception backwards. This is advocated by some materialistic doctrines which claim to be progressive. Fuller treatment of this subject follows later on, when we comment on Verse 59 of this *sūrah*. Here, we limit our discussion to the angels who are part of the world which lies beyond our human senses.

The Qur'ān tells us about some of the qualities and attributes of the angels. These are sufficient for us to formulate a proper concept of them and of our relationship with them. They are a species of God's creation who submit themselves totally to God and who obey Him all the time without hesitation. They are near to God although we do not know what sort of proximity is meant here. "*They say: 'The Most Gracious has taken to Himself a son!' Limitless is He in His glory! No; they are but His honoured servants. They do not speak until He has spoken, and they act at His behest. He knows all that lies before them and all behind them. They do not intercede for any but those whom He has already graced with His goodly acceptance, since they themselves stand in reverent awe of Him.*" (21: 26–8) "*Those that are with Him are never too proud to worship Him and never grow weary of that. They extol His limitless glory by night and day, without ever flagging.*" (21: 19–20)

They carry God's Throne and surround it on the Day of Judgement. We do not know how this happens, because we only know what God has revealed to us of the world beyond: "*Those who bear God's Throne and those who stand around it extol their Lord's limitless glory and praise and believe in Him.*" (40: 7) "*You will see the angels surrounding the Throne, extolling their Lord's glory and praise. Judgement would have been passed in justice on all, and the word will be spoken: all praise is due to God, the Lord of all the worlds.*" (39: 75)

They provide the keepers of the heavens and hell, receive the inhabitants of the first with greetings and prayer, while they receive those bound to hell with reproach and warnings of great suffering. "*In throngs the unbelievers shall be urged on towards hell, till, when they reach it, its gates will be opened and its keepers will ask them: 'Have there not come to you messengers from among yourselves who proclaimed to you your Lord's revelations and warned you of the coming of this your Day [of Judgement]?' They will answer: 'Yes, indeed!' And thus the sentence of suffering would have already fallen due upon the unbelievers. They will be told, 'Enter the gates of hell, therein to abide!' How vile an abode for those who were given to false pride. But those who were God-fearing will be urged on in throngs to Paradise till, when they reach it, they will find its gate wide open; and its keepers will say to them, 'Peace be to you! Well have you done: enter this Paradise, herein to abide'.'' (39: 71–3) "We have appointed none but angels to guard the Fire." (74: 31)*

The angels deal with people on earth in various ways. They watch over them by God's decree and they follow their deeds and keep a record of everything that human beings do or say. They also cause them to die when their time is over: *"He alone holds sway over His servants. He sends forth guardians to watch over you until, when death approaches any one of you, Our messengers cause him to die. They leave no part of their duty unfulfilled."* (Verse 61) *"Each has guardian angels before him and behind him, who watch him by God's command."* (13: 11) *"Each word he utters shall be noted down by a vigilant guardian."* (50: 18)

Angels also deliver God's revelations to His messengers (peace be upon them all). God has also informed us that Gabriel (peace be upon him) is the one chosen among them to fulfil this task: *"He sends down angels with this Divine inspiration, [bestowed] by His will on any of His servants He may wish: 'Warn [mankind] that there is no deity but Me: so fear Me'."* (16: 2) *"Say: Whoever is an enemy of Gabriel should know that he revealed it [the Qur'ān] to your heart by God's leave..."* (2: 97) God describes Gabriel as one who has been endowed with power. He confirms that His Messenger, Muḥammad, has seen Gabriel in his angelic form twice, while he has seen him in various shapes and forms when he gave him other revelations: *"Consider the star when it sets, this fellow man of yours has not gone astray, nor is he deluded. He does not speak out of his own fancy. That [which he conveys to you] is but a revelation with which he is inspired. He is taught by one who is very mighty, [an angel] endowed with surpassing power, who manifested himself in his true shape and nature, appearing on the uppermost horizon, and then, drew near, and came close, until he was within two bows' length or even closer, and revealed to His servant that which he revealed. The servant's heart did not deny*

*what he saw. Will you, then, contend with him as to what he saw?
And indeed he saw him a second time, by the lote-tree of the farthest
limit, near to the garden of promise."* (53: 1–15)

The angels also join the believers giving them support and help,
steadying their feet in their great, unabating battle against evil and
tyranny. They busy themselves with what happens to the believers.
They glorify their Lord, pray to Him to forgive the sins of those who
believe in Him. In their supplication for the believers, which is
mentioned in the Qur'ān, they appear to be so caring, kind and loving.
They also give the believers, at the time of their death, the happy news
that they are going to heaven. When they arrive in the next world,
they also give them their happy news and greet them in heaven.

On the other hand, they receive the unbelievers in hell with reproach
and warning of their impending suffering. They may also fight against
them in the battle that rages on between truth and falsehood. When
they die, they pluck out their souls in a manner which afflicts and
humiliates the unbelievers.

The angels have also had a relationship with human beings ever since
the creation of Adam, the first man. This relationship extends
throughout life until the hereafter. References to this relationship
abound in the Qur'ān.

There is, then, a wide expanse in which human life is linked to the
life of the supreme society of angels. It provides a broader vision and
understanding of this universe and enables man to feel his existence,
his actions and reactions in a much wider world. In this way what we
witness in our world is closely related to the world beyond.

Those who wish to deprive man of this world, and of the expanse
of the realm that lies beyond our human perception, have nothing but
evil in store. They want to confine man to the narrow, material world,
thus forcing him into the animal world. God has given man the ability
of conception, which enables him to understand what no animal can
understand, allowing him to live in a wider realm of knowledge and
feeling, giving him the facility to look at this world through his heart
and mind, and helping him to purify himself as he moves towards this
spreading light.

In their pre-Islamic days, the Arabs held all sorts of misconceptions,
but they were nevertheless better placed than the advocates of today's
materialism who deride the whole idea of a world beyond. These
describe believing in an imperceptible world as naïve, unscientific. They

consider the two mutually exclusive. We will discuss their claims, which are devoid of any scientific or religious substance when we comment on Verse 59. Here we are only speaking briefly about the angels.

We wonder: what does science divulge to those who claim to believe only in 'scientific' rationalism to make them categorically deny the existence of the angels, making them outside the realm of belief? Science cannot preclude the existence of life, of a type other than the one that exists on earth, on other planets or stars which differ from earth in nature, conditions and atmosphere. How can they deny the existence of such worlds when they have no single evidence to prove that they do not exist?

In this, we are not asking them to submit to the rule of our faith or to God's words. We are simply asking them to submit to the dictates of their own 'science', which they have made into a deity. Although they can provide no evidence based on their science, they persist in their totally unscientific denial. Yet it is no exaggeration to say that the imperceptible world which they deny is the very truth which human knowledge has come to recognise, even in our world which we touch and see.

When God's Message is Met with Derision

This passage concludes with a reference to what happened to those who derided God's messengers. The new rejecters of the faith are called upon to reflect on the fate of those who preceded them. They are told to travel all over the earth to see for themselves the fate of earlier unbelievers, because that tells them of God's law which never fails: "*Indeed other messengers have been derided before your time, but those who scoffed at them were eventually overwhelmed by the very thing they have derided.*" (Verse 10)

Having shown their attitude as stubborn rejection and their suggestions as marks of total ignorance, and having established that God's refusal to act on their suggestions is an aspect of His mercy and forbearance, the *sūrah* refers to the treatment received by earlier messengers. Such reference has a dual purpose. It firstly provides some solace to the Prophet who was at the receiving end of their obstinate rejection of the truth. It reassures him that God will certainly punish those who deride and scoff at His messengers. It tells him that such rejection is not a new phenomenon. Earlier messengers received similar treatment from their peoples, but those who scoffed at them were soon to suffer God's punishment. Ultimate victory belongs to the Truth.

Secondly, it reminds the Arabs who rejected the Prophet's message of the fate of their earlier counterparts. A similar fate awaits them if they persist in their ridicule and rejection. God's punishment destroyed earlier generations who were much more powerful and who enjoyed greater wealth. This reference, then, shakes their hearts violently.

Let us reflect a little here on this Qur'ānic directive: "*Say: Go all over the earth and see what was the fate of those who denied the truth.*" (Verse 11) To travel all over the earth for the simple objective of reflection and drawing lessons on the basis of past events and on history told by one generation to the next was something totally new to the Arabs. It shows how great was the gulf between their level of ignorance and the much higher level of intelligence, knowledge and reflection to which Islam carried them. They used to travel for trade and to earn their living. Travelling to gain knowledge and draw lessons was unheard of. This new Islamic method took them by the hand, elevating them from the depths of their ignorance and gently coaxing them along the road to the high zenith they were soon to achieve.

Moreover, it was totally new for mankind in that period of time to try to interpret human history according to methodical and well-defined rules based on cause and effect, such as those pointed out by the Qur'ān to the Arabs. All people can easily observe these laws and formulate their own concept of premises, stages and results. Up to that period in time, the best that people knew of history was the recording of events and narratives about customs and social habits. No particular method, whether analytic or synthetic, was followed to determine links between events or to relate results to premises. The Qur'ān elevated mankind to a new horizon and gave them a method to analyse and reflect upon the events of human history. This method does not represent a stage in the development of human knowledge. Rather, it is the only method which can give us a true picture of human history.

A period of one quarter of a century is insufficient to bring about a dramatic development in economic conditions. Those who are amazed at the great advances achieved by the Arabs in such a short period of time from the outset of the Islamic message will cease to be amazed if they switch their attentions away from seeking economic factors for this change. They should try instead to discover the secret of this advancement in the new Divine method which God, in His wisdom, gave them through His Messenger, Muḥammad (peace be upon him). It is in this method that the secret of the miracle experienced by the Arabs lies. Any attempt to find the secret with the false deity created by modern materialism, namely, economy, will remain futile. For what dramatic economic development took place in Arabia to explain the formulation of new concepts and beliefs, systems of government, methodical thought, moral values, new social status and new fields of knowledge which the Arabs witnessed within just a quarter of a century? None, it was simply the Qur'ān and its message.

The Qur'ān established a new system of thought. Totally unknown to man previously, this system was and is both unique and valid for all times. It is the one pointed out by numerous Qur'ānic verses, such as that with which this passage concludes: "*Say: Go all over the earth and see what was the fate of those who denied the truth.*" (Verse 11) A similar pointer is an earlier verse in this passage: "*Do they not see how many a generation We have destroyed before them – people whom We had made more powerful in the land than We have made you, and for whom We sent down abundant water from the sky, and made rivers flow at their feet? Yet We destroyed them for their sins, and raised up another generation in their place.*" (Verse 6)

3

A Commitment to Mercy

Say: To whom belongs all that is in the heavens and on earth? Say: To God. He has committed Himself to bestow grace and mercy. He will certainly gather you all together on the Day of Resurrection, about which there is no doubt. Those who squandered their own souls will not believe. (12)

قُل لِّمَن مَّا فِى ٱلسَّمَٰوَٰتِ وَٱلۡأَرۡضِ قُل لِّلَّهِ كَتَبَ عَلَىٰ نَفۡسِهِ ٱلرَّحۡمَةَ لَيَجۡمَعَنَّكُمۡ إِلَىٰ يَوۡمِ ٱلۡقِيَٰمَةِ لَا رَيۡبَ فِيهِ ٱلَّذِينَ خَسِرُوٓاْ أَنفُسَهُمۡ فَهُمۡ لَا يُؤۡمِنُونَ ۝

To Him belongs whatever takes its rest in the night or in the day. He alone hears all and knows all. (13)

۞ وَلَهُۥ مَا سَكَنَ فِى ٱلَّيۡلِ وَٱلنَّهَارِ وَهُوَ ٱلسَّمِيعُ ٱلۡعَلِيمُ ۝

Say: Am I to take for my master anyone but God, the Originator of the heavens and the earth, who gives nourishment to all and Himself needs none? Say: I am commanded to be the first of those who surrender themselves to God, and not to be among those who associate partners with Him. (14)

قُلۡ أَغَيۡرَ ٱللَّهِ أَتَّخِذُ وَلِيّٗا فَاطِرِ ٱلسَّمَٰوَٰتِ وَٱلۡأَرۡضِ وَهُوَ يُطۡعِمُ وَلَا يُطۡعَمُ قُلۡ إِنِّىٓ أُمِرۡتُ أَنۡ أَكُونَ أَوَّلَ مَنۡ أَسۡلَمَ وَلَا تَكُونَنَّ مِنَ ٱلۡمُشۡرِكِينَ ۝

Say: Indeed I would dread, were I to disobey my Lord, the suffering of an awesome day. (15)

قُلْ إِنِّى أَخَافُ إِنْ عَصَيْتُ رَبِّى عَذَابَ يَوْمٍ عَظِيمٍ ﴿١٥﴾

He who is spared that shall have received His grace. This will be a manifest triumph. (16)

مَن يُصْرَفْ عَنْهُ يَوْمَئِذٍ فَقَدْ رَحِمَهُ وَذَلِكَ ٱلْفَوْزُ ٱلْمُبِينُ ﴿١٦﴾

If God were to expose you to affliction, none can remove it but He. And if He were to bless you with good fortune – well, He has power over all things. (17)

وَإِن يَمْسَسْكَ ٱللَّهُ بِضُرٍّ فَلَا كَاشِفَ لَهُۥ إِلَّا هُوَ وَإِن يَمْسَسْكَ بِخَيْرٍ فَهُوَ عَلَىٰ كُلِّ شَىْءٍ قَدِيرٌ ﴿١٧﴾

He alone holds sway over all His creatures, and He alone is truly wise, all-aware. (18)

وَهُوَ ٱلْقَاهِرُ فَوْقَ عِبَادِهِۦ وَهُوَ ٱلْحَكِيمُ ٱلْخَبِيرُ ﴿١٨﴾

Say: What is weightiest in testimony? Say: God is witness between me and you. This Qur'ān has been revealed to me that I may thereby warn you and all whom it may reach. Will you in truth bear witness that there are other deities beside God? Say: I bear no such witness. Say: He is but one God. I disown all that you associate with Him. (19)

قُلْ أَىُّ شَىْءٍ أَكْبَرُ شَهَٰدَةً قُلِ ٱللَّهُ شَهِيدٌ بَيْنِى وَبَيْنَكُمْ وَأُوحِىَ إِلَىَّ هَٰذَا ٱلْقُرْءَانُ لِأُنذِرَكُم بِهِۦ وَمَنۢ بَلَغَ أَئِنَّكُمْ لَتَشْهَدُونَ أَنَّ مَعَ ٱللَّهِ ءَالِهَةً أُخْرَىٰ قُل لَّآ أَشْهَدُ قُلْ إِنَّمَا هُوَ إِلَٰهٌ وَٰحِدٌ وَإِنَّنِى بَرِىٓءٌ مِّمَّا تُشْرِكُونَ ﴿١٩﴾

Overview

The early passages in this *surah* sound like waves following one another in quick succession. Rising high and with a deep, mysterious rhythm, this third wave comes after a discussion about denying the truth of Islam, turning away from it, meeting its advocates with derision and ridicule. The discussion in the earlier passage included very strong threats and a reminder of the fate of earlier nations that took a similar attitude to God's messages. The first passage, representing the first wave, discussed the truth of Godhead as reflected in the creation of the wide universe and highly complex human beings. This new wave also discusses the same truth of Godhead but it includes different aspects, employing different rhythms and a new inspiration. Thus, the discussion on denying the truth comes in between the opening and the present passages, and this adds to its unpleasant reality.

In the opening passage, Godhead is reflected in the creation of the heavens and earth, darkness and light, the creation of man out of clay, his first term of life, and the setting of another term for resurrection. It made clear that the whole universe submits itself to God, whose knowledge of mankind includes what everyone does both in public and in private. None of these qualities is approached in the *surah* in a theoretical, philosophical or theological way. Rather, the approach aims to establish what they mean to human life: complete and total faith in God alone, entertaining no doubts about Him whatsoever, and acceptance that His Godhead comprises all aspects of the universe and human life. Thus, human submission to God's sovereignty in all affairs becomes the natural and logical option in the same way as the universe submits to the same sovereignty.

In this new wave, the reality of Godhead is shown in a variety of aspects: ownership, direct action, the provision of sustenance, care, overwhelming power, bringing benefit and causing harm. Again, we do not see a theoretical, philosophical or theological approach here. The aim is to define the meaning of all these aspects in human life: namely, the unity of allegiance and worship as a practical demonstration of the unity of submission. Thus, when God's Messenger is directed to denounce the very thought of having any master other than God, this denunciation is based first of all on the fact that it is God who provides nourishment while He needs none. It is also based on the fact that the acknowledgement of a master other than God is contrary to His orders requiring him to submit himself to God alone.

The presentation of the reality of Godhead in this form and for this objective is accompanied by a host of powerful and inspiring effects. It starts with explaining that God owns all, provides sustenance to all creatures while He needs nothing from anyone. It then refers to the great suffering the mere avoidance of which represents an act of mercy granted by God and a great success. It also mentions God's power to administer benefit or harm, His authority over all creatures, and His infinite wisdom. All this is associated with a powerful rhythm, provided by the repeated Divine order, 'Say... Say... Say...'.

When the presentation is completed, the conclusion is given with increased rhythm, calling out witnesses to God's oneness and denouncing the very thought of associating partners with Him, all this within a clear demarcation of positions. Here again the strong rhythm is enhanced by the repeated order, 'Say... Say... Say...'. Thus, the passage delivers a sense of awe and seriousness.

A Commitment Made by God

> Say: To whom belongs all that is in the heavens and on earth? Say: To God. He has committed Himself to bestow grace and mercy. He will certainly gather you all together on the Day of Resurrection, about which there is no doubt. Those who squandered their own souls will not believe. To Him belongs whatever takes its rest in the night or in the day. He alone hears all and knows all. (Verses 12–13)

Here, the *sūrah* adopts an attitude of confrontation that aims to state the issues very clearly before drawing the lines that separate the believers from all others. It gives the Prophet certain instructions to take up this confrontation with those who are fully aware that God is the Creator of the whole universe, but who, nevertheless, worship other beings even though these have no power to create anything equal to Him. That is, they associate partners with Him whom they claim have a say in how they conduct their lives. The Prophet is instructed to confront them with a question about the ownership, which follows creation, of everything in the heavens and on earth. As the question is put, it is meant to include every single element in the whole universe. It is followed by a statement of fact over which they did not and could not argue. The Qur'ān tells us elsewhere that they used to acknowledge it fully: "*Say: To whom belongs all that is in the heavens and on earth? Say: To God.*" (Verse 12)

Despite the depth of their ignorance, which resulted in deviant concepts that devalued their quality of life, the Arabs in their pre-Islamic days were superior in this particular aspect to later-day *jāhiliyyah*. This new *jāhiliyyah* shuts its mind to this fact while the Arabs used to recognise and admit that God owned everything in the heavens and on earth. However, they did not bring that recognition to its logical conclusion which would have required them to acknowledge God's total authority over what He owns and that the only proper way to use what God has created is to obtain His permission and to act according to His law. Because of this, the Arabs were described as idolaters and their lifestyle as ignorant. How then should those who deny God's authority to legislate for human existence and, instead, exercise that authority themselves, be described? They must be given a description other than that of idolatry. God describes them as unbelievers, as wrongdoers and transgressors, no matter how strongly they claim to be Muslims and regardless of what religion is entered on their birth certificates.

The Qur'ānic verse follows this statement asserting God's ownership of the heavens and earth by stating that "*He has committed Himself to bestow grace and mercy.*" (Verse 12) He is the sole, undisputed owner of the whole universe. He, however, out of His generosity and by His own will, has committed Himself to bestow grace and mercy. No one could suggest this exercise of bestowing grace to Him or require it of Him, apart from His absolutely free-will and His compassionate lordship over the universe. Grace and mercy provide the basic rules in His treatment of, and judgement over, His servants both in this present life and in the life to come. Believing in this rule is one of the constituents of the Islamic concept of life. Even when God tests His servants with hardship, His mercy takes precedence. Indeed, the test is meant to prepare a group of them for the fulfilment of the trust He assigns to them after they have proven their dedication to His cause and preparedness to sacrifice themselves for it. He actually sorts out the good from the bad among them: those among them who are keen to follow God's Messenger distinguish themselves from those who turn back on their heels. The exercise of mercy and the bestowing of grace in all this are clearly manifest.

If we were to try to make an exhaustive list of the incidents and occasions wherein God bestows His mercy and how it is reflected in life, we would need to devote our whole lives to it. Indeed, generations can come and go before this task could be accomplished. In every moment God's grace is showered over people. We have only identified that mercy which is reflected in hard tests, because often people do not see it as such. We have no intention to attempt a full list of the occasions and the incidents where God's mercy is brought into action. We will instead only make some brief references to it. However, we need to reflect a little on the way this Qur'ānic statement is phrased: "*He has committed Himself to bestow grace and mercy.*" (Verse 12) The same statement is repeated again in Verse 54 of this *sūrah* with a slight variation: "*Your Lord has committed Himself to bestow grace and mercy.*"

What immediately attracts our attention in this statement is the fact that God, the Creator, the Owner, the Almighty who has power over all His servants, has granted them the favour of making the exercise of His mercy and grace a commitment to which He has bound Himself out of His own free-will. This is a great fact, one which we can hardly contemplate let alone appreciate. There is, however, yet another favour here which attracts our attention. This is manifested in the fact that He has also favoured His servants by telling them about this commitment. Who are human beings that they deserve the favour of being told of what God has willed, and for the communication to be given in God's own words through His Messenger? It is nothing short of a great favour that can only be bestowed by God, the Most Gracious.

When we reflect on this fact in this way, we feel a mixture of surprise and happiness that no words can describe. Indeed, such facts and the effects they have on the human mind are indescribable in human language. Humans, however, can appreciate these facts even though they may not be able to define them.

To appreciate this fact forms a part of our understanding of the nature of Godhead and the relationship between God and His servants. It is a pleasant, comforting and reassuring understanding which makes us wonder at those perverted minds which level accusations at Islam because it rejects the very idea of God having a son. Islam has no time for such insupportable visions. At the same time, it describes the relationship of grace and mercy between God and His servants in a way that has a profound effect on peoples' hearts and minds. God's mercy is extended to all His servants throughout their lives. Here, we can only refer to some of its main aspects. It is reflected in the very existence of mankind who originate from where they do not know and who are given a noble position, easily recognised in the qualities God bestows on many of His servants. It is also reflected in the forces and resources of the universe which God has made subservient to man. This is, indeed, the broader view of the meaning of the provisions God has given to man to enable him to live in comfort and affluence. It is further reflected in granting man the ability to learn and to make his talents and abilities responsive to the world around him. The result is the knowledge man achieves through God's grace and on account of which some miscreants reject God's existence. Again, the knowledge God has given to man is part of the grace He has bestowed on him.

God's grace is clearly seen in the role God has assigned to man as His vicegerent, and the care He takes of him by sending messengers to him to give him guidance. Nevertheless, God treats man with forbearance despite his stubborn refusal to listen to the warnings of God's messengers. It is so easy for God to punish him but God's grace oversteps His punishment.

It is further reflected in the fact that God forgives man his sins every time he repents of them. In the same vein, we can mention the fact that when God punishes man, His punishment is administered on the basis of what is exactly equivalent to his bad deeds. On the other hand, God rewards man for his good deeds at least ten times their value and He may increase that manifold for whomever He wills. Furthermore, a good deed erases bad ones. All this is part of God's grace because no human being can earn admission into heaven on the basis of his or her actions alone, unless God bestows His mercy on them. God's Messenger states that this also applies to him, thereby acknowledging man's shortcomings and God's grace.

It is only appropriate to acknowledge that it is impossible for us to attempt to make an exhaustive list of the aspects of God's mercy and grace. Suffice it to say that it is beyond human ability to fully reflect on and appreciate the full significance of one moment in which God opens the gates of His mercy to His servant so as to give him security and reassurance. To describe such a moment and the feelings it generates is a much harder task.

An Outline of Divine Mercy

Let us now consider a number of *aḥādīth* which give us an insight into how the Prophet portrayed God's grace so as to make it properly appreciated by ordinary people.

Abū Hurayrah quotes the Prophet as saying: "When God created His creation, He wrote in a book which He keeps with Him above the Throne: My grace overspeeds My anger." (Related by al-Bukhārī and Muslim with slight variations.) In another version related by al-Bukhārī, the last sentence is quoted as, "My grace oversteps My anger."

Both al-Bukhārī and Muslim relate on the authority of Abū Hurayrah that God's Messenger said that: "God has made mercy into one hundred parts. He then retained ninety-nine parts and placed on earth one part. It is from that one part that creatures show mercy to one another, to the extent that a female animal lifts its hoof away from its young in order not to harm it."

Muslim also relates on the authority of Salmān that God's Messenger said: "God has one hundred acts of mercy. One of these is the one by which creatures show mercy to one another. The other ninety-nine parts are reserved to the Day of Judgement."

In yet another *ḥadīth* related by Muslim, we read: "When God created the heavens and the earth, He also created one hundred mercies, each one of them filled the space between the heavens and the earth. He placed one mercy on earth. It is through this that a mother is compassionate to her baby, and so are wild beasts and birds. On the Day of Judgement, God complements them with this one mercy."

This is an inspiring description by the Prophet, one which makes it easy for the human mind to visualise the extent of God's grace. We only need to reflect on how mothers are so kind-hearted to their youngsters and the sympathy and kindness people show towards the very young and very old, the sick and the invalid, and to relatives and friends. We should also contemplate how birds and animals sometimes manifest their mercy to one another in amazing ways. Now let us consider that all this mercy is the result of a single part out of one hundred parts of God's mercy. We can, thus, appreciate the extent of God's abounding, and inexhaustible grace.

Time after time, the Prophet spoke to his Companions about God's grace, reminding them that its benefits go to His servants. 'Umar ibn al-Khaṭṭāb reports that once a group of slaves was sent to the Prophet in Madinah. A woman slave was seen walking fast with her breast oozing with milk. She found a young boy among the slaves, picked him up and put him to her breast to feed him. The Prophet put this question to his Companions: "Do you think that this woman would throw her boy in the fire?" They replied: "No! By God, she would not if she has any way of avoiding that." He said: "God is more merciful to His servants than this woman to her child." (Related by al-Bukhārī and Muslim.) How could it be otherwise when the woman's kindness to her child is produced by her share of a single mercy God has placed into the world out of one hundred He has created?

Having taught his Companions this important fact and its great significance in such an inspiring way, God's Messenger moved them on another step so that they became merciful in their dealings with others and so that they were compassionate to one another and to all living things. The Prophet wanted them to enjoy the happiness of being merciful, just as they were happy to appreciate the extent of God's grace.

ʿAbdullāh ibn ʿAmr quotes the Prophet as saying: "The merciful are granted mercy by God. Show mercy to those on earth so that you are shown mercy by the One in heaven." (Related by Abū Dāwūd and al-Tirmidhī.) Jarīr quotes God's Messenger as saying: "God does not bestow His grace on those who do not show mercy to people." (Related by al-Bukhārī, Muslim and al-Tirmidhī.) Abū Hurayrah quotes the Prophet as saying: "No one but a miserable creature is deprived of mercy." (Related by Abū Dāwūd and al-Tirmidhī.)

Abū Hurayrah also reports that God's Messenger (peace be upon him) kissed al-Ḥasan ibn ʿAlī, his grandson, when al-Aqraʿ ibn Ḥābis was in the Prophet's presence. Al-Aqraʿ said: "I have ten children but I never kissed any one of them." The Prophet looked at him and said: "Mercy is not granted to one who is not merciful." (Related by al-Bukhārī and Muslim.)

In teaching his Companions, the Prophet did not stop at extending mercy to mankind. He was fully aware that God's grace encompasses everything, and that the believers are required to cultivate within themselves the moral principles which form the attributes of God. Man does not attain his full humanity unless he is merciful to every living thing. The Prophet's instructions in this regard were, as always, highly inspiring. Abū Hurayrah quotes the Prophet as saying: "A man was travelling along a road when he was very thirsty. He found a well, so he went down into it to drink. As he came up he found a gasping dog who was apparently so thirsty that he licked the dust. The man thought, 'this dog is now as thirsty as I was a short while ago'. Therefore, he went down the well again and filled his shoe with water. Holding it in his mouth, he came up and gave the water to the dog to drink. God rewarded him for his action by forgiving him. "The Prophet's audience asked: 'Messenger of God, are we to be rewarded for kindness to animals?" He answered: "You get a reward for every kindness you do to any living creature." (Related by al-Bukhārī, Muslim and Mālik.)

In another report, a prostitute is mentioned as having seen a dog walking to and fro in front of a well on a very hot day. His tongue was hanging out because of his thirst. She used her shoe to give him water to drink. So, God forgave her because of her kindness.

'Abd al-Raḥmān ibn 'Abdullāh transmits the following report by his father, who says: "We were travelling with God's Messenger when we saw a small bird with two chicks. We took the chicks away. The bird came over us lowering her wings and flying close to the earth. When the Prophet came over, he asked, 'Who has taken the chicks of this bird? Give her back her chicks.' He also saw that we burnt a number of ant dwellings. When we owned up to the fact in response to his question, he said, 'No one may punish any creature with fire except the Lord of the Fire'." (Related by Abū Dāwūd.)

Abū Hurayrah quotes the Prophet as saying: "An ant bit one of the earlier prophets, so he ordered the ant dwellings to be burnt. Through inspiration God asked him: If you are bitten by an ant, would you burn a whole nation which glorifies God?" (Related by al-Bukhārī and Muslim.)

Such was the Prophet's method in cultivating among his Companions a keen sense of appreciation of Qur'ānic guidance. This enabled them to appreciate how limitless God's grace is, through their own mercy to one another. It was clear to them that all aspects of mercy in their world come only from one out of a hundred parts of God's mercy.

When All Gather for Judgement

When this concept of mercy is engrained in a Muslim's thinking, it leaves a profound impact on his life, his view of things and his manners and moral values. A full study of such impact is beyond the scope of this commentary. Therefore, we have to be content with only a few very brief observations.

When a Muslim truly appreciates the significance of God's commitment to being merciful to His servants, he experiences a profound sense of reassurance which remains with him even when he goes through periods of hardship and severe trials that are enough to turn people away from their Lord. A believer is certain that at every moment and in every situation and condition, God's grace is present and sure to be bestowed. He knows that his Lord does not put him to the test because He has abandoned him or denied him His mercy. God does not deny His grace to anyone who sincerely hopes to receive it. It is human beings who deny themselves God's mercy when they disbelieve in Him and reject His grace. A believer's reassurance that God's grace is close at hand fills his heart with strength, perseverance, hope and comfort. He knows that he is in good, caring hands and he enjoys the comfort of God's grace as long as he does not go far astray.

Moreover, when a believer recognises this fact in this particular manner, his sense of modesty in front of God is enhanced. Hoping for God's mercy and forgiveness does not motivate people to disobey God as some would have us believe. Indeed, it makes a believer very shy in his dealings with God, the Much-Forgiving, the Merciful. A person who is tempted to disobey God because of God's mercy is one who has not experienced the true taste of being a believer. For example, some Sufis or mystics claim that they deliberately indulge in sin, in order to enjoy the sweetness of God's forbearance, forgiveness and mercy. This is twisted logic, which is alien to the proper nature of a believer.

A true recognition by a believer of God's unfailing grace is bound to leave a very strong influence on his moral values and manners. He knows that he is required to cultivate within himself the same manners and values as God. As he recognises that despite his shortcomings, slips and mistakes, he still enjoys an abundance of God's grace, he learns that he must show mercy to others, forgive them their mistakes and treat them with forbearance. It is to strengthen this principle that the Prophet tried to cultivate a sense of mercy in his Companions.

One of the aspects of God's mercy which is stated in the Qur'ānic verse is that God has decreed that all people will be gathered together on the Day of Judgement. This undoubted gathering is certainly an aspect of His grace. It tells us that for certain, God looks after His servants whom He has created for a particular purpose, and placed them in charge of this earth for a definite objective. He has not created them in vain and has not abandoned them altogether. He has made the Day of Resurrection the end of their journey, as travellers arrive at their destination. He will then give them the reward of their endeavours and compensate them for their toil in this life. Nothing is lost and no one is without reward on the Day of Judgement. In taking such care of His servants, an important aspect of God's grace is discerned. Other aspects are manifest in the fact that God's punishment of any sin is equivalent to it, but He rewards a person with ten times the value of his good deeds, and may multiply that further to whomever He wills. He may also forgive any slips or sins to whom He chooses of His servants.

Before God favoured the Arabs with this religion and elevated them to its noble level, they used to deny the Day of Resurrection in the same way as the proponents of the present-day *jāhiliyyah* deny it. Hence, this fact of gathering God's creatures has been expressed in the most emphatic style: "*He will certainly gather you all together on the Day of Resurrection, about which there is no doubt.*" (Verse 12)

The only losers on that day are those who have not believed during this life. These shall not gain anything to compensate for their loss, because they have lost everything. Indeed, they have lost themselves and are no longer capable of anything. After all, man tries to make a gain for himself. When he has lost his own soul, what can he gain? And for whom? "*Those who squandered their own souls will not believe.*" (Verse 12)

Since they have forfeited their souls, they no longer have what they need in order to believe. It is a very apt and accurate description of a real condition. Those who reject this religion, in spite of its profound appeal to human nature and despite its irrefutable arguments and all the signs and pointers which direct them to faith, must have already lost their share of uncorrupted nature. Their receptive and responsive systems must have either been totally destroyed or locked up and screened over. In such a condition, they lose themselves and they are unable to believe since they no longer have the souls that will respond to faith. This is the underlying explanation of their refusal to believe despite all the evidence around them supporting faith. Alas! This is what determines their destiny on the Day of Resurrection. That destiny is the greatest loss of all that comes in consequence of their having lost themselves.

The *sūrah* then refers to all creatures in terms of time, as it has referred to them in terms of place in the preceding verse. It states that God, limitless is He in His glory, owns them all, has full knowledge of them and hears everything they say and do: "*To Him belongs whatever takes its rest in the night or in the day. He alone hears all and knows all.*" (Verse 13)

The Arabic term used in the Qur'ānic verse and rendered here by the phrase 'takes its rest' also means 'to dwell, stop moving, etc.'. The reference in the verse is then made to every creature that rests at night or in the day. As such, it includes all creatures. The Qur'ānic verse states the fact that they all belong to God alone. This is the second statement of this fact although it came in the first verse in terms of place: "*Say: To whom belongs all that is in the heavens and on earth? Say: To God.*" (Verse 12) The reference here, in the second verse, is made in terms of time: "*To Him belongs whatever takes its rest in the night or in the day. He alone hears all and knows all.*" (Verse 13) This tendency to include all, and to use every aspect, is perfectly familiar in the Qur'ān.

The final comment is that which concerns God's attributes of hearing all and knowing all. It implies having complete and perfect knowledge of all these creatures and all that is said about them by the unbelievers. The pagan Arabs used to acknowledge that the Creator and the Owner is one. Nevertheless, they claimed for their false gods a portion of the fruits, cattle and children as will be told later, in Verse 136 of this *sūrah*. Hence, their acknowledgement of God's ownership of everything is stated clearly here so that they will be confronted with it later on as part of a reference to what they assign to those partners they associate with God. Moreover, the establishment of this fact of God's ownership of everything is given here as a prelude to the statement that God has mastery over everything and all creatures since He is the owner of all, who hears and knows everything that is said and done.

God's Oneness: The Fundamental Question

So far, the basic fact that God is the only Creator and the only owner of everything that exists in the universe has been established. This is now followed by a strong denunciation of seeking support from, or addressing worship to, anyone other than God. All such deeds contradict the fundamental fact of submission to God since they are acts of polytheism that do not fit with Islam. A number of God's attributes are also stated here, including that He is the Creator of the heavens and earth, the sustainer of all, the Almighty. The general air of awe is enhanced by a mention of God's severe punishment.

> *Say: Am I to take for my master anyone but God, the Originator of the heavens and the earth, who gives nourishment to all and Himself needs none? Say: I am commanded to be the first of those who surrender themselves to God, and not to be among those who associate partners with Him. Say: Indeed I would dread, were I to disobey my Lord, the suffering of an awesome day. He who is spared that shall have received His grace. This will be a manifest triumph. If God were to expose you to affliction, none can remove it but He. And if He were to bless you with good fortune – well, He has power over all things. He alone holds sway over all His creatures, and He alone is truly wise, all-aware.* (Verses 14–18)

This is, indeed, the basic issue: taking God alone for our Master, or *waliy*, in every sense of the word. He alone is the Lord to be worshipped. We submit to Him as He is the only Sovereign. No support may be sought from anyone other than Him. In every grave situation, we appeal to Him alone for help. This is the basic question of faith. When we take Him as master, in every sense of the word, and submit to Him alone, we are true Muslims. Those who associate others with Him in any aspect of His mastery are guilty of associating partners with God. This is something that cannot be entertained by any Muslim.

This fundamental issue is stated in these verses in the strongest terms and is contained within a powerful rhythm: *"Say: Am I to take for my master anyone but God, the Originator of the heavens and the earth, who gives nourishment to all and Himself needs none? Say: I am commanded to be the first of those who surrender themselves to God, and not to be among those who associate partners with Him."* (Verse 14)

This Qur'ānic verse reflects human nature's powerful logic. To whom does mastery belong and who alone is to be viewed as patron, if not the Creator who has originated the heavens and the earth? To whom, if not to the One who provides sustenance and nourishment to every creature in the heavens and on earth while He Himself needs none? *"Say: Am I to take for my master anyone but God"*, when such are His attributes? What logic allows that anyone other than God be taken as master? If it is help and support that one needs from a master, then God, the originator of the heavens and the earth has the supreme power in both. If the objective of taking a master is to get provisions and sustenance, then it is God who provides sustenance to all creatures in the universe. How then can mastery be attributed to anyone other than the Almighty who provides for all?

This is followed by another instruction to the Prophet: *"Say: I am commanded to be the first of those who surrender themselves to God, and not to be among those who associate partners with Him."* (Verse 14) To submit oneself to God and not to associate partners with Him means that we must not accept anyone other than God as a master. To do so is to be guilty of polytheism and polytheism cannot be equated with Islam.

It is all a single issue that admits no equivocation. Either we turn to God alone, receive His instructions, submit to Him and obey Him, seek His support, worship Him alone, and acknowledge only His authority over all matters, pledge our loyalty and allegiance to Him in both worship and law-making and thus become Muslims, or we claim that any one of His creatures has a say or partnership with Him in any of these matters and we, thus, become guilty of polytheism. Needless to say, Islam, i.e. submission to God, and the association of partners with Him cannot exist side by side.

God's Messenger (peace be upon him) was commanded to declare all this without ambiguity. He was ordered to face the unbelievers with it, that is those who were trying to persuade him to accept a compromise and allow a place in his faith for their gods in return for their acceptance of it. They also tried to obtain a concession from him such that some of them were allowed certain attributes of Godhead in order that they could retain their prestige and safeguard their interests. Had he afforded them this concession and allowed them in particular the authority to forbid things or make them lawful, they would have offered to stop opposing him, would have made him their chief, given him much of their wealth and married him to the prettiest of their girls. They tried hard, waving a stick in one hand, representing torture, hardship and war, and holding a carrot of reconciliation and peace in the other.

In reply to this dual attempt, the Prophet was commanded to make this powerful and decisive denunciation of their beliefs and to state the principles of Islam in the clearest of terms. He was also ordered to warn and frighten them, declaring at the same time how seriously he viewed the whole issue and how he dreaded God's punishment, should he be guilty of disobedience to Him: "*Say: Indeed I would dread, were I to disobey my Lord, the suffering of an awesome day. He who is spared that shall have received His grace. This will be a manifest triumph.*" (Verses 15–16)

This verse is a faithful portrayal of the feelings of God's Messenger in respect of the commandments he received from God, and how he truly feared God's punishment. To be spared that punishment is considered an act of grace bestowed by God and a clear triumph for the recipient over all temptation. In addition, these two verses violently shook the hearts of the unbelievers at that time, as they continue to do at all times. They describe the torment of the Day of Judgement as something fearsome, moving fast towards its victim and surrounding him before claiming him altogether. The only way to avert it is through the power of the Almighty who diverts it away. As we view this scene depicted in this verse, we hold our breaths, waiting for the final image.

But why should man take a master for himself other than God? Why does he allow himself to sink into paganism when he has been forbidden to do so? Why does he not do what he is commanded to do, namely to submit himself to God? Why does he expose himself to the grievous torment which follows upon such disobedience? Does he think that people will come to his help if he experiences misfortune? Or does he hope to receive kindness from them? All this can only be granted to him by God, who has supreme power and who can cause everything to happen and who holds sway over all His creatures. It is He alone who grants and denies people's wishes according to His wisdom and His knowledge of their conditions: "*If God were to expose you to affliction, none can remove it but He. And if He were to bless you with good fortune – well, He has power over all things. He alone holds sway over all His creatures, and He alone is truly wise, all-aware.*" (Verses 17–18)

Here we see how the Qur'ān penetrates the depth of the human soul to touch on its latent desires and innermost fears. It brings all this into the open and subjects it to the light of faith which distinguishes good from evil. It presents the issues clearly and defines the nature of Godhead succinctly. This fits well with the importance of the central question with which the *sūrah* deals at this point and which the Qur'ān tackles on many occasions.

A Testimony to Settle All Issues

Now comes the climax of this passage, which employs a profound rhythm so as to re-emphasise the right attitude of a believer. The final verse of the passage serves as a clear statement of position, a warning and a move away from everything that has an element of setting partners with God. The style here is both strong and decisive: "*Say: What is weightiest in testimony? Say: God is witness between me and you. This Qur'ān has been revealed to me that I may thereby warn you and all whom it may reach. Will you in truth bear witness that there are other deities beside God? Say: I bear no such witness. Say: He is but one God. I disown all that you associate with Him.*" (Verse 19)

This verse is made up of a series of short statements which follow each other in very quick succession. This, to give us quick images of the different attitudes which can be held in relation to the central issue. Nevertheless, the painting is so vivid that we can see all expressions on the faces of the characters drawn and we can even penetrate their thoughts. What we see first is a command given by God to His Messenger. This is immediately followed by a scene wherein God's Messenger confronts the unbelievers who are associating partners with God and who want him, i.e. the Prophet, to endorse their falsehood before they accept his message. They imagine that such an exchange is feasible and that Islam and idolatry can exist side by side in someone's heart. It is sad to say that some people still think that this is possible. They argue that a person can submit himself to God while he conducts his life on the basis of teachings he receives from other sources and while he acknowledges the authority of other powers and seeks the help and patronage of other beings.

Thus, God's Messenger (peace be upon him) confronts the unbelievers. He makes it clear to them that he and they follow two separate roads that cannot meet. He outlines the difference between what he advocates of believing in God's oneness and submitting to Him and their beliefs and practices which associate partners with God. He tells them that the starting points of both camps are so wide apart that no compromise between them can be worked out unless they abandon their beliefs and accept His faith.

This confrontation is depicted in a public scene calling for an open testimony: "*Say: What is weightiest in testimony?*" (Verse 19) Who is the best witness in the whole universe? Who is the One whose testimony refutes every other argument? Who has the final word? In order to make the generalisation total so that nothing in the whole universe is discounted as a possible witness, the question is asked in this manner: "*What is weightiest in testimony?*" (Verse 19)

The Prophet is ordered to put the question, and he is also ordered to provide the answer. The addressees themselves acknowledge that there is no other answer to give: "*Say: God.*" (Verse 19) Yes, indeed. God – limitless is He in His glory – is the One who provides the weightiest testimony. He tells the truth and He is the best to provide the final answer to all issues and questions. When He has made His testimony, all matters are settled.

Having declared this indisputable fact, that God's testimony is strongest and weightiest, the Prophet declares that God Almighty is the witness between them and Him in this central issue: "*God is witness between me and you.*" (Verse 19) The Arabic text admits a break in this statement, making it more in line with the general scene and giving it a more powerful and dramatic effect. In the first instance, the sentence is given in the same way as it is rendered in the translation: "*Say: God is witness between me and you.*" (Verse 19) If we break it up, it reads as follows: "*Say: What is weightiest in testimony? Say: God. [He] is witness between me and you.*" (Verse 19)

When the principle of referring to God for arbitration in this central issue has been established, the Prophet declares to the unbelievers that God's testimony is included in the Qur'ān which He has revealed to him to warn them as well as everyone who comes to know of the Qur'ān during the Prophet's lifetime or subsequently. Thus, the Qur'ān is taken in evidence against them and against all those whom it reaches, because it contains God's testimony in this central issue which provides the basis of human existence and universal existence as a whole. "*This Qur'ān has been revealed to me that I may thereby warn you and all whom it may reach.*" (Verse 19)

Thus, every human being who becomes aware of the Qur'ān and what it contains in a language he understands has been duly warned. He incurs God's punishment if he rejects the message of Islam after it has been conveyed to him. A person who does not know the language of the Qur'ān and, therefore, cannot understand its message is not held accountable in the same way. However, Muslims are deemed to be at fault for not conveying the message of the Qur'ān to others in a language which they know well enough to understand the true meaning of this testimony.

Having made it clear to them that God's testimony is included in the Qur'ān, the Prophet goes on to sum up this testimony in a challenging way which discards the unbelievers' own testimony, since it is fundamentally at variance with God's own. The Prophet also declares to them that he totally rejects their assertions and believes them to be false. He further declares that he firmly believes in the oneness of God, the Supreme Lord of the universe. As such, he parts company with them at the outset and dissociates himself most emphatically from their polytheism: "*Will you in truth bear witness that there are other deities beside God? Say: I bear no such witness. Say: He is but one God. I disown all that you associate with Him.*" (Verse 19)

With such powerful rhythm and short, emphatic sentences, the Qur'ānic text touches people's hearts in a way no other style can do. I, therefore, do not wish to make any comment which could affect its flow and powerful impact.

A Perfectly Clear Attitude

However, I wish to discuss the central question in this passage, namely that of faith and its fundamental principle: God's oneness and the break with unbelievers. Those of us today who belong to the Muslim community should reflect very deeply on this passage and the way it tackles this central issue. The small community of true believers today are faced with well entrenched *jāhiliyyah* throughout the world, in the same way as the first generation of Muslims were when these verses were revealed. In the light of these verses, the proper attitude to be adopted by the Muslim community must be defined now as it was defined then.

The situation of mankind today is in many ways identical to what it was at the time when the Qur'ān was revealed to the Prophet Muḥammad (peace be upon him). At that time, Islam, as a faith and a code of living was established on a central principle which required people to declare their acceptance that 'there is no deity other than God'. It is a declaration which has a special meaning as outlined by Rab 'ī ibn 'Āmir, a messenger sent by a Muslim army commander to Rustom, the Persian commander, before the two armies fought a decisive battle. The latter asked him what brought the Muslims out of their land. He answered: "It is God who ordered us to march out so that we may help to free those who are willing to be freed from the worship of creatures to the worship of God alone, and from the restrictions of this present life to the expanse of its universal link with the life to come, and from the oppression exercised by other religions to the justice of Islam." That Muslim messenger was keenly aware that Rustam and his people did not consider their emperor, Khusraw, as the lord who created the universe, nor did they offer worship rituals to him. They simply acknowledged him as the sovereign who enacted laws for them. As such, they made themselves subservient to him in the particular sense that is diametrically opposed to Islam. Thus, the Muslim messenger informed the Persian commander that the Muslims were fulfilling God's orders to help free people from situations where one group of them worship another. They do so by attributing to rulers an essential quality of Godhead, i.e. sovereignty and what it imparts of authority to legislate, and implementing their legislation in practice, which is a form of religion. The mission of the Muslim armies was to free people so that they would worship God alone and enjoy the justice of Islam.

We are today in a situation similar to that which prevailed when the religion of Islam declared to mankind that 'there is no deity other than God'. Human beings have reverted to the worship of other creatures and accepted the oppression of different forms of religion and abandoned the principle of God's oneness in its true sense. It is true that some groups of people still make the declaration on mosque minarets that 'there is no deity other than God', but they hardly know its true sense, and as such, they do not mean it. Nor do they reject the claims of others to sovereignty, which is synonymous with Godhead. It does not matter whether individuals, legislative councils or nations claim the authority. For none of these is a god to exercise that authority. It is only the relapse of humanity into *jāhiliyyah* that assigns to such creatures the attributes of Godhead. As such, humanity no longer manifests a firm belief in God's oneness or total devotion to Him alone.

This applies to all mankind, including those everywhere in the world, who repeat the declaration of God's oneness from minarets without giving it its true meaning or putting it into practice. These incur a bigger sin, one which is more severely punishable on the Day of Judgement, because they have sunk back into the worship of creatures after they have received proper guidance and embraced the true faith.

The advocates of Islam should reflect deeply on these verses, starting with the one which outlines the relationship of patronage: *"Say: Am I to take for my master anyone but God, the Originator of the heavens and the earth, who gives nourishment to all and Himself needs none? Say: I am commanded to be the first of those who surrender themselves to God, and not to be among those who associate partners with Him."* (Verse 14) Such reflection would bring home to them that to take anyone other than God for a patron or master, submitting to him and seeking his help, is contrary to Islam. It is, indeed, the sort of idolatry from which Islam endeavours to free mankind. They will also come to know that the first manifestation of such a relationship is to accept laws enacted by any being other than God, whether they relate to faith or practical life. Needless to say, all mankind are in this position today. Hence, the advocates of Islam must define their objective to free all mankind from subservience to other creatures so that they submit to God alone. In carrying out their noble task, they face the same sort of ignorance as that faced by God's Messenger when he received the Qur'ān from God.

Moreover, the advocates of Islam need to contemplate the basic facts outlined in the following verses: *"Say: Indeed I would dread, were I to disobey my Lord, the suffering of an awesome day. He who is spared that shall have received His grace. This will be a manifest triumph. If God were to expose you to affliction, none can remove it but He. And if He were to bless you with good fortune – well, He has power over all things. He alone holds sway over all His creatures, and He alone is truly wise, all-aware."* (Verses 15–18)

Anyone who faces ignorance, its tyranny, might, deviousness, arrogance, corruption and wickedness needs to keep these facts in mind and preserve these feelings in his heart as a precaution against falling into sin as also to ward off the terrible punishment which awaits sinners. This will enhance his conviction that the only one who can benefit or harm him is God, who holds sway over all His servants and whose judgement cannot be overturned. The task of establishing Islam anew in the face of the overwhelming opposition posed by *jāhiliyyah* is hard indeed, requiring a long and enduring struggle. It cannot be undertaken by anyone who does not keep the above facts in mind and who does not nurture the aforementioned feelings.

When the advocates of Islam have made certain what their present task is, they need to adopt the same decisive attitude of dissociating themselves totally from the type of idolatry practised by societies that are deep in *jāhiliyyah*, and to seek the right witnesses for their stand. They should say what God's Messenger was commanded to say in this position, and to confront *jāhiliyyah* with it in the same way as the Prophet did in fulfilment of what he was bidden by God: *"Say: What is weightiest in testimony? Say: God is witness between me and you. This Qur'ān has been revealed to me that I may thereby warn you and all whom it may reach. Will you in truth bear witness that there are other deities beside God? Say: I bear no such witness. Say: He is but one God. I disown all that you associate with Him."* (Verse 19)

This is the word of truth which must be stated loudly, decisively and without ambiguity. When the advocates of Islam have declared it in this way, they must turn to God in full realisation that He has power over all things. Even the mightiest of tyrants are weaker than flies, for they cannot retrieve anything a fly takes away from them. With all their might, they cannot harm or benefit anyone unless God lets them. God always prevails in whatever be His purpose. Most people, however, do not know this fact.

The advocates of Islam must also be certain that they will not triumph or enjoy the fruits of God's promise to grant them power or establish them in the land, unless they part company with *jāhiliyyah* at the outset. They must first confront tyranny and *jāhiliyyah* in the clearest of terms.

The Qur'ān was not revealed to confront a single situation at a particular moment in history. It is an approach which cannot be restricted by the limitations of time and place. Whenever the Muslim community finds itself in a situation similar to that which prevailed at the time of the revelation of the Qur'ān, it must adopt this approach. As we have already said, we face today the same situation which prevailed at the time the Qur'ān was revealed. Therefore, an unshakeable certainty of the truth of this religion, a complete awareness of God's absolute power and a categorical rejection of falsehood and its advocates must constitute part of the strength of the Muslim community. *"God is the best guardian and of those who show mercy He is the most merciful."* (12: 64)

4

Preference to Remain Blind

Those to whom We had given revelations know this as they know their own sons. But those who have squandered their own souls will never have faith. (20)

الَّذِينَ ءَاتَيْنَهُمُ الْكِتَبَ يَعْرِفُونَهُ كَمَا يَعْرِفُونَ أَبْنَاءَهُمُ الَّذِينَ خَسِرُوٓا أَنفُسَهُمْ فَهُمْ لَا يُؤْمِنُونَ ۝

Who is more wicked than one who invents a falsehood about God or denies His revelations? The wrongdoers shall never achieve success. (21)

وَمَنْ أَظْلَمُ مِمَّنِ افْتَرَىٰ عَلَى اللَّهِ كَذِبًا أَوْ كَذَّبَ بِـَٔايَـٰتِهِۦٓ إِنَّهُۥ لَا يُفْلِحُ الظَّـٰلِمُونَ ۝

One day We shall gather them all together, then We shall say to those who associate partners with God: "Where, now, are those partners which you have been claiming?" (22)

وَيَوْمَ نَحْشُرُهُمْ جَمِيعًا ثُمَّ نَقُولُ لِلَّذِينَ أَشْرَكُوٓا أَيْنَ شُرَكَاؤُكُمُ الَّذِينَ كُنتُمْ تَزْعُمُونَ ۝

They will have no contention then other than to say, "By God, our Lord, we have never associated partners with Him." (23)

ثُمَّ لَمْ تَكُن فِتْنَتُهُمْ إِلَّآ أَن قَالُوا وَاللَّهِ رَبِّنَا مَا كُنَّا مُشْرِكِينَ ۝

Behold how they have lied to themselves and how they have been forsaken by whatever they have fabricated. (24)

انظُرْ كَيْفَ كَذَبُوا عَلَىٰٓ أَنفُسِهِمْ وَضَلَّ عَنْهُم مَّا كَانُوا يَفْتَرُونَ ۝

Some of them listen to you. But over their hearts We have laid veils which prevent them from understanding what you say, and into their ears, deafness. Were they to see every sign, they would still not believe in it. When they come to you to contend with you, the unbelievers say: "This is nothing but fables of the ancients." (25)

وَمِنْهُم مَّن يَسْتَمِعُ إِلَيْكَ وَجَعَلْنَا عَلَىٰ قُلُوبِهِمْ أَكِنَّةً أَن يَفْقَهُوهُ وَفِىٓ ءَاذَانِهِمْ وَقْرًا وَإِن يَرَوْا۟ كُلَّ ءَايَةٍ لَّا يُؤْمِنُوا۟ بِهَا حَتَّىٰٓ إِذَا جَآءُوكَ يُجَٰدِلُونَكَ يَقُولُ ٱلَّذِينَ كَفَرُوٓا۟ إِنْ هَٰذَآ إِلَّآ أَسَٰطِيرُ ٱلْأَوَّلِينَ ﴿٢٥﴾

They forbid [others] to listen to it and go far away from it. They ruin none but themselves, though they do not perceive it. (26)

وَهُمْ يَنْهَوْنَ عَنْهُ وَيَنْـَٔوْنَ عَنْهُ وَإِن يُهْلِكُونَ إِلَّآ أَنفُسَهُمْ وَمَا يَشْعُرُونَ ﴿٢٦﴾

If you could but see them when they will be made to stand before the Fire! They will say: "Would that we could return! Then we would not deny our Lord's revelations, but would be among the believers." (27)

وَلَوْ تَرَىٰٓ إِذْ وُقِفُوا۟ عَلَى ٱلنَّارِ فَقَالُوا۟ يَٰلَيْتَنَا نُرَدُّ وَلَا نُكَذِّبَ بِـَٔايَٰتِ رَبِّنَا وَنَكُونَ مِنَ ٱلْمُؤْمِنِينَ ﴿٢٧﴾

Indeed, that which in the past they used to conceal will manifest itself to them; and if they were to return to life they would go back to that which they have been forbidden. They are indeed liars. (28)

بَلْ بَدَا لَهُم مَّا كَانُوا۟ يُخْفُونَ مِن قَبْلُ وَلَوْ رُدُّوا۟ لَعَادُوا۟ لِمَا نُهُوا۟ عَنْهُ وَإِنَّهُمْ لَكَٰذِبُونَ ﴿٢٨﴾

They say: "There is nothing beyond our life in this world, and we shall never be raised to life again." (29)

وَقَالُوٓا۟ إِنْ هِىَ إِلَّا حَيَاتُنَا ٱلدُّنْيَا وَمَا نَحْنُ بِمَبْعُوثِينَ ﴿٢٩﴾

If you could but see them when they are made to stand before their Lord! He will say: "Is this not the truth?" They will say: "Yes, indeed, by our Lord!" He will then say, "Taste, then, the suffering in consequence of your having refused to believe'." (30)

وَلَوْ تَرَىٰٓ إِذْ وُقِفُواْ عَلَىٰ رَبِّهِمْ قَالَ أَلَيْسَ هَٰذَا بِٱلْحَقِّ قَالُواْ بَلَىٰ وَرَبِّنَا قَالَ فَذُوقُواْ ٱلْعَذَابَ بِمَا كُنتُمْ تَكْفُرُونَ ۝

Lost indeed are they who deny that they will have to meet God. When the Last Hour comes suddenly upon them, they cry, "Alas for us! We have neglected much in our life-time!" And they will be carrying their burdens on their backs. Evil indeed is that with which they are burdened. (31)

قَدْ خَسِرَ ٱلَّذِينَ كَذَّبُواْ بِلِقَآءِ ٱللَّهِ حَتَّىٰٓ إِذَا جَآءَتْهُمُ ٱلسَّاعَةُ بَغْتَةً قَالُواْ يَٰحَسْرَتَنَا عَلَىٰ مَا فَرَّطْنَا فِيهَا وَهُمْ يَحْمِلُونَ أَوْزَارَهُمْ عَلَىٰ ظُهُورِهِمْ أَلَا سَآءَ مَا يَزِرُونَ ۝

The life of this world is nothing but a sport and a passing delight. Surely the life in the hereafter is by far the better for those who are God-fearing. Will you not, then, use your reason? (32)

وَمَا ٱلْحَيَوٰةُ ٱلدُّنْيَآ إِلَّا لَعِبٌ وَلَهْوٌ وَلَلدَّارُ ٱلْأَخِرَةُ خَيْرٌ لِّلَّذِينَ يَتَّقُونَ أَفَلَا تَعْقِلُونَ ۝

Overview

This new wave or round takes us back to the confrontation with the unbelievers who deny the truth of the Qur'ān and refuse to believe in resurrection and life after death. This time, however, it does not describe their stubborn rejection; nor does it remind them of the destruction of earlier generations who took the same attitude before them. Instead, it holds before their eyes their destiny on the Day of Resurrection which they deny, and the recompense they will be made to suffer in their next life which they refuse to accept, both described in the most vivid of scenes. It confronts them with all this when they are gathered together, putting to them questions full of reproach, and loaded with amazement at their attitude: *"Where, now, are those partners which you have been claiming."*? (Verse 22) They are overwhelmed by fear, realising their weakness, helpless and bewildered. They swear by God, acknowledging that He is the only Lord: *"By God, our Lord, we have never associated partners with Him."* (Verse 23)

Once again they are confronted with their past attitude as they stand before the fire. Worried, afraid, repentant and full of sorrow, they say: *"Would that we could return! Then we would not deny our Lord's revelations, but would be among the believers."* (Verse 27) The same confrontation is repeated again as they stand before their Lord, overwhelmed by shame, sorrow and fear. He, in His majesty, will ask them: *"Is this not the truth?"* (Verse 30) They will humbly answer: *"Yes, indeed, by our Lord!"* (Verse 30) But this admission will have come too late to be of any benefit to them, for God will say to them: *"Taste, then, the suffering in consequence of your having refused to believe."* (Verse 30)

The same confrontation is made time and again, until eventually they realise that they have lost everything. They carry their burdens on their backs, crying in grief for having refused to believe in the hereafter and for having squandered their chances.

Scene after scene the terrible outcome is shown in a way that shakes hearts. It opens both eyes and minds to the truth presented to them by God's Messenger in the Book which they deny. However, those who have received revelations in the past recognise its truth, just like they know their own children.

Wilful Denial of Known Facts

"Those to whom We had given revelations know this as they know their own sons. But those who have squandered their own souls will never have faith." (Verse 20) The Qur'ān mentions on several occasions that the people who received earlier revelations, i.e. the Jews and the Christians, recognize the Qur'ān and the truthfulness of the Prophet Muḥammad's message as well as the fact that the Qur'ān was revealed to him by God. At times, the people of these earlier revelations are confronted by this fact because of their hostile attitude towards the Prophet and Islam. At other times, the Arab idolaters are told this so that they realize that the people of earlier revelations, are fully aware of

the nature of revelation, recognize the Qur'ān and that the Prophet Muḥammad (peace be upon him) tells only the truth when he states that God revealed it to him in the same way as He bestowed messages from on high to earlier prophets.

Since this verse was most probably revealed in Makkah, its reference to the people of earlier revelations suggests that it was addressed to the idolaters, emphasizing that the people of earlier revelations recognize the Qur'ān as they recognize their own sons. It is true that the majority of them do not believe in it but this is only because they have squandered their own souls. In this, they are the same as the pagan Arabs who rejected this faith and, thereby, also squandered their souls. Both the preceding and following verses also speak of the idolaters, a fact which lends weight to the view that it is a Makkan revelation.

Commentators on the Qur'ān generally suggest that this verse means that the people of earlier revelations know that the Qur'ān is truly revealed by God, and that the Prophet was truly a messenger of God to whom the Qur'ān was bestowed from on high. This is undoubtedly part of the meaning of this verse. However, a glance at the history and attitude of the people of earlier revelations towards the Islamic faith indicates another aspect to the meaning of this verse which God wants the Muslim community to fully understand.

Since the people of earlier revelations recognize the validity of the Qur'ān as a message revealed by God, they are fully aware of its powerful effect, undoubted authority, the goodness it produces, the impetus it gives to its followers, and the moral values and the system it establishes. They take all this into account and realise that they cannot co-exist with the advocates of this faith. They know the truth of this message and their own falsehood. It is clear to them that the *jāhiliyyah* into which they have sunk and their deviant morals and systems cannot be tolerated by Islam. Hence, the battle between their *jāhiliyyah* and Islam is inevitable and it will continue to rage until God's authority prevails on earth and all people submit to Him. In this way, all submission is to God alone.

The people of earlier revelations are fully aware of this fact and recognise it in this religion of ours as readily as they recognise their own children. Generation after generation, they study this faith in depth, trying to identify its strengths and how it penetrates people's hearts and minds. They vigorously seek a way to destroy its driving force and sow seeds of doubt in its followers' minds. They try to distort it and prevent people from having full knowledge of it. This religion of Islam moves to destroy falsehood and *jāhiliyyah* and repel those who usurp God's authority. Its aim is to make mankind submit to God alone. They, however, try to reduce it to a mere academic exercise, lifeless research and futile discourse in divinity and theology. They try to find ways and means to mould Islamic concepts in forms and colours that are alien to the nature of Islam, raising in front of its people the delusion that their faith is respected. They also work tirelessly to fill the vacuum that remains when faith is drastically weakened with other concepts and concerns. All this, so as to remove the sentimental traces of faith from the hearts of Muslims.

The people of earlier revelations study this religion of Islam in depth, but they do not undertake such a study in search of the truth, or to be fair to its followers, as some naïve Muslims think when they come across a good word about Islam by an Orientalist. They are out to discover a vulnerable point in this religion through which they hope to put an end to it. They want to block its ability to enter into people's hearts and minds. They want to know how best to resist it and how to utilize its methods in order to substitute for it some hollow concepts. It is to achieve these goals that they study it in full, to the extent that they recognize it as they do their own children. It is our duty to know this and to realise that we should be the ones who know our own faith as we know our own children.

The history of fourteen centuries of Islam gives credence to the fact stated in this verse of the Qur'ān: *"Those to whom We had given revelations know this as they know their own sons."* (Verse 20) This fact, however, appears most true in this period of history, when we see that an average of one book a week is written about Islam in a foreign language. All this research testifies to the thorough knowledge of the people of earlier revelations of our religion, its nature, history, strengths and the methods to resist and distort it. Needless to say, most of these authors do not state their intentions openly because they realise that an open attack on Islam has always provoked resistance. They are aware that the movements that rose up to repel armed aggression against Islam, represented in imperialism, had a religious basis. Even an intellectual attack on Islam is bound to make people rally to its defence. Hence, most of them resort to more wicked methods, praising this religion in order to win the confidence of their readers before presenting their poisonous ideas. This religion, they tell us, is great; but it has to develop its concepts and systems in order to match those of modern civilization. It must not object to recent developments in social practices, methods of government and moral standards. It should demonstrate itself in the form of personal faith leaving the theories, practices and experiences of modern civilization to regulate our practical lives. In this way, it would give its blessings to whatever false lords decree. As such, it would remain great.

Such authors try further to give an impression of fairness and objectivity by extolling the strengths of Islam. They, however, are simply drawing the attention of their own people to Islam's strengths so that they know where to direct their attacks in future and how to suppress Islam altogether.

The secrets of the Qur'ān will continue to reveal themselves to its followers, as long as they try to understand it and contemplate its leanings. They, however, should go into the battle of faith armed with the lessons of history, aware of the full significance of the present and equipped with the light God has provided in order to show us the truth and enlighten our way.

A Contention Contrary to Reality

Who is more wicked than one who invents a falsehood about God or denies His revelations? The wrongdoers shall never achieve success. One day We shall gather them all together, then We shall say to those who associate partners with God: "Where, now, are those partners which you have been claiming?" They will have no contention then other than to say, "By God, our Lord, we have never associated partners with Him." Behold how they have lied to themselves and how they have been forsaken by whatever they have fabricated. (Verses 21–4)

These verses place in front of the idolaters' eyes the truth of their attitudes and practices, as they are viewed by God Almighty. It begins with a rhetorical question to establish the fact of their wrongdoing as they fabricate lies against God. They profess to follow His faith, as preached by the Prophet Abraham. They further allege that what they make lawful or forbidden of meat, food and worship rituals, which will be detailed in Verses 136–40, have been ordered by God, when they have not. Similarly, some of those who describe themselves as

Muslims today falsely claim to follow the Divine faith preached by the Prophet Muḥammad (peace be upon him). The fact is that they enact rules and laws, bring about situations and establish values by which they claim for themselves God's authority. They allege that all these inventions are nothing other than the divine faith. Some people who have bartered away their faith for a dwelling in hell also endorse their false claims. They also reject the divine revelations which the Prophet brought them, deny their truth, claiming that they have not been bestowed from on high. Conversely, they claim that their own practices, immersed in *jāhiliyyah*, have been sanctioned by God. All this still happens today in many societies.

God denounces all this and describes it as the worst injustice: "*Who is more wicked than one who invents a falsehood about God or denies His revelations? The wrongdoers shall never achieve success.*" (Verse 21) Reference is made here to idolatry as injustice in order to enhance its most horrible image. Indeed, it is the most frequent description of idolatry in the Qur'ān. Moreover, it is accurate since idolatry is an act of injustice perpetrated against the truth, against oneself and against mankind in general. It is an offence against God's own right to be worshipped alone, without partners, and against oneself as it leads the perpetrator to ruin. It is also an offence against mankind who are thus led away from the path of submission to God alone in order to establish regimes and conditions that ruin human life altogether. As such, idolatry is a great injustice, as it is described by the Lord of all the worlds. Neither idolatry nor the idolaters will, however, achieve any success: "*The wrongdoers shall never achieve success.*" (Verse 21) Here God states the full facts and the end result of idolatry and the idolaters, or injustice and the wrongdoers. What short-sighted people may see of the affluence that some enjoy in the short run cannot be described as success or prosperity because it is no more than a short-lived situation which leads to eventual ruin. Who can be more truthful than God?

As an example of their loss, their situation on the Day of Resurrection is described very vividly: "*One day We shall gather them all together, then We shall say to those who associate partners with God: 'Where, now, are those partners which you have been claiming.'? They will have no contention then other than to say, 'By God, our Lord, we have never associated partners with Him.' Behold how they have lied to themselves and how they have been forsaken by whatever they have fabricated.*" (Verses 22–4)

There are numerous forms and types of idolatry and idolaters and the partners they associate with God. A naïve image of people worshipping statues, stones, trees, etc. is by no means the only form of idolatry. In essence, associating partners with God is to acknowledge any one of the qualities attributable to God alone as belonging to others as well, whether such quality relates to His conduct or control of events, destinies, or to the offering of worship rituals, or to the enactment and implementation of man-made laws. All these are forms of idolatry practised by different groups of unbelievers who associate different forms of partners with God.

The Qur'ān describes all these forms as polytheism or idolatry. It portrays scenes from the Day of Judgement which depict many of these and show that the destiny and punishment of different types of idolatry are the same in this life and in the life to come.

The pagan Arabs used to practise all types of idolatry. They believed that some types of God's creation have a say in the conduct of events and the determination of destinies, through intercession which is binding on God. These were the angels. Others, like the *jinn*, they claimed, had the ability to harm them, whether they acted on their own initiative or were manipulated by sorcerers and fortune-tellers. They also assigned abilities to the spirits of their forefathers. Idols were symbols of all these creatures. They attributed to fortune-tellers the ability to talk to these idols which would then issue their decrees of prohibition or permissibility. The truth, then, was that the fortune-tellers themselves were the partners they associated with God.

Idolatry was practised in the form of addressing worshipful rituals to those idols and presenting offerings to them, which actually went to the monks and fortune-tellers themselves. Some borrowed from the Persians the belief that planets have a say in the running of events and, therefore, they addressed their rituals to them. They also practised a third type of idolatry by enacting for themselves, through their monks and notables, laws of which God does not approve. They used to claim that these represented God's law in the same way as some people do today.

In this scene of gathering and confrontation, all types of idolaters are questioned about the partners they associate with God. These other deities are nowhere to be seen, nor can they avail their worshippers of anything: "*One day We shall gather them all together, then We shall say to those who associate partners with God: 'Where, now, are those partners which you have been claiming.'"* (Verse 22) We almost behold the scene with our own eyes: the gathering of all creatures and the question to which no answer is given.

The awesome scene has its effect: human nature is rid of all that has blinded it and it realises that no partners with God have ever existed. They have to face up to their test and to make the truth appear before all. In that awesome situation, they will have no contention other than to say: *"By God, our Lord, we have never associated partners with Him."* (Verse 23) As they realise the truth, they abandon their past in total and acknowledge the Lordship of God alone. They disown their idolatry when it is too late. Their acknowledgement of the truth cannot save them because it is time for reward or punishment, not for action. They cannot go back to life, rather they are faced with what they used to do during their life on earth. The Prophet is invited to wonder at their situation as God states that they have lied to themselves when they associated partners with God, for He has no partners. On the Day of Judgement, their falsehood fails them and they have no option but to acknowledge the truth: *"Behold how they have lied to themselves and how they have been forsaken by whatever they have fabricated."* (Verse 24)

This is the interpretation I find most logical concerning their oaths on the Day of Judgement, made in the presence of God, that they did not associate partners with Him. On that Day they dare not utter any falsehood against God and cannot make a false oath deliberately. On that Day, they hide nothing from God. It is simply that their nature sees the truth for what it is and falsehood leaves no trace whatsoever in their senses. Hence, the invitation by God to wonder at their lies to themselves which, on the Day of Judgement, leave no mark on their minds or senses. God knows best the meaning of His words. Here, we only present a possible interpretation.

The *sūrah* goes on to describe how some of the unbelievers stubbornly block their minds as they listen to the Qur'ān. Having resolved to reject it altogether, they argue with the Prophet alleging that the Qur'ān is nothing but fables told by the ancients. They turn away from it and they forbid others to listen to it. Having depicted the attitude they adopt in this life, the Qur'ān describes their miserable state as they are made to stand before the fire of hell, facing the horror of their destiny, powerless, and without support. The only thing they can do is wish to go back to life in order to change those views and practices which led them to this horrible end. Their wishes, however, are rejected as petty and childish.

> *"Some of them listen to you. But over their hearts We have laid veils which prevent them from understanding what you say, and into their ears, deafness. Were they to see every sign, they would still not believe in it. When they come to you to contend with you, the unbelievers say: "This is nothing but fables of the ancients." They forbid [others] to listen to it and go far away from it. They ruin none but themselves, though they do not perceive it. If you could but see them when they will be made to stand before the Fire! They will say: "Would that we could return! Then we would not deny our Lord's revelations, but would be among the believers". Indeed, that which in the past they used to conceal will manifest itself to them; and if they were to return to life they would go back to that which they have been forbidden. They are indeed liars.* (Verses 25–8)

Here, we have two contrasting scenes: the one in this life is characterized by stubborn rejection, while the other, in the hereafter, is a situation of profound regret. They are portrayed in such a way so as to help awaken human nature that has been left to rust for a long time. If only human nature would open up to the Qur'ān and reflect on its message, it would gain the chance to be spared a fearful destiny.

"Some of them listen to you. But over their hearts We have laid veils which prevent them from understanding what you say, and into their ears, deafness. Were they to see every sign, they would still not believe in it." (Verse 25) This is a description of a particular type of people who listen but do not understand as if they do not have minds to help them comprehend, or ears to help them hear. This type of person may exist any time, anywhere. Their listening to what is being said has no effect whatsoever. Their ears do not function and their comprehension is sealed, so that the meaning of what they hear does not register with them.

"Were they to see every sign, they would still not believe in it. When they come to you to contend with you, the unbelievers say: This is nothing but fables of the ancients'." (Verse 25) Their eyes are open, but they do not seem to see, or what they see delivers no message to their minds.

What has happened to them, then? What prevents them from responding when they have ears, eyes, and minds? God tells us: "*Over their hearts We have laid veils which prevent them from understanding what you say, and into their ears, deafness. Were they to see every sign, they would still not believe in it.*" (Verse 25) It is God who has willed that their faculty of comprehension remains unable to grasp the truth and that their hearing does not function. We should try, then, to understand the wisdom behind God's will.

God, limitless is He in His glory, says: "*Those who strive hard for Our cause, We shall most certainly guide onto paths that lead to Us.*" (29: 69) He also says: "*By the Soul and its moulding, and inspiration with wickedness and piety. Successful is the one who keeps it pure and ruined is the one who corrupts it.*" (91: 7–10) It is God's will that He guides those who strive to follow His guidance, and that anyone who purges his soul from corruption will be successful. Those people have neither sought guidance nor tried to make use of their natural responses. These are the two things people need to do to ensure that God will guide them and help them give the proper responses. They started by knocking their nature out of action and, in consequence, God has placed a veil between them and His guidance. It is God's will, then, that people should bear the consequences of their initial attitude and action. Everything occurs according to God's will. It is His will to guide those who seek guidance and to grant success to those who work to purify themselves. It is also His will to place veils over the hearts and minds of those who turn away from His message and to make them deaf and unresponsive to the signs they see. Those who try to put the blame for their sins and their disbelief on God's will surely make a fraudulent claim. God confronts them with the truth as He reports and derides their claims: "*Those who associate partners with God say, 'Had God so wished, neither we nor our forefathers would have worshipped any other than Him, nor would we have declared anything forbidden without a commandment from Him.' Those before them said the same. Do the Messengers have to do anything other than to clearly deliver the Message? Indeed, We have raised a Messenger in every community, [who said to them]: 'Worship God and shun the Evil One.' Among them were some whom God graced with His guidance, while others were inevitably doomed by their error. Go, then, about the earth and observe what was the end of those who gave the lie to the truth.*" (16: 35–6) It is clear from these verses that God rejects their claims: it was inevitable that they should fall prey to grievous error after they had been given sufficient warnings to mend their ways.

People have often raised questions about predestination, compulsion and free choice, man's will, etc. They have made of these topics an academic debate which they tackle on the basis of their own assumptions. Their approach is contrary to the simple and straightforward Qur'ānic exposition of these questions. The Qur'ān states that everything takes place by God's will, and that man chooses the line he follows and that his choice is part of his nature, endowed to him by God. The direction he chooses to follow will entail certain consequences in this life and in the life to come. These consequences are part of God's will. Hence, the ultimate power behind everything is God's will which dictates the consequences of the freedom of choice God has given to man. Anything that goes beyond this simple statement is false.

All indicators to the truth and pointers to the right way and to faith were displayed in front of the idolaters. The Qur'ān repeatedly drew their attention to countless signs and indications which they recognise within themselves and in the world around them. Had they only thought objectively about these, they would have awakened to the truth and responded to it. But they have made no effort to receive guidance. On the contrary, they suppressed their own nature, and in consequence, God placed a veil between them and proper guidance. They did not go to the Prophet with open hearts, ears and eyes in order to listen, see and reflect. They went to argue and dispute: "*When they come to you to contend with you, the unbelievers say: 'This is nothing but fables of the ancients.'*" (Verse 25)

They were well aware that the Qur'ān bears no resemblance to such fables or legends which speak of supernatural events that happen to heroes and deities and which constitute a part of the beliefs of idolatrous communities. In their attempts to justify their rejection of the message of Prophet Muḥammad (peace be upon him), they give all types of false arguments. Since the Qur'ān recited to them by the Prophet contains stories about former prophets and their nations, as well as the fate of those who, in the past, denied God's messages, the unbelievers claimed that the Qur'ān was no more than the fables of the ancients. What a futile claim based on the least convincing of arguments.

Truth and Fables

In order to give more credence to their false description of the Qur'ān and to turn people away from it, a man like Mālik ibn al-Naḍr, who had learnt some Persian epics about Rustam and other Persian legendary heroes, used to sit at a short distance from the Prophet when he recited the Qur'ān. After the Prophet Muḥammad (peace be upon him) had finished, Mālik ibn al-Naḍr used to say to his audience: "If Muḥammad could tell you some fables of the ancients, I can tell you better ones." He would then relate to them some of the epics and histories he had learnt, hoping that in this way, he could prevent them from listening to the Qur'ān. Indeed, the chiefs of Makkah who commanded a position of authority and respect used to forbid others to listen to the Qur'ān, and they tried to stay away from its reading so that they did not submit to its powerful logic and irrefutable argument. In other words, they feared to be influenced by it: "*They forbid [others] to listen to it and go far away from it. They ruin none but themselves, though they do not perceive it.*" (Verse 26)

In this battle between the powerful authority of truth and the feeble structure of falsehood, it was not enough that a man like Mālik ibn al-Naḍr sat down to relate the epics and histories of the ancients. Instead, the Quraysh chiefs forbade their followers from listening to the Qur'ān and they also distracted themselves lest they too be unable to resist its influence. A story mentioned in the history of the Prophet about al-Akhnas ibn Sharīq, Abū Sufyān ibn Ḥarb and 'Amr ibn Hishām, and their secret listening to the Qur'ān is well known.[1]

All this effort which they exerted to refrain and prevent others from listening to the Qur'ān and allowing themselves to be influenced by it or respond to it was a recipe for disaster: "*They ruin none but themselves, though they do not perceive it.*" (Verse 26) Whom would a person ruin if all his efforts were geared towards preventing himself and others from listening to proper guidance and following the right way that ensures salvation?

Poor and wretched indeed are those who take such a goal for themselves, even though they may appear to other people as very powerful and having much influence. Wretched indeed they are because

---

1. A full report of this incident is given in the next chapter. – Editor's note.

their efforts ensure their own ruin both in this life and in the life to come. At times, it may appear to them and to others that they are on a winning course, but this is all delusion.

A Wish Availing Nothing

If we want to know the ultimate end of their efforts, we need only look at the result: "*If you could but see them when they will be made to stand before the Fire! They will say: 'Would that we could return! Then we would not deny our Lord's revelations, but would be among the believers.'*" (Verse 27)

This is the scene which contrasts with their situation in this life. Now they are in a state of regret, humility and total loss. This is compared with their attitude when they turned away from guidance, using their power to force others to also turn away, and boasting about their own strength and influence.

"*If you could but see them when they will be made to stand before the Fire!*" (Verse 27) Now they cannot turn away, use their argumentation, or repeat their falsehoods. If we were to see them ourselves in such a position, we would be sure to see something fearful. Their dearest wish would be: "*Would that we could return! Then we would not deny our Lord's revelations, but would be among the believers.*" (Verse 27) They know that the Qur'ān is God's revelation, and their desire to return to earth is such that they may have a second chance when they no longer deny these revelations. They claim that they would make sure that they would be among the believers.

All these are wishes that have no way of coming true. They do not know their own nature, which will always reject the faith. When they say that if they could return they would be believers is nothing but a lie, because it does not match with what they would do if their wishes were answered. They only make these assertions because they have come to realize how wicked and evil they are. What they used to conceal from their followers in order to portray an image of themselves as successful and prosperous is now laid bare: "*Indeed, that which in the past they used to conceal will manifest itself to them; and if they were to return to life they would go back to that which they have been forbidden. They are indeed liars.*" (Verse 28)

God knows their nature very well and He is fully aware that they will stubbornly continue in their falsehood. He is also fully aware that it is only the fearsome situation in which they find themselves as they stand by the fire that causes them to utter such wishes and to make these promises. But the real situation is this: *"If they were to return to life, they would go back to that which they have been forbidden. They are indeed liars."* (Verse 28) They are, thus, left to their miserable destiny. This answer confronts them with the truth as they endure their humiliation.

Contrasting Concepts and Values

The *sūrah* now opens two new pages to draw two contrasting scenes. The first looks at this present life where the unbelievers make their assertions that there will be no resurrection, accountability or reward. The other is in the hereafter when they are stood before their Lord, and He asks them about the positions they adopted in their first life: *"Is this not the truth?"* (Verse 30) The very question jolts them violently. They answer in complete humility: *"Yes, indeed, by our Lord!"* (Verse 30) They are then put face to face with what awaits them of painful suffering. The *sūrah* goes on to portray how overwhelmed they are in the Last Hour, caught unawares, after they disbelieved in the meeting with their Lord. They are full of sorrow, carrying their burdens on their backs. This is concluded with a statement showing the real value of this life as opposed to the life to come, according to God's true measure.

> *They say: "There is nothing beyond our life in this world, and we shall never be raised to life again." If you could but see them when they are made to stand before their Lord! He will say: "Is this not the truth?" They will say: "Yes, indeed, by our Lord!" He will then say, "Taste, then, the suffering in consequence of your having refused to believe." Lost indeed are they who deny that they will have to meet God. When the Last Hour comes suddenly upon them, they cry, "Alas for us! We have neglected much in our lifetime!" And they will be carrying their burdens on their backs. Evil indeed is that with which they are burdened. The life of this world is nothing but a sport and a passing delight. Surely the life in the hereafter is by far the better for those who are God-fearing. Will you not, then, use your reason?"* (Verses 29–32)

The concept of resurrection, reward and retribution in the life to come is central to the Islamic faith. Indeed, it ranks second only to the concept of Godhead as the foundation upon which the structure of Islam as a faith, law, system and code of conduct is built. God tells the believers in the Qur'ān that He has perfected their religion for them and completed with it the grace He has bestowed on them and has chosen it for them as a faith. It is then, a complete and coherent way of life in which the ideological concept is in perfect harmony with the moral values it upholds, as well as the laws and regulations it proclaims. All these are based on the same basic foundation: the Islamic concept of Godhead and the life hereafter.

According to Islam, life is not the short period of time which an individual lives, nor is it the limited period which represents the lifespan of a nation. Indeed, it is not even the longer period of time which represents the duration of human existence in this world. Life, in the Islamic view, has a much longer time span, much wider horizons and a much deeper and varied context than the period of time which is assigned to it by those who overlook the next world and do not believe in it.

According to Islam, life stretches out to include this present life of ours and the life to come, which is of a duration unknown to anyone but God. Compared to it, human life on earth is no longer than an hour in a day's work. It also stretches out in space to include this earth on which we live and added to it a paradise which is as vast as the heavens and the earth, as well as a hell which can accommodate the majority of people across all the generations that have existed and will exist on earth.

It stretches out further to add to this world's existence which we know another about which we know nothing except what God has told us. Its true nature is only known to God. This latter existence starts from the moment of our birth and reaches its fullness in the abode of the hereafter. When we speak of death and the hereafter, we are actually speaking of things the nature of which God has kept to Himself. Human existence continues in these worlds in forms and patterns known only to God alone.

Life has a further extension in its essence: it includes the type familiar to us in our world and other types which will be experienced in the next world, in heaven and hell. These types will have tastes and sensations that are different from what we know now. Compared to it, this present life is less than even the span of a mosquito's wings.

In the Islamic concept, humanity extends into these dimensions of time and place and into these deeper levels of worlds and existences. It is in proportion to its understanding of this fact that its appreciation of all existence, life, bonds, values and concerns becomes more profound. By contrast, the people who do not believe in the hereafter continue to have a very narrow and limited concept of the universe and human existence. They continue to confine their concepts, values and struggle to their very narrow corner in this world.

This difference in outlook leads to the adoption of different values and systems. It tells us clearly that this religion of Islam is a complete and coherent way of life. We can appreciate the importance of belief in a second life to its conceptual, ideological, moral, behavioural and legal structure. A man who lives in such a vast expanse of time, place, world and feelings is totally different from one who lives in a narrow corner and has to fight others for it, awaiting no compensation for that from which he is deprived and no reward for what he does in this present world, apart from his life on earth and what he receives during it from his fellow human beings.

A profound and varied concept will, by nature, elevate human concerns and refine human aspirations. This will, by itself, lead to the adoption of moral values and behaviour different from those which are characteristic of people living in their own narrow corners. When we adopt this profound concept, based on absolute justice in the life to come, and when we realize that a much larger compensation awaits us than what is here missed out on, then those who adopt this concept work hard to establish the truth and ensure that goodness prevails. They know that this is what God wants them to do and that reward and compensation are based on the fulfilment of God's bidding. When any human being believes in the hereafter as Islam views it, his manners and behaviour are set on the right footing. Similarly, all systems and laws acquire the right orientation; and what is more is that people will not allow them to be abused or corrupted. This is because people realise that if they keep quiet when they see corruption around them, they not only miss out on the benefits and goodness of this life, but they are deprived of reward in the hereafter. Thus, they lose in both worlds.

Some people are quick to speak against belief in the hereafter, claiming that it causes people to adopt a negative attitude towards this life, exerting no effort to improve it. They abandon it to dictators and their corrupt regimes, because they prefer to aspire to the blessings of the hereafter. This is an unfair criticism, one which combines injustice with ignorance. They group belief in the hereafter as advocated in Church concepts that have deviated from Christianity under the same classification as its Islamic concept. In the Islamic view, this life is where you place your investment in order to reap the benefits in the hereafter. To strive to put this life on the right course, to purge it from evil and corruption, to repel all assaults on God's authority, to smash tyrants and ensure justice and goodness to all people are the keys to the hereafter. It opens, for those who so strive, the gates to heaven and compensates them for everything they sacrifice during their struggle against evil and for the harm they may suffer.

How is it possible that the followers of such a faith could abandon this life and allow it to stagnate, deviate or become corrupt? How could they allow injustice and tyranny to establish their roots and spread? How could they allow it to remain backward, undeveloped when they aspire to receive reward from God in the hereafter? That reward is not given for a negative attitude.

The Only Faith Worthy of Man

There were periods of time when people adopted a negative attitude allowing corruption, evil, injustice, tyranny, ignorance and backwardness to prevail in their life while claiming at the same time that they were Muslims. They did this only because their understanding of Islam was faulty and their belief in the hereafter was shaken and weakened. Their negative attitude could not be the result of a true understanding of this faith or the belief that they have to face God on the Day of Judgement. No one who believes in this inevitable meeting with God and understands the nature of this religion can adopt a negative attitude towards life or allow himself to remain backward or to accept evil, corruption and tyranny.

While going through life, a true Muslim feels that he is bigger and more sublime than life itself. He may enjoy its comforts or ignore them, knowing that they are lawful and permissible to him in this life, placed at his disposal on the Day of Judgement when no one else can claim them. He strives to promote and improve this life and to use its potentials and abilities, happy in the knowledge that this is the duty assigned to him by God when He placed him in charge of the earth. He fights evil, corruption and injustice willingly, bearing any hardship and making every sacrifice, including his own life, knowing that he is simply adding to his credit in the hereafter. Understanding his religion well, he knows that this life is the one in which the seeds are planted, for the fruits to be reaped in the hereafter. There is simply no way to success in the life to come which does not go through this world of ours. True, this life is very small and cheap, but it is part of God's grace which makes it a stage towards the greatest blessings and grace He bestows on man.

Every detail in the Islamic system takes due account of the life to come, and the broadness, beauty and elevation it imparts to people's visions and concepts. It also adds to the refinement, purity and forbearance which are inherent in the Islamic moral code. It enhances its followers' determination to establish what is right and to prevent evil and avoid disobedience to God. It helps set human activities on the right course. For all that, Islamic life is not properly achieved without a firm belief in the hereafter. Hence, the great emphasis placed in the Qur'ān on the fact that we will be raised up for our next life.

In their ignorance, as much as because of it, the pagan Arabs could not conceive of a second life or believe in it. They could not simply imagine another world, different from this present one of ours. They could not conceive how a human being could aspire to horizons beyond the physical world. Their concepts and feelings were not much different from those of animals. It is the same situation we witness today in the modern type of *jāhiliyyah*, whose exponents describe as 'scientific'.

"*They say: 'There is nothing beyond our life in this world, and we shall never be raised to life again.'*" (Verse 29) God knows very well that beliefs of this type do not allow the emergence of a noble type of human life. The limited scope of beliefs makes man strongly attached to the earth and to that which is physical and tangible in it, just like animals. Our limited time span and area tend to loosen a forceful desire to seek a self-aggrandisement which enslaves man to worldly pleasures. His physical desires are set loose without restraint. He feels that unless he satisfies his profane desires, which can hardly be elevated above those of animals, he misses out on his pleasure without hope of compensation. Systems and regimes are established on earth based on a very selfish and narrow view of time and space. This leads to a life devoid of justice and compassion. War becomes the order of the day with individuals, classes and races fighting one another. It is a jungle type of life, not that much different from the world of wild animals and brutal beasts. All this is there for us to see in the world of modern 'civilization'! It is evident everywhere.

God has been aware all along of these facts. Hence why He wanted to assign to a certain community the role of leading mankind to the summit where human dignity can be seen in full play in real life. God knows that this community cannot fulfil its task unless it brings its concepts and values out of its hole in that narrow corner, the earth, and places them over a vast horizon. That community must move out of the narrowness of this world to the expanse which combines this life with the life to come. Hence, the emphasis is placed by Islam on the future life; firstly because it is real – for God always tells the truth; and secondly because believing in it is essential for the completeness of man's existence, in ideology, morality, behaviour, systems and legal code.

This accounts for the strong and deep rhythm which we notice in this part of the *sūrah* which runs like a very fast river. God knows well that it is within human nature to respond to such a strong and deep rhythm. It opens up its receptive elements, awaiting instructions, in order to respond to them. We must not forget, however, that everything that is mentioned about the hereafter is simply the truth.

> *If you could but see them when they are made to stand before their Lord! He will say: "Is this not the truth?" They will say: "Yes, indeed, by our Lord!" He will then say, "Taste, then, the suffering in consequence of your having refused to believe."* (Verse 30)

This is the eventual destiny of those who claimed that there was nothing beyond our present life and that they would never he raised up again. It is a miserable, shameful, humiliating destiny as they are brought before their Lord, having persistently denied that they would face Him. They cannot stir. They are depicted as if they were led by the neck until they are stood in that awesome surrounding, facing the questioning: "*Is this not the truth?*" (Verse 30). What a humiliating question! There is only one possible reply: "*Yes indeed, by our Lord!*" (Verse 30). Now they are face to face with their Lord, on the occasion that they most stubbornly refused to believe in.

In a summary way, which most befits the awesome scene, the divine order is given, sealing their fate: "*He will then say: Taste, then, the suffering in consequence of your having refused to believe.*'" (Verse 30) This is the most suitable destiny for those who denied themselves the comfort of a wider human concept, following instead an exceedingly narrow material concept. They have refused to raise themselves to the level that fits a noble humanity. They conducted their lives on the basis of their profane, hollow concept. By so doing, they actually earned their own punishment and this fits with the nature of those who deny the hereafter.

What the Unbelievers Actually Reject

The scene portraying the final outcome decreed by God is now complemented with a statement of the truth of its causes: "*Lost indeed are they who deny that they will have to meet God. When the Last Hour comes suddenly upon them, they cry, 'Alas for us! We have neglected much in our lifetime!' And they will be carrying their burdens on their backs. Evil indeed is that with which they are burdened.*" (Verse 31)

It is indeed an utter loss because it includes the loss of this world, since they have spent their lifetime caring only for what is petty, low and profane, and the loss of the hereafter as we have already seen. Those deluded, ignorant people have not taken any precautions against what comes to them as a sudden shock: "*When the Last Hour comes suddenly upon them, they cry, 'Alas for us! We have neglected much in our lifetime!*'" (Verse 31) They are then portrayed as overladen donkeys: "*And they will be carrying their burdens on their backs.*" (Verse 31) Indeed, animals are in a better situation because they carry ordinary loads, while these have loads of sin. Animals are unloaded and set free to relax, while these march with their loads to hell, followed by the rebuke: "*Evil indeed is that with which they are burdened.*" (Verse 31)

The passage then portrays a terrible scene which strikes fear in the listener's heart, followed by one of complete and utter loss. These two scenes are then followed by a statement of the real weight and value of this life and the life hereafter according to God's measure: "*The life of this world is nothing but a sport and a passing delight. Surely the life in the hereafter is by far the better for those who are God-fearing. Will you not, then, use your reason?*" (Verse 32) This is the final value of each of the two lives. It could not be otherwise, when we compare an hour in a day's work on this small planet with eternity in God's vast dominion. What value other than a pastime could be attached to an hour's work in this life when it is compared to the seriousness of the great world beyond.

This evaluation is absolute in nature, but it does not create any tendency to neglect this life or approach it in an isolationist or negative way. There has certainly been some of this among some Sufi or mystic movements, but this tendency has no roots in the proper Islamic vision. It is simply borrowed from some Christian clerical concepts, Persian and Greek ideologies as they found their way into Islamic society.

The great practical examples history gives us of how the Islamic concept of life works in practice have never been negative or isolationist in attitude. You have only to look at the generation of the Prophet's Companions who were able to subdue the evil tendency within themselves and overcome the prevailing systems of *jāhiliyyah*, represented by powerful empires. That generation, which understood the true value of this life as it is in God's measure, was the same generation which set out to work for the hereafter and accomplished in the process feats that left great positive effects on human life. That generation lived a life of immense activity, great power and unstoppable momentum.

The proper evaluation of the two lives according to God's measure gave them the benefit of not being enslaved by the pleasures of this life. They mastered this life and made use of it for God's cause, to ensure that His authority remains supreme. They gave worldly pleasures no chance to enslave them. Thus, they were able to fulfil their task of building a proper and sound structure for human life. At no time did they aim to enjoy more of the pleasures of this world but instead aimed to win in the hereafter. With this driving aim, they were able to excel over the rest of mankind in this life and to ensure that they will excel them in the hereafter.

The nature of the hereafter is something which has not been explained to us in detail. Therefore, believing in it gives us a broader vision and nobler thinking. To work for it ensures better results for the God-fearing which can easily be recognized by those who use their reason: *"Surely the life in the hereafter is by far the better for those who are God-fearing. Will you not, then, use your reason?"* (Verse 32)

Those who deny the hereafter, simply because it is imperceptible, are only ignorant people who claim to have sound knowledge. Human knowledge today has no longer any certainty other than the certainty of what lies beyond our world and what is imperceptible.

5

The Dead Cannot Hear

We know too well that what they say grieves you. Yet it is not you that they charge with falsehood; but it is God's revelations that the wrongdoers deny. (33)

قَدْ نَعْلَمُ إِنَّهُ لَيَحْزُنُكَ ٱلَّذِى يَقُولُونَ فَإِنَّهُمْ لَا يُكَذِّبُونَكَ وَلَكِنَّ ٱلظَّالِمِينَ بِـَٔايَـٰتِ ٱللَّهِ يَجْحَدُونَ ﴿٣٣﴾

Other messengers were charged with falsehood before your time, but they patiently endured all those charges and abuse, until Our help came to them. There is no power that can alter God's words. You have already received some of the history of those messengers. (34)

وَلَقَدْ كُذِّبَتْ رُسُلٌ مِّن قَبْلِكَ فَصَبَرُوا۟ عَلَىٰ مَا كُذِّبُوا۟ وَأُوذُوا۟ حَتَّىٰ أَتَىٰهُمْ نَصْرُنَا وَلَا مُبَدِّلَ لِكَلِمَـٰتِ ٱللَّهِ وَلَقَدْ جَآءَكَ مِن نَّبَإِى۟ ٱلْمُرْسَلِينَ ﴿٣٤﴾

If you find it so distressing that they turn their backs on you, seek, if you can, a chasm to go deep into the earth or a ladder to the sky by which you may bring them a sign. Had God so willed, He would have gathered them all to [His] guidance. Do not, therefore, allow yourself to be one of the ignorant. (35)

وَإِن كَانَ كَبُرَ عَلَيْكَ إِعْرَاضُهُمْ فَإِنِ ٱسْتَطَعْتَ أَن تَبْتَغِىَ نَفَقًا فِى ٱلْأَرْضِ أَوْ سُلَّمًا فِى ٱلسَّمَآءِ فَتَأْتِيَهُم بِـَٔايَةٍ وَلَوْ شَآءَ ٱللَّهُ لَجَمَعَهُمْ عَلَى ٱلْهُدَىٰ فَلَا تَكُونَنَّ مِنَ ٱلْجَـٰهِلِينَ ﴿٣٥﴾

Only those that can hear will surely answer. As for the dead, God will bring them back to life, then to Him shall they return. (36)

إِنَّمَا يَسْتَجِيبُ ٱلَّذِينَ يَسْمَعُونَ وَٱلْمَوْتَىٰ يَبْعَثُهُمُ ٱللَّهُ ثُمَّ إِلَيْهِ يُرْجَعُونَ ۞

They say: "Why has no sign been sent down to him from his Lord?" Say: God is well able to send down any sign, but most of them are devoid of knowledge. (37)

وَقَالُوا۟ لَوْلَا نُزِّلَ عَلَيْهِ ءَايَةٌ مِّن رَّبِّهِۦ قُلْ إِنَّ ٱللَّهَ قَادِرٌ عَلَىٰٓ أَن يُنَزِّلَ ءَايَةً وَلَٰكِنَّ أَكْثَرَهُمْ لَا يَعْلَمُونَ ۞

There is not an animal that walks on earth and no bird that flies on its wings but are communities like your own. No single thing have We left out of the book. Then to their Lord shall they all be gathered. (38)

وَمَا مِن دَآبَّةٍ فِى ٱلْأَرْضِ وَلَا طَٰٓئِرٍ يَطِيرُ بِجَنَاحَيْهِ إِلَّآ أُمَمٌ أَمْثَالُكُم مَّا فَرَّطْنَا فِى ٱلْكِتَٰبِ مِن شَىْءٍ ثُمَّ إِلَىٰ رَبِّهِمْ يُحْشَرُونَ ۞

Those who deny Our revelations are deaf and dumb, groping along in darkness. Whomever God wills, He lets go astray; and whomever He wills, He guides along a straight path. (39)

وَٱلَّذِينَ كَذَّبُوا۟ بِـَٔايَٰتِنَا صُمٌّ وَبُكْمٌ فِى ٱلظُّلُمَٰتِ مَن يَشَإِ ٱللَّهُ يُضْلِلْهُ وَمَن يَشَأْ يَجْعَلْهُ عَلَىٰ صِرَٰطٍ مُّسْتَقِيمٍ ۞

Overview

In this new round or wave, an address is made to the Prophet (peace be upon him). It begins with God, limitless is He in His glory, consoling and comforting him. He, honest and truthful, was particularly distressed at the charges of falsehood that were laid at his door. Here, he is told by his Lord that they never thought him a liar, but used this as a ploy to maintain their stubborn denial of God's signs and their rejection of the faith. He is also comforted with the information that earlier messengers of God were similarly accused of falsehood and subjected to abuse, and that they endured all this with patience. Eventually, they were given God's help to triumph, in accordance with the consistent laws He has set in operation. When the comforting and reassurance are over, the address makes clear the essential truth concerning God's message. It moves according to God's will and His laws. Its advocates have nothing to do with it other than to convey it to people and to make it clear. Other than that, it is God who decides what happens to it. Hence, its advocates, including the Prophet himself, have nothing to decide other than to continue with their task, without hastening its moves or suggesting anything to God. They are not to pay any attention to people's suggestions concerning its strategy, the proofs that may be given of its truth or the miracles needed to prove it. The point is that those who are alive and have the power of hearing will respond. On the other hand, those whose hearts are dead will not. The ultimate decision belongs to God: He may give people life or keep them dead until they return to Him on the Day of Judgement.

The people the Prophet was addressing demanded a miracle like the ones granted earlier prophets. God is certainly able to give them such a miracle, but He, in His wisdom, does not wish to do so. If the Prophet is so distressed by their turning away, then let him try, by his own human effort, to bring them such a miracle. God is the Creator of all living creatures, and He knows all their secrets and the differences in their nature. He leaves those human beings who reject His message to wander in the deep darkness, deaf and dumb. He leaves some to go astray and guides others to the truth, according to His infallible knowledge of His different creatures.

Honest No Doubt

We know too well that what they say grieves you. Yet it is not you that they charge with falsehood; but it is God's revelations that the wrongdoers deny. (Verse 33)

The pagan Arabs with their idolatrous beliefs, particularly those of them who took upon themselves the unworthy task of opposing the message of Islam, had no doubt that Muḥammad (peace be upon him) was telling the truth. They have known him to be truthful and honest. They knew that he had never told a lie before starting to convey God's message. Those who were most hardened in their opposition to him did not doubt the truthfulness of his message either. They knew that the Qur'ān could not have been authored by a human being. They, nevertheless, stubbornly refused to declare their belief or to embrace a new faith. Their reason for rejecting it was not that they could not believe the Prophet; rather, it was their realisation that his message threatened their positions and influence. Hence, they decided to deny God's revelations and to stick to their idolatrous beliefs. There are numerous reports that clearly state the reasons behind the Quraysh's attitude. We will now look at just a few of these.

Ibn Ishāq reports on the authority of al-Zuhrī that three of the Quraysh's notables, namely, Abū Sufyān, Abū Jahl and al-Akhnas ibn Sharīq, protected by the cover of darkness, took their separate ways to listen to God's Messenger as he recited the Qur'ān during his night worship. They sat just outside his house, listening to his recitation of the Qur'ān. Each was on his own, thinking that no one would know about his action. One can only assume that their motivation was either to try to judge Muḥammad's message objectively, or to learn the truth about it, or to listen to the superb literary style of the Qur'ān. As the day began to break, each of them returned the way they had come such that their clandestine activities would not be found out. However, their individual plans were foiled when the three happened, by chance, to meet with each other. There was no need to ask each other what they were doing. There was only one reason for their presence there at that particular time. Therefore, they counselled each other against such action: "Should some of your followers see you", one of them said, "you would stir doubts in their minds".

The following night they did the same, and once again they met at the break of day. Again they counselled each other against their 'irresponsible' action. Nevertheless, the third night each of them again went to sit outside the Prophet's home and listen to the Qur'ān. When they met in the morning, they were ashamed of themselves. One of them suggested that they should give each other their word of honour not to come again. They did so before going home.

Later that morning al-Akhnas ibn Sharīq went to see Abū Sufyān in his home. He asked him what he thought about what he had heard Muḥammad reciting. Abū Sufyān said: "I heard things which I know and recognize to be true, but I also heard things whose nature I cannot understand." Al-Akhnas said that he felt the same. He then left and went to Abū Jahl's home to put the same question to him.

Abū Jahl's answer was totally different. For once, he was candid and honest with himself and his interlocutor:

> I will tell you about what I heard! We have competed with the clan of 'Abd Manāf for honours: they fed the poor, and we did the same; they provided generous support to those who needed it and we did the same. When we were together on the same level, like two racehorses running neck and neck, they said that one of their number was a Prophet receiving revelations from on high! When can we attain such an honour? By God, we shall never believe in him.[1]

Knowing the Truth

Commenting on the Qur'ānic verse, "*We know too well that what they say grieves you. Yet it is not you that they charge with falsehood; but it is God's revelations that the wrongdoers deny*" (Verse 33), al-Ṭabarī quotes the following report on the authority of al-Suddī: "On the day of the Battle of Badr, al-Akhnas ibn Sharīq said to his tribesmen, the Zuharh people, 'Muḥammad is your sister's son, and you are the ones who defend their nephew. If he is truly a Prophet, why would you fight him today? And if he is a liar, you should repel aggression against your nephew. Wait until I meet Abū al-Ḥakam, i.e. Abū Jahl. Should Muḥammad be victorious, you will return home safely, but if he is defeated, your people will do you no harm.' [It was on that day that he was nicknamed al-Akhnas, while his real name was Ubayy.] He went to meet Abū Jahl and spoke to him in private: 'Tell me about Muḥammad: is he telling the truth, or is he a liar? There is no one from the Quraysh listening to this conversation between us.' Abū Jahl said: 'By God, Muḥammad is telling the truth. Muḥammad never told a lie in his life. But what would happen, should the descendants of Quṣayy add prophethood to their other honours, such as holding the banner

---

1. Ibn Isḥāq, *Muhammad, The Life of the Prophet,* as quoted in A. Salahi, *Muhammad: Man and Prophet,* London, 1995, pp. 161–2.

in war, providing water for the pilgrims, etc. What will remain for the rest of the Quraysh?'"[2] All this then explains the statement made in the above verse.

In considering this report, we have to realise that this incident took place on the day of the Battle of Badr, nearly two years after the Prophet had settled in Madinah, while the *sūrah* and this verse are Makkan revelations, i.e. they precede this incident. To account for this, we have to understand that commentators on the Qur'ān might report an event and cite a particular verse in connection with it, but this is not to say that the verse in question was revealed on that occasion. Rather it explains the verse in relation to life events.

The following report is given by Ibn Isḥāq in his history of the Prophet's life: One day, as 'Utbah was sitting with a group of Quraysh notables, he noticed the Prophet sitting alone close to the Ka'bah. 'Utbah suggested to his friends: "Shall we go to Muḥammad and make him some offers? He may accept one or the other. If he does, we will give him that and put an end to our problem with him".

This idea was greeted with unanimous approval. As 'Utbah sat with the Prophet he addressed him: "My nephew, you know you command a position of high esteem and noble birth among us. You have brought into the life of your community something very serious indeed. You have thus caused disunity to creep into their ranks; you have belittled their ideals, ridiculed their gods and their religion and spoken ill of their forefathers. Now listen to me. I am making you some offers which I would like you to consider. You may, perhaps, find some of them acceptable."

The Prophet asked him to make his proposals, and listened attentively. 'Utbah said: "My nephew, if you have started this affair hoping to make money out of it, we are all willing to give you some of our own wealth so that you would be the richest among us. If it is honour and position you want, we will make you our master and seek your advice in all matters. If it is a throne you are after, we will make you our king. If, on the other hand, you are possessed and are unable to resist what overwhelms you, we will spare no expense in seeking a medical cure for you."

When 'Utbah stopped speaking, the Prophet asked him whether he had finished. As 'Utbah affirmed that he had, the Prophet asked him

---

2. Al-Ṭabarī, *Jāmi' al-Bayān,* Dar al-Fikr, Beirut, 1984, Vol. 7, p. 182.

to listen to what he had to say. The Prophet then recited the first 38 Verses of *Sūrah* 41 of the Qurʾān. ʿUtbah listened attentively. When the Prophet had finished his recitation, he prostrated himself in humble devotion to God, before saying to ʿUtbah: "You have heard what I have to say and you can make up your own mind."

ʿUtbah left quietly and went to his people, who realized as they saw him approaching that a change had come over him. They looked up at him curiously, listening to his words: "I have heard something the like of which I have never heard in my life. It is neither poetry nor sorcery. Take up the suggestion I am making to you, and lay the blame for the outcome at my door. Leave this man alone. What I have heard from him will certainly bring about great events. Should the rest of the Arabs kill him, you would have been spared the trouble. If he wins, whatever glory he achieves will be yours." They retorted: "He has certainly bewitched you." He said: "I have stated my opinion, and you can do as you wish."[3]

In his commentary on the Qurʾān, al-Baghawī reports a different ending for the above incident. He mentions that, "as the Prophet recited the opening passage of *Sūrah* 41, he read up to Verse 13, stating: '*Should they turn their backs on you, say to them, I am warning you against a calamity like those that befell the peoples of ʿĀd and Thamūd.*' At this point ʿUtbah placed his hand on the Prophet's mouth and appealed to him by his blood relationship with the Quraysh. He then went home and did not go out to see his people. When they spoke to him about this, he mentioned the warning he had heard from the Prophet and said: 'I stopped him putting my hand on his mouth and appealed to him by our kinship. You know that Muhammad does not lie. I feared that a calamity might befall you.'"[4]

Making False Accusations

Another incident reported by Ibn Isḥāq took place close to the pilgrimage season. A meeting attended by a large number of Makkans and chaired, as it were, by al-Walīd ibn al-Mughīrah, defined their

---

3. A. Salahi, op. cit., pp. 106–7.

4. Al-Baghawī, *Maʿālim al-Tanzīl*, Vol. 4, p. 110.

According to Ibn Kathīr, this version is somewhat less authentic as its chain of transmission includes ʿAbdullāh al-Kindī who is classified as rather weak.

strategy for a defamation campaign. In his opening address, al-Walīd said: "Now that the pilgrimage season is approaching, people will start arriving from all over the place. They must have heard about your friend [meaning the Prophet]. So you had better agree what to say when you are asked about him. We must guard against having too many opinions, particularly if they are mutually contradictory."

When his audience asked his advice as to what they should say, he preferred to listen to their suggestions first. What concerned al-Walīd most was that the opinion they would come out with should take account of the fact that Muḥammad was asking people to listen to the Qur'ān, God's message, expressed in the most beautiful language and employing the most powerful of styles. The description they would attach to Muḥammad should also account for his persuasive, eloquent argument.

Descriptions like 'fortune-teller', 'madman', 'poet' and 'magician' were proposed. None was considered convincing by al-Walīd, who pointed out weaknesses in each, one after the other. He told his people that what Muḥammad said was nothing like what was said by such men. When nobody could suggest anything more plausible, they asked al-Walīd to come up with a better suggestion.

He said: "What Muḥammad says is certainly beautiful. It is like a date tree with solid roots and rich fruit. Every one of these suggestions you have made is bound to be recognized as false. The least disputable one is to claim that he is a magician who repeats magic words which make a man fall out with his father, mother, wife and clan". They all approved of al-Walīd's suggestion and set about preparing their propaganda campaign to make the pilgrims wary of Muḥammad and unwilling to meet him.[5]

Another report mentions that al-Walīd ibn al-Mughīrah met the Prophet once and the Prophet read him some passages of the Qur'ān. Al-Walīd seemed to have been favourably influenced by what he had heard. News of this was communicated to Abū Jahl who went straight to al-Walīd and said: "Uncle, your people are starting a collection of money for you!" Surprised, al-Walīd asked the reason for this. Abū Jahl said: "They want to give you that money because you went to Muḥammad trying to find what you may get out of him." (Abū Jahl

---

5. A. Salahi, op. cit., pp. 111–12.

was making this insinuation knowing that al-Walīd would be on the defensive because his pride would not allow him to appear in this light at all.) Al-Walīd answered: "All the Quraysh are aware that I am the richest among them." Abū Jahl then offered the following advice: "Then you should say something about him to reassure your people that you disagree with what he says and that you are fully against it."

Al-Walīd said: "What shall I say? None of you is a better judge of poetry than I. None of you can appreciate the finer points of poetry as I do. By God, what he says has no similarity with poetry. It is sweet, fine, overpowering and cannot be excelled." Abū Jahl said: "By God, your people will not be satisfied unless you denounce him." Al-Walīd asked for time to think the matter over. When he had done so, he came up with the idea of describing the Qur'ān as sorcery handed down from olden times.[6] There is a reference to this in the Qur'ān: "*Leave Me alone [to deal] with the one whom I created alone, and to whom I have granted vast wealth and thriving children. I have made his progress smooth and easy; yet he greedily desires that I shall give him more. By no means! Because he has stubbornly denied Our revelations, I shall constrain him to endure a painful uphill climb. He reflects and meditates. Confound him how he meditates! Again, confound him how he meditates! He then looks around him, and then he frowns and glares; and in the end he turns his back in scornful pride and says: 'This is but sorcery handed down [from olden times]. This is nothing but the word of a mere mortal!' I shall cast him in the Fire. Would that you knew what the Fire is like! It leaves nothing, it spares no one; it burns the skin of men. It is guarded by nineteen keepers.*" (74: 11–30)

Another version of this story suggests that when al-Walīd showed signs of appreciating the Qur'ān some people in Makkah said: "If al-Walīd will desert his religion, all the Quraysh people will follow suit." Abū Jahl then said: "I will take care of him." He then went to him and said what we have learned of in the above reports. When al-Walīd came up with his ill-conceived suggestion, he justified it in the following words: "It is sorcery. We all see how it causes friction between a man and his family, children and members of his household."

All these reports confirm that these unbelievers did not think that the Prophet Muḥammad (peace be upon him) was telling them

---

6. Al-Ṭabarī, op. cit., Vol. 14, p. 156.

something untrue when he conveyed God's message to them. They only persisted with their disbelief for the sort of reasons indicated in these reports and because they realized that the triumph of Muḥammad's message meant that they would have to give up their authority which rightly belonged to God, and which they had unfairly and unjustifiably usurped. They knew their language very well and they perfectly understood the meaning of the declaration that there is no deity other than God, which is the cornerstone of the Islamic faith. They simply did not want to put that declaration into practice, because it meant an all-out rebellion against any authority, other than that of God, which aimed to regulate human life. God certainly tells the truth when He says: "*We know too well that what they say grieves you. Yet it is not you that they charge with falsehood; but it is God's revelations that the wrongdoers deny.*" The term 'wrongdoers' refers to the unbelievers, and is frequently used in the Qur'ān in this context.

Who Gives a Favourable Response?

Having given the Prophet this consolation, the *sūrah* reminds him of what happened to past messengers, some of whose history is given in the Qur'ān. They endured abuse and hardship with patience and moved along the way God had shown them until they were granted victory by God. This is, then, an assertion that meeting affliction was only natural for God's messengers. The outcome must never be precipitated even though the advocates of the divine message may be subjected to torture, abuse, denial and other hardships: "*Other messengers were charged with falsehood before your time, but they patiently endured all those charges and abuse, until Our help came to them. There is no power that can alter God's words. You have already received some of the history of those messengers.*" (Verse 34)

Advocates of God's message have continued along the same difficult way, overcoming numerous hurdles. They move along with steady steps, opposed by wrongdoers of all sorts, rejected by those who have chosen to go astray and their followers. Harm may be inflicted on some of those advocates, pressure, torture, and death. Yet the advocates of the truth will move on, maintaining their way, undeterred. The outcome remains the same, long as it may take. At the end of the road awaits victory, granted by God: "*Other messengers were charged with falsehood before your time, but they patiently endured all those charges and abuse, until Our help came to them. There is no power that can alter God's words. You have already received some of the history of those messengers."* (Verse 34)

These are words said by God to His Messenger, Muḥammad, (peace be upon him) to remind and console him. However, these words show the advocates of Islam who will come after the Prophet the way they have to travel and the role they have to play. Indeed, the difficulties they are to expect are held up before their eyes. They are also told what to expect at the end of the road.

These verses make clear that the same rules apply to all divine messages. In fact, these messages constitute a single and integral unity. The majority of people reject the message as false and inflict hardship on its advocates who, in turn, face all this with patience and perseverance. The ultimate outcome, however, is victory, which comes at the time determined by God. That outcome is not precipitated by the fact that honest and devoted advocates have to bear hardship and rejection, or that hardened criminals are able to inflict torment on innocent, defenceless people. Nor is it hastened by the fact that a totally dedicated advocate of faith is keen to see his people follow divine guidance, simply because he loves them and feels distressed when he sees them in their erroneous ways, knowing what punishment awaits them in the life to come. God does not hasten things because anyone of His creatures is over enthusiastic to see the end. There is simply no way that God's words can be altered, whether they relate to the ultimate victory or the appointed time. What we have here is a statement combining seriousness and decisiveness with consolation and reassurance.

Seriousness is further heightened in order to counter what might have been entertained by God's Messenger of a keen, kindly desire to make his people recognise guidance. It also deals with any hope he may have entertained that their request for a sign, so that they may accept God's message, might be answered. The same desire was similarly entertained by other Muslims at the time, as later verses in this *sūrah* explain. This was a perfectly natural human desire. However, in order to make a final statement about the nature of this message, its method, the roles of earlier messengers and people in its promotion and progress, the Qur'ān makes this very clear delineation of the right attitude: *"If you find it so distressing that they turn their backs on you, seek, if you can, a chasm to go deep into the earth or a ladder to*

117

the sky by which you may bring them a sign. Had God so willed, He would have gathered them all to [His] guidance. Do not, therefore, allow yourself to be one of the ignorant. Only those that can hear will surely answer. As for the dead, God will bring them back to life, then to Him shall they return." (Verses 35–6)

These are majestic words, portraying an awesome scene. We cannot appreciate fully the whole idea unless we recall vividly that these are words addressed by God, the Lord of all worlds, to his noble Prophet who has shown maximum perseverance and who is one of the small number of messengers endowed with the strongest resolve. He patiently endured all that his people tried to inflict on him. He never uttered a prayer akin to that of the Prophet Noah, despite his long and arduous suffering. He is being told how God's law works. If he finds their rejection and aversion too much to cope with and wants to bring them a miraculous sign, then he is free to do so. He may, in the process, try to find a chasm to go deep into the earth or a ladder to ascend to heaven for the purpose.

That people should follow divine guidance does not depend on their having a miraculous sign or receiving any clear proof. This was not what they found lacking in Muḥammad's message. Had it been God's will, he would have united them all under His guidance, either by making their nature akin to that of angels, so that they could follow proper guidance, or by directing their hearts to enable them to receive such guidance and respond to it. Alternatively, He could, if He so wished, accomplish something of a miraculous nature in the face of which they would have to give up their stubborn rejection. There are other ways and means and all of them are within God's ability.

However, in His superior wisdom, God has created man for a particular purpose of His own, giving him certain abilities that are different from those of angels. This has meant that man should contain within himself a varying ability to receive guidance and pointers to faith and able to make different responses to them. He has a range of ability to determine his direction so that justice is maintained, as he receives reward for following guidance or punishment for his deliberate error. For this reason, God has not brought all mankind together to His guidance by a decree He promulgates. He has only commanded them to follow His guidance, and given them the ability to choose either to obey or disobey Him. At the end, everyone will have his fair reward. The Prophet is told to keep this in mind and not to ignore it: "*Had God so willed, He would have gathered them all to [His] guidance. Do not, therefore, allow yourself to be one of the ignorant.*" (Verse 35) What a decisive word given by way of comment on a situation which requires such a decisive finality.

This is followed by an explanation of the nature God has given to mankind, and their different attitudes to His guidance which lacks no proof: "*Only those that can hear will surely answer. As for the dead, God will bring them back to life, then to Him shall they return.*" (Verse 36)

In their attitude to the truth sent down by God from on high and preached by His Messenger, people can be divided into two groups: one who are alive, opening up their receptive faculties and responding to divine guidance. They find such guidance to be strong, clear, consistent with human nature and easily heard. Hence, there is no problem with responding to it: "*Only those that can hear will surely answer.*" (Verse 36)

The other group are dead, their nature out of order and, as such, they cannot listen or respond. They do not lack any evidence of the truth, because the evidence is inherent in it. Once it touches human nature, response is certain. What this group actually lack is to have their nature awakened and their responses activated. The Prophet can do nothing to such people. Proofs have no use for them. Their case is left to God. He may raise them up if they show that they deserve to be brought to life. By the same token, however, He may not raise them up at all in this life. He may leave them dead despite their moving about in this world, until they return to Him in the hereafter: "*As for the dead, God will bring them back to life, then to Him they shall return.*" (Verse 36)

This is, then, the full explanation of responding to guidance or rejecting it. It sets out all the issues clearly, outlining the role of God's Messenger and leaving the ultimate decision to God who accomplishes what He wills.

Who Needs Miraculous Evidence?

The *sūrah* then refers to the unbelievers' request that a sign in the form of something supernatural be sent down to the Prophet. It points out that such a request betrays ignorance of God's law and the mercy

He shows them by not responding to their request. Were they to continue with their rejection after a supernatural sign is given them, they would be destroyed.

What they requested was a physical miracle such as those given to earlier messengers. They were not satisfied with the permanent sign embodied in the Qur'ān, which heralds the ultimate stage of mankind's maturity. It makes a final address to man's mature mind. Moreover, its significance is not limited to the generation that sees it, as is the case with material miracles; its miraculous message will continue to address the human intellect until the Day of Judgement.

As they made their requests for a miracle, they overlooked the divine law which brought immediate punishment to those who continued to deny divine messages after a miraculous sign had been given them. They simply did not appreciate God's kindness by not responding to their request, when He knew that they would continue to deny Him, as earlier people had done. That would have sealed their fate. God wanted to give them an extended chance to believe in Him. Those who continue to reject faith may have children who grow up as believers. Needless to say, they did not thank God for His grace in giving them such an extended chance.

The *sūrah* mentions their request and comments that most of them do not know what it entails or the reason for its rejection. It states that God is certainly able to give them the miraculous sign they want, but His wisdom and grace have stopped the woeful doom that is certain to follow: "*They say: 'Why has no sign been sent down to him from his Lord?' Say: God is well able to send down any sign, but most of them are devoid of knowledge.*" (Verse 37)

The Qur'ān then begins another gentle approach to awaken their senses, inviting them to reflect on the numerous pointers to faith which they see all around them: "*There is not an animal that walks on earth and no bird that flies on its wings but are communities like your own. No single thing have We left out of the book. Then to their Lord shall they all be gathered.*" (Verse 38)

Human beings are not the only residents of this universe, so as to consider that they come into existence by sheer coincidence, or that human life is meaningless. There are numerous creatures in the world and they all have their lives regulated in a way that indicates careful planning and elaborate design. Moreover, they all confirm the oneness of the Creator and the consistency of His law of creation.

All animals that walk on earth, be they insects, reptiles, or vertebrates and all flying creatures, including every winged insect or bird, and indeed every living creature, belong to a community which shares certain characteristics and a particular way of life, just as human beings do. God has not left any type of His creation without providing it with an elaborate plan to organize its existence and without taking account of what it does with its life. At the end, all creatures are gathered to their Lord for judgement.

This short verse, which makes an all-important statement about life and the living, has a strong effect on our hearts as it describes God's complete supervision, elaborate planning, total knowledge and superior power. We cannot elaborate here on each of these aspects, because such elaboration is beyond the scope of this work. What we need to say is that directing our attentions to the system of creation, God's management and knowledge of them and His ultimate gathering of them to Himself, is much greater than providing physically miraculous signs, seen only by one isolated generation.

This round concludes with a statement that God's will and law remain operative when people choose either to follow His guidance or to go astray: "*Those who deny Our revelations are deaf and dumb, groping along in darkness. Whomever God wills, He lets go astray; and whomever He wills, He guides along a straight path.*" (Verse 39)

This is indeed a reiteration in a new form, using a different scene, of what has been stated earlier in this passage concerning the fact that only those who listen attentively will respond, while those who are dead can make no response. Those who deny God's signs which are present all over the universe, and who also deny God's revelations, do so because their receptive faculties have been knocked out of order. They are deaf, unable to hear; dumb, unable to speak; groping in total darkness, unable to see. This is not a description of their physical status, because they indeed have eyes, ears and mouths. It is rather that their faculty of comprehension is not working, which makes their senses of no value, as if they cannot receive or transmit any signal. This is an apt description because God's revelations have their own inherent effect, if they are only properly received. Only a person whose nature has been corrupted turns away from them because he is no longer able to benefit by guidance or rise to the higher level of life which divine revelations promote.

God's will is seen to work behind all this. It is God's will which has determined that this particular species of creation, known as man, has the dual ability to follow guidance or go astray, according to his own free choice, not as a result of any compulsion. This is how God lets whomever He wills go astray and how He helps whomever He wills follow the straight path. His will helps everyone who strives to implement divine guidance, while it abandons and lets go astray anyone who stubbornly rejects guidance. It does no injustice to anyone.

A human being may follow guidance or may allow himself to go astray: both possibilities are part of his nature. Both directions have been created by God's will. Similarly, the consequences that follow upon a person's choice to follow one way or the other are also determined by God's will which is active, absolute. Reckoning, judgement and reward are based on man's choice of the course he follows. That choice is of his own making, although the ability to choose either has been planted in him by God's will.

A System Bearing No Comparison

Having looked at this passage, we need to take a short pause to point out the extent of the directives it contains to all advocates of God's message throughout all generations. These directives transcend the historical occasion which required them to be issued. They delineate a system of advocating God's faith that applies to all advocates, free of all constraints of time and place. We cannot, in this commentary, speak about this system in detail. We will only indicate its main features.

The road the advocates of Islam have to follow is tough and full of hardship. Although God will undoubtedly grant victory to the truth, this victory comes at the time God, in His wisdom, chooses. Moreover, God keeps the timing of this victory to Himself, giving no information of it to anyone, not even His Messenger. The hardship along this road has two basic sources. The first is the denial and rejection with which the message of Islam is confronted at the beginning, as well as the harm inflicted on its advocates. The second source is the natural human desire felt by every advocate to guide people to the truth he himself has experienced, his enthusiasm to support the truth and his desire to see it victorious. Contending with this desire is no less difficult than facing up to denial, rejection and the infliction of harm.

We see in this passage how the Qur'ān tackles both aspects. It states that those who reject this faith and try to suppress it know full well that they are only called upon to follow the truth. They realise that the Messenger who conveys it to mankind tells the truth. Nevertheless, they refuse to respond. Indeed they persist, for certain ulterior motives, in their stubborn rejection. They realize that this truth has an intrinsic evidence to support it: it addresses human nature which responds to it positively once it is alive and receptive: "*Only those that can hear will surely answer.*" (Verse 36) Those, on the other hand, who oppose the truth have dead hearts and they themselves are "*deaf and dumb, groping along in darkness*". (Verse 39) The Messenger cannot make those who are dead or deaf hear. An advocate of the truth is not required to bring the dead back to life. This is something only God can do. On the other hand, God is certain to grant victory to His message. But that victory comes at the right time, according to God's law and by His will. God's law cannot be precipitated or changed with regard either to the certainty of ultimate victory, or to its timing. God does not hasten things simply because the advocates of His message, or even His messengers are made to endure rejection, harm and suffering. Indeed, an advocate of God's cause is required to submit himself to God's will, without trying to precipitate it. He is also required to show patience in the face of adversity and to demonstrate his certainty of the ultimate victory.

The Qur'ān also defines the role of God's Messenger, as also successive generations of advocates of Islam. All that is required of them is to convey God's message and to follow the road God has chosen for them, despite the hardships they may have to face. People's responses to the same are beyond their terms of reference. People follow guidance or error in accordance with a divine law that will never change, even to accommodate God's Messenger's desire to get some of those whom he loves to follow the guidance he brings them from God. Nor will this law change as a result of his distress at what is done by those whom he must confront. His own person is not considered here. He will not be accountable for the number of those who follow guidance as a result of his efforts. He is judged on the basis of his efforts and his obedience of his instructions. What happens to people afterwards is determined by their Lord: "*Whomever God wills, He lets go astray; and whomever He wills, He guides along a straight path.*" (Verse 39) "*Had God so willed, He would have gathered them all to [His] guidance. Do not, therefore, allow yourself to be one of the ignorant."* (Verse 35)

As we have already explained, an advocate of God's message may not act on the suggestions of people whom he addresses nor can he force the divine method. He must not try to adapt Islam to his own liking. The unbelievers used to request miracles, as was expected at their time. Such requests are mentioned in several places in this *sūrah* and in other *sūrahs* as well: *"They say: 'Why has not an angel been sent down to him?'"* (Verse 8) *"They say: 'Why has no sign been sent down to him from his Lord?'"* (Verse 37) *"They swear by God most solemnly that if a miracle be shown to them they would believe in it."* (Verse 109)

In other *sūrahs* we have even more amazing suggestions: *"They say: 'We shall not believe in you till you cause a spring to gush forth for us from the earth, or [till] you have a garden of date trees and vines, and you cause running waters to flow through it, or till you cause the sky to fall upon us in pieces, as you have threatened, or till you bring God and the angels face to face before us, or till you have a house of gold, or you ascend to heaven. Indeed we shall not believe in your ascent to heaven until you bring a book for us to read.'"* (17: 90–3) *"Yet they say: 'What sort of messenger is this [man] who eats food and goes about in the market-place? Why has not an angel been sent down to him, to act as a warner together with him? Or, [why has not] a treasure been granted to him? Or, he should at least have a garden, so that he could eat from its fruits.'"* (25: 7–8)

The Qur'ānic directive in this passage makes it clear to God's Messenger and the believers that they must not entertain any desire to have a miraculous sign given to them, regardless of its type. The Prophet is told in plain terms: *"If you find it so distressing that they turn their backs on you, seek, if you can, a chasm to go deep into the earth or a ladder to the sky by which you may bring them a sign. Had God so willed, He would have gathered them all to [His] guidance. Do not, therefore, allow yourself to be one of the ignorant. Only those that can hear will surely answer. As for the dead, God will bring them back to life, then to Him shall they return."* (Verses 35–6) Those believers who entertained the desire to have the unbelievers' request for a sign granted, when those unbelievers vowed that they would certainly believe once they saw such a sign, have been told: *"Miracles are in the power of God alone. How can you tell that even if one is shown to them, they may still not believe? We will turn their hearts and eyes away [from the truth] since they did not believe in it the first time. We shall leave them to blunder about in their overweening arrogance.*" (Verses 109–10) The believers should know that those who deny the truth do not lack a sign nor is it true that they cannot find evidence to support the truth. The believers also know that this religion follows a set pattern which does not change. It is far too sublime to modify its methods in accordance with the desires of those who make whatever suggestions come into their heads.

This leads us to the wider implication of this Qur'ānic directive which is not limited to any particular period of time, or concerned with a particular incident or suggestion. Times change, and so do people's desires and suggestions. The advocates of the divine faith must not allow themselves to be swayed by people's desires. Indeed, it is the tendency to respond to other people's suggestions that makes some of the advocates of Islam in our time try to shape the Islamic faith into a theory similar to man-made ones. These, as we know, are shown, with the passage of time, to be full of defects and contradictions. It is the same desire which makes some advocates of Islam try to fashion the Islamic system into a theoretical system or draft laws regulating certain situations of modern *jāhiliyyah* that have nothing to do with Islam. They do this in order to counter what people say about Islam to the effect that it is merely a faith that has nothing to do with the practical affairs of society. Some of the advocates of Islam try to provide people with such theoretical drafts while the people themselves continue to follow their own ways, unwilling to implement God's law or abide by it. All such attempts are contemptible and must not be entertained by any advocate of Islam.

Even more contemptible is the attempt of those who try to impart certain colours to Islam because they happen to be popular at a particular period of time, such as describing Islam as socialist or democratic, etc. They think that they are doing Islam a service by donning it with such colours. Socialism is a man-made economic and social doctrine. Like any other such system, whether it be democracy or whatever, it may be right or it may be wrong in its details. Islam is a way of life that includes an ideological concept and economic, social and executive systems. It is made by God and, as such, is free of all defects. How much of a true Muslim is the person who seeks to justify God's system by showing it as akin to human systems, or who seeks to make God acceptable to people by endorsing their statements?

The Islamic Doctrine's Starting Point

All that the Arab idolaters did in their ignorant days was that they took for their patrons certain creatures hoping that the latter could win them favour with God: *"And yet they who take for their protectors other beings beside Him, say: 'We worship them for no other reason than that they bring us nearer to God.'"* (39: 3) This manner of seeking favour for oneself with God by being patronized by some of His servants is described in the Qur'ān as idolatrous. What description would then fit those who are guilty of a much more ghastly practice as they try to win favour for God, limitless is He in His glory, with His servants by associating His message with a man-made doctrine or code of practice?

Islam has its own distinctive characteristics while socialism and democracy are what they are. Islam is a code of living devised by God and it admits no title or description other than that given to it by God Himself. Socialism and democracy are man-made systems based on human experience. If people want to choose them, then they must be fully aware of the basis of their choice. A believer who advocates the implementation of the faith chosen by God must never allow himself to yield to the temptation of anything that happens to be temporarily fashionable, deluding himself that he is doing the divine faith a favour.

I would like to put a question to those whose faith has sunk so low in their valuation and who have no true understanding of the Divine Being. If you present Islam to people today associating it with socialism and democracy because these are fashionable trends in this present time, you should remember that capitalism was, for a period of time, people's favourite system when it replaced the feudal system. Similarly, there were periods of time when absolute power was a desirable pattern of government, particularly when the objective was the unification of small provinces into a national set-up as happened in the cases of Germany and Italy under Bismark and Mazzini. Only time will tell what sort of social system and method of government will be preferred in the future. So, what sort of colour will you be giving Islam tomorrow in order to present it to people in the guise they like most?

It is no coincidence that the Qur'ānic directives make it clear that the advocates of Islam must think highly of their faith and refuse to consider futile suggestions. They must not try to delude themselves and present this faith to people under any name or description which does not belong to it, or to give it any method other than its own. God has no need of anyone. Those who do not respond to Islam by way of submitting themselves to God alone are not needed by this faith, nor does God have any need of anyone, be he obedient or disobedient to Him.

Moreover, this religion has its own distinctive characteristics and constituent elements which God wants to prevail in human society. Similarly, it has its own distinctive method of operation and its particular style of addressing human nature. The One who bestowed this religion from on high and gave it its distinctive characteristics and constituent elements, as well as its method of operation, is the One who has created man and who knows what man's innermost soul whispers within him. All glory and praise be to Him.

In this passage, we have one of the various ways in which the Qur'ān addresses human nature. It establishes a link between human nature and the existence of the universe, leaving the latter to work its full inspiration on it. God knows that when such inspiration, profound and strong as it is, touches human nature it will certainly respond: "*Only those that can hear will surely answer.*" (Verse 36)

The pattern which we have in this passage begins in this way: "*They say: 'Why has no sign been sent down to him from his Lord?' Say: God is well able to send down any sign, but most of them are devoid of knowledge.*" (Verse 37) This verse reports what is said by those who denied God's revelations and demanded a miracle which would have had a temporary effect on their own generation. It then refers to the destruction which would have followed, had the suggestion been acted upon. God is certainly well able to accomplish any miracle, but it is the bestowing of His mercy that prevents it. It is His wisdom that precludes acting on their suggestion. Then, suddenly, their attention is made to turn from their little world to the wide expanse of the universe with all the great signs which they see in the universe around them and which are far greater than the one they demanded. The signs in the universe are permanent, available for all generations to behold: "*There is not an animal that walks on earth and no bird that flies on its wings but are communities like your own. No single thing have We left out of the book. Then to their Lord shall they all be gathered.*" (Verse 38)

This is a great fact which at that time, when humanity had not developed and regulated its branches of science, they could understand by mere observation alone. They could see animals, birds and insects grouping in communities, each of which has its own characteristics and rules. As human knowledge develops, this fact has greater application, but human knowledge cannot add to its basis. Relevant to it, however, is the fact that God's knowledge is absolute and total and it is He who manages everything in the universe. The facts that people can observe around them testify to the great truism of God's oneness and His Lordship over all the universe. Could the physical miracle they demanded provide more than that? They have the great miracle of creation in front of them. They see its manifestations and effects in every direction they turn.

In this particular example, the Qur'ānic method presents human nature neither with theoretical or dialectic argument, nor any material or logical theory. It only puts it face to face with practical existence, what is perceptible of it and what is imperceptible. It then invites human nature to react to it and respond to its inspiration within a well-defined and regulated system, so that it does not lose its way.

It then provides the following comment on the attitudes of those who deny such magnificent signs; "*Those who deny Our revelations are deaf and dumb, groping along in darkness. Whomever God wills, He lets go astray; and whomever He wills, He guides along a straight path.*" (Verse 39) What an apt description of the rejecters for they are indeed deaf and dumb, groping along in darkness. The Qur'ānic verse states God's law with regard to guidance and error, stating that God's will operates either way in accordance with the nature God has given to man.

We, thus, have a full concept of man's position. We have a clear idea of the appropriate method of presenting Islam to others. We also have a definitive statement of how an advocate of Islam should operate and make his address to human beings in all situations and at all times.

6

To Avert Sudden Punishment

Say: If God's punishment befalls you or the Hour comes upon you, can you see yourselves calling upon anyone other than God? [Answer me] if you are truthful! (40)

قُلْ أَرَءَيْتَكُمْ إِنْ أَتَنكُمْ عَذَابُ ٱللَّهِ أَوْ أَتَتْكُمُ ٱلسَّاعَةُ أَغَيْرَ ٱللَّهِ تَدْعُونَ إِن كُنتُمْ صَدِقِينَ ﴿٤٠﴾

No, on Him alone you will call, whereupon He will, if He so wills, remove the ill which caused you to call on Him; and you will have forgotten all those you associate as partners with Him. (41)

بَلْ إِيَّاهُ تَدْعُونَ فَيَكْشِفُ مَا تَدْعُونَ إِلَيْهِ إِن شَآءَ وَتَنسَوْنَ مَا تُشْرِكُونَ ﴿٤١﴾

Indeed We sent messengers before your time to other nations, and visited them with misfortune and hardship so that they might humble themselves. (42)

وَلَقَدْ أَرْسَلْنَا إِلَىٰٓ أُمَمٍ مِّن قَبْلِكَ فَأَخَذْنَهُم بِٱلْبَأْسَآءِ وَٱلضَّرَّآءِ لَعَلَّهُمْ يَتَضَرَّعُونَ ﴿٤٢﴾

If only, when the misfortune decreed by Us befell them, they humbled themselves! Rather, their hearts were hardened and Satan made their deeds seem goodly to them. (43)

فَلَوْلَآ إِذْ جَآءَهُم بَأْسُنَا تَضَرَّعُوا۟ وَلَكِن قَسَتْ قُلُوبُهُمْ وَزَيَّنَ لَهُمُ ٱلشَّيْطَنُ مَا كَانُوا۟ يَعْمَلُونَ ﴿٤٣﴾

Then, when they had clean forgotten what they had been reminded of, We threw open to them the gates of all good things, until just when they were rejoicing in what they had been granted, We suddenly took them to task; and they were plunged into utter despair. (44)

فَلَمَّا نَسُوا۟ مَا ذُكِّرُوا۟ بِهِۦ فَتَحْنَا عَلَيْهِمْ أَبْوَٰبَ كُلِّ شَىْءٍ حَتَّىٰٓ إِذَا فَرِحُوا۟ بِمَآ أُوتُوٓا۟ أَخَذْنَٰهُم بَغْتَةً فَإِذَا هُم مُّبْلِسُونَ ﴿٤٤﴾

Thus the last remnant of the wrongdoing people was wiped out. All praise is due to God, the Lord of all the worlds. (45)

فَقُطِعَ دَابِرُ ٱلْقَوْمِ ٱلَّذِينَ ظَلَمُوا۟ وَٱلْحَمْدُ لِلَّهِ رَبِّ ٱلْعَٰلَمِينَ ﴿٤٥﴾

Say: Do but consider, if God should take away your hearing and your sight and seal your hearts, what deity but God is there to restore them to you. See how varied and multifaceted We make Our signs, and yet they turn away! (46)

قُلْ أَرَءَيْتُمْ إِنْ أَخَذَ ٱللَّهُ سَمْعَكُمْ وَأَبْصَٰرَكُمْ وَخَتَمَ عَلَىٰ قُلُوبِكُم مَّنْ إِلَٰهٌ غَيْرُ ٱللَّهِ يَأْتِيكُم بِهِ ٱنظُرْ كَيْفَ نُصَرِّفُ ٱلْءَايَٰتِ ثُمَّ هُمْ يَصْدِفُونَ ﴿٤٦﴾

Say: Do but consider, if God's punishment befalls you suddenly or in a perceptible manner, would any but the wrongdoing folk be destroyed? (47)

قُلْ أَرَءَيْتَكُمْ إِنْ أَتَىٰكُمْ عَذَابُ ٱللَّهِ بَغْتَةً أَوْ جَهْرَةً هَلْ يُهْلَكُ إِلَّا ٱلْقَوْمُ ٱلظَّٰلِمُونَ ﴿٤٧﴾

We send Our messengers only as bearers of good news and as warners. Those who believe and act righteously shall have nothing to fear, nor shall they grieve. (48)

وَمَا نُرْسِلُ ٱلْمُرْسَلِينَ إِلَّا مُبَشِّرِينَ وَمُنذِرِينَ فَمَنْ ءَامَنَ وَأَصْلَحَ فَلَا خَوْفٌ عَلَيْهِمْ وَلَا هُمْ يَحْزَنُونَ ﴿٤٨﴾

But those that deny Our revelations shall be afflicted with suffering as a result of their sinful deeds. (49)

وَٱلَّذِينَ كَذَّبُواْ بِـَٔايَـٰتِنَا يَمَسُّهُمُ ٱلۡعَذَابُ بِمَا كَانُواْ يَفۡسُقُونَ ﴿٤٩﴾

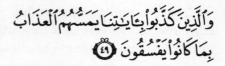

Overview

In this new wave, the *sūrah* puts the idolaters' nature face to face with God's might; indeed, it puts them face to face with their own nature when it confronts the prospect of being smitten by God's might. What happens to human nature when it is overwhelmed by the terrible prospects ahead? It is certain to shed all its burdens, whether of false concepts or false deities, and turn to its true Lord, whom it knows well. It appeals to Him alone for help to be saved from the impending doom.

The *sūrah* takes the idolaters by the hand to show them how earlier communities were destroyed. Along the way, it describes how God's law and His will operate. It makes clear how, after those earlier communities had rejected God's messengers and denied their messages, they were set one test after another, sometimes with hardship and misfortune, and sometimes with comfort and affluence. They were given chance after chance to wake up from their deep slumber. When they had had all their chances, remained oblivious to trials and hardship, and were deluded by the comforts and pleasures they enjoyed, God's will came into operation. Punishment overtook them suddenly: *"Thus the last remnant of the wrongdoing people was wiped out. All praise is due to God, the Lord of all the worlds."* (Verse 45)

Just as this scene that violently shakes people's hearts begins to disappear, a new scene shows them exposed to God's might. Their hearing and sight are taken away and their hearts are sealed off. They cannot find a deity other than God to replace their faculties of hearing, seeing and comprehension.

Against the background of these two awesome scenes, they are told about the role of the messengers who are sent to give good news and to warn. That is all they are required to do. They do not bring any miraculous events, or respond to suggestions and requests. They simply convey the messages entrusted to them. Some people believe and do well, and, as a result, they are safe, experiencing no fear or grief. Others deny the messengers and turn away, and, in consequence, they are exposed to punishment. The choice is open to all: either to believe or disbelieve. The end result is made clear.

The Only Hope

> Say: If God's punishment befalls you or the Hour comes upon you, can you see yourselves calling upon anyone other than God? [Answer me] if you are truthful! No, on Him alone you will call, whereupon He will, if He so wills, remove the ill which caused you to call on Him; and you will have forgotten all those you associate as partners with Him. (Verses 40-1)

Here we have one of the various methods the Qur'ān employs to address human nature in order to present to it the Islamic faith. We have already seen how the Qur'ān draws people's attentions to the elaborate system of life and the multitude of living creatures, and how God's knowledge is total, flawless, absolute. Here, the Qur'ānic address makes use of God's power and how human nature reacts when it reflects on any aspect of God's might, shaking off all traces of idolatry. Thus, human nature regains its freedom and tears off what used to prevent it from acquiring proper knowledge of its Lord and believing in His oneness: "*Say: If God's punishment befalls you or the Hour comes upon you, can you see yourselves calling upon anyone other than God? [Answer me] if you are truthful!*" (Verse 40)

Human nature is, thus, put face to face with the possibility of total destruction which may come as punishment in this life, or with the totally unexpected arrival of the Last Hour. Once human nature is made to visualize this eventuality, it responds positively to the truth. God knows that such a positive response remains latent within it. Human nature is shaken as it must own up to the truth it knows. God puts the question to the unbelievers, demanding a verbal answer to express their true, natural feelings: "*can you see yourselves calling upon anyone other than God? [Answer me] if you are truthful!*" (Verse 40)

The *sūrah* then states the true answer which corresponds to their natural feelings, although they may not give it verbal expression: "*No, on Him alone you will call, whereupon He will, if He so wills, remove the ill which caused you to call on Him; and you will have forgotten all those you associate as partners with Him.*" (Verse 41)

Thus, all thoughts of idolatry are forgotten. The fearful prospect lays human nature bare, and thus it turns to God alone for security. Its knowledge of the true Lord is deeply rooted within it. Idolatrous beliefs are no more than a superficial, thin covering that beclouds human nature through external factors. When human nature is shaken by this fearful prospect, this covering falls off and the truth comes to the surface. Thus, man's natural reactions operate and he turns to His Lord, praying to be spared that fate to which it has no answer.

Within this description of the natural human reaction to the prospect of God's punishment, we are told of God's response. He may, if He so pleases, respond to their supplication and remove what they fear. His will is free, unrestrained. It is His choice whether to respond to them or not and whether to remove the ill they fear in full or in part. In this, the only operative factors are His knowledge, wisdom and will.

Having outlined the attitude of human nature towards idolatry, into which it sinks as a result of deviation from the right path, it is pertinent to ask about its attitude towards atheism and the denial of God's existence altogether. As I have said on several occasions, I have serious doubts that those who profess to be atheists, completely denying the existence of God, truly believe what they say. I doubt that anyone created by God can sink so deep into ignorance as to obliterate totally the distinctive mark of the hand that originated him, when he continues to have within him the same mark reflected in every one of his cells. Atheism is simply the result of long suffering at the hands of the Church, and the brutal struggle against it. The Church resorted to oppressive practices and denied natural human impulses at the same time as churchmen indulged in deviant pleasures.

That long history of suffering, endured for centuries by Europe, was responsible for pushing the Europeans into their professed atheism, simply to flee from their tormentors. Besides, Jewish forces have exploited this historical legacy to tempt the Christians away from their faith so that they spread immorality and its attendant misery among them. This facilitates what the Zionist Jews see as the manipulation of the 'asses', to use the expression as contained within the Talmud and the Protocols of the Elders of Zion. It would have been impossible for those evil forces to achieve any of this, or to drive people to atheism, without the exploitation which occurred during that grim period of European history.

These tireless efforts have been given their most striking picture in the efforts of Communism, itself a Jewish invention. Despite all the work of the Soviet Communists, over more than half a century, using all the state suppressive agencies, to spread atheism, the Russian people themselves continue to indicate that deep at heart they yearn to have a faith based on belief in God. Stalin himself, described by his successor Khrushchev as exceedingly brutal, was forced into a period of truce in his fight against the Church. This was during the Second World War when Stalin was forced to release the Russian Archbishop. The war left him no option but to admit that faith in God was deeply entrenched in human nature. His own view and that of the few atheists wielding power with him was of little account.

The Jews have tried, with the help of the 'asses' from among the Christians they used, to spread atheism among the nations which professed to follow the Islamic faith. Although Islam was considerably weakened among the people of the Muslim world, their attempt, pioneered by Kemal Ataturk, the hero of Turkey, could achieve very little despite all the praise and glory they heaped on it and its hero. Numerous books have been written in praise of this leading experience. More recently, they have tried to benefit from the lessons of the Ataturk experience. They no longer give any new experience an atheistic colour. Indeed, they give it an Islamic banner so that it does not represent a shock to human nature as was the case with Ataturk's experience. However, they put under that banner everything they want of immorality, promiscuity and all that filth, as well as all the machinery which works to destroy the proper human element in the Muslim world.

The fact remains that human nature recognises its Lord well and submits to Him declaring its belief in His oneness. Should it fall for a while under a covering that screens facts and prevents it from seeing them, all that covering will fall off once human nature is shaken by a calamity. It regains its vision and returns to its Lord, humble, submissive, believing. All the schemes of the enemies of faith require no more than a clear declaration of the truth, and they will soon collapse. Human nature thus returns to faith. Evil will not have total mastery while there remains on the face of this earth people who will make this declaration. By the grace of God, there will always remain people to make this declaration of the truth, no matter how the advocates of falsehood try to wipe them out.

Trials Serve as Reminders

Indeed We sent messengers before your time to other nations, and visited them with misfortune and hardship so that they might humble themselves. If only, when the misfortune decreed by Us befell them, they humbled themselves! Rather, their hearts were hardened and Satan made their deeds seem goodly to them. Then, when they had clean forgotten what they had been reminded of, We threw open to them the gates of all good things, until just when they were rejoicing in what they had been granted, We suddenly took them to task; and they were plunged into utter despair. Thus the last remnant of the wrongdoing people was wiped out. All praise is due to God, the Lord of all the worlds. (Verses 42–5)

These verses place before our eyes an historical example of how people expose themselves to God's might and what happens to them in consequence. God gives them one chance after another and issues them with successive reminders, but they still forget. If the trials they encounter do not persuade them to turn to God and implore Him, and if His grace which they enjoy does not prompt them to be grateful and to guard against evil, then their nature has become irremediably corrupt and their lives are no longer worth extending. God's punishment befalls them and their world is destroyed: "*Indeed We sent messengers before your time to other nations, and visited them with misfortune and hardship so that they might humble themselves. If only, when the misfortune decreed by Us befell them, they humbled themselves! Rather, their hearts were hardened and Satan made their deeds seem goodly to them.*" (Verses 42–3)

Human history has known many such nations and the Qur'ān gives us accounts of them which date back to periods long before recorded history. Such history is new and it contains only a small portion of human history on earth. Short as it is, this history recorded by human beings is full of misrepresentation and falsehood. It is also marked by its inability to take full account of all factors which influence the movement of human history. Some of these lie deep in the human soul, while others remain beyond the realm of what is perceptible by man. Only some of these factors are made visible, but these are nevertheless not identified or interpreted properly or correctly. Indeed, people cannot distinguish the false from the true in these factors. For any human being to claim that he has full knowledge of human history, can interpret it 'scientifically' and is able to predict its inevitable future events is to say the greatest lie a human being may utter. Nevertheless, some people do make such claims. What is even more amazing is that some people believe such claims. Had the claimant said that he is mainly relating what he 'expects' to happen, not what is 'inevitable', his claim may be reasonable. When a liar finds people gullible enough to believe him, he will certainly invent lies to tell them.

God certainly tells the truth. He also knows what happened and the reasons that led to it. Out of His grace, He tells His servants some aspects of the working of His law and how His will operates, so that they may take heed. They are, thus, placed in a position of knowing the interaction of inner factors and manifest reasons that have led to the events of history. They can then have a realistic expectation of what will happen in accordance with God's law which God has revealed to them and which never changes.

In these verses we have a full outline of an example that has repeated itself several times: communities that have received God's messengers but rejected their messages. God then tested them with hardship and tribulation that involved their lives, properties and general situations. Such hardship and tribulation obviously fell short of the punishment of total destruction to which reference is made in the preceding verse.

The Qur'ān mentions a specific example of these communities and the tribulations visited upon them in the account it gives of Pharaoh and his people: "*Most certainly did We afflict Pharaoh's people with drought and poor harvests, so that they might take heed. But whenever something good came their way, they would say, 'This is but our due'; and whenever affliction befell them, they would blame their evil fortune on Moses and those who followed him. Surely, their ill fortune had been decreed by God, though most of them did not know it. They said [to Moses]: 'Whatever sign you may produce before us in order to cast a spell on us, we will not believe in you.' So We plagued them with floods, locusts, lice, frogs, and blood: clear signs all; but they continued in their arrogance, for they were evil-doing folk."* (7: 130–3)

This is just one of numerous examples to which this Qur'ānic verse refers. God visited these people with hardship and tribulation so that they might awaken to the truth. He wanted them to examine their situation. The hardship might have prompted them to appeal to God in all humility, and might have helped them to get rid of their arrogance and to pray with open, sincere hearts. Had they done so, God would certainly have opened the gates of His mercy to them. But they did not turn back to God. The hardship did not soften their hearts, open their minds and help them rid themselves of their stubbornness. Satan continued to portray their erring ways to them as fair and appealing: *"Their hearts were hardened and Satan made their deeds seem goodly to them."* (Verse 43)

When hardship fails to make a human being turn to God for help, that person's heart is certainly hardened. Its natural receptive quality is no longer functioning. It does not feel the compunction which normally brings life back to hearts and makes them fully receptive. God puts His servants through a test of hardship. He who is alive will be awakened by it and it is he who returns to his Lord. The hardship is, thus, an act of mercy which God has committed Himself to bestow on His servants. He who is dead will benefit nothing by it. Indeed, it leaves him without any excuse for his attitude. He is made more miserable by it since it serves as an introduction to God's punishment.

The communities whose history God relates to His Messenger and his followers have benefited nothing by the trials to which they were put. They made no appeal to God. They did not mend their erring ways but persisted with their rejection of the truth, which Satan portrayed to them as good and proper. God then allowed them a respite and gave them provisions in plenty: *"Then, when they had clean forgotten what they had been reminded of, We threw open to them the gates of all good things, until just when they were rejoicing in what they had been granted, We suddenly took them to task; and they were plunged into utter despair."* (Verse 44)

People may be tested with a life of plenty just as they may be tested with hardship. Indeed, God may test both His obedient servants and those who are disobedient, either with abundance or with hardship. The test of abundance is even harder and more difficult to endure. A believer who is tested with hardship perseveres and shows his steadfastness, and when he is tested with abundance, he is grateful to his Lord. Thus, whatever happens to him, the result is certainly good. The Prophet says: "Wonderful is the lot of a believer. Whatever may happen brings him good. This applies to no one other than a believer, because when good fortune comes his way, he is grateful and that is good for him. When misfortune befalls him, he endures patiently and that is good for him." (Related by Muslim.)

Those communities who rejected God's messengers and whose histories are given in the Qur'ān were on a different course. They were reminded of the proper attitude but they ignored it. When their destruction was inevitable, God visited them with hardship and tribulation so that they would awaken and mend their ways, but they did not. He then put them to the test of abundance. The Qur'ān gives us a very vivid description of how they were put to that test: "*We threw open to them the gates of all good things.*" (Verse 44) All provisions, luxuries and power are shown here flowing like unhindered floods. They come to them without any need for them to put in even the smallest of effort.

We have here a wonderful scene depicting a state full of life in the inimitable style of the Qur'ān. "*We threw open to them the gates of all good things, until just when they were rejoicing in what they had been granted.*" (Verse 44) They enjoyed abundance of provisions and endless luxuries, but showed no gratitude to God for the grace He had bestowed on them. All they cared for was to indulge in the pleasures of this world, leaving no room in their lives for higher concerns. This corruption of their hearts and morals was followed by a corruption of their systems, and this naturally led to corruption being the mark of their lives. That was enough to trigger God's law which never fails: "*We suddenly took them to task; and they were plunged into utter despair.*" (Verse 44)

God's punishment befell them when they were fully drunk with the pleasures of this life. They were left confused, hopeless, unable to think where to turn. They were destroyed: "*Thus the last remnant of the wrongdoing people was wiped out.*" (Verse 45) The Arabic text refers to the very last one of each of these communities. If this one was wiped out then everyone else faced the same destiny. The phrase, 'the wrongdoing people', means here those who associated partners with God. This is a frequently used expression in the Qur'ān referring to idolatry as wrongdoing and idolaters as wrongdoers.

"*All praise is due to God, the Lord of all the worlds.*" (Verse 45) This comes by way of commenting on the destruction of the people who did wrong, or rather those who associated partners with God, after they were put to different tests. Can we think of any blessing greater than the eradication of the wrongdoers from the face of the earth or imagine an act of grace shown to God's servants better than such a purge? Praise, then, must be offered to God for this blessing.

God allowed this law to operate for the people of Noah, Hūd, Ṣāliḥ, Lot, as well as the followers of Pharaoh, the Greeks, the Romans and many others. Beyond the rise of each of these civilizations and their decline and destruction lies this secret destiny and the operation of God's law. This is the proper and true interpretation of the events of history known to us.

These communities attained standards of civilization, power and affluence which were equal, if not in certain respects superior, to what is enjoyed today by the mighty communities of the world, intoxicated as they are with their power. Their might deceives those who do not know God's law that operates tests of hardship and abundance. These communities cannot even imagine that God is simply putting them to a test. As they look at them, other communities may be dazzled with the great power and affluence they enjoy. They think that God has given these communities everything when they refuse to worship Him, rebel against His authority, claim His attributes for themselves, spread corruption on earth and deal unjustly with people after they have usurped God's authority.

When I was in the United States,[1] I could see with my own eyes, the practical manifestation of this Qur'ānic statement: "*Then, when they had clean forgotten what they had been reminded of, We threw open to them the gates of all good things.*" (Verse 44) The scene

---

1. The author was given an Egyptian government scholarship in the US to do a Masters Degree. He lived there for two years, from 1949–51, and wrote a book on his observations of American society, but it was never published in full. Extensive quotations from it are made in his other works. – Editor's note.

portrayed in this verse of provisions flowing unchecked cannot be seen anywhere on earth as clearly as it can be seen there. I also witnessed the arrogance of these people, imparted to them by their wealth. They behaved as if that abundance was always exclusive to the white man. I saw them treating coloured people, especially those who were Muslim, with hateful arrogance and much brutality. Their conceit surpassed by far that of the Nazis of whom the Jews have made a symbol of arrogance.

As I witnessed all this, I used to remember this Qur'ānic verse, expecting God's law to come into operation. Indeed, I could see it coming to catch people unaware: "*Until just when they were rejoicing in what they had been granted, We suddenly took them to task; and they were plunged into utter despair. Thus the last remnant of the wrongdoing people was wiped out. All praise is due to God, the Lord of all-worlds.*" (Verses 44–5)

After the Prophet Muḥammad's mission, God suspended the punishment of total destruction. However, other types of punishment remain in force. Mankind today, particularly those nations enjoying abundance, experience different types of punishment, in spite of their affluence.

The psychological problems, spiritual vacuum, sexual perversion and immorality suffered by these communities today almost negate the effects of the great productivity and affluence they enjoy. They impart to the lives of these communities an air of worry, stress and total misery. In addition, we hear every now and then about political scandals when state secrets are sold in return for enjoying pleasures or indulging in perversion. These are simply the forerunners that herald unfailing punishment.

This is only the beginning. The Prophet certainly tells the truth as he says: "When you see that God has given a person plenty of what he likes in this world, despite his sinful practices, know that it is only a temptation and a test." He then quoted the Qur'ānic verse: "*Then, when they had clean forgotten what they had been reminded of, We threw open to them the gates of all good things, until just when they were rejoicing in what they had been granted, We suddenly took them to task; and they were plunged into utter despair.*" (Related by Ibn Jarīr and Ibn Abī Ḥātim.)

It is necessary to point out that God's law of destroying falsehood and evil requires that the truth be established on earth in the shape of a community. When this happens, God causes the truth to overwhelm falsehood and it is, thus, totally destroyed. The advocates of the truth must never sit idle, waiting for God's law to operate, without putting in any effort. If they do this, then they disqualify themselves as advocates of the truth. The truth can only be represented by a community that exerts all its efforts to implement God's law and overpower those who claim for themselves God's attributes and authority. This is the most basic element of the truth. *"Had it not been for the fact that God repels one group of people by another, the earth would have been utterly corrupted."* (2: 251)

Important Points for Reflection

As the *sūrah* moves on, it puts those who associate partners with God face to face with His might and how it may strike them personally, taking away their hearing and eyesight and sealing their hearts. They are defenceless against it, and they can find no deity other than God to return what God may take away from them. The scene depicted here is very vivid, showing them their total powerlessness against God's might. It also paints for them the stark reality of those partners they associate with God when they have to face a truly grave situation. The scene shakes them violently. God, the Creator of human nature knows how far it is affected by this scene and the truth it describes. Human nature realizes that God is able to take away people's hearing and sight and seal their hearts. None of these organs can then function at all. Should He do this, there is no other deity to reverse what He has done.

As this scene sends a shiver into people's hearts, it shows how hollow and erroneous the concept of idolatry is. The *sūrah* wonders at those who are shown different, wide-ranging and multi-faceted signs, beckoning them to faith, and yet still they turn away. Here, their attitude is painted in the image of a camel which has a particular disease in its legs, causing it to limp outwardly as it walks. The scene was familiar to the Arabs who were the first to be addressed by the Qur'ān. It fills us with a feeling of contempt for those who turn away: *"See how varied and multifaceted We make Our signs, and yet they turn away!"* (Verse 46)

They are hardly allowed to take their breath before they are put face to face with another possibility that may well not be far away from them. They are shown their own destruction as they are indeed the wrongdoers, a term which is often used interchangeably with those who associate partners with God. The scene here paints the destruction of the wrongdoers when they are taken unawares or when God's punishment is inflicted on them in open daylight: "*Say: Do but consider, if God's punishment befalls you suddenly or in a perceptible manner, would any but the wrongdoing folk be destroyed?*" (Verse 47)

Divine punishment may come in any form and in any situation. Whether it comes suddenly when least expected or it comes gradually, in broad daylight when they are fully prepared, total destruction would be the lot of the wrongdoing folk, a description often used in the Qur'ān to refer to the idolaters. This punishment will be visited on them alone. They cannot protect themselves against it whether it comes suddenly or openly, for they are too weak to repel it. Nor can any of the partners they associate with God spare them this punishment, because those partners are among God's servants who are equally weak and powerless.

The *sūrah* raises this prospect before them, so that they may take the necessary steps to avoid it before it happens. Limitless is God in His glory: He knows that this prospect touches certain cords within human nature which know and truly fear what it entails.

When this passage of warning has reached its peak, having portrayed several scenes, making inspiring comments on each of them and giving serious warnings which have their effect on people's hearts, it is concluded with a statement outlining the task of God's messengers. Their communities demand supernatural miracles but their duty is merely to convey a message, bringing happy news and giving stern warnings. They have no say in people's fate, which is determined by the attitudes people choose to adopt for themselves: "*We send Our messengers only as bearers of good news and as warners. Those who believe and act righteously shall have nothing to fear, nor shall they grieve. But those that deny Our revelations shall be afflicted with suffering as a result of their sinful deeds.*" (Verses 48–9)

This faith of Islam began by preparing mankind for a stage of maturity which would enable it to use fully God's great gift. With such usage people recognise and understand the truth which the Qur'ān reveals and to which it directs human intellect. Numerous signs pointing to this truth are present everywhere in the universe, as well as in the different stages of life and in every aspect of creation.

To attain such maturity requires a complete departure from the stage of physical miracles which confront those who deny the truth with what forces them to submit. Instead, the human intellect is directed to observe the final touches of what God creates in the whole universe. These are indeed miraculous, but they are permanent miracles upon which the whole universe is founded. The human mind is addressed with a superb book revealed by God, which is absolutely miraculous in its style, method and the social set-up it aims to create. This set-up remains unique, with nothing similar having ever existed previously or since.

For the human intellect to be familiar with this new high level which the departure from physical miracles represents, man has undergone careful education and instruction. This was necessary for man to begin to read the open book of the universe with his mind, under divine guidance and according to Qur'ānic directives and the Prophet's teachings. Such reading should combine positive realism with the recognition of what lies beyond the realm of human perception. It should steer away from those abstract concepts that characterise a part of Greek and Christian philosophies, as well as the materialistic concepts which pervaded parts of Greek philosophy as well as Indian, Egyptian, Buddhist and Magian philosophies. Needless to say, it also required the discarding of naïve materialism characterized by some ignorant Arabian beliefs.

Part of that education was represented by the definition of the task of God's Messenger and the nature of his role with regard to the divine message. The Messenger is a human being to whom God assigned the task of giving happy news as well as warnings. When he had completed that, his task was fulfilled and the response was left to human beings to determine. God's will operates through this response and the reward or punishment is determined on its basis. He who believes and does good works need not worry about what he may encounter, or grieve over what he might have done. If he has slipped, he will be forgiven. If he has done well, he will be rewarded for it. But those who deny the signs the Prophet has brought, and to which their attention has been drawn, will have to be punished for their disbelief, or for "their sinful deeds", to use the relevant reference in this passage. We should remember that the Qur'ān often uses the terms 'wrongdoing' and 'sinful deeds' to denote associating partners with God and total disbelief.

The result is a plain concept, which has no complication or ambiguity, and a clear outline of the Prophet's task and his terms of reference. According to this concept, all attributes of Godhead are given to God alone. Everything happens by God's will. But within that framework, man is given freedom of action and is required to account for what he chooses. The divergent destinies of God's obedient servants and those who disobey Him are described in perfect clarity. All legends and arbitrary concepts that have prevailed in *jāhiliyyah* societies about the role of the Messenger are shown to be false. All this helps elevate mankind to maturity without letting it drift into the maze of abstract philosophies and futile arguments which continue to waste the energy of the human mind for generation after generation.

7

Accountability and Grace

Say: I do not say to you that God's treasures are with me; nor do I know what is beyond the reach of human perception; nor do I say to you that I am an angel. I only follow what is revealed to me. Say: Can the blind and the seeing be deemed equal? Will you not reflect? (50)

قُل لَّا أَقُولُ لَكُمْ عِندِى خَزَآئِنُ ٱللَّهِ وَلَا أَعْلَمُ ٱلْغَيْبَ وَلَا أَقُولُ لَكُمْ إِنِّى مَلَكٌ إِنْ أَتَّبِعُ إِلَّا مَا يُوحَىٰٓ إِلَىَّ قُلْ هَلْ يَسْتَوِى ٱلْأَعْمَىٰ وَٱلْبَصِيرُ أَفَلَا تَتَفَكَّرُونَ ۝

Warn with this [Qur'ān] those who fear that they will be gathered to their Lord, when they shall have none to protect them from Him or to intercede with Him, so that they may be God-fearing. (51)

وَأَنذِرْ بِهِ ٱلَّذِينَ يَخَافُونَ أَن يُحْشَرُوٓا۟ إِلَىٰ رَبِّهِمْ لَيْسَ لَهُم مِّن دُونِهِۦ وَلِىٌّ وَلَا شَفِيعٌ لَّعَلَّهُمْ يَتَّقُونَ ۝

Do not drive away those who call on their Lord morning and evening, seeking only to win His pleasure. You are in no way accountable for them, just as they are in no way accountable for you. Should you drive them away, you would be among the wrongdoers. (52)

وَلَا تَطْرُدِ ٱلَّذِينَ يَدْعُونَ رَبَّهُم بِٱلْغَدَوٰةِ وَٱلْعَشِىِّ يُرِيدُونَ وَجْهَهُۥ مَا عَلَيْكَ مِنْ حِسَابِهِم مِّن شَىْءٍ وَمَا مِنْ حِسَابِكَ عَلَيْهِم مِّن شَىْءٍ فَتَطْرُدَهُمْ فَتَكُونَ مِنَ ٱلظَّٰلِمِينَ ۝

It is in this way that We try some of them by means of others, so that they may say: "Are these the ones upon whom God has bestowed His favour from among us?" Does not God know best as to who is truly grateful? (53)

وَكَذَٰلِكَ فَتَنَّا بَعْضَهُم بِبَعْضٍ لِّيَقُولُوٓاْ أَهَٰٓؤُلَآءِ مَنَّ ٱللَّهُ عَلَيْهِم مِّنۢ بَيْنِنَآ أَلَيْسَ ٱللَّهُ بِأَعْلَمَ بِٱلشَّٰكِرِينَ ۝

When those who believe in God's revelations come to you, say: Peace be upon you. Your Lord has committed Himself to bestow grace and mercy: if any of you does a bad deed out of ignorance, and then repents and mends his ways, He will be much-forgiving, merciful. (54)

وَإِذَا جَآءَكَ ٱلَّذِينَ يُؤْمِنُونَ بِـَٔايَٰتِنَا فَقُلْ سَلَٰمٌ عَلَيْكُمْ كَتَبَ رَبُّكُمْ عَلَىٰ نَفْسِهِ ٱلرَّحْمَةَ أَنَّهُۥ مَنْ عَمِلَ مِنكُمْ سُوٓءًۢا بِجَهَٰلَةٍ ثُمَّ تَابَ مِنۢ بَعْدِهِۦ وَأَصْلَحَ فَأَنَّهُۥ غَفُورٌ رَّحِيمٌ ۝

Thus do We make plain Our revelations; so that the path of the evildoers may be clearly distinct. (55)

وَكَذَٰلِكَ نُفَصِّلُ ٱلْءَايَٰتِ وَلِتَسْتَبِينَ سَبِيلُ ٱلْمُجْرِمِينَ ۝

Overview

Yet another round of confrontation with the idolaters concerning the truth of the divine message and the nature of the Messenger gets underway in this passage. It seeks to rectify preconceived ideas among mankind generally about God's messages and messengers. Such ideas had been further distorted during periods of ignorance among the Arabs and other communities, such that they had moved away from the truth of prophethood, revelation, and messengers. They had even added legends, superstitions, myths and the like to confuse the whole issue with sorcery, fortune-telling, the *jinn* and even with madness. Thus, a Prophet would be asked to predict the future, produce miracles and do what a medium or a sorcerer normally does.

The Islamic faith does away with all this nonsense, presenting its ideology in clear, simple and practical terms. It purges the concept of prophethood of all the myths and superstitions that had been attached to it in practically all *jāhiliyyah* communities, including those introduced by different Jewish and Christian sects. All these had badly distorted the image of prophets and prophethood.

The Qur'ān then presents the Islamic faith to people free of all temptations or adornments that are alien to it. The Messenger advocating it is an ordinary human being, who has no access to God's treasures, no knowledge of what lies beyond the reach of human perception, and who makes no claim to be an angel. He receives his message only from his Lord, and follows nothing other than what is revealed to him. Those who accept his message are the most honourable in God's view. It is his duty to be with them, welcome them and convey to them the fact that God has committed Himself to bestow mercy and grace and to grant forgiveness. He must also warn those whose consciences are alert to the truth of the life to come, so that they may work hard and become God-fearing. So, these two aspects represent his full role, in the same way as the facts of his humanity and of his being the recipient of revelations represent the nature of his status as a messenger of God. When we bear this in mind, we have the correct concept of both his nature and role. What is more, the path followed by the evil-doers becomes very distinct. Truth and falsehood go their separate ways, all confusion and ambiguity are clarified, and believers and unbelievers are aware of what separates them.

Intertwined with these facts, the *sūrah* outlines certain aspects of Godhead and how they relate to God's Messenger and to people generally. It adds certain points about following God's guidance, and going astray. To be aware of the truth of Godhead is to have good sight and to be unaware of what it is to be blind. Moreover, God has committed Himself to mercy, which means that He forgives those of His servants who ignorantly slip into error but then repent and mend their ways. He wants the way of the evil-doers to be clearly marked, so that those who believe or choose to turn their backs on faith may do so after having received clear evidence of the truth. Everyone takes his stance once all confusion has been removed.

A Call for Proper Reflection

*Say: I do not say to you that God's treasures are with me; nor do I
know what is beyond the reach of human perception; nor do I say*

to you that I am an angel. I only follow what is revealed to me. Say: Can the blind and the seeing be deemed equal? Will you not reflect? (Verse 50)

Stubborn in their rejection of Islam, the people of the Quraysh demanded that the Prophet (peace be upon him) perform a miracle for them so as to win their acceptance. As we have already mentioned, they were certain that he was truthful. Indeed, they had no doubt about that. Nevertheless, they demanded, on occasion, that he transform the two hills of al-Ṣafā and al-Marwah into gold! At times, they demanded that both hills be removed from Makkah altogether so as to have in their place a fertile area which could yield crops and fruits. At other times, they demanded that they be informed of what would happen in the future. Alternatively, they demanded that an angel be sent down to endorse the Prophet's message, or that a written statement be sent down to him from on high.

All these demands were simply a cover-up for their stubborn rejection. They were born out of the myths, superstitions and legends which were associated with the status and role of a prophet, as conceived by *jāhiliyyah* societies. The closest of these to them were the myths and legends held by the Jews and Christians after they had deviated from the truth preached to them by God's messengers.

A number of false prophecies were commonly held in *jāhiliyyah* societies, claimed by false prophets and believed by those deceived by them. These included prophecies with origins based in sorcery, fortune-telling, astrology and hallucination. Such false prophets claimed access to withheld information through contact with the *jinn* and other spirits. They further claimed an ability to influence natural phenomena through prayers, supplications, charms or other methods. Falsehood is a common feature of all these, although they may differ in type, form, rites and methods.

Prophecies based on magic are largely concerned with the manipulation of evil spirits in order to gain knowledge of the world beyond or to manipulate events. On the other hand, prophecies by fortune-tellers are assumed to be the fruit of a relationship with the gods who do not obey the fortune-teller. They answer his prayers and supplication by granting access to the world of the unknown, when he is either asleep or awake, or by giving him some guidance through special features or dreams. Nevertheless, not all prayer and supplication are answered. Both types of prophecy remain different from that associated with being possessed. Sorcerers and fortune-tellers are fully aware of what they request and they try to achieve it through supplication and insistent prayer. A possessed person or a madman has no control of himself. He simply hallucinates and repeats what he does not mean or may not even understand. When this type of prophecy is common in a particular community, it is often the case that such a possessed person is accompanied by an interpreter who claims to know what he means and explain his symbols. In ancient Greece, they called such a possessed person *manti* and his companion who spoke for him 'prophet'. European languages have borrowed this term in all its connotations to refer to prophets and prophecies. Fortune-tellers and possessed people rarely agree, unless the fortune-teller is the one who interprets what the possessed person says and provides the key to his symbols. More often, however, they fall into dispute because they have two different social roles and widely different backgrounds. A possessed person is a rebel who does not conform to social values and traditions. A fortune-teller, on the other hand, is conservative by nature and often receives his knowledge from his parents and forefathers. Fortune-telling is normally seen in areas where there are temples and hermitages in nearby and remote areas. Possession is not limited to this area, because it may occur in the wilderness as well as in urban areas.[1]

Prophets were numerous among the Israelite tribes. It is understood that in their successive generations, they were similar to the Sufi shaikhs of modern times. In certain cases, they were numbered in their hundreds. They used similar methods to those used nowadays by Sufis who aspire to being possessed, through physical mortification or through listening to music. In Samuel, Book I: 19 we read that, "Saul

---

1. A.M. Al-'Aqqād, *Ḥaqā'iq al-Islām wa Abāṭīl Khuṣūmih*, [Arabic], Cairo, p. 60. We should mention here that we disagree with the author's line explaining the development of human concepts of Godhead and prophethood as reflected in different religions, including the divine ones, until it reaches its full maturity under Islam. The fact is that these concepts are the same in all true divine messages, regardless of the distortions that crept into them over time. The Qur'ān, a perfect record, establishes this very clearly. We uphold this and disregard what Western theologians may assume. – Author's note.

sent messengers to take David. When they saw the company of the prophets in a frenzy, with Samuel standing in charge of them, the spirit of God came upon the messengers, and they also fell into a prophetic frenzy. When Saul was told, he sent other messengers, and they also fell into a frenzy… He [i.e. Saul] too stripped off his clothes, and he too fell into a frenzy before Samuel. He lay naked all that day and all that night."

> Also in Samuel we read this promise: "You shall meet a group of prophets descending from the hill, with a tambourine, a flute and a lute in front of them. They will be in a prophetic frenzy and the spirit of God will come upon them. You will be in a prophetic frenzy with them and will become a different man."

> Prophecy was passed from father to son, as mentioned in the Second Book of Kings: "the prophet's children said: Eliasha, ahead of you is the place where we are staying. It has become too small for us. Let us go to Jordan."

> They also had a service attached to the army in certain places. It is mentioned in Chronicles I: "David and the army commanders assigned the tribe of Asaf for service together with other prophets and gave them lutes, rebabs and cymbals."[2]

Ignorant communities, including those that deviated from the proper concept elaborated by the divine messages, were rife with such false ideas about the nature of prophethood and prophet. People expected anyone who claimed to be a prophet to come up with such miracles. They required him at times to make prophecies and at other times to influence natural phenomena, either through fortune-telling or sorcery. Indeed, it was in this vein that the pagan Arabs in Makkah made their demands of the Prophet Muḥammad (peace be upon him). To rectify such misconceptions, the Qur'ān makes repeated statements on the nature of the divine message and the Messenger conveying it. One of these statements is the one we are currently discussing: *"Say: I do not say to you that God's treasures are with me; nor do I know what is beyond the reach of human perception; nor do I say to you that I am an angel. I*

---

2. Al-ʿAqqād, ibid., p. 66.

only follow what is revealed to me. Say: Can the blind and the seeing be deemed equal? Will you not reflect?" (Verse 50)

The Prophet (peace be upon him) is commanded by his Lord to introduce himself as an ordinary human being who entertains nothing of the misconceptions that prevailed in *jāhiliyyah* communities about the nature of prophets and prophethood. He is further commanded to present his faith free of any temptation: no wealth is promised and no wild claims are made. It is simply a faith conveyed by a Messenger who is granted divine guidance. He follows nothing but divine revelations informing him of things that he has not known. He does not possess God's treasures in order to make rich gifts to those who follow him. Nor does he know what has been hidden in order to inform his followers of what may happen in the future. Nor is he an angel, nor can he meet their demands that God sends them an angel. He is simply a human Messenger preaching a faith that is clear, pure and simple.

This faith is the one to which human nature responds. It is the foundation of this life and the guide to happiness in the life to come and to earning God's pleasure. It requires neither decoration nor adornment. Whoever wants it for itself may have it, and it will be to him the most supreme of all values. On the other hand, a person who wants quick material gain out of it does not understand it or appreciate its value. Hence, it gives him nothing.

Which Path the Prophet Follows

The Prophet is, therefore, ordered to present it to people as it is, without adornment or temptation. It requires none of these. Those who adopt it should know that they are not going to gain any material wealth or position by it. They shall have no distinction over other people except through their good actions. They are only opting for divine guidance which is much more valuable than wealth, position or distinction. *"Say: I do not say to you that God's treasures are with me; nor do I know what is beyond the reach of human perception; nor do I say to you that I am an angel. I only follow what is revealed to me."* (Verse 50)

When they accept and adopt this, they should know that they bring themselves out of darkness and blindness into light and enlightenment: *"Say: Can the blind and the seeing be deemed equal? Will you not reflect?"* (Verse 50) Besides, following divine revelations is, in itself, following proper guidance. A person who is left without such guidance remains blind. This is stated plainly in this verse. What role, then, is left to the human mind?

From the Islamic point of view, the answer to this question is very simple. The mind with which God has endowed man is able to receive His revelation and comprehend it. This is its role. Moreover, it is the opportunity available to man to follow God's guidance and to be equipped with the proper, infallible criterion.

When the human mind is left to its own devices, isolated from divine guidance, it is exposed to deviation, blurred vision, miscalculation and error. This is due to its very nature, which tends to look at the universe as small, separate parts, and not as a complete whole. It limits its outlook to individual events, experiences and situations. As such, it cannot acquire a comprehensive view of the universe from which to derive conclusions and establish a comprehensive and balanced system. Isolated from divine guidance, the human mind continues to experiment, change views and systems, vacillate between action and reaction, wavering between one extreme and another. In doing so it tramples over some honoured human beings and destroys noble human faculties. If it would only follow divine revelations, it would spare humanity all this evil. Experiments and changes would then be limited to things, materials, appliances and machines, which constitute the natural field where the human mind can have its full play. Any losses incurred in this field are material losses, not human beings.

There is another factor which exposes the human mind to all this. That is the desires and whims that have been made part of the human constitution. These require a discipline that guarantees that they play their part in the continuity and development of human life. They must not be allowed to go beyond that level, because they would then contribute to the erosion and destruction of human life. The discipline cannot come from our human mind alone, because it wavers under the pressures of desires and whims. A discipline to control the human mind and to protect it from error is needed. Only this can serve as a point of reference before any new experience for the purposes of evaluating such experience.

Some people claim that the human mind is essentially right, just like divine revelations. They maintain that since both the mind and revelation have been made by God, they must be in agreement. Such arguments are advanced by human philosophers, but they have no divine foundations.

Other people claim that the human mind can play the role of revelation. But even if they claim this for the most intelligent person to have ever walked the earth, they contradict what God has said. God has made His own revelation and His message the basis for accountability. He has not defined that basis as the human mind or as human nature, despite the fact that human nature tends to seek its Lord and believe in Him. God knows that when left to its devices, the human mind may err, and human nature may deviate. The only way to prevent such error and deviation is to follow the guidance provided by God's revelations, because with this guidance we have both light and enlightenment.

Likewise, some people claim that philosophy can put the human mind in a position where it has no need for religion, or that humanity will not need divine guidance if it opts for science, which is, after all, a product of the human mind. Such claims rely on no true evidence and no practical example in the real world. Practical life testifies to the fact that human systems, based either on philosophical doctrines or scientific progress, have led man to endure a most miserable life, even in the most affluent of societies where production and income are at their maximum and where the means of comfort are plentiful. The alternative to this is not a life based on ignorance and spontaneity. Anyone who claims this must have vested interests. Islam offers a way of life that provides the human mind with safeguards against its own defects and against the pressures of desires and whims. It also establishes for man foundations and rules to ensure a direct and honest approach to wider knowledge and progressive scientific achievements. It also ensures a straightforward and clean, practical life based on divine law. As such, man becomes free from any pressure that leads to the adoption of deviant concepts or methods.

Equipped with divine revelation and guidance, the human mind can see things clearly. Deprived of them, it is blind. We note that in the Qur'ānic verse, the statement that the Prophet follows only what is revealed to him from on high is immediately followed by a reference to blindness and clear sight. It concludes with an exhortation to think and reflect: *"I only follow what is revealed to me. Say: Can the blind and the seeing be deemed equal? Will you not reflect?"* (Verse 50) Such a sequence is particularly significant. Reflection is certainly needed, and the Qur'ān calls on people to reflect. However, reflection must be guided by divine revelation so that it remains enlightened. There is no virtue in reflection that is blind, groping in the dark, without guidance.

When the human mind uses its faculties within the framework provided by divine revelation, it has a very wide field in which to play its role. It has the whole universe to reflect upon, which includes both the realms of the perceptible and the imperceptible, as well as the whole human soul and all aspects of life. Divine revelation does not restrain the movement of the human mind except to prevent it from following a deviant method or from succumbing to evil desires. Indeed, divine revelation provides continuous motivations for the working of the human mind. When God has endowed man with his great gift, the mind, He has required him to use it actively and provided him with guidance so that he can steer himself away from deviation and error.

A Warning Loud and Clear

Warn with this [Qur'ān] those who fear that they will be gathered to their Lord, when they shall have none to protect them from Him or to intercede with Him, so that they may be God-fearing. Do not drive away those who call on their Lord morning and evening, seeking only to win His pleasure. You are in no way accountable for them, just as they are in no way accountable for you. Should you drive them away, you would be among the wrongdoers. It is in this way that We try some of them by means of others, so that they may say: "Are these the ones upon whom God has bestowed His favour from among us?" Does not God know best as to who is truly grateful? When those who believe in God's revelations come to you, say: Peace be upon you. Your Lord has committed Himself to bestow grace and mercy: if any of you does a bad deed out of ignorance, and then repents and mends his ways, He will be much-forgiving, merciful. (Verses 51–4)

It is a mark of the Islamic faith that it pays little regard to worldly values and petty human considerations. God's Messenger (peace be upon him) has been commanded to present it to human beings as it is, without decoration, adornment or tempting promises. He was also commanded to pay particular attention to those who are likely to respond positively to his call and to ally himself with those who receive it well, willing to make a sincere effort to win God's pleasure. He was not to attach any weight to the values of a *jāhiliyyah* society. His task was to warn those who fear what may happen to them when they are gathered to their Lord, on the Day of Resurrection, when they shall have none to support or intercede for them. The fact remains that no one can intercede with God unless he is given permission to do so. Even with this permission, he can only intercede on behalf of those for whose benefit God allows intercession. Those who genuinely fear what will happen on that day have a strong claim to know the warning with which God's Messenger has been sent. They are more likely to benefit by it and respond to it.

If the Prophet explains it to them, they may be able to avoid in this life what may expose them to God's punishment in the life to come. The warning with which the Prophet has been sent outlines to them what they must avoid and gives them the motivation to do so: "*Warn with this [Qur'ān] those who fear that they will be gathered to their Lord, when they shall have none to protect them from Him or to intercede with Him, so that they may be God-fearing.*" (Verse 51)

"*Do not drive away those who call on their Lord morning and evening, seeking only to win His pleasure.*" (Verse 52) The Prophet is also ordered not to drive away those who pray to God and who call on Him with sincerity, every morning and every evening, seeking only to please Him. This is an example of dedication, love and good manners. A person does not address his worship and supplication to God alone unless he is truly dedicated. He does not seek only God's pleasure unless he profoundly loves Him. When he combines the two qualities of worshipping God alone and seeking only His pleasure, he will have adopted the sort of manners worthy of a true believer.

It is reported that some of the Arabian 'notables' felt it unbecoming of them to respond to the Islamic call because the Prophet Muḥammad (peace beupon him) kept his door open to poor and unsupported people such as Ṣuhayb, Bilāl, 'Ammār, Khabbāb, Salmān, Ibn Mas'ūd and others. These were poor people who could not change their sweat-stained clothes when they visited him. Their social position did not qualify them to be in the same meeting place as the Quraysh chiefs. Therefore, the chiefs asked the Prophet to drive them away, but he refused. They suggested to him that he should meet the two groups separately in order to give the chiefs their privileges, just as they enjoyed them in pre-Islamic society. Keen as he was to persuade them to accept Islam, the Prophet considered the possibility of granting their request. His Lord made His command clear to him: "*Do not drive away those who call on their Lord morning and evening, seeking only to win His pleasure.*" (Verse 52)

Saʿd ibn Abī Waqqāṣ, a prominent Companion of the Prophet, reports: "Six of us were with the Prophet (peace be upon him) when the unbelievers said to him: drive away these so that they are not encouraged to go above their standing with us. With me were ʿAbdullāh ibn Masʿūd, a man from the Hudhayl, Bilāl and two others." The Prophet felt whatever God might have let him feel. He was deep in thought when God revealed to him the verse stating: "*Do not drive away those who call on their Lord morning and evening, seeking only to win His pleasure*". [Related by Muslim.] Those Quraysh chiefs spoke ill of the poor whom the Prophet received well. They pointed to their poverty and weakness and claimed that their presence with God's Messenger was the reason behind the negative attitude adopted by the upper classes towards Islam. God gave his final ruling on this question, totally refuting their claims: "*You are in no way accountable for them, just as they are in no way accountable for you. Should you drive them away, you would be among the wrongdoers.*" (Verse 52)

Each is accountable for himself. If those individuals were of straitened means, then that is what God gave them. You, Prophet, have nothing to do with it. Similarly, whether you are rich or poor is not of anyone else's concern. Wealth or poverty have nothing to do with faith and its criterion for determining people's positions. The Prophet is told that if such people were driven away from his company on account of their financial status, he would not be attaching to such considerations their value as determined by God's measure. Hence, he would be a wrong-doer. Far be it from the Prophet to be so.

The result of this was to let those who were rich in character, although financially poor, remain with the Prophet, occupying their rightful positions which they had earned by virtue of their faith and their pursuit of God's pleasure. They did so through calling on Him and by appealing to Him. Islamic values were thus given supremacy.

The arrogant Quraysh chiefs were not impressed. They wondered: how could God choose the poor and the weak to grant them guidance in preference to us? Had it been true that the message Muḥammad preached was a message of goodness, they would not have been ahead of us in embracing it. God would have certainly guided us to it before them. They wondered: is it possible that God would grant them His favours in preference to us, when we are the people exercising power and enjoying wealth and high position in this city. This was, indeed, a test God set for those proud people. They were hardened on account of their wealth and distinguished family backgrounds. Yet they fared very badly because they could not appreciate the true nature of this faith and the type of social order it wanted people to establish. Needless to say, the social order that Islam establishes takes humanity by the hand to elevate it to heights it cannot attain through any other means. When Islam was allowed to have its full play in the life of Arabia, the Arabs rose to heights they could not have imagined possible at the time. Indeed, even today, they cannot be imagined possible even by the most advanced of democratic systems.

The Most Deserving of God's Grace

"*It is in this way that We try some of them by means of others, so that they may say: 'Are these the ones upon whom God has bestowed His favour from among us?'*" (Verse 53) This is a rhetorical question asked by the arrogant Arab chiefs. The Qur'ān provides the perfect answer: "*Does not God know best as to who is truly grateful?*" (Verse 53) It is an answer loaded with pointed connotations. It clearly suggests that following right guidance is a reward given by God to those whom He knows to be truly grateful. In this way, they are favoured with this particular aspect of divine grace. No amount of gratitude is sufficient in return for this act of grace. God, however, accepts the best that His servants can do and rewards them for it. His reward is always exceedingly generous.

The answer also suggests that accepting faith is a blessing that has nothing to do with the values that may prevail in any society following man-made systems. God bestows it on those whom He knows to be grateful for it, even though they may be poor and have no influence. Human values have no weight on God's scales.

It is clear from God's answer to that arrogant question that it is those people's sheer ignorance that gives rise to their objection to the selection of people on whom God bestows His grace. Those who raise the question do not realise that God bestows this favour on the basis of His perfect knowledge. It is He who knows those who deserve such a favour from among His servants. Such ignorant objections also betray the objectors' bad manners.

God commands His Messenger to be the one who starts by greeting those on whom God has bestowed the grace of being among the early Muslims; the very ones whom the Quraysh chiefs ridiculed. The

Prophet is further commanded to give them the happy news that God has committed Himself to grant them His mercy, as He will forgive those among them who mend their ways after having committed any bad deed out of ignorance. "*When those who believe in God's revelations come to you, say: Peace be upon you. Your Lord has committed Himself to bestow grace and mercy: if any of you does a bad deed out of ignorance, and then repents and mends his ways, He will be much-forgiving, merciful.*" (Verse 54)

Having given them the blessing of adopting the faith, and promised them easy reckoning on the Day of Judgement, God now honours them with His mercy. Indeed, He commits Himself to showing mercy to those who believe in Him. He also commands His Messenger (peace be upon him) to convey to them this commitment. God's grace is so plentiful that it ensures forgiveness of all bad deeds, once those who commit them repent and mend their ways. The qualification mentioned here, which describes a bad deed as being committed 'out of ignorance', is interpreted by scholars as intrinsic to committing sins. All human sins are committed 'out of ignorance'. According to this interpretation, this statement includes every bad deed: once the person who has done it repents and mends his ways, he will be forgiven. Other statements support this interpretation as they describe forgiveness as surely forthcoming upon repentance and doing well. This is the practical exercise of grace, which God has committed Himself to bestow.

It is useful to mention here some of the reports about the circumstances which led to the revelation of these verses. Together with the Qur'ānic statements, these reports indicate the great departure Islam brought about in human life. It enables human beings to attain a summit far higher than any they would otherwise be able to reach.

Al-Ṭabarī relates on the authority of Ibn Mas'ūd: "A group of Quraysh notables passed by the Prophet when he was with a group of Muslims who were of low status in Makkan society, including Ṣuhayb, 'Ammār, Bilāl and Khabbāb. The notables said to the Prophet: 'Muḥammad, are you happy to be with these from among your people? Are these the ones upon whom God has bestowed His favour from among us? Are we to follow these? Drive them away, for if you do so, we may follow you'. God then revealed the Qur'ānic verses which states: "*Do not drive away those who call on their Lord morning and evening, seeking only to win His pleasure.*" (Verse 52) "*It is in this way that We try some of them by means of others, so that they may say: 'Are*

*these the ones upon whom God has bestowed His favour from among us?'
Does not God know best as to who is truly grateful?"*[3] (Verse 53)

Al-Ṭabarī also attributes to Khabbāb, one of the Prophet's
Companions, the following report of the incident which led to the
revelation of Verse 52:

> Al-Aqraʿ ibn Ḥābis of the tribe of Tamīm and 'Uyaynah ibn Ḥiṣn
> of the Fazār once found the Prophet sitting with Bilāl, Ṣuhayb,
> 'Ammār, Khabbāb and others who commanded no influence in
> Arabian society. They looked on them with contempt. They said
> to the Prophet: "We would like you to establish a special time for
> us so that the Arabs will recognize our high position. Delegations
> come to you from all parts of Arabia and we feel ashamed to be
> seen with such people. When we come to see you, tell them to
> leave. When we depart, you may sit with them if you wish." The
> Prophet agreed. They said: "Could you put this in writing for
> us." The Prophet asked for a sheet of writing material and called
> 'Alī to write the same down. We were sitting a little further away.
> Then Gabriel, the angel, was sent down with these verses: "*Do
> not drive away those who call on their Lord morning and evening,
> seeking only to win His pleasure. You are in no way accountable for
> them, just as they are in no way accountable for you. Should you
> drive them away, you would be among the wrongdoers. It is in this
> way that We try some of them by means of others, so that they may
> say: 'Are these the ones upon whom God has bestowed His favour
> from among us?' Does not God know best as to who is truly grateful?
> When those who believe in God's revelations come to you, say: 'Peace
> be upon you. Your Lord has committed Himself to bestow grace and
> mercy.'*" (Verses 52–4) The Prophet dropped the sheet and called
> us. We went to him and he said: "*Peace be upon you. Your Lord has
> committed Himself to bestow grace and mercy*". Thereafter, we used
> to sit with him. When he wished to leave, he would stand up and
> go. But then God revealed to him the verse: "*Contain yourself in
> patience with those who call on their Lord morning and evening,
> seeking His countenance. Let not your eyes pass beyond them in
> quest of the beauties of the life of this world.*" (18: 28) After that
> God's Messenger would sit with us. When it was his usual time

---

3. Al-Ṭabarī, *Jāmiʿ al-Bayān*, Dār al-Fikr, Beirut, 1984., Vol. 7, p. 200.

to leave, we would leave first so that he could leave, if he so wished.[4]

Subsequent to the revelation of these verses, the Prophet would always be the first to greet them, every time he saw them. He would say: "Praise be to God who has made among my followers some people whom I am ordered to be the first to greet".

An authentic report related by Muslim mentions that Abū Sufyān passed by Salmān, Ṣuhayb, Bilāl and others. They said: "The swords of God's soldiers have not taken their dues from this enemy of God." Abū Bakr said: "Do you say this about the leader of the Quraysh?" He then mentioned this to the Prophet who said: "Abū Bakr, you may have offended them. If you have, then you have offended your Lord." Abū Bakr then went to them and said, "Brothers! Have I offended you?" They said, "No. May God forgive you, brother."

To Bridge a Wide Gulf

We need to cast another long look at this whole passage, as it is of exceeding importance to humanity as a whole. Its verses have a much greater significance than the listing of values and theoretical principles on human rights. They represent something great that has been achieved in human life when this faith took humanity by the hand to bridge a very wide gulf. In just one stage of history, humanity attained the brightest summit. Despite its long retreat from that summit, the greatness and reality of that achievement cannot be taken lightly. Since humanity has reached that summit once, it can certainly repeat its performance. The summit remains there. Human beings and the religion of Islam remain the same. What is needed is the determined resolution to try again and the confidence that the summit is once again attainable.

---

4. Al-Ṭabarī, ibid., Vol. 7, p. 201

In his famous commentary on the Qur'ān, Ibn Kathīr comments: "The authenticity of this ḥadīth is questionable, because this verse was revealed in the Makkan period, while al-Aqraʿ ibn Ḥābis and ʿUyaynah embraced Islam long after the Prophet's migration to Madinah." I cannot agree with Ibn Kathīr's comments. There is no doubt that these two men said what they did before they embraced Islam. They could not after all have said such a thing after they had become Muslims. Hence, it might be that they did not accept Islam when their suggestion was refused, but then they embraced it much later. – Author's note.

I may add that Ibn Kathīr's objection is perhaps more valid, because when the Prophet was still in Makkah he went to meet pilgrims from other tribes. He did not receive Arab delegations referred to in this report until late in his Madinan period. – Editor's note.

These verses draw for humanity the rising curve, marking each stage in order to show the low level of ignorance at which the Arabs were situated before Islam took them to the highest summit. When they attained it, they took the rest of mankind with them.

The depths in which the Arabs, and the whole of humanity, lived in their days of ignorance is brought before our eyes as the Quraysh chiefs say to the Prophet, with an overtone of reproach: "Muḥammad, are these the ones you have chosen for company from among your people? Are these the ones upon whom God has bestowed His favour from among us? Are we to be the followers of these? Drive them away for, then, we may consider following you." We see it again in the way al-Aqra' and 'Uyaynah looked contemptuously on the early Companions of the Prophet such as Bilāl, Ṣuhayb, 'Ammār, Khabbāb and other seemingly unsuitable people. The two chiefs said to the Prophet: "We would like you to establish a special time for us so that the Arabs will recognize our high position. Delegations come to you from all parts of Arabia and we feel ashamed to be seen with such people. When we come to see you, tell them to leave. When we depart, you may sit with them if you wish."

This is the uglier face of ignorance and its petty values, which attach importance to social standing and considerations of wealth and class. Those individuals despised by the Arabian chiefs were either non-Arabs, or they lacked wealth and social standing. The same values prevail in all *jāhiliyyah* societies, even modern ones.

Islam attaches no value whatsoever to all these considerations. For Islam has come from on high, and did not spring from the earth. Indeed, the earth represents that low level which could not have supported such a new and noble plant. Islam gives a specific order to the first person to carry out Islamic orders, Muḥammad (peace be upon him), the recipient of divine revelations who belonged to the leading family of the top clan, Hāshim, of the leading Arabian tribe, the Quraysh, and to Abū Bakr, the Prophet's Companion and successor, concerning those people of very low status. For these individuals abandoned allegiance to anyone and dedicated themselves to the service of God alone. That enabled them to attain all those spectacular achievements.

If the low depth of ignorance is represented by the suggestions of the Quraysh chiefs and the feelings of al-Aqra' and 'Uyaynah, the great height of Islam is delineated by God's order to His Messenger (peace be upon him): "*Do not drive away those who call on their Lord morning and evening, seeking only to win His pleasure. You are in no way accountable for them, just as they are in no way accountable for you. Should you drive them away, you would be among the wrongdoers. It is in this way that We try some of them by means of others, so that they may say: 'Are these the ones upon whom God has bestowed His favour from among us?' Does not God know best as to who is truly grateful? When those who believe in God's revelations come to you, say: 'Peace be upon you. Your Lord has committed Himself to bestow grace and mercy: if any of you does a bad deed out of ignorance, and then repents and mends his ways, He will be much-forgiving, merciful.'"* (Verses 52–4) It is also highlighted by the Prophet's attitude towards those weaker individuals whom God has ordered him to be the first to greet and to stay with until they leave. This order is given to none other than Muḥammad ibn 'Abdullāh, God's Messenger, the best and most noble creature that ever lived.

The height of Islam is also represented by the way those individuals looked at their position with God. They considered their swords as God's swords and they were not impressed by Abū Sufyān, the elder and chief of the Quraysh. His rank among Muslims was a low one, since he was among those pardoned by the Prophet as they accepted Islam when Makkah surrendered to him. Their high position was earned by their early acceptance of Islam, when that acceptance exposed them to a great deal of suffering. When Abū Bakr took issue with them concerning Abū Sufyān, the Prophet warned him that he might have angered them and by so doing he might have incurred God's displeasure. How splendid. No comment is adequate here. We can only reflect on this totally new outlook on social status. Abū Bakr goes to those very individuals to make sure that he has not angered them. He says to them: "Brothers! Have I offended you?" They said, "No. May God forgive you, brother."

What a great achievement for humanity! What a great divide separates the new situation, with all its new values, concepts and feelings from what prevailed in the days of ignorance! The earth remained the same, with the same environment, the same people, and the same economy. The only difference is that something has been sent down from on high to human beings. The revelations combined power and authority. They addressed human nature in its purity. It signalled those lurking at the bottom to start their march up to the great heights, the scaling of which was made possible with Islam.

Yet humanity has now retreated from that summit and has tumbled back to its lower depths. We see in New York, Washington, Chicago, Johannesburg and other centres of 'civilisation' a later-day prevalence of the same stinking bigotry based on ties of race, colour, nationhood and class.

At the same time, Islam remains at the summit telling mankind that, by God's grace, it can lift itself out of the mud and aspire to a bright, glorious future. To do this, it has to listen to the divine guidance and to implement the code embodied in this religion of Islam. For it is this that ensures for mankind a place up there at the summit.

Within the approach I have set myself in this work, I cannot elaborate much further. Nevertheless, I repeat my call on people to reflect in depth on these Qur'ānic statements in order to visualize the great expanse which opens up for human beings as they start to climb up from the depths of ignorance to the great heights, guided by Islam. They should then reflect on the great difference between that and how low they can sink when they respond to the beckoning of materialistic civilisation, which is totally devoid of faith and its spiritual dimensions. Such reflection should be enough to make people understand where the implementation of Islam will lead them today, after they have experienced the multiple failure of a great many doctrines, creeds, systems, concepts and situations. All these have been invented by men in isolation from divine guidance. Hence, they have failed to guide mankind again to the summit or to ensure a proper standard of human rights. In contrast, we see Islam giving people a sense of reassurance as it accomplishes that great departure without strife, persecution, conflict or extraordinary measures that deny people their basic rights. It employs no special measures of terror, torture, hunger, poverty or any element of suffering which people experience as they try to move from one man-made system to another. Nevertheless, under all these systems, people subjugate one another and endure much misery.

We have to satisfy ourselves with these comments and try to appreciate the powerful effect of the Qur'ānic statement and its strong implications.

Tearing Off the Masks of Evildoing

Now we come to the conclusion of this passage which has outlined very clearly the nature of the last message revealed by God and the task assigned to His last Messenger. It has further outlined the essentials of faith as they are, unadorned, giving us an insight into the values and principles Islam wants to establish in human life and those it wants to abolish. At the conclusion of this passage we are reminded that this detailed outline is given on purpose in order to lay down everything very clearly and to leave no room for confusion. Thus, the truth will be known to everyone, without any need for miraculous proofs. Such clarity is provided by the Qur'ānic approach, of which this passage is an example.

The final verse in this passage is expressed in two short clauses: the first refers to all signs of guidance, pointers to faith and statements of the truth that have been given so far in this *sūrah*: "*Thus do We make plain Our revelations*". The second clause in this short verse fills us with wonder: "*So that the path of the evildoers may be clearly distinct.*" (Verse 55)

This statement tells us that the Qur'ānic approach endeavours to clarify the truth and states it very plainly, but its purpose is not merely to make the path of the believers clearly distinct. It also endeavours to clearly and plainly portray falsehood so that the path of the evildoers is also clearly distinct. Clarity of the one necessitates clarity of the other.

This approach of the Qur'ān has been chosen by God as it is most effective with the human mind. God knows that believing in the truth requires knowledge of falsehood and adding total certainty to faith requires a clear-cut distinction between falsehood and evil on the one hand and truth and goodness on the other. The momentum a believer requires in his advocacy of the truth is not merely generated by his feeling that he follows the truth. The extra power is given by realizing that opposition to his efforts comes from falsehood, advocated by the evildoers, who have always been the ones to oppose prophets. As God states in another verse: "*Thus, against every prophet We have set up an enemy from among the evildoers.*" (25: 31) Thus, the Prophet Muḥammad and the believers know for certain that those opposing them are none other than evildoers.

It is an important objective of the Qur'ānic approach that evil and falsehood be very clearly identified, so that the truth and goodness become clear and distinct. Confusion about the first may lead to confusion about the second because the two move along paths that cannot meet. Therefore, every Islamic movement should begin with a clear identification of the methods and features of the believers, as well as those of the evildoers. This identification should be based on what we see in the real world, not confined to theories and an abstract world. The advocates of Islam should be able to know who are the believers in their community and who are the evildoers.

Such total clarity and complete distinction was witnessed when Islam confronted the unbelievers in Arabia. The path of Muslims was that marked out by God's Messenger and those supporting him. Those who did not join them followed the path of the unbelievers and evildoers. Even with this clear demarcation, the Qur'ān was being revealed, in absolute clarity, to make the path of the evildoers readily apparent and clearly distinct. Moreover, whenever Islam confronted polytheism, atheism or other creeds that have deviated from earlier religions distorted by human beings, each of the two paths was clearly marked out. No confusion was possible.

The greatest difficulty that confronts the Islamic movements of today is represented by what we see in the lands that used to belong to Islam, where the Islamic faith was supreme. We find all over this area people of Islamic descent, but both the land and its people have abandoned Islam in reality, although they continue to claim to be Muslims. They disown the basic Islamic principles in faith and practice, although they may think that they still believe in Islam as a faith. We know that Islam is essentially the belief outlined by the declaration that there is no deity other than God. This declaration entails an unshakeable belief that God alone is the Creator of the whole universe who manages all its affairs, and that to Him alone all acts of worship, and indeed all human activities, should be addressed. From Him alone should people receive their laws and according to His wishes they should conduct all their affairs. Anyone who does not declare his belief that there is no deity other than God, realizing the full significance of this declaration does not actually bear witness to this fact and has not yet become a Muslim, although he may have a Muslim name. Any land that does not implement the declaration that, "There is no deity other than God", in its full significance is not a land which submits to Islam.

The real difficulty encountered by the Islamic movements of today is represented by the ambiguity and lack of clarity associated nowadays with the concept of God's oneness as the basic principle of Islam. This has led to a corresponding ambiguity of what constitutes this belief. Thus, the path of the true believers is not as clearly distinct from the path of the evildoers as it should be. Titles and features have been muddled up. No clear demarcation of ways and methods is made.

The forces hostile to Islam are aware of this and they are busy adding to the confusion and deepening it. Thus, when Muslims nowadays raise their voices advocating clear distinction, a grave accusation is levelled at them, namely, that they consider fellow Muslims as unbelievers! They face severe punishments for their 'crime', as social tradition is given the final say on who is a Muslim and who is not. Needless to say, the ultimate arbiter in all this is God and His Messenger.

The greatest difficulty facing the advocates of Islam in every new generation is represented by this first stumbling block. Advocacy of a faith must begin by making the path of the believers clearly distinct from that of the evildoers. The advocates of Islam must raise their voices loud with the word of the truth. They must fear no blame or reproach. They must pay no attention to anyone who claims that they classify Muslims as unbelievers.

Islam is not as wet as some people think. It has its clearly distinctive features. It is represented by the declaration that there is no deity other than God, bearing fully the significance we have just outlined. Anyone who does not believe in it fully, and does not implement it in human life as it should be, runs the risk of being judged by God and His Messenger as unbeliever, evildoer and transgressor: *"Thus do We make plain Our revelations; so that the path of the evildoers may be clearly distinct."* (Verse 55)

The advocates of Islam must pass this hurdle and must have a clear view of the basic issues. This enables them to pool all their efforts and use all their potential in the service of the call they advocate, unimpeded by any confusion or ambiguity. They cannot achieve this unless they believe with full certainty that they themselves are the Muslims and those who oppose them and turn people away from God's path are evildoers. The point is that they will not be able to endure the difficulties along their way unless they are clear in their minds that they are fighting the battle of faith against unfaith. They must realize to the full that they follow one religion while the rest of their people follow another: *"Thus do We make plain Our revelations; so that the path of the evildoers may be clearly distinct."* (Verse 55) God always tells the truth.

8

The Extent of God's Knowledge

Say: I am forbidden to worship those beings whom you invoke instead of God. Say: I do not follow your whims, for then I would have gone astray, and would not be on the right path. (56)

قُلْ إِنِّى نُهِيتُ أَنْ أَعْبُدَ ٱلَّذِينَ تَدْعُونَ مِن دُونِ ٱللَّهِ قُل لَّآ أَتَّبِعُ أَهْوَآءَكُمْ قَدْ ضَلَلْتُ إِذًا وَمَآ أَنَا۠ مِنَ ٱلْمُهْتَدِينَ ٥٦

Say: I take my stand on a clear evidence from my Lord, yet you deny Him. It is not in my power [to produce] that which you so hastily demand. Judgement rests with God alone. He declares the truth and He is the best of arbiters. 57)

قُلْ إِنِّى عَلَىٰ بَيِّنَةٍ مِّن رَّبِّى وَكَذَّبْتُم بِهِۦ مَا عِندِى مَا تَسْتَعْجِلُونَ بِهِۦٓ إِنِ ٱلْحُكْمُ إِلَّا لِلَّهِ يَقُصُّ ٱلْحَقَّ وَهُوَ خَيْرُ ٱلْفَٰصِلِينَ ٥٧

Say: If that which you so hastily demand were in my power, the case between me and you would have been decided. But God knows best as to who are the wrongdoers. (58)

قُل لَّوْ أَنَّ عِندِى مَا تَسْتَعْجِلُونَ بِهِۦ لَقُضِىَ ٱلْأَمْرُ بَيْنِى وَبَيْنَكُمْ وَٱللَّهُ أَعْلَمُ بِٱلظَّٰلِمِينَ ٥٨

With Him are the keys to what lies beyond the reach of human perception: none knows them but He. He knows all that the land and sea contain; not a leaf falls but He knows it; and neither is there a grain in the earth's deep darkness, nor anything fresh or dry but is recorded in a clear book. (59)

﴾وَعِندَهُۥ مَفَاتِحُ ٱلْغَيْبِ لَا يَعْلَمُهَآ إِلَّا هُوَ ۚ وَيَعْلَمُ مَا فِى ٱلْبَرِّ وَٱلْبَحْرِ ۚ وَمَا تَسْقُطُ مِن وَرَقَةٍ إِلَّا يَعْلَمُهَا وَلَا حَبَّةٍ فِى ظُلُمَٰتِ ٱلْأَرْضِ وَلَا رَطْبٍ وَلَا يَابِسٍ إِلَّا فِى كِتَٰبٍ مُّبِينٍ ٥٩﴿

It is He who causes you to be like the dead at night, and knows what you do in the daytime. He raises you again to life each day in order that a term set by Him be fulfilled. In the end, to Him you must return; and then He will tell you all that you have done. (60)

وَهُوَ ٱلَّذِى يَتَوَفَّىٰكُم بِٱلَّيْلِ وَيَعْلَمُ مَا جَرَحْتُم بِٱلنَّهَارِ ثُمَّ يَبْعَثُكُمْ فِيهِ لِيُقْضَىٰٓ أَجَلٌ مُّسَمًّى ۖ ثُمَّ إِلَيْهِ مَرْجِعُكُمْ ثُمَّ يُنَبِّئُكُم بِمَا كُنتُمْ تَعْمَلُونَ ٦٠

He alone holds sway over His servants. He sends forth guardians to watch over you until, when death approaches any one of you, Our messengers cause him to die. They leave no part of their duty unfulfilled. (61)

وَهُوَ ٱلْقَاهِرُ فَوْقَ عِبَادِهِۦ ۖ وَيُرْسِلُ عَلَيْكُمْ حَفَظَةً حَتَّىٰٓ إِذَا جَآءَ أَحَدَكُمُ ٱلْمَوْتُ تَوَفَّتْهُ رُسُلُنَا وَهُمْ لَا يُفَرِّطُونَ ٦١

They are then brought back to God, their true Lord Supreme. Indeed, His alone is all judgement; and He is most swift in reckoning. (62)

ثُمَّ رُدُّوٓا۟ إِلَى ٱللَّهِ مَوْلَىٰهُمُ ٱلْحَقِّ ۚ أَلَا لَهُ ٱلْحُكْمُ وَهُوَ أَسْرَعُ ٱلْحَٰسِبِينَ ٦٢

Say: Who is it that saves you from the dark dangers of land and sea, when you call out to Him humbly and in secret: "If He will but save us from this peril, we will most certainly be grateful"? (63)

قُلْ مَن يُنَجِّيكُم مِّن ظُلُمَٰتِ ٱلْبَرِّ وَٱلْبَحْرِ تَدْعُونَهُۥ تَضَرُّعًا وَخُفْيَةً لَّئِنْ أَنجَىٰنَا مِنْ هَٰذِهِۦ لَنَكُونَنَّ مِنَ ٱلشَّٰكِرِينَ ٦٣

Say: God alone saves you from these and from every distress; and still you associate partners with Him. (64)

قُلِ ٱللَّهُ يُنَجِّيكُم مِّنْهَا وَمِن كُلِّ كَرْبٍ ثُمَّ أَنتُمْ تُشْرِكُونَ ٦٤

Say: It is He alone who has the power to let loose upon you suffering from above you and from beneath your feet, or to divide you into disputing groups, causing the one to suffer at the hands of the other. See how We make plain Our revelations so that they may understand. (65)

قُلْ هُوَ ٱلْقَادِرُ عَلَىٰٓ أَن يَبْعَثَ عَلَيْكُمْ عَذَابًا مِّن فَوْقِكُمْ أَوْ مِن تَحْتِ أَرْجُلِكُمْ أَوْ يَلْبِسَكُمْ شِيَعًا وَيُذِيقَ بَعْضَكُم بَأْسَ بَعْضٍ ٱنظُرْ كَيْفَ نُصَرِّفُ ٱلْءَايَٰتِ لَعَلَّهُمْ يَفْقَهُونَ ٦٥

Overview

In this new round the *sūrah* again picks up the theme of the true nature of Godhead, after having discussed in the previous passage the nature of God's message and the Messenger to whom it is entrusted. The discussion in Chapter 7 ended with a clear demarcation of the separate paths followed by the believers and the evildoers.

In this passage the nature of Godhead is brought out clearly in a number of areas which we will first outline very briefly. It is first of all clear in the Prophet's heart as he knows that he has clear evidence given him by God. He is absolutely certain of this evidence, and his firm belief will not admit any doubts as a result of the attitude of unbelievers who deny his message. Hence, he devotes himself to his faith, and takes his stand away from his people. His certainty that they are in deep error is as strong as his certainty of the truth that he is rightly guided. (Verses 56–7)

The nature of Godhead manifests itself in God's forbearance when He does not act on the unbelievers' requests for a physical miracle. Should He give them such a miracle and should they continue to disbelieve, their continued rejection of the truth would ensure their total destruction. Had the Prophet been able to grant them what they hastily demanded, he would have done so. As a human being, he would have been fed up with their stubborn rejection. To allow them an indefinite chance is an aspect of God's grace, one which reflects His Godhead. (Verse 58)

Again, the nature of Godhead is clearly reflected in God's knowledge that encompasses everything that takes place throughout the universe. This is described in a way that cannot apply to anyone other than God, and cannot be painted by anyone but Him. (Verse 59)

Moreover, the truth of Godhead is seen in the fact that God holds sway over all His creatures in all situations, whether asleep or awake, in life and after death, in this present world and in the next one. (Verses 60–2)

Finally, it is manifested in the nature of the unbelievers themselves. When they are overwhelmed by serious danger, they call for help on none other than God. Yet, they associate partners with Him, forgetting that the one to whom they appeal for delivery from danger is able to inflict punishment on them that none can remove. (Verses 63–5)

A Law Not to Be Violated

Say: I am forbidden to worship those beings whom you invoke instead of God. Say: I do not follow your whims, for then I would have gone astray, and would not be on the right path. Say: I take my stand on a clear evidence from my Lord, yet you deny Him. It is not in my power [to produce] that which you so hastily demand. Judgement rests with God alone. He declares the truth and He is the best of arbiters. Say: If that which you so hastily demand were in my power, the case between me and you would have been decided. But God knows best as to who are the wrongdoers. (Verses 56–8)

This passage is particularly inspiring. It seeks to influence the addressees by stating the true nature of Godhead, explaining its different aspects, using varying cadences and a most effective style. One particularly inspiring feature is the use of the address form, "Say…

Say... Say...", making it profoundly clear that this is an address to God's Messenger (peace be upon him). He is required to deliver his Lord's message as it is revealed to him. We are told with absolute clarity that the Messenger does not have or follow anything other than this message and seeks none other than its guidance: *"Say: I am forbidden to worship those beings whom you invoke instead of God. Say: I do not follow your whims, for then I would have gone astray, and would not be on the right path."* (Verse 56)

God commands His Messenger to declare to the unbelievers that his Lord forbids him to worship those beings on whom they call instead of God and whom they make partners with God. He is forbidden to follow their whims. The fact is that they invoke those beings, giving them a divine status, as a result of their whims and caprice. This cannot be the outcome of any certain knowledge or any truth. If he responded to their whims, he too would then go astray and find no guidance whatsoever. Their whims can only cause him and them to deviate from the path of the truth and to lose their way altogether.

God instructs his Messenger to put the issues so clearly to the unbelievers and to explain to them how his way and their way cannot meet. Indeed, this is not the first time God issues such an order to His Messenger in this *sūrah*. Earlier, He ordered him to say: *"Will you in truth bear witness that there are other deities beside God? Say: I bear no such witness. Say: He is but one God. I disown all that you associate with Him."* (Verse 19)

The unbelievers used to try to tempt God's Messenger (peace be upon him) to endorse their beliefs in return for their endorsement of his faith. They suggested to him that he should bow to their deities and, likewise, they would prostrate themselves before his, as if this could ever happen, and as if idolatry and Islam, with its emphasis on submission to God alone, could exist side by side in the heart of any one person, or worship of God alone could join hands with the worship of other beings. Nothing of this could ever be imagined. God is the One who is least in need of any partners. He requires His servants to submit to Him alone. He makes it clear to them that He will never accept their submission if they allow any traces of polytheism to creep into it.

Let us now consider an important linguistic usage in this verse: *"Say: I am forbidden to worship those beings whom you invoke instead of God."* (Verse 56) This statement makes it clear that the Prophet must tell the unbelievers that he is forbidden to worship any of their idols or any other beings they worship. This applies to whatever being is invoked besides God. However, the rules of Arabic grammar indicate that use of the relative pronoun 'whom' in this statement is significant. Normally, its usage is limited to beings with minds of their own. Had the prohibition only meant idols and similar inanimate objects, the relative pronoun 'what' would have been used instead. The reference here must, then, include some intelligent beings to justify the use of the relative pronoun 'whom'. This interpretation is consistent with the practical facts and with general Islamic terminology in this respect.

In practice, the Arab idolaters did not only worship idols. They also associated *jinn*, angels and human beings as partners with God. The partnership they ascribed to human beings manifested itself only in giving those human beings the authority to legislate. They set for them their norms and traditions and arbitrated in their disputes, in accordance with the prevailing customs and what they thought fit. We need, then, to look at how this is described in Islamic terminology. Islam considers all this as a form of idolatry. When human beings are given the authority to regulate people's affairs in accordance with their own legislation, they are actually considered equal to God. This is as strongly forbidden in Islam as any actual prostration before idols. Both actions are manifestations of polytheistic beliefs. Both ascribe divinity to beings other than God.

The Prophet is then ordered by God to declare to those idolaters who deny the absolute oneness of their Lord his own firm belief and unshakable conviction that God is the only Lord in the universe and that He sends down revelations to him: *"Say: I take my stand on a clear evidence from my Lord, yet you deny Him. It is not in my power [to produce] that which you so hastily demand. Judgement rests with God alone. He declares the truth and He is the best of arbiters."* (Verse 57)

This is, indeed, what earlier prophets and messengers felt. They expressed it in similar terms. The Prophet Noah used practically the same wording: *"Think, my people! If I take my stand on a clear evidence from my Lord and He has favoured me with grace from Himself, to which you have remained blind, can we force it upon you when you are averse to it?"* (11: 28) Similarly did the Prophet Ṣāliḥ speak to his people, the Thamūd: *"Think, my people! If I take my stand on a clear evidence from my Lord and He has bestowed on me His grace, who will save me from God, should I disobey Him? You are, in such case, only augmenting my ruin."* (11: 63) Abraham said it somewhat differently: *"His people argued with him. He said: 'Do you argue with me about God, when it is He Who has given me guidance?'"* (Verse 80) The Prophet Jacob stated the same idea to his children: *"When the bearer of good news arrived [with Joseph's shirt], he laid it over his face; and he recovered his sight. He said: 'Did I not say to you that I know from God something that you do not know?'"* (12: 96)

This is, then, the nature of Godhead as it is fully understood by God's most obedient servants. They feel its truth bringing them total reassurance and unshakeable faith. When the unbelievers in Arabia demanded miracles from the Prophet Muḥammad (peace be upon him), God commanded him to declare this truth as he felt it, putting it clearly in front of those unbelievers: *"Say: I take my stand on a clear evidence from my Lord, yet you deny Him."* (Verse 57)

They also demanded that the Prophet accomplish for them some miracle or let God's scourge loose on them so that they could believe that what he preached was revealed by God. He was ordered, in response, to declare to them the true nature of his message and what it meant to be God's Messenger. He was commanded to make an absolutely clear distinction between this and the nature of Godhead. He had to declare that he had no control whatsoever over what they tried to hurry. It is controlled only by God. He himself was only a messenger, not a deity: *"It is not in my power [to produce] that which you so hastily demand. Judgement rests with God alone. He declares the truth and He is the best of arbiters."* (Verse 57)

Hastening the punishment of the unbelievers when they continued to deny God even after miraculous proof had been given them is in effect a judgement put into effect. Hence, it belongs to God who tells the truth and who arbitrates between the one who advocates the truth and those who deny His message. No creature has been given any such authority to judge others.

The Prophet thus denies that he himself has any power or any say in what judgement God passes against His servants. The Prophet is no more than a human being who receives revelations which he conveys, discharging his duty as a warner. God alone passes judgement. That is the perfect distinction between the nature of God and His attributes on the one hand and the nature of His servants on the other.

The Prophet is then ordered to explain to them a particularly effective argument about how the whole affair rests with God and operates according to His will. Had the accomplishment of miracles, including the subsequent administration of punishment been within his power, then, as a human being, he could not have refused it as they were insisting so strongly on a miracle. Since such a decision belongs to God alone, He treats them with forbearance and withholds miracles so that they do not put themselves in a position whereby their own destruction becomes inevitable, as happened to earlier communities: "*Say: If that which you so hastily demand were in my power, the case between me and you would have been decided. But God knows best as to who are the wrongdoers.*" (Verse 58) Human beings have a limited capacity for forbearance. It is only God, the Supreme, the Almighty who can show such forbearance to human beings when they persist with their disobedience and boastful rejections.

God certainly tells the truth. We see some people behaving in a way which totally exhausts our patience and makes us absolutely angry. Nevertheless, God forbears with them, lets them enjoy His provisions, feeds them and gives them abundance. In such a situation, one can only say: "My Lord, how forbearing You are!" This is, indeed, what Abū Bakr said when the unbelievers in Arabia beat him so badly that his nose could not be distinguished from his eye. God forbears with them when He knows them full well: "*God knows best as to who are the wrongdoers*". When He gives them a respite, He certainly has a purpose behind His decision. He forbears with them when He is certainly able to respond to their suggestions and to let loose His scourge to destroy them.

Knowledge Unlimited

Developing the point of God's knowledge of who are the wrongdoers, and continuing with the explanation of the nature of Godhead, the *sūrah* gives us an image of this knowledge as it pertains to one of its unique areas, namely, that of *ghayb*. This term will be explained presently.

> "*With Him are the keys to what lies beyond the reach of human perception: none knows them but He. He knows all that the land and sea contain; not a leaf falls but He knows it; and neither is there a grain in the earth's deep darkness, nor anything fresh or dry but is recorded in a clear book.*" (Verse 59)

This is an image of God's complete knowledge that leaves out nothing in terms of time or place, land, sea or sky, in the depths of the world or in the wild expanse of space, including what is dead or alive, dry or fresh, green or withering away. But how prosaic is our own description as compared to the fine Qur'ānic portrayal? Wholly inadequate when the latter combines within itself a purely arithmetic statement with a profoundly inspiring image!

This short verse causes our human imagination to come to life trying to explore the horizons of what we know and what lies beyond our knowledge. We try to imagine the limitless nature of God's knowledge as it encompasses the whole universe and goes far beyond what we know of that universe. We are in awe as we receive one image after another from all directions and as we try to lift the curtains drawn over what is kept hidden, whether it relates to the past, the present or the future. This is a complete world extending beyond our imagination. But the keys to all of it are with God, and He alone knows them. Our minds may try to discover what has so far been unknown to us in the land or at sea, realizing that everything in them is perfectly known to God. We visualize the leaves that drop from the trees: innumerable as they are, yet every single one of them, wherever it falls, is seen by God. Every single grain, buried in the darkest depths of the earth, is beheld by God who sees everything, whether fresh or dry, dead or alive, anywhere in the universe. Nothing escapes God's knowledge.

Minds are left dizzy as they contemplate the picture this verse draws of God's knowledge. Its lines are infinite, stretching endlessly in time and place, across the visible and the unseen. This endless expanse, which exhausts our minds to just imagine, is painted with absolute precision in only a few words.

Every time we look at this short verse, we cannot fail to recognize its miraculous style which tells of the author of the Qur'ān. One look at its subject matter is sufficient to make us absolutely certain that this is something no human being would say. Human intelligence does not stretch to limitless horizons when it describes perfect, unfailing knowledge. Instead, the human intellect has different characteristics and set limits, because its images reflect its own concerns. Why should human beings care about the number of leaves falling from the trees all over the globe? Why should they bother about grains buried in the deep dark recesses of the earth? What concern is it to them to know everything that is fresh or dry? People simply do not care about falling leaves, let alone about counting them. They care about the seeds they plant, hoping to have a good harvest. Otherwise, they would not care about the grains buried in the earth. They certainly like to use what they have of fresh and dry things, but none of these matters is thought of as evidence of perfect knowledge. It is only the Creator who knows and cares about every falling leaf, buried grain and the like, as He does about other things, fresh or dry.

No human being could ever contemplate that each falling leaf, each buried grain, every fresh object and also every dry one should be recorded in a clear book. They cannot see any benefit to them from keeping such a record. But the Sovereign of the whole universe is the One who has all that recorded because everything in the whole universe, large or small, visible or hidden, distant or close, apparent or unknown, is part of His dominion and, as such, is accounted for.

This is an expansive scene, one which leaves a profound effect on the human mind. The human intellect does not even try to paint such a scene comprising the leaves falling from every tree throughout the world and every grain hidden in the soil and every fresh and dry thing on earth. Indeed, neither our eyes nor our imagination care to visualize it in the first place. Nevertheless, it is a powerful scene that tells us much about God's knowledge, reminding us that God oversees and records everything. His will takes care of what is large or small, highly important or infinitely insignificant, visible or hidden, distant or close, apparent or unknown.

Those of us who react to what we experience and have the talent of expression are keenly aware of our human limitations to visualize and express things. We know from personal experience that it does not occur to any human mind to paint such a scene and that no human being can use such a mode of expression. I invite anyone who disputes this to look into everything that human beings have ever written in an attempt to see if human literary talent has ever ventured in this direction. Indeed, this verse and similar ones in the Qur'ān are sufficient for us to know the Author of this glorious book.

If we look at the artistic excellence in this verse, we soon realize that it surpasses everything that human beings have ever attempted: "*With Him are the keys to what lies beyond the reach of human perception: none knows them but He.*" (Verse 59) The verse takes us first into the unfathomable reaches of the world beyond, stretching into time and place, as well as the past, present and future and into what takes place both in this life and in our imagination.

"*He knows all that the land and sea contain.*" (Verse 59) The picture here is of the seen world, stretching infinitely over the horizon so that the world we see is stretched into an infinite existence to provide harmony with the limitless nature of the world beyond.

"*Not a leaf falls, but He knows it.*" (Verse 59) This depicts the movement of death, the fall from above and disappearance after the end of life.

"*Neither is there a grain in the earth's deep darkness.*" (Verse 59) This depicts the movement of growth and life, starting in the deep and going up onto the surface. We see how the dead quickens and the moving forward with vigour.

"*Nor anything fresh or dry but is recorded in a clear book.*" (Verse 59) This is an overall generalization that comprises both life and death, the thriving and the withering away of everything that lives on earth. Who other than God would begin with such material in order to paint such an expansive scene? And who would give it such beauty and harmony to add to its excellence? Who other than God can do that?

Beyond Our Perception

We need now to say a word about the first clause in this verse, which states: "*With Him are the keys to what lies beyond the reach of human perception: none knows them but He.*" (Verse 59)

It is important to define what we describe in English as lying "beyond the reach of human perception" and the keys to it as being known only to God. This expression is given in the Arabic text in one word, *ghayb*, which is an essential element of the Islamic concept of faith, existence and life. The term is derived in Arabic from a root which denotes "absence, disappearance, hiding, shielding from people's senses and understanding".[1]

We need to speak about *ghayb* because it is frequently contrasted nowadays with 'science' and what is 'scientific'. The Qur'ān states that there is something to describe as *ghayb* which lies beyond the reach of human perception, and that the keys to this world are known only to

---

1. Many translators of the Qur'ān have chosen to render it in English as "unseen, invisible or hidden". I feel that the rendering of Muhammad Asad, "What lies beyond the reach of human perception", is closer to its true sense, because *ghayb* suggests a world that we cannot fathom by any means of knowledge acquisition. – Editor's note.

God. The Qur'ān also states that the knowledge man has been given is scanty, but sufficient for man and appropriate for his potential. Beyond the factual knowledge given them by God, people only indulge in guesswork, which is no substitute for the truth. God states that He has set into operation certain laws for this universe, and He has taught man how to understand some of these laws and deal with them according to his ability. He further states that He will reveal to man of these laws what strengthens his faith. This does not violate the unchangeable laws of nature or affect the world that remains beyond the reach of human perception. Nor does it affect God's absolute will or the fact that everything occurs in accordance with His will. We will now touch briefly on these facts.

In the Qur'ān, God often describes the believers as those who believe in what lies beyond the reach of human perception. This quality is indeed essential to faith: "*This [the Qur'ān] is the Book, there is no doubt about it, a guidance for the God-fearing, who believe in what lies beyond the reach of human perception, observe prayers and give of what We bestow upon them. [They are] those who believe in what has been revealed to you and what was revealed before you, and are certain of the hereafter. Those follow their Lord's guidance, and they shall surely prosper.*" (2: 2–5)

To believe in God (limitless is He in His glory) is to believe in what lies beyond the reach of human perception. It is not possible for human beings to comprehend the nature of God. When they believe in Him, they recognize the results of His actions, but they cannot conceive His nature or what He works. Similarly, the life to come also lies beyond the reach of human perception. Everything that relates to the Day of Judgement: the reckoning, the reward, and the punishment – all belong to the world beyond. We believe in all these because God has told us about them.

The *ghayb* which we are required to accept in order to have true faith includes other facts mentioned in the Qur'ān as God describes the believers and their faith: "*The Messenger believes in what has been revealed to him by his Lord, and so do all the believers. Each one of them believes in God, His angels, His books, and His messengers. We make no distinction between any of His messengers. And they say, 'We hear and we obey. Grant us Your forgiveness, our Lord; to You we shall all return.'*" (2: 285) Every believer, then, must also believe in what God has revealed to His Messenger (peace be upon him) which includes some

178

knowledge of the *ghayb* which God imparts to His Messenger, in a measure He determines, as explained in another Qur'ānic verse: "*He alone knows what lies beyond the reach of human perception, and He does not reveal it to anyone except those whom He chooses to be His messengers.*" (72: 26–7)

Believing in the angels is also part of believing in the imperceptible, because we only know about angels what God has chosen to tell us. In addition, we have to believe in God's will and its operation. That is also part of *ghayb*.

Man is, however, surrounded by imperceptibles in every direction. Part of this relates to time: past, present and future. Another part exists within man himself, and more is available in the universe. What does man know about the origin of this universe, its existence, nature and motion? What does he know about life and its cycles? All this lies beyond his perception. Indeed, man does not know what occurs within him at the present moment, let alone what occurs during the next moment or in the universe with its atoms and electrons, etc.

The human intellect floats in an ocean of the unknown, stopping every now and then at little islands which, to him, represent the landmarks of his world. Without God's grace and His will to make this world subservient to man and to teach him a number of the rules of nature, man would not have been able to do anything. But he remains ungrateful to God: "*Few of My servants are truly grateful.*" (34: 13) Indeed, some men these days boast of the scanty knowledge God has given them and the laws of nature He has shown them to claim that "man stands alone"[2] and that he is in no need of God. Sometimes, man's boasting suggests that science is the opposite of the imperceptible and that scientific thinking contrasts with imperceptibility. The two, as he claims, are opposite extremes.

It is useful here to cast a glance at what some scientists have said about *ghayb*, remembering that man has only been given scanty knowledge. We do not need to look at what they say in order to confirm what God has said. A believer does not confirm a divine statement by a human one. We simply quote these scientists in order to put their statements in front of the eyes of those who are always talking about science, as the opposite of *ghayb* or the imperceptible. In this way,

---

2. This is the title of a book by Julian Huxley, an atheist author. – Author's note

they may realize that they need to increase their knowledge in order to live in their world, and not to be left behind. This enables them to realize that the existence of *ghayb* is the only scientific fact that is proven by human experience and scientific achievement.

They would thus realize that, in the light of recent discoveries and experiments, 'scientific' goes hand in hand with 'imperceptible'. What truly contrasts with believing in what lies beyond the reach of human perception is ignorance. It is a sort of ignorance that might have been acceptable in the last three centuries, but it is certainly unacceptable in the twentieth century.

Describing the 'facts' proven by science generally, a contemporary American scientist says:

> Science is tested knowledge, but it is still subject to human vagaries, illusions and inaccuracies. It is legitimate only within the confines of its own areas. It is rigidly restricted to quantitative data for description and prediction. It begins and ends with probability, not certainty. Its results are approximations subject to 'probable error,' especially in measurements and correlations. Its products are tentative and are modified frequently by new data. There is *finality* in scientific inferences. The scientist says: "Up to the present, the facts are thus and so." [3]

This sums up the nature of all scientific conclusions. Since these conclusions are the ones which man arrives at, working with his available means and within his own world which remains limited in comparison to the everlasting existence, these conclusions have a human mark. Like man, they are of limited scope, liable to error and admit of amendment.

Man arrives at his conclusions through experiment and analogy. He begins with a limited experiment and then generalizes his conclusions by comparison, all of which can only lead a scientist to admit a probability, not a certainty. One way of arriving at a certainty is to apply the result of a particular experiment to everything with the same nature, occurring at any time and under any conditions. This is not available to man. The only way to arrive at a certainty and absolute

---

3. Merritt Stanley Congdon, "The Lesson of the Rosebush", a paper in *The Evidence of God in an Expanding Universe*, Ed. J.C. Monsma, G.P. Putnam's Sons, New York, 1958, p. 34.

truism is through divine guidance. What this boils down to is that we have the certainties that God has chosen to give us through His messengers. Beyond these, human knowledge remains within the range of what is probable, not what is certain.

Scientific and Imperceptible

Ghayb exists all around us, beyond the realm of our knowledge which continues to be based on probabilities. Man looks at the universe around him and continues to work out hypotheses and theories about its origin, nature and movement, and about time and place, their inter-relationship with each other and with what takes place in the universe. Man also tries to think about life: its source, origin, nature, continuity, the factors and forces that influence it and how it relates to material existence. He also thinks about himself: how is man different from matter and what distinguishes him from other living things? How did he come to exist on this earth; and how does he behave? What is human intellect, and what are its distinctive features? What happens to him after death? Even if we take the human body: what occurs inside it of chemical interactions at every moment and how do such interactions happen?

All these belong to the realm of *ghayb*. Science stops at its peripheries, unable to penetrate through them even to assign relative probabilities to different hypotheses. We will leave aside for the moment the subjects which scientists do not care to enlist among their priorities and preoccupations, such as the nature of Godhead and the nature of God's other creatures, such as angels and *jinn*, the nature of death, and the hereafter. It is sufficient for our purposes to speak only about that sort of *ghayb* which is closer to us. Here also we find science acknowledging its limited ability. Let us take one or two examples.

The first example concerns the atom which, according to modern science, is the basic unit in the structure of the universe. Yet it is not the smallest unit, because it consists of protons with a positive electric charge, electrons with a negative charge and neutrons with a static charge. With an atomic fusion, electrons are released, but they do not stick to a uniform behaviour in a laboratory. At one time, they move like waves of light, and at another like missiles. We cannot determine their future behaviour in advance. This is subject to the law of probability. The same differences of behaviour apply to a single atom and a group of atoms forming a small unit.

Sir James Jeans, a prominent British physicist says:

> The old science had confidently proclaimed that nature could follow only one road, the road which was mapped out from the beginning of time to its end by the continuous chain of cause and effect; state A was inevitably succeeded by state B. So far the new science has only been able to say that state A may be followed by state B or C or D or by innumerable other states. It can, it is true, say that B is more likely than C, C than D, and so on; it can even specify the relative probabilities of states B, C and D. But, just because it has to speak in terms of probabilities, it cannot predict with certainty which state will follow which; this is a matter which lies on the knees of the gods – whatever gods there be.[4]

This, then, is what is meant by *ghayb*, which relates to God's will into which human knowledge cannot penetrate. All that human knowledge and scientific experiment can reach are only peripheries. Further than that, it cannot go. Professor Jeans gives the example of radiation and how the atoms of the radium are transformed into lead and helium. Throughout this process, they are subject to laws which remain closed to human knowledge:

> It is known that the atoms of radium, and of other radio-active substances, disintegrate into atoms of lead and helium with the mere passage of time, so that a mass of radium continually diminishes in amount, being replaced by lead and helium. The law which governs the rate of diminution is very remarkable. The amount of radium decreases in precisely the same way as a population would if there were no births, and a uniform death-rate which was the same for every individual, *regardless of his age*. Or again, it decreases in the same way as the numbers of a battalion of soldiers who are exposed to absolutely random undirected fire. In brief, old age appears to mean nothing to the individual random atom; it does not die

---

4. James Jeans, *The Mysterious Universe*, Cambridge University Press, 1931, pp. 18–19.

because it has lived its life, but rather because in some way fate knocks at the door.[5]

To take a concrete illustration, suppose that our room contains two thousand atoms of radium. Science cannot say how many of these will survive after a year's time, it can only tell us the relative odds in favour of the number being 2000, 1999, 1998, and so on. Actually the most likely event is that the number will be 1999; the probabilities are in favour of one, and only one, of the 2000 atoms breaking up within the next year.

We do not know in what way this particular atom is selected out of the 2000. We may at first feel tempted to conjecture it will be the atom that gets knocked about most or gets into the hottest places, or what not, in the coming year. Yet this cannot be, for if blows or heat could disintegrate one atom, they could disintegrate the other 1999, and we should be able to expedite the disintegration of radium merely by compressing it or heating it up. Every physicist believes this to be impossible; he rather believes that every year fate knocks at the door of one radium atom in every 2000, and compels it to break up; this is the hypothesis of "spontaneous disintegration" advanced by Rutherford and Soddy in 1903.[6]

What example may illustrate the imperceptible operation of God's will better than the disintegration of atoms, in which neither the atoms nor anyone on earth has any say or choice.

We observe that the scientist who has given us this example is not trying to prove the operation of God's will. Indeed, he tries hard to counter the pressure of the conclusions to which scientific research leads. The truth of *ghayb* in the Islamic sense stares him and all scientists in the face.

The truism of *ghayb*, or the imperceptible, also imposes itself on the rules governing the emergence of life. Professor Russell Charles Artist, Professor of Biology at Frankfurt-on-the-Main, Germany, says:

---

5. This is what this scientist says, but we are concerned only with the scientific conclusion he is describing. His view that the death of radium atoms occurs at random does not concern us. We know that these atoms die by God's will at a specified time, which He has set for a particular purpose. "Every age has a term decreed." (13: 38.) This law stated in the Qur'ān applies to the atom of radium and to every living thing. People die when the time appointed for each one of them is over.

6. James Jeans, op. cit., pp. 18–19.

Many theories have been brought forward in the attempt to derive living cells from inanimate matter. Certain investigators are claiming that life has originated through the protogene, or through an aggregation of large protein molecules, which may leave the impression that at last the gap between the lifeless and the living has been spanned. Actually it must be admitted that all attempts to produce living matter experimentally from inanimate matter have failed utterly.

Furthermore, it is not by direct evidence that the one who denies the existence of God proves to a waiting world that a fortuitous aggregation of atoms and molecules is life, capable of maintaining and directing itself as do the cells described here. Not at all. He accepts this as a *belief*. It is his private interpretation of the facts visible to us all, that an accidental concourse brought the first cell into being. But this is to accept an even greater miracle than to believe that Intelligence called it into being!

I maintain that each of these single cells (each a system so intricate and delicate that its complete functioning has so far escaped our study), and all the trillions of them on this earth, definitely present a justifiable inference – one of Mind, or Intelligence, or Thought, which we call God. Science both admits and accepts this inference.

I believe firmly that there is a God.[7]

We have quoted this example here only to emphasise that the secret of life and its origin belongs to the realm of what God has withheld from our knowledge. All human explanations are only hypothetical. God tells the truth when He says: "*I did not call them to witness at the creation of the heavens and the earth, nor at their own creation.*" (18: 51)

We take a giant stride to look at man and his life. One drop of man's semen contains about 60 million sperms, all of which race to fertilize the female egg. No one knows which of these millions will win the race, because that is part of God's will to which human beings have no access, not even the couple involved. The fertilized egg produces the foetus. The chromosomes in the female egg are all female, while those in the sperm have male and female characteristics. Hence, the

---

7. R.C. Artist, "Trillions of Living Cells Speak Their Message", in *The Evidence of God in an Expanding Universe*, op. cit., p. 124.

sex of the child is determined by the male chromosomes. This is again subject to God's will. No human being can influence it in any way, not even the child's parents: *"God knows what every female bears, and by how much the wombs may fall short [in gestation], and by how much they may increase. With Him every thing has its definite measure. He knows all that lies beyond the reach of human perception and all that anyone may witness. He is the great One, the highly exalted."* (13: 8–9) *"To God alone belongs the dominion over the heavens and the earth. He creates whatever He wills: He bestows the gift of female offspring on whomever He wills, and the gift of male offspring on whomever He wills; or He gives both male and female (to whomever he wills), and causes to be barren whomever He wills: truly, He is all-knowing, infinite in His power."* (42: 49–50) *"He creates you in your mothers' wombs, one act of creation after another, in threefold depths of darkness. Thus is God, your Lord: to Him belongs all dominion; there is no deity other than Him. How, then, can you lose sight of the truth?"* (39: 6)

The above are three examples showing how human knowledge in the twentieth century recognizes *ghayb*, acknowledging what lies beyond the reach of human perception. Those who remain influenced by the attitude of past generations continue to say that *ghayb* and science are contradictory. Science in this twentieth century readily admits that its conclusions are only statements of probabilities. The only certainty is that there is a world that cannot be reached by human perception.

The Imperceptible and the Nature of Islamic Faith

Before we conclude we need to say a few words on the nature of *ghayb* as understood in the Islamic faith.

The Qur'ān, the basic source of Islamic faith, states very clearly that there is a world beyond the reach of human perception and another world that can be perceived. Not everything around man is *ghayb*, and not all forces of the universe are unknown. There are certain laws that operate in the universe without fail. Man can know some of these in as much as this knowledge can be tolerated or is needed by him to fulfil his role on earth.

God has given him the power to know this much of the laws of the universe and to manipulate these forces in accordance with these laws. He will then be able to accomplish his mission and make use of the potentials of the earth and promote life.

Side by side with these constant laws, God's will operates free of all restrictions. It is God's will that sets these laws in operation every time they operate. Theirs is not a purely automatic motion. Although they operate in accordance with the rules God has set for them, it is God's will that operates them. That will is part of *ghayb*, which is not known to anyone with any degree of certainty. The maximum that people can know of it remains within the range of assumptions and probabilities. Science readily admits this.

Millions of processes and interactions occur within man at every given moment, all of which are, to him, imperceptible, while he is also unaware of millions of processes and interactions occurring in the world around him. Indeed, the imperceptible engulfs the past, the present and the future as they relate to man or to the universe. This works side by side with the constant laws of nature some of which are known to man, who benefits by them regularly and scientifically as he works to fulfil his role. Man comes into this world against his will and without any prior knowledge of his arrival here. He departs from it unwillingly and without any knowledge of his departure time. This applies to every living thing. No matter how much man increases his knowledge, this will remain the same. The Islamic mentality is a scientific one and it believes in the imperceptible, because science recognizes the imperceptible and accepts its existence.

Denying it is an exercise of ignorance in spite of all the claims of those who make such a denial. The Islamic mentality combines believing in what lies beyond the reach of human perception, the secrets of which are known only to God, with the belief in the constant laws of nature. Hence, a Muslim benefits by scientific achievements. At the same time, he remains at peace with the fact that there is a complete world which our faculties cannot fathom, and which is known only to God who determines how much He reveals of it to those whom He chooses.

It is animals that cannot comprehend anything beyond the reach of their senses. When a person believes in *ghayb*, he elevates himself to the rank of man who realizes that the universe is far greater and wider than the limited scope of his senses. Such a belief represents a great departure in an individual's perception of the nature of existence, the forces operating in the universe, and the Power which controls all that. This belief has a profound effect on man's own life. A person confining his concerns to the limited field in which his senses operate has a much narrower outlook than that of one who recognizes his place in the spacious universe which is far greater, in time and space, than whatever he can imagine in his limited life. He, therefore, recognizes that beyond all this existence there is a greater Truth, namely, the Supreme Being who gives the universe its existence, whom we cannot see with our eyes and whose nature we cannot comprehend with our minds.

Believing in the imperceptible is the point which signals the elevation of man high above the world of animals. However, those among us who have a materialistic outlook, and these can be found in every age, want man to sink back to the rank of animals where there is no recognition of anything beyond what the senses can perceive. Yet they call this progress, when it is actually a set-back against which God protects the believers. Their distinctive characteristic is that "they believe in what lies beyond the reach of human perception". Praise be to God for His grace.

Those who reject the belief in the imperceptible as contrary to scientific progress also speak of 'historical inevitability', as if the future is certain. As we have seen, scientists today speak of probabilities, and tell us that there are no inevitabilities. Karl Marx used to speak about inevitabilities, but which of his prophecies has been realized? He predicted that England was certain to become communist, because it was the leading nation in industrial progress. As such, it was the leading capitalist country where the labour force suffered most. Communism was adopted instead by countries which were industrially backward, such as Russia, China and a handful of other nations. Likewise, Lenin and Stalin predicted that war was inevitable between the capitalist and the communist blocs. Their successor, Khrushchev, raised instead the banner of peaceful coexistence.

We need not dwell much on these prophecies. They are too trivial to merit any discussion. There is only one certainty, which is that of the world that lies beyond the reach of human perception. Everything else belongs to the world of probabilities. There is also one inevitability, which is that God's will shall come to pass. His will is part of the *ghayb* known only to Him. Nevertheless, there are constant laws of nature which man may study and recognize, and even utilize for his benefit. At the same time, the door remains open for God's will to operate as He chooses. This is the absolute certainty. *"This Qur'ān guides to the path that is straightest."* (17: 9)

Having emphasized that God's knowledge includes everything in the universe, the *sūrah* cites one aspect of this absolute knowledge which relates to man himself, and another aspect which asserts God's absolute power over everything in the universe: *"It is He who causes you to be like the dead at night, and knows what you do in the daytime. He raises you again to life each day in order that a term set by Him be fulfilled. In the end, to Him you must return; and then He will tell you all that you have done."* (Verse 60) In a few simple words, this verse explains that all human life is in God's hands, within His knowledge and subject to His will. This includes people's sleep and awakening, death and resurrection, reckoning and judgement. The description follows the inimitable method of the Qur'ān in portraying everything vividly, alive. Thus it is able to touch people's hearts with every image drawn and every movement described.

"It is He who causes you to be like the dead at night." (Verse 60) It is then a form of death that occurs to people when they are overtaken by sleep. Their senses do not operate, their minds stop functioning and their consciousness stops. Human beings cannot yet discover the secret of what happens to them when they sleep, although they know its effects. This is, then, one of the numerous forms of *ghayb* that engulfs human life. As they sleep, human beings lose all their power, including their consciousness. They are in God's hands, as they are certainly all the time. He alone can bring them back to life. How weak we are in comparison to Him.

"He knows what you do in the daytime." (Verse 60) Whatever good or evil we do, and whatever our hands take or leave, is known to God. None of our movements is left out.

"He raises you again to life each day in order that a term set by Him be fulfilled." (Verse 60) It is He who awakens you in the day from your slumber so that you complete the term He has appointed for each one of you. This covers the status of human beings within the range set by God. His will is inescapable.

"In the end, to Him you must return." (Verse 60) You return to Him just like sheep coming back to their shepherd at the end of the day. *"Then He will tell you all that you have done."* (Verse 60) This is when the record that includes everything is laid open. Absolute justice is then administered to all.

Although this is a short verse composed of a few words, it nonetheless includes a long sequence of scenes and images, statements of fact and wide-ranging connotations. Who other than God can produce such a style? What is miraculous if this is not a miracle? Yet those who reject the faith choose not to see it in its true colour. They demand instead a physical miracle despite the fact that this would inevitably be followed by God's punishment, should they continue to reject Him afterwards.

When All Efforts Are of No Avail

An important feature of Godhead is that which combines absolute power over all creation and a constant, alert watch. That which combines the predetermination of the life span of every individual, and our inescapable destiny with the final reckoning which is both prompt and unfailing. All this belongs to the realm of those imperceptibles which encompass human life.

> He alone holds sway over His servants. He sends forth guardians to watch over you until, when death approaches any one of you, Our messengers cause him to die. They leave no part of their duty unfulfilled. They are then brought back to God, their true Lord Supreme. Indeed, His alone is all judgement; and He is most swift in reckoning. (Verses 61–2)

"*He alone holds sway over His servants.*" (Verse 61) All power belongs to Him, and all creatures are subject to His power. In front of Him, they are powerless. In front of the Almighty, they are no more than submissive slaves. This is the truth confirmed by the realities of human life. Despite all the freedom of action they are given and the degree of knowledge they are allowed, and the ability instilled in them to fulfil the task assigned to them, their every breath is allowed them in accordance with a specific measure; their every action is subject to God's power. Such is the basic law of human life which they cannot violate, although this law may manifest itself each time in accordance with a specific divine will. This even applies to every individual breath or action.

"*He sends forth guardians to watch over you.*" (Verse 61) The nature of those guardians is not mentioned here. Elsewhere in the Qur'ān, we are told that they are angels who record everything we do. The point here is to impart a feeling that there is a close supervision over everyone. No single person is left all alone, not even for a moment. Watchers count and record every word we say, every action we do and every movement we make. When we imagine this, we are at the height of our alertness.

"*Until, when death approaches any one of you, Our messengers cause him to die. They leave no part of their duty unfulfilled.*" (Verse 61) The same atmosphere is generated again by a different image. Every soul is left until a particular moment which always remains unknown to it, although it is specified by God. It can be neither advanced nor delayed. Every soul has an angel close at hand watching over it, counting its every breath, mindful of his task and never neglecting anything. He is a guardian angel. At the appointed moment, when the human soul is fully preoccupied with its affairs the guardian completes his task and the messenger delivers his message. As we think of this, we are bound to shiver as we feel that we are totally in the hands of a destiny which remains unknown to us. We realize that we could meet death at any moment.

"*They are then brought back to God, their true Lord Supreme.*" (Verse 62) He is indeed our true Lord, while all other deities are false. It is He who has originated us and given us our lives, keeping us all the time under His unfailing supervision. He then gathers us back to Him for final judgement: "*Indeed, His alone is all judgement; and He is most swift in reckoning.*" (Verse 62) It is He alone who reckons and judges. Both His judgement and reward are readily delivered. The reference to His speed here is meant to make us feel that we are not given even a short period of grace before we are held to account.

This sort of image which is outlined by the basic Islamic concept of life, death, resurrection, reckoning and reward, is sufficient to ensure that a Muslim acknowledges without hesitation God's authority to rule over people's lives on earth. The reckoning, reward and judgement in the hereafter are based on what people actually do in this life. People cannot be held to account for what they do here in this world unless they are given a law which details for them what is lawful and what is forbidden. This explains the need for a single authority over both this life and the life to come.

When a law other than that of God's is enforced in this world, how can people be judged in the hereafter? According to the law they implemented here? Or according to the divine law which they did not implement?

Human beings must realize that God will hold them to account on the basis of His own law. They must be aware that if they do not conduct their lives and establish their relationships as well as their worship, according to God's law, then this will be the first thing for which they have to account. They will be questioned why have they not chosen God as their Lord on earth, preferring instead to claim other deities? This means that they will have to account for denying God or associating partners with Him. This they do by following God's law in matters of worship but adopting a different law in their social, political and economic systems as well as their interactions, dealings and relationships. We know that God forgives whomever He pleases, but only that which is short of associating partners with Him.

The Only Saviour

They are then called upon to listen to the voice of their very nature. Indeed, human nature recognizes the truth of Godhead and turns to God alone when it faces dangers and difficulties. The *sūrah* paints for them their nature when they are in distress, and describes how they go against its appeals when they go through a period of ease and comfort.

This is all portrayed in a short, fast, clear scene, producing a profound effect. They are reminded that great distress is not limited to the Day of Resurrection when they have to face their reckoning. They, indeed, go through periods of great distress in the deep darkness of land and sea. At such moments, they turn only to God, recognizing that only He can save them. Still they revert to their erring ways in periods of ease: "*Say: Who is it that saves you from the dark dangers of the land and sea, when you call out to Him humbly and in secret: If He will but save us from this peril, we will most certainly be grateful? Say: God alone saves you from these and from every distress; and still you associate partners with Him.*" (Verses 63–4) At times, it is sufficient to visualize danger and remember distress to soften people's hearts and help them restrain their wild desires. People can then remember their feelings of weakness as they remember God's grace when He alleviates their distress.

"*Say: Who is it that saves you from the dark dangers of land and sea, when you call out to Him humbly and in secret: 'If He will but save us from this peril, we will most certainly be grateful?'*" (Verse 63) Such an experience is well known to everyone who has gone through a period of distress or witnessed and observed what people in distress feel. There are indeed many types of darkness involving perils of different types on land and at sea. It is not necessary that the night should spread its mantle for darkness to prevail: losing one's way and danger are two types of darkness and what awaits people on land and at sea is screened from them by darkness. Wherever people find themselves in the midst of darkness they realize that they must turn only to God, praying to Him in earnest or appealing to Him in private. At such a moment, human nature sheds its burden and comes face to face with the truth implanted deep inside it, that is the truth of God's oneness. Therefore, it turns to God alone, addressing Him without any partners, because it recognizes then the absurdity of idolatry and polytheism and the non-existence of any partners with God. At such a moment, those who are in distress are quick to make solemn pledges: "*If He will but save us from this peril, we will most certainly be grateful.*" (Verse 63)

God commands His Messenger to remind them of the truth: "*Say: God alone saves you from these and from every distress.*" (Verse 64) There is no one to respond to them other than He, and no one else to remove their distress. But the Prophet is also commanded to remind them of their singularly queer attitude: "*Still, you associate partners with Him.*" (Verse 64)

Diverse Ways to Expound Revelations

The *sūrah* reminds them of God's power which could smite them after they have been saved. It is not like a momentary distress which is not replaced once it is over. They are reminded of God's unlimited ability to bring about suffering that they cannot endure: "*Say: It is He alone who has the power to let loose upon you suffering from above you and from beneath your feet, or to divide you into disputing groups, causing the one to suffer at the hands of the other. See how We make plain Our revelations so that they may understand.*" (Verse 65)

To visualize suffering coming from above or from beneath in overwhelming force has a much more powerful effect on the human mind than to visualize it coming from the right or the left. Anyone may imagine that he can resist the latter type coming sideways, but the type of suffering which is brought down from above or which overwhelms people from beneath must be irresistible. In its inspiring style, the *sūrah* adds this forceful effect as it states in plain terms that God is able to overwhelm people with suffering from any direction and in any method He chooses. It then adds another type of suffering which is slow and long lasting. This type does not destroy them all in a flash, but lingers with them so that they experience it day after day and night after night: "*[He has the power] to divide you into disputing groups, causing the one to suffer at the hands of the other.*" (Verse 65)

This is an image of long-lasting suffering which they bring upon themselves and make each other experience. God allows them to split into hostile groups which can hardly be distinguished, one from the other. There is no clarity of separating lines. These groups are in a state of constant hostility, argument and dispute. Therefore, they bring suffering upon one another.

In many periods of its history, humanity has experienced this type of suffering, whenever it deviated from the divine method, allowing people, in their weakness and ignorance, to conduct human life in accordance with their desires. Thus we find people groping in the dark as they devise their own systems, laws and values for human life. This is followed by one group trying to impose these systems, laws and values on others. The result is that one group may resist and those who have power try to crush their resistance. The desires, ambitions and concepts held by different groups would thus be involved in a bitter conflict, with one group made to suffer the tyranny of another. Thus, mutual hatred becomes widespread. When you analyze this state of affairs, you are bound to conclude that it is caused by the fact that humanity does not apply the same standard given them by their Supreme Lord to whom all human beings must submit. While people may not find it easy to recognise the authority of others, none of them feels himself humiliated when he submits to God alone.

The most terrible situation in human life is that in which some human beings claim for themselves the rights of Godhead and try to impose these in practice on the rest of mankind. This is the sort of confused situation which splits people into hostile groups: on the surface, they may appear to be one community, but in reality some of them are subservient to others. One group wields power, using it in a tyrannical way because they are not restrained by God's law. The others are embittered and nurse their grudges. Both groups are made to suffer the might and tyranny of each other. They do not form a single nation although they may not be easily distinguished, one from the other. When we look at mankind today, we realize that the whole world is engulfed by this slow, long-lasting suffering.

This leads us to consider the attitude of the advocates of Islam. They must form a community which moves swiftly to distinguish itself from the state of *jāhiliyyah* surrounding it from all directions. *Jāhiliyyah* refers to every situation, regime, community and society which does not implement God's law or which does not recognize that Godhead and sovereignty belong to God alone. The advocates of Islam must abandon any *jāhiliyyah* society, fully aware that they are completely distinguished as a community from those in their society who prefer to maintain ways and implement laws, systems and values different from those bestowed from on high.

Only if the advocates of Islam distinguish themselves in this way can they spare themselves the suffering with which God threatens those who reject His call: "*[He has the power] to divide you into disputing groups, causing the one to suffer at the hands of the other.*" (Verse 65) This mental distinction of the advocates of Islam applies by necessity to faith, feelings and code of living. It must continue until Islam is established in a geographical area and is an authority that extends protection to all advocates of Islam. Those advocates of the divine faith must feel themselves to be the Muslim community, and that all others who refuse to accept their method belong to the world of *jāhiliyyah*.

They should make their attitude clear to all people, telling them that their dispute with them is over faith and their code of living. They then pray to God to judge between them and their people in accordance with the truth. Unless the advocates of Islam make this distinction, the threat made here by God applies to them. They remain a group in a society which is not clearly distinguished from others. They are then made to endure the slow, long-lasting suffering.

Such total distinction may require the advocates of Islam to make sacrifices and endure hardships. But these will never be anywhere near what happens to them if their attitude is not distinguished from the rest of the community, and if they are lost in the un-Islamic society surrounding them.

When we review the history of the call to the divine faith pioneered by God's messengers, we are certain that God will not grant victory to his messengers and their followers until the advocates of the divine faith have distinguished themselves from the rest of their people over the basic issue of submission to God alone. They must also implement the code of living He has chosen for His servants. Such a split over faith and a practical constitution is always the starting point.

We must realize that the divine method has only a single way to follow. It cannot choose today a path other than that followed by God's messengers (peace be upon them all) throughout history: "*See how We make plain Our revelations so that they may understand.*" (Verse 65) We pray to God to include us among those who understand as He expounds to them His revelations.

9

Point of Separation

Your people have rejected this [i.e. the Qur'ān], although it is the very truth. Say: I am not responsible for you. (66)

وَكَذَّبَ بِهِۦ قَوْمُكَ وَهُوَ ٱلْحَقُّ قُل لَّسْتُ عَلَيْكُم بِوَكِيلٍ ﴿٦٦﴾

Every piece of news has a time set for its fulfilment, as you will come to know. (67)

لِّكُلِّ نَبَإٍ مُّسْتَقَرٌّ وَسَوْفَ تَعْلَمُونَ ﴿٦٧﴾

Whenever you see those who indulge in vain discourse about Our revelations, turn away from them until they talk of other things. Should Satan ever cause you to forget, do not, once you remember, stay with such wrong-doing folk. (68)

وَإِذَا رَأَيْتَ ٱلَّذِينَ يَخُوضُونَ فِىٓ ءَايَٰتِنَا فَأَعْرِضْ عَنْهُمْ حَتَّىٰ يَخُوضُوا۟ فِى حَدِيثٍ غَيْرِهِۦ وَإِمَّا يُنسِيَنَّكَ ٱلشَّيْطَٰنُ فَلَا تَقْعُدْ بَعْدَ ٱلذِّكْرَىٰ مَعَ ٱلْقَوْمِ ٱلظَّٰلِمِينَ ﴿٦٨﴾

Those who are God-fearing are in no way accountable for them. It is their duty, however, to admonish them, so that they may become God-fearing. (69)

وَمَا عَلَى ٱلَّذِينَ يَتَّقُونَ مِنْ حِسَابِهِم مِّن شَىْءٍ وَلَٰكِن ذِكْرَىٰ لَعَلَّهُمْ يَتَّقُونَ ﴿٦٩﴾

Stay away from those who, beguiled by the life of this world, take their religion for a pastime and a sport; but remind them with this (Qur'ān), lest every human being should be held in pledge for whatever he has done, when he shall have none to protect him from God, and none to intercede for him. If he were to offer any conceivable ransom, it shall not be accepted from him. Those are the ones who are held in pledge for what they have done. Scalding water shall they drink, and grievous suffering awaits them because they were unbelievers. (70)

وَذَرِ ٱلَّذِينَ ٱتَّخَذُوا۟ دِينَهُمْ لَعِبًا وَلَهْوًا وَغَرَّتْهُمُ ٱلْحَيَوٰةُ ٱلدُّنْيَا وَذَكِّرْ بِهِۦٓ أَن تُبْسَلَ نَفْسٌۢ بِمَا كَسَبَتْ لَيْسَ لَهَا مِن دُونِ ٱللَّهِ وَلِىٌّ وَلَا شَفِيعٌ وَإِن تَعْدِلْ كُلَّ عَدْلٍ لَّا يُؤْخَذْ مِنْهَآ أُو۟لَـٰٓئِكَ ٱلَّذِينَ أُبْسِلُوا۟ بِمَا كَسَبُوا۟ لَهُمْ شَرَابٌ مِّنْ حَمِيمٍ وَعَذَابٌ أَلِيمٌۢ بِمَا كَانُوا۟ يَكْفُرُونَ ﴿٧٠﴾

Overview

This passage re-endorses the issues elaborated upon in Chapter 8. It was the Prophet's own people who rejected his message although it was the very truth. Hence, all relations between him and his people were severed. He is instructed to declare to them that he could not be responsible for their erring ways. He had to leave them to their inevitable destiny. He is further instructed not to sit with them when they engage in idle talk about religion, taking it as a sport and fun, showing no due respect to it. His instructions are very clear: he has to remind and warn them, convey his message to them and explain to them what they will have to face on the Day of Judgement. However, he must realize that although they are his people, they belong to two different nations. No considerations of nationality, race, clan or family are of much value in Islam. It is faith that causes relationships to be established or severed. When the bond of faith is established all other bonds may establish their roots. When the bond of faith is severed, however, no other ties can be established.

Consistent Attitude

Your people have rejected this [i.e. the Qur'ān], although it is the very truth. Say: I am not responsible for you. (Verse 66)

The passage starts with an address to God's Messenger (peace be upon him) which gives him and all believers who follow him complete confidence and reassurance that his message is the very truth. His people may persist in rejecting it and describing it as lies. This should not, however, affect him in any way. His people are not to arbitrate on this. The final word belongs to God. He states that this message is the truth. Hence, its rejection by any group of people is of no consequence.

God then instructs His Messenger to dissociate himself from his people, making his attitude clear to them. He is also to inform them that he has no say over their fate. Neither is he responsible for their behaviour, nor can he guide their hearts. That is not up to him. Once he has conveyed to them his message, he has discharged his duty and he has to leave them to their inevitable destiny. Everything comes to its appointed end, and they will come to know the result of their efforts: "*Every piece of news has a time set for its fulfilment, as you will come to know.*" (Verse 67) Although this is a very general statement, providing no details, it is nonetheless intimidating.

The believers have that reassurance imparted to them by their knowledge that what they follow is the very truth and that evil is doomed to failure, even though it may appear very powerful. They are confident that God will destroy those who deny His message, at the time He has appointed for them. They realise that what God has said will undoubtedly come true, and that every living thing is certain to meet its destiny. The advocates of Islam who face a similar rejection from their own people and who are made to feel as though they are strangers among their own families and who, as a consequence, endure much hardship and endless affliction need such confidence and reassurance and this the Qur'ān gives them in plenty.

The Prophet is further commanded not to sit with the unbelievers, even for the sake of explaining his message or reminding them of God and their need to believe in Him, especially if he finds them engaged in idle talk about divine revelations. If they talk about religion in any way other than with respect and seriousness, or make it, by word or deed, an object of fun, he must remove himself from their company.

If he were to do otherwise, his action could be construed as an implicit acceptance of what they do. Alternatively, it may be taken as a carelessness with the faith, when a Muslim should place his religion at the top of what he cherishes. Should he forget all this and sit with them, he must immediately upon remembering the correct approach rise up and leave their company: *"Whenever you see those who indulge in vain discourse about Our revelations, turn away from them until they talk of other things. Should Satan ever cause you to forget, do not, once you remember, stay with such wrongdoing folk."* (Verse 68)

This order to the Prophet, which could be interpreted as applying to all Muslims, was issued in Makkah where the Prophet's task was limited to the advocacy of his faith. At that time, the Prophet was not ordered to fight anyone. Indeed, the approach was to avoid all physical conflict with the unbelievers wherever that was possible. Nevertheless, the Prophet was ordered not to sit with them if they spoke disrespectfully of God's revelations. Should he forget and sit with them, then, he should leave them immediately upon remembrance. All Muslims, according to some reports, were ordered likewise. The term, 'wrongdoing folk', used here refers to the unbelievers, as it is frequently used in the Qur'ān.

When Islam established its state in Madinah, the Prophet's attitude towards the unbelievers was totally different. The Prophet could resort to every type of struggle, even war, in order to ensure that submission to God prevailed. No one was to be allowed to engage in idle talk or vain discourse concerning God's revelations.

The *sūrah* then asserts the complete separation between believers and unbelievers, in the same way as this was established between the Prophet (peace be upon him) and those who associate partners with God. Responsibilities are different and so are destinies: *"Those who are God-fearing are in no way accountable for them. It is their duty, however, to admonish them, so that they may become God-fearing"*. This means that there is simply no common responsibility between the God-fearing and the unbelievers. They are two separate communities or nations, although they may belong to the same race and the same nationality. These considerations are of little consequence in God's view. The God-fearing are a nation on their own, and the unbelievers are a totally different nation. Those who fear God share nothing of the burden of the wrongdoers and they are accountable for none of their deeds. They only try to remind them of their duty towards God in the hope that they follow suit and join their camp. If they continue to reject the faith based on God's oneness, then there is nothing to share between the two camps.

This is indeed, the attitude of Islam as stated clearly by God. Anyone may choose a different stance, but he must know first that by so doing he abandons the divine faith altogether.

When Support is in Short Supply

The *sūrah* continues to reiterate the complete distinction between the two communities, outlining the limits within which dealings and interactions may be conducted.

> *Stay away from those who, beguiled by the life of this world, take their religion for a pastime and a sport; but remind them with this (Qur'ān), lest every human being should be held in pledge for whatever he has done, when he shall have none to protect him from God, and none to intercede for him. If he were to offer any conceivable ransom, it shall not be accepted from him. Those are the ones who are held in pledge for what they have done. Scalding water shall they drink, and grievous suffering awaits them because they were unbelievers.* (Verse 70)

This verse re-emphasises the distinction between the two communities, making several important points.

1. The Prophet, and indeed every Muslim, is commanded to ignore, by word and deed, those who treat religion as a pastime and as idle play. This description applies to anyone who does not give his faith respect by making it the basis of all aspects of his life: worship, beliefs, practices, moral values, and a legal code. It also applies to anyone who describes the principles and legislations of this faith in derogatory terms, such as those who ridicule the concept of *ghayb*, or believing in the world beyond the reach of human perception, which is an essential part of the Islamic faith. The same is the case with people who talk disrespectfully of *zakāt* which is one of the pillars upon which the structure of Islam is built, or describe morality and chastity as the values of rural and feudal societies, and those who speak disapprovingly of the Islamic rules of marriage, or describe as fetters the sort of guarantees God has given to Muslim women to help them

maintain their chastity. It applies above all to those who deny God's absolute sovereignty and His authority to legislate for human life in political, social, economic and legal fields, claiming that human beings may legislate for themselves without reference to God's law. All those are included as ones who, *'take their religion for a pastime and a sport'*. Every Muslim is commanded to stay away from them except to remind them of their duty towards God. They are among the wrongdoers and unbelievers described in this verse as ones who are *'held in pledge for what they have done'*. They are threatened with having to drink boiling water and having to endure painful suffering for their disbelief.

2. The Prophet, and indeed every Muslim is further instructed to remind these people of God and warn them against being held in pledge and destroyed in consequence of what they have done. They are to be reminded that they cannot enjoy any support against God, and no one can intercede with Him on their behalf. No ransom will be accepted from them. The Qur'ānic style here is exceedingly beautiful and effective: *"Remind them with this (Qur'ān), lest every human being should be held in pledge for whatever he has done, when he shall have none to protect him from God, and none to intercede for him. If he were to offer any conceivable ransom, it shall not be accepted from him."* (Verse 70) Every single soul will have to account for itself, without support, and when no ransom is of any use. As for those who have taken their religion in jest and been beguiled by the life of this world, they are already held in pledge for what they have done. Their doom is sealed: *"Those are the ones who are held in pledge for what they have done. Scalding water shall they drink, and grievous suffering awaits them because they were unbelievers."* The scalding water, which boils in their throats and stomachs, and the painful suffering which ensues are a fitting recompense for their ridicule of faith.

3. Speaking of the unbelievers, God describes them as *'Those who take their religion for a pastime and a sport'*. Is it truly *their* religion? This description fits perfectly those who declared their acceptance of Islam and then treated their religion as an object of ridicule. There were some people like that to whom the appellation 'hypocrites' was given, but they were in Madinah. Can the same statement apply to unbelievers who did not embrace Islam in

the first place? Well, Islam is the religion of all mankind, including those who do not believe in it, since it is the only faith God accepts from human beings ever since the revelation of the message preached by the Prophet Muḥammad, the last of all messengers. Hence, anyone who rejects it actually rejects his own faith. Hence, it is significant that the possessive pronoun is used in the beginning of this verse: *"Stay away from those who take their religion for a pastime and a sport."* It is most probably, and God knows best, a reference to the fact that Islam is a religion for all mankind. Whoever makes fun of it, even though he may be an idolater, actually makes fun of his own religion.

We probably still need to explain who are meant by the term 'idolaters'. They are those who claim that any being has a share of God's attributes. This may take the form of believing in the existence of deities other than God, or offering worship and performing rituals to anyone other than God, or acknowledging the authority to legislate to anyone besides God. Needless to say, the term idolaters also includes those who claim for themselves any of these, however strongly they may profess to be Muslims. We should then be clear about who belongs to our faith.

4. The last point concerns the limits within which it is permissible to sit with the wrongdoers, or idolaters, and those who take religion as an object of fun and ridicule. As we have already mentioned, this is permissible only when it is done to remind them of divine faith and to warn them against disobeying God. It can have no other purpose. Once we realize that they engage in idle talk about God's revelations or treat them as an object of ridicule we must leave their company immediately. In commenting on this verse, al-Qurṭubī explains the rulings mentioned in the Qur'ān: "This verse provides an answer in God's Book to anyone who claims that high standing Imams and their followers may have social contacts with wrongdoers, or may try to protect themselves by pretending to accept their views as correct."[1]

Our view is that the Qur'ānic verse allows mixing with the wrongdoers in order to admonish and warn them, and to correct their

---

1. Al-Qurṭubī, *Al-Jāmi' li-Aḥkām al-Qur'ān*, Vol. 7, p. 12.

erring views. Mixing with them and keeping quiet about what they say and do in order to protect ourselves is unacceptable, because it imparts an impression of accepting falsehood and rejecting the truth. In addition, it deceives people and degrades the divine faith and its advocates. Such a situation is totally unacceptable.

Al-Qurṭubī quotes a few statements by other scholars: "Ibn Khuwayz Mindād says: 'Anyone who engages in vain discourse about God's revelations should be boycotted, whether he is a believer or an unbeliever. Our colleagues also disallow entry into the land ruled by the enemy or entry into their churches and temples, as well as mixing socially with unbelievers and those who invent deviant practices and claim them to be Islamic. It is also not permissible to be sympathetic to them or to argue with them. One of these inventors once said to Abū 'Imrān al-Nakha'ī: "Let me say one word to you". Al-Nakha'ī turned away, saying: "Not even half a word". The same attitude was reported of Ayyūb al-Sakhtiyānī. Al-Fuḍayl ibn 'Iyāḍ says: "If one loves a person who practises deviant inventions, God will cause his good actions to be wasted and will cause his conviction to be shaky. A person who gives his daughter in marriage to a deviant inventor is unkind to her, and one who mixes with such a person has no share of wisdom. If God knows a person to truly dislike deviant inventors, I hope He will forgive him his sins." The Prophet is quoted by his wife, 'Ā'ishah as saying: He who respects a person practising deviant inventions actually helps to destroy Islam'.[2]

All these statements speak about a person who practises deviant inventions, although he continues to believe in the divine faith. Needless to say, he is in a much better position than the person who claims for himself the attributes of Godhead by promulgating laws that are in conflict with divine law, or one who acknowledges his authority to do so. Such claims indicate total disbelief or polytheism. Early scholars did not have to deal with such situations after the establishment of Islam. No one made any such claims while saying at the same time that he was Muslim. This was unknown until the French occupation of Egypt under Napoleon when the majority of people turned their backs on their faith. Obviously, the statements of past scholars do not apply to the present situation which exceeds by far what they have described and the rulings they made concerning it.

---

2. Al-Qurṭubī, ibid., p. 133.

10

Sovereign of All the Worlds

Say: Shall we invoke, instead of God, something that can neither benefit nor harm us, and shall we turn back on our heels after God has given us guidance, like one whom the satans have lured away in the land, blunders along perplexed. Yet he has companions who call out to him, "Come to us for guidance." Say: In truth, God's guidance is the only guidance. We are commanded to surrender ourselves to the Lord of all the worlds. (71)

قُلْ أَنَدْعُواْ مِن دُونِ ٱللَّهِ مَا لَا يَنفَعُنَا وَلَا يَضُرُّنَا وَنُرَدُّ عَلَىٰٓ أَعْقَابِنَا بَعْدَ إِذْ هَدَىٰنَا ٱللَّهُ كَٱلَّذِي ٱسْتَهْوَتْهُ ٱلشَّيَٰطِينُ فِي ٱلْأَرْضِ حَيْرَانَ لَهُۥٓ أَصْحَٰبٌ يَدْعُونَهُۥٓ إِلَى ٱلْهُدَى ٱئْتِنَا قُلْ إِنَّ هُدَى ٱللَّهِ هُوَ ٱلْهُدَىٰ وَأُمِرْنَا لِنُسْلِمَ لِرَبِّ ٱلْعَٰلَمِينَ ۝

And to attend regularly to prayers and to fear Him. It is to Him you all shall be gathered. (72)

وَأَنْ أَقِيمُواْ ٱلصَّلَوٰةَ وَٱتَّقُوهُ وَهُوَ ٱلَّذِىٓ إِلَيْهِ تُحْشَرُونَ ۝

He it is who has created the heavens and the earth in truth. Whenever He says, "Be," it shall be. His word is the truth. All sovereignty shall be His on the Day when the trumpet is blown. He knows all that is beyond the reach of human perception, and all that is manifest. He alone is truly wise, all-aware. (73)

وَهُوَ ٱلَّذِى خَلَقَ ٱلسَّمَٰوَٰتِ وَٱلْأَرْضَ بِٱلْحَقِّ وَيَوْمَ يَقُولُ كُنْ فَيَكُونُ قَوْلُهُ ٱلْحَقُّ وَلَهُ ٱلْمُلْكُ يَوْمَ يُنفَخُ فِي ٱلصُّورِ عَٰلِمُ ٱلْغَيْبِ وَٱلشَّهَٰدَةِ وَهُوَ ٱلْحَكِيمُ ٱلْخَبِيرُ ۝

Overview

This short passage of three verses is characterized by a powerful rhythm. It begins with a statement of the essential characteristics of Godhead and a denouncement of those who turn away from guidance to sink back into disbelief and their associating partners with God. It portrays a person who is totally lost, bewildered, not knowing where to turn, and this emphasizes the meaning of turning away from faith after having believed in God. The passage then emphasizes that God's guidance is the only true guidance. It ends on a high note as it speaks of God's total sovereignty and His complete authority over all creation. On the Day of Resurrection, even the most hardened atheists cannot entertain any doubt about His complete sovereignty, and then to Him all creation returns.

Bewilderment After Guidance

Say: Shall we invoke, instead of God, something that can neither benefit nor harm us, and shall we turn back on our heels after God has given us guidance, like one whom the satans have lured away in the land, blunders along perplexed. Yet he has companions who call out to him, "Come to us for guidance." Say: In truth, God's guidance is the only guidance. We are commanded to surrender ourselves to the Lord of all the worlds.' (Verse 71)

The passage starts with the instruction, '*Say*'. This is used often in this *sūrah* to formulate a recognition that all authority belongs to God and that the Prophet Muḥammad (peace be upon him) is the one chosen to convey a message and warn people against its rejection. As it imparts a feeling of the seriousness of the message, we are also made to understand that the Prophet does no more than what he is bidden. He implements his instructions with complete dedication.

"*Say: Shall we invoke, instead of God, something that can neither benefit nor harm us?*" (Verse 71) This is an order to the Prophet to tell the unbelievers that what they do is to invoke and appeal to beings other than God, allowing those beings to lead them where they please, when they cannot actually benefit or harm them in any way. This is true, whether those beings whom they invoke are idols of stone, trees, spirits, angels, devils or other human beings. They only have one quality in common, namely, that they can bring no benefit and cause no harm. Every movement in the universe occurs by God's will. Hence, what God does not sanction cannot take place. Nothing happens except what He approves of. Thus, the Prophet is instructed to denounce every type of worship, submission or appeal to anyone other than God and to make it clear that every action of this sort is absolutely absurd.

This instruction to the Prophet might have been given by way of reply to the suggestions made by the unbelievers to the Prophet for working out a compromise whereby he would join them in invoking their deities in return for their joining him in worshipping his Lord. On the other hand, it might have been an outright denunciation of the practices of the idolaters and a declaration by the Prophet and the believers that their way could have no meeting point with that followed by the unbelievers. Either way, the final result is the same. We have a strong denunciation of this absurdity which no human intellect can accept once it is freed of inherited traditions and prevailing values and is allowed to judge objectively for itself.

To emphasise the association of partners with God and to strengthen its denunciation, the *sūrah* portrays these beliefs in contrast to the concept of God's oneness and submission to Him alone. It is to this concept that He has guided the believers: "*Say: Shall we invoke, instead of God, something that can neither benefit nor harm us, and shall we turn back on our heels after God has given us guidance?*" (Verse 71) To revert to idolatry is, then, a turning back on one's heels in a retrogressive movement after one has achieved considerable progress.

This is followed by a vividly realistic and inspiring scene: "*Like one whom the satans have lured away in the land, blunders along perplexed. Yet he has companions who call out to him, 'Come to us for guidance.'*" (Verse 71) The scene is full of life. It describes the loss and bewilderment that inevitably overwhelms any person who reverts to idolatry after having believed in God's oneness. He finds himself torn between believing in the Supreme Lord who has no partners, and numerous deities who are powerless. He is confused, unable to determine where to turn for guidance. He is lost, bewildered. How miserable is his lot for being lured away, perplexed and for committing blunders. The word 'lure' is highly descriptive. The person we see in this scene does not follow the direction into which he is lured in order to establish a well-defined objective, even though it leads to error. He has, on the other side, friends and companions who have followed proper guidance, and who beckon him to come over to them. Between the lure of the devils and the beckoning of his guided companions this person continues to blunder along, unable to determine where to go and which side to join. His psychological suffering looms large, so much so that we actually feel it as it is described.

Every time I read these verses I can see this scene in front of me and feel all the confusion, hesitation and bewilderment with which it overflows. But that was merely a mental exercise. More recently, I have known real-life cases that answer this description very accurately. All the confusion was there to see and all the suffering to feel. These were examples of people who had known the faith and experienced what it meant to believe, but who then turned back on their heels in order to worship false deities, under the pressure of fear or temptation. No matter how strong or otherwise their faith was, their turning back subjected them to this utter misery. As I saw these people, the full import of these verses became much clearer to me.

The scene is followed by a clear statement outlining the right way which all people should follow: "*Say: In truth, God's guidance is the only guidance. We are commanded to surrender ourselves to the Lord of all the worlds, and to attend regularly to prayers and to fear Him.*" (Verses 71–2) This decisive statement fits perfectly with the psychological situation described here. When someone fully appreciates the type of bewilderment the Qur'anic verse describes and the suffering of anyone who so experiences such bewilderment, he is ready to receive with reassurance such a decisive statement and accept it without hesitation. "*Say: In truth, God's guidance is the only guidance.*" (Verse 71) This is an absolute certainty. Whenever people abandon this guidance and replace it with man-made concepts, regimes, laws and values they find themselves lost in absolute bewilderment.

Guidance Followed by Complete Submission

God has given man the ability to recognize and appreciate some of the laws of nature, its forces and potentials so that he may be able to use these in discharging the task assigned to him of building the earth and promoting human life and civilization. But man has not been granted by God the ability to get to the core of the absolute truths of the universe or to fathom the world which lies beyond the reach of his perceptions. This world includes the workings of his own mind and soul, and even the workings of his own organs and the causes which enable his body to function properly, according to a definite system and a particular fashion.

Hence, man is in need of divine guidance concerning everything that relates to his own nature, including faith, morals, values and standards, systems and laws. Only with such guidance can man regulate his life as it should be regulated. Whenever man adopts God's guidance, he finds himself following the right track, because '*God's guidance is the only guidance*'. Whenever man abandons God's guidance completely or deviates from it partially in order to replace it with something else, he loses his way. This is due to the fact that whatever is in conflict with God's guidance represents error and loss. There is simply no third cause: "*What is in conflict with the truth other than error.*" (10: 32)

Humanity continues to endure the terrible effects of going astray, for these are inevitable when mankind moves away from God's guidance. Indeed, this is the one historical inevitability which is certain to take place because, unlike those inevitabilities claimed by the advocates of different philosophies, this one is determined by God. Anyone who wishes to look closely at the misery to which people expose themselves when they deviate from God's guidance does not need to look far. That misery is everywhere for us to see. Those who are endowed with insight and intelligence continue to raise their voices to warn against it.

The Qur'ānic verse states clearly that human beings must submit themselves to God alone, offer worship to Him and continue to fear Him alone: "*We are commanded to surrender ourselves to the Lord of all the worlds, and to attend regularly to our prayers and to fear Him.*" (Verses 71–2)

The instructions given to the Prophet Muḥammad (peace be upon him) are such that he has to declare in absolute clarity that God's guidance is the only guidance. As such, we are commanded to submit to the Lord of all the universe, because to Him alone all the worlds submit. Why should man be the only exception out of all creation when everything in the universe submits to God's absolute Lordship? The reference made here to the fact that God is 'the Lord of all the worlds' comes at the right time. It emphasizes an undeniable fact that all the worlds, whether known or unknown to us, submit to the laws God has set in operation and cannot break away from them. Biologically, man is also subject to the laws of nature. What he needs to do, then, is to submit also in the area in which he has been given a choice: to follow guidance or to sink in error. When man chooses to submit to God in the same way as he does biologically, all his affairs will be set aright, because harmony will be established between his constitution and his action, between his body and his soul, between his present life and his life to come. The declaration made by God's Messenger and his followers that they have complied with the commandment to surrender themselves to God is enough to inspire anyone to open his mind and make himself ready to respond to the divine instruction.

After the declaration of surrender to the Lord of all the worlds is given, some of the duties required of man are given in terms of acts of worship and attitudes: *"Attend regularly to prayers and to fear Him."* (Verse 72) The most essential thing, then, is complete submission to God and the acknowledgement of His Lordship over the universe. The offering of worship and the moulding of conscious attitudes follow from this, because these cannot be done properly unless they are based on the solid foundation of man's submission to God.

The final note in this passage brings together a number of essential components of the concept of faith, namely, resurrection, creation, wisdom and awareness of all that takes place in the universe. All these are attributes so that our concept of God is properly formulated: *"It is to Him you all shall be gathered. He it is who has created the heavens and the earth in truth. Whenever He says, 'Be,' it shall be. His word is the truth. All sovereignty shall be His on the day when the trumpet is blown. He knows all that is beyond the reach of human perception, and all that is manifest. He alone is truly wise, all-aware."* (Verses 72–3)

Since all creation will be gathered before the Lord of all the worlds, submission to Him alone is absolutely essential. It is only wise that people should consider their future in the light of the fact that they will inevitably be gathered to God. They better submit to Him, as all the worlds and all creation do, before they are brought to account in front of Him. We see how the fact of resurrection is used here to convince people that it is in their best interests to submit to God right at the beginning. Especially since they have no option but to submit to Him in the end.

"He it is who has created the heavens and the earth in truth." (Verse 73) This is another undeniable fact mentioned here to influence people into choosing the right course of submission to God. If they do, they only surrender to the One who has created the heavens and the earth. Needless to say, the one who creates is the one who owns, controls and determines the destiny of the heavens and the earth and all that lives in or on them. Moreover, this creation has been made *'in truth'*. This is to refuse all the conjectural theories advanced by philosophers, particularly Plato and the Utopians, which suggest that this physical world of ours is a delusion and has no real substance. The Qur'ānic statement goes further than refuting such theories. It makes it clear that the truth is an essential element in the foundation, as well as the destiny of this universe. The truth which people seek and to which they turn is supported by the truth which is essential in the nature of existence. Thus, it becomes an overpowering force which sweeps all falsehood away. Indeed, falsehood cannot establish any roots in the structure of the universe. It is only *'like an evil tree torn out of the earth and shorn of all its roots'*. Falsehood is like swelling foam surfacing over running water: it has no substance. This is again a profoundly powerful statement of fact.

A believer feels that the truth which he advocates and feels within himself is directly linked to the greater truth manifested in the universe, and this, in turn, is directly linked to the absolute truth of God. In another *sūrah*, we read this Qur'ānic statement: *"Indeed, God is the ultimate truth."* (22: 62) Equipped with this realization a believer views falsehood as no more than a large bubble which is certain to explode. Falsehood may indeed manifest itself as large and powerful and able to cause believers much harm. The fact remains, however, that it has no root to support its structure. It soon disappears and becomes forgotten as if it never existed.

When an unbeliever contemplates this truth, he is bound to experience a feeling of awe. He may give up his falsehood and accept God's guidance.

"Whenever He says, 'Be,' it shall be." (Verse 73) His power dominates all, and His will is unrestrained. He creates, changes and replaces as He pleases. This fact is mentioned here for a dual purpose: it helps the proper formulation of the correct concept of faith in the believers' hearts and it inspires those who are called upon to submit to God, the Lord of all the worlds, the Creator of everything,

the One who says to anything He wishes to create, "Be", and it is instantly there.

"*His word is the truth.*" (Verse 73) This fact applies to God's word, "*Be*", which causes creation. This His commandment that all creation should submit to Him alone, this His word providing legislation for mankind to implement, and this His word which tells us about the past, present and future, the origin of creation, resurrection, reckoning and reward. In all this, His word is the truth. Hence, those who associate with Him partners that can cause no benefit or harm, those who follow the bidding of anyone other than Him, or who adopt any philosophy other than that of the divine faith, or who implement any legislation other than His code are advised to surrender themselves to Him alone.

"*All sovereignty shall be His on the Day when the trumpet is blown.*" (Verse 73) On the Day of Resurrection, the trumpet is sounded in a way that no human being has thus far heard. It is part of what God has kept to Himself. The nature of that trumpet and how people respond to it remain unknown to anyone other than God. The reports available to us suggest that it is a horn-like trumpet, made of light. It is blown by an angel. As the dead in their graves hear it, they immediately rise up. Indeed, this is the second blow given on that trumpet. The first one causes all creatures in the heavens and on earth to be stunned, with the exception of those God chooses to exempt. This is mentioned in verse 68 of *Sūrah* 39: "*The trumpet will be sounded, and all creatures that are in the heavens and all that are on earth will fall down senseless, unless they be such as God wills to exempt. And then it will be sounded again, and they all stand up and will begin to see.*" These descriptions of the trumpet and the effects of its blowing make it clear to us that it is something different from what human beings have seen or heard on this earth or what they visualize. It belongs to the world that lies beyond the reach of human perception. We know about it only by virtue of what God has chosen to inform us of its shape and effect. We confine ourselves to this information so as not to indulge in speculation which lacks solid foundation.

On that day when the trumpet is sounded, even the rejecters and the blind will begin to see and realize that all sovereignty belongs to God alone. No one has any power other than Him. No will can operate other than His. Hence, those who in this life refuse to submit to Him willingly are well advised to change their attitude before they have to submit to His absolute power on the day when the trumpet is blown.

"*He knows all that is beyond the reach of human perception, and all that is manifest.*" (Verse 73) His knowledge is perfect, absolute. It includes everything that is kept away from us as well as that which we see in the universe. Nothing of people's affairs and no part of their lives can be hidden from Him. Again, they will follow good counsel if they surrender themselves to Him, worship Him and be God-fearing. This fact is mentioned here for its own sake and is used as something with which to influence those who reject the faith.

"*He alone is truly wise, all-aware.*" (Verse 73) He conducts all the affairs of the universe which He has created, as well as the affairs of the creatures over whom He has absolute power in this life and in the life to come. All that He does is characterized by wisdom and is based on unbounded knowledge. When they submit to His law, they will enjoy the happiness that is imparted to their lives by His wisdom. They will bring themselves out of their loss and bewilderment to enjoy His guidance and learn happiness from His wisdom.

11

Guidance for All Nations

Thus Abraham said to his father Āzar: "Do you take idols for gods? I see that you and your people have obviously gone astray." (74)

﷽ وَإِذْ قَالَ إِبْرَٰهِيمُ لِأَبِيهِ ءَازَرَ أَتَتَّخِذُ أَصْنَامًا ءَالِهَةً إِنِّي أَرَىٰكَ وَقَوْمَكَ فِي ضَلَٰلٍ مُّبِينٍ ۝

Thus did we give Abraham an insight into [God's] mighty dominion over the heavens and the earth; so that he may become a firm believer. (75)

وَكَذَٰلِكَ نُرِي إِبْرَٰهِيمَ مَلَكُوتَ ٱلسَّمَٰوَٰتِ وَٱلْأَرْضِ وَلِيَكُونَ مِنَ ٱلْمُوقِنِينَ ۝

When the night drew its shadow over him, he saw a star; and he exclaimed: "This is my Lord!" But when it set, he said: "I do not love things that set." (76)

فَلَمَّا جَنَّ عَلَيْهِ ٱلَّيْلُ رَءَا كَوْكَبًا قَالَ هَٰذَا رَبِّي فَلَمَّا أَفَلَ قَالَ لَا أُحِبُّ ٱلْآفِلِينَ ۝

Then when he beheld the rising moon, he said: "This is my Lord!" But when it set, he said: "If my Lord does not guide me, I will most certainly be one of those who go astray." (77)

فَلَمَّا رَءَا ٱلْقَمَرَ بَازِغًا قَالَ هَٰذَا رَبِّي فَلَمَّا أَفَلَ قَالَ لَئِن لَّمْ يَهْدِنِي رَبِّي لَأَكُونَنَّ مِنَ ٱلْقَوْمِ ٱلضَّآلِّينَ ۝

Then when he beheld the sun rising, he said: "This is my Lord! This is the greatest of all!" But when it also set, he said: "My people, I disown all that you associate with God." (78)

إِنِّي وَجَّهْتُ وَجْهِيَ لِلَّذِي فَطَرَ السَّمَٰوَٰتِ وَالْأَرْضَ حَنِيفًا وَمَا أَنَا مِنَ الْمُشْرِكِينَ ۝

"I have turned my face with pure and complete devotion to Him who brought the heavens and the earth into being. I am not one of those who associate partners with God." (79)

His people argued with him. He said: "Do you argue with me about God, when it is He who has given me guidance? I do not fear those beings you associate with Him, [for no evil can befall me] unless my Lord so wills. My Lord embraces all things within His knowledge; will you not, then, reflect?" (80)

"And why should I fear anything you worship side by side with Him, when you are not afraid of associating with God partners without His ever giving you any warrant? Which of the two parties has a better right to feel secure, if you happen to know?" (81)

"Those who believe and do not taint their faith with wrong-doing are the ones who will feel secure, as they follow the right path." (82)

This was Our argument with which We furnished Abraham against his people. We raise whom We will, degree after degree. Your Lord is Wise, All-Knowing. (83)

وَتِلْكَ حُجَّتُنَآ ءَاتَيْنَـٰهَآ إِبْرَٰهِيمَ عَلَىٰ قَوْمِهِۦ نَرْفَعُ دَرَجَـٰتٍ مَّن نَّشَآءُ إِنَّ رَبَّكَ حَكِيمٌ عَلِيمٌ ﴿٨٣﴾

We bestowed on him Isaac and Jacob, and We guided each of them as We had guided Noah before them. Among his offspring were [the Prophets] David, Solomon, Job, Joseph, Moses and Aaron. Thus do We reward those who do good. (84)

وَوَهَبْنَا لَهُۥٓ إِسْحَـٰقَ وَيَعْقُوبَ كُلًّا هَدَيْنَا وَنُوحًا هَدَيْنَا مِن قَبْلُ وَمِن ذُرِّيَّتِهِۦ دَاوُۥدَ وَسُلَيْمَـٰنَ وَأَيُّوبَ وَيُوسُفَ وَمُوسَىٰ وَهَـٰرُونَ وَكَذَٰلِكَ نَجْزِى ٱلْمُحْسِنِينَ ﴿٨٤﴾

And Zachariah, John, Jesus and Elijah; who were all righteous. (85)

وَزَكَرِيَّا وَيَحْيَىٰ وَعِيسَىٰ وَإِلْيَاسَ كُلٌّ مِّنَ ٱلصَّـٰلِحِينَ ﴿٨٥﴾

And Ishmael, Elisha, Jonah and Lot. Every one of them did We favour above all people. (86)

وَإِسْمَـٰعِيلَ وَٱلْيَسَعَ وَيُونُسَ وَلُوطًا وَكُلًّا فَضَّلْنَا عَلَى ٱلْعَـٰلَمِينَ ﴿٨٦﴾

And [We exalted likewise] some of their forefathers, their offspring and their brethren. We chose them and guided them to a straight path. (87)

وَمِنْ ءَابَآئِهِمْ وَذُرِّيَّـٰتِهِمْ وَإِخْوَٰنِهِمْ وَٱجْتَبَيْنَـٰهُمْ وَهَدَيْنَـٰهُمْ إِلَىٰ صِرَٰطٍ مُّسْتَقِيمٍ ﴿٨٧﴾

Such is God's guidance; He bestows it on whomever He wills of His servants. Had they associated partners with Him, in vain would certainly have been all that they ever did. (88)

ذَٰلِكَ هُدَى ٱللَّهِ يَهْدِى بِهِۦ مَن يَشَآءُ مِنْ عِبَادِهِۦ وَلَوْ أَشْرَكُوا۟ لَحَبِطَ عَنْهُم مَّا كَانُوا۟ يَعْمَلُونَ ﴿٨٨﴾

On these did We bestow revelation, wisdom and prophethood. If this generation were to deny this truth, We have certainly entrusted it to others who will never deny it. (89)

أُوْلَـٰٓئِكَ ٱلَّذِينَ ءَاتَيْنَـٰهُمُ ٱلْكِتَـٰبَ وَٱلْحُكْمَ وَٱلنُّبُوَّةَ فَإِن يَكْفُرْ بِهَا هَـٰٓؤُلَاءِ فَقَدْ وَكَّلْنَا بِهَا قَوْمًا لَّيْسُوا۟ بِهَا بِكَـٰفِرِينَ ﴿٨٩﴾

Those are the ones whom God has guided. Follow, then, their guidance, [and] say: "No reward do I ask of you for this. It is but an admonition to all mankind." (90)

أُوْلَـٰٓئِكَ ٱلَّذِينَ هَدَى ٱللَّهُ فَبِهُدَىٰهُمُ ٱقْتَدِهْ قُل لَّآ أَسْـَٔلُكُمْ عَلَيْهِ أَجْرًا إِنْ هُوَ إِلَّا ذِكْرَىٰ لِلْعَـٰلَمِينَ ﴿٩٠﴾

No true understanding of God have they when they say: "God has never revealed anything to any human being." Say: Who, then, revealed the Book which Moses brought to people as a light and a guidance? You transcribe it on sheets to show around, while you suppress much. You have been taught [by it] what neither you nor your forefathers had ever known. Say: God, and leave them to their play and foolish chatter. (91)

وَمَا قَدَرُوا۟ ٱللَّهَ حَقَّ قَدْرِهِۦٓ إِذْ قَالُوا۟ مَآ أَنزَلَ ٱللَّهُ عَلَىٰ بَشَرٍ مِّن شَىْءٍ قُلْ مَنْ أَنزَلَ ٱلْكِتَـٰبَ ٱلَّذِى جَآءَ بِهِۦ مُوسَىٰ نُورًا وَهُدًى لِّلنَّاسِ تَجْعَلُونَهُۥ قَرَاطِيسَ تُبْدُونَهَا وَتُخْفُونَ كَثِيرًا وَعُلِّمْتُم مَّا لَمْ تَعْلَمُوٓا۟ أَنتُمْ وَلَآ ءَابَآؤُكُمْ قُلِ ٱللَّهُ ثُمَّ ذَرْهُمْ فِى خَوْضِهِمْ يَلْعَبُونَ ﴿٩١﴾

This is a blessed book which We have revealed, confirming what came before it, that you may warn the Mother City and all who dwell around it. Those who believe in the life to come do believe in it, and they are ever-mindful of their prayers. (92)

وَهَـٰذَا كِتَـٰبٌ أَنزَلْنَـٰهُ مُبَارَكٌ مُّصَدِّقُ ٱلَّذِى بَيْنَ يَدَيْهِ وَلِتُنذِرَ أُمَّ ٱلْقُرَىٰ وَمَنْ حَوْلَهَا وَٱلَّذِينَ يُؤْمِنُونَ بِٱلْءَاخِرَةِ يُؤْمِنُونَ بِهِۦ وَهُمْ عَلَىٰ صَلَاتِهِمْ يُحَافِظُونَ ﴿٩٢﴾

Who could be more wicked than one who invents a falsehood about God, or says: "This has been revealed to me," when nothing has been revealed to him? Or one who says, "I can reveal the like of what God has revealed"? If you could but see the wrongdoers when they are in the throes of death and the angels stretch out their hands [and say]: "Give up your souls!" Today you shall be rewarded with a humiliating punishment for having attributed to God something that is untrue and, in your arrogance, scorned His revelations. (93)

وَمَنْ أَظْلَمُ مِمَّنِ ٱفْتَرَىٰ عَلَى ٱللَّهِ كَذِبًا أَوْ قَالَ أُوحِىَ إِلَىَّ وَلَمْ يُوحَ إِلَيْهِ شَىْءٌ وَمَن قَالَ سَأُنزِلُ مِثْلَ مَا أَنزَلَ ٱللَّهُ وَلَوْ تَرَىٰ إِذِ ٱلظَّٰلِمُونَ فِى غَمَرَٰتِ ٱلْمَوْتِ وَٱلْمَلَٰٓئِكَةُ بَاسِطُوٓا۟ أَيْدِيهِمْ أَخْرِجُوٓا۟ أَنفُسَكُمُ ٱلْيَوْمَ تُجْزَوْنَ عَذَابَ ٱلْهُونِ بِمَا كُنتُمْ تَقُولُونَ عَلَى ٱللَّهِ غَيْرَ ٱلْحَقِّ وَكُنتُمْ عَنْ ءَايَٰتِهِ تَسْتَكْبِرُونَ ﴿٩٣﴾

And now, indeed, you have come to Us individually, just as We created you in the first instance; and you have left behind all that We conferred on you. Nor do We see with you those intercessors of yours whom you had claimed to be partners in your affairs. Broken are the ties which bound you, and that which you have been asserting has failed you. (94)

وَلَقَدْ جِئْتُمُونَا فُرَٰدَىٰ كَمَا خَلَقْنَٰكُمْ أَوَّلَ مَرَّةٍ وَتَرَكْتُم مَّا خَوَّلْنَٰكُمْ وَرَآءَ ظُهُورِكُمْ وَمَا نَرَىٰ مَعَكُمْ شُفَعَآءَكُمُ ٱلَّذِينَ زَعَمْتُمْ أَنَّهُمْ فِيكُمْ شُرَكَٰٓؤُا۟ لَقَد تَّقَطَّعَ بَيْنَكُمْ وَضَلَّ عَنكُم مَّا كُنتُمْ تَزْعُمُونَ ﴿٩٤﴾

Overview

Here begins a very long passage which stretches across twenty-one verses but which constitutes a single unit, tackling one subject, which is indeed the main theme running throughout the whole *surah*. As has already been explained, the *surah* establishes this theme on a solid foundation, strengthened by a comprehensive explanation of the nature

217

of Godhead, servitude to God and the links between them. The approach adopted here, however, is different from the one we encountered earlier in the *sūrah*. Here, we find a story followed by comments, coupled with a number of inspiring elements. One element used here that deserves particular mention is an elaborate scene depicting our approaching deaths.

This long passage provides a vivid picture of the long procession of the faithful, beginning with the Prophet Noah and travelling down the ages until the time of the Prophet Muḥammad (peace be upon them both). Before this procession is shown, the nature of Godhead is outlined as instinctively perceived by a saintly servant of God, the Prophet Abraham (peace be upon him). We have a splendid scene of unperverted human nature seeking the true Lord, whose presence it clearly senses, although at the surface it comes face to face with distortions and misconceptions. It continues its search until it can formulate a proper and correct concept that corresponds to the true image it has deep down of its true Lord. From within it, it has strong proof of that concept which is more firmly founded than what is superficially apparent. This is outlined in the argument Abraham advances to refute his people's theories, after he has been reassured that his new concept is the true one.

The *sūrah* continues with the long procession of the faithful, led by the noble prophets and messengers. As we look attentively at this procession, all concepts of polytheism and all the arguments of those who reject the truth are shown to be worthless. All the faithful across all ages are seen as constituting one nation and one community, the later generations of which follow the same guidance received by earlier generations. Thus, considerations of time, place, race, nationality, lineage or colour are seen to be of no value whatsoever. The tie that links all the faithful is the single faith preached by the noble prophets (peace be upon them all).

This is a splendid picture followed by a powerful commentary making it clear that whoever turns his back on God's guidance shall find that all his deeds avail him nothing. People are required to follow the divine guidance outlined by the prophets who seek no wages for teaching their people. They only fulfil the mission entrusted to them by God.

This is followed by a denunciation of those who claim that God neither sent messengers nor vouchsafed revelations to any human being.

It denounces those who do not hold God in the position He deserves, because they claim, in effect, that He abandons people to their own devices. These are they who rely on their finite reason, influenced as it is by their desires and shortcomings, to come up with codes and concepts to implement in their lives. Needless to say, this does not fit with God's Lordship, knowledge, wisdom, justice and grace. Indeed, all these attributes of Godhead require that He sends messengers to His servants and that He gives some of them revelations so that they guide mankind to their Lord and keep their nature pure from any influences that blind them to the truth. An example of this is the book revealed to Moses. Another example is the Qur'ān which endorses all past divine revelations.

As this long passage draws to a close, it denounces those who indulge in false fabrications, claiming that they receive revelations when they do not, or who claim that they are able to produce revelations similar to those God has given to His messengers. Some of the opponents of Islam have indeed made such claims: from receiving inspiration and revelation from God to claiming full prophethood.

The passage concludes with a picture of the unbelievers facing the moment of truth as death approaches them. *"And now, indeed, you have come to Us individually, just as We created you in the first instance; and you have left behind all that We conferred on you. Nor do We see with you those intercessors of yours whom you had claimed to be partners in your affairs. Broken are the ties which bound you, and that which you have been asserting has failed you."* (Verse 94) It is a scene that sends fear into people's hearts and shows the unbelievers' humiliation as part of their punishment for rejecting the truth and concocting false fabrications.

An Instinctive Rejection of Idolatry

Thus Abraham said to his father Āzar: "Do you take idols for gods? I see that you and your people have obviously gone astray." Thus did we give Abraham an insight into [God's] mighty dominion over the heavens and the earth; so that he may become a firm believer. When the night drew its shadow over him, he saw a star; and he exclaimed: "This is my Lord!" But when it set, he said: "I do not love things that set." Then when he beheld the rising moon,

219

he said: "This is my Lord!" But when it set, he said: "If my Lord does not guide me, I will most certainly be one of those who go astray." Then when he beheld the sun rising, he said: "This is my Lord! This is the greatest of all!" But when it also set, he said: "My people, I disown all that you associate with God. I have turned my face with pure and complete devotion to Him who brought the heavens and the earth into being. I am not one of those who associate partners with God." (Verses 74–9)

This is a splendid scene which the *surah* uses to portray healthy human nature initially rejecting all ignorant concepts of idolatry. To undistorted nature, idolatry is no more than an unfounded and totally unacceptable superstition. Rejecting it without hesitation, human nature begins to seek its true Lord with vigorous activity. It has an innate feeling of the Lord, although it has no well-formulated concept of Him. Hence, it looks up to anything that presents itself as a possible manifestation of God. Soon it discovers that such an object cannot be the true Lord. It does not correspond to what is deeply implanted within human nature of the reality and nature of God and His attributes.

It then experiences the truth revealing itself and shining within. This gives man his greatest joy. He declares his unshakeable belief as he realizes the complete and total correspondence between his innate picture of the Lord and the reality he has consciously discovered. All this is shown in the splendid scene of Abraham and his search for his Lord. In a few short verses, the great experience of Abraham is outlined. As faith establishes its firm roots within him, he declares his belief, fearing no opposition or objection. He is not prepared to make any compromise with his father, family, clan or nation. Every believer must, then, adopt the same attitude as Abraham who faced up to his father and his people with undeniable firmness: "*Thus Abraham said to his father Āzar: 'Do you take idols for gods? I see that you and your people have obviously gone astray.'*" (Verse 74)

This is the instinctive argument of nature voiced by Abraham who had not yet consciously recognized his true Lord. When human nature is free of deviation and perversion, it simply cannot accept that those idols worshipped by Abraham's people were gods. It should be remembered here that the ancient Chaldeans, who lived in Iraq at that time, used to worship idols as well as the stars and planets. To

Abraham, the deity to be worshipped, to whom people turn for help
in all situations, and who has created all living things, cannot be an
idol made of stone or wood. It is obvious that those idols cannot
create, listen, respond or provide sustenance. Hence, they are not
worth worshipping. Indeed, they cannot be considered as deities even
if they are given the limited role of being intermediaries between the
Lord of the universe and human beings. Such a set-up and practices
are, then, all erroneous. Abraham (peace be upon him) recognized
this instinctively at the first instant. Indeed, he provides a complete
example of human nature as created by God: pure, and free of
perversion. It confronts error and deviation with clarity and
decisiveness, stating the whole truth, since the matter is one of faith:
"*Do you take idols for gods? I see that you and your people have obviously
gone astray.*" (Verse 74)

Abraham, the best natured of all people, forbearing, tolerant and
fine-mannered, as we gather from his frequent descriptions in the
Qur'ān, makes a clear and strong declaration to his father. It would
have been expected that his attitude towards his father would be rather
different but the question here is one of faith. This supersedes all ties
of parenthood and the duties of a son towards his father. It simply
overrules the dictates of parenthood and generosity. We should not
forget that Abraham is the example that God orders Muslims to follow.
This story is related here in the Qur'ān so that it should be followed
by Muslims for all generations to come.

As he demonstrated such a fine, pure nature dedicated to the truth,
Abraham deserved that God reveal to him some of the secrets of the
universe and some of the pointers to the truth that He has placed
everywhere around us. "*Thus did we give Abraham an insight into
[God's] mighty dominion over the heavens and the earth; so that he may
become a firm believer.*" (Verse 75)

Nature's Way to the Truth

When Abraham demonstrated that he was not prepared to pervert
his nature or becloud his vision, and that he was determined to reject
falsehood and follow the truth, God showed him some aspects of the
kingdom of the heavens and the earth. He let him into some of the
secrets of the universe, so that he could reflect on some of the great
signs of the truth with which the world around us abounds. Thus, he

would be able to make the correct linkage between his pure nature and the pointers to the right faith and guidance. This would then enable him to move from the stage of rejecting falsehood to the stage of conscious recognition of God, the true Lord.

This is indeed the proper line to be followed by human nature. It should demonstrate a consciousness unaffected by false ideas and an open mind which studies the miraculous working of God's power. Such contemplation is certain to benefit by the lessons of what God has created in the universe and receive proper guidance from God as a result.

Let us follow this very interesting journey with Abraham's pure nature. Easy and comfortable as it may appear, it is certainly a tough and demanding journey starting from the point of instinctive belief and ending with a conscious acceptance of faith. It is the sort of faith that initiates action, defining a task to fulfil and a law to implement. God does not abandon human beings or require them to achieve that degree of faith using their reason alone. He shows it to them, clearly outlined in the messages with which He sends His messengers. Thus, He makes the message, not human nature or intellect, the basis of their accountability and the determinant of their destiny. In this, His perfect knowledge of human nature works in conjunction with His justice and His grace.

We should remember that Abraham was God's chosen friend, the father of the nation that includes all people who surrender themselves totally to God Almighty.

"*When the night drew its shadow over him, he saw a star; and he exclaimed: 'This is my Lord!' But when it set, he said: 'I do not love things that set.'*" (Verse 76) The *sūrah* portrays here an image of Abraham as he begins to have serious doubts and then rejects the idols worshipped by his community. He was fully preoccupied with the question of faith. As we read the Qur'ānic expression, '*When the night drew its shadow over him*', we see the whole image rising before our eyes. It is as if the night covers Abraham alone, isolating him from all other beings, so that he remains alone with his thoughts and the issue that preoccupies him: "*When the night drew its shadow over him, he saw a star; and he exclaimed: 'This is my Lord!'*" (Verse 76)

As we have already said, his people worshipped the stars and planets as well as idols. As he despaired of recognizing his true Lord among those idols, he might have hoped to find Him among the other things which his people worshipped. He was certainly aware of the sort of beliefs his people entertained particularly the worship of stars. Nor was this the first time he saw a star. On this night, however, the star spoke to him in an entirely new fashion. The inspiration of the star was in line with Abraham's preoccupations: "*He said: 'This is my Lord.'*" Its shining light and its elevation made the star more plausible to be the Lord than the idols worshipped on the ground. But he soon realized the error in his thinking: "*But when it set, he said: 'I do not love things that set.'*" (Verse 76) The star, then, sets and can no longer be seen by ordinary creatures. Who, then, will take care of all these creatures when it sets?

Certainly the star cannot be the Lord, because the Lord is always present. This is the simple logic of nature. It cares nothing for theoretical hypotheses or questions of logic. It is simple and decisive. It expresses the instinctive, natural reaction: "*I do not love things that set.*" (Verse 76) The relationship that exists between nature and the Lord is one of love, and Abraham's nature has no love for things that set. The deity that nature loves does not set at any time.

"*Then when he beheld the rising moon, he said: 'This is my Lord!' But when it set, he said: 'If my Lord does not guide me, I will most certainly be one of those who go astray.'*" (Verse 77) This is a very similar experience, as if Abraham has never seen the moon before, and does not know that his people worshipped the moon. To him on that particular night, it was something new: "*He said: 'This is my Lord.'*" Its light spreads all over the place: it is a beautiful light singling it out in the sky. Nevertheless, it sets, while the Lord, as Abraham knows Him instinctively through his unadulterated nature, does not set.

At this moment, Abraham realizes that he needs help from his true Lord, the existence of whom he feels in the depths of his soul. He loves his Lord although he has not yet recognized Him in his consciousness. Therefore, he feels he will remain astray unless his Lord helps him with His guidance and shows him the way. Hence, when he sees the moon setting, he says: "*If my Lord does not guide me, I will most certainly be one of those who go astray.*" (Verse 77)

> *Then when he beheld the sun rising, he said: "This is my Lord! This is the greatest of all!" But when it also set, he said: "My people, I disown all that you associate with God. I have turned my face with*

pure and complete devotion to Him who brought the heavens and the earth into being. I am not one of those who associate partners with God.' (Verses 78–9)

This is Abraham's third experience with stars, and it is with the sun, the largest, brightest and hottest of visible stars. The sun rises and sets every day, but now it appears to Abraham as something brand new. He is searching for the Lord whom he can recognize with certainty and who can give him reassurance. After his long search, he feels that now he can make a decision: *"This is my Lord! This is the greatest of all!"* (Verse 78) But the sun also sets.

At this moment, everything becomes clear. Contact is made between pure nature and God, the true Lord. Light shines within his searching heart and spreads over the visible world and over man's reason and consciousness. At this moment, Abraham finds his true Lord and realizes that there is complete identity between what he feels deep in his heart and his new, clear concept. He realizes that his Lord is not a bright planet, a rising moon or a shining sun. He is not one to be seen with the human eye or felt with other physical senses. He is the one recognized by man's heart, nature, reason and consciousness all alike. He is the one seen everywhere in the universe, the creator of everything eyes behold, senses feel and intellects recognize.

At this point Abraham realizes that there can be no meeting point between him and his people while they continue to worship their false deities. With complete clarity, he dissociates himself from all that they worship and from their methods and philosophies. It should be remembered that they were not atheists who denied God completely, but were rather used to associating those false deities as partners with God. Abraham, on the other hand, turned to God alone. Thus, when the sun set, he said: *"My people, I disown all that you associate with God. I have turned my face with pure and complete devotion to Him who brought the heavens and the earth into being. I am not one of those who associate partners with God."* (Verses 78–9)

This is a firm and decisive decision taken by Abraham who now turns with complete devotion to God, entertaining no hesitation or doubt. How can he do otherwise, when the identity is complete between what he feels deep in his heart and the conclusions he has arrived at after such a long and meaningful search?

A Stronger Claim to Security

Once again we see with our eyes the splendid scene of faith when it is clearly manifest, with established roots and shining over man's whole being. Man is thus reassured, at ease with himself and with the universe around him. The full splendour of this scene comes to its climax in the verses that follow.

We witness the case of the Prophet Abraham as he realizes with all his consciousness the truth of his Lord. He has complete peace of mind as he feels that God has taken him by the hand to guide him to the straight path. His people come to him with their arguments about his declared belief in God's oneness and to warn him against what their idols and deities might inflict on him: "*His people argued with him. He said: 'Do you argue with me about God, when it is He who has given me guidance? I do not fear those beings you associate with Him, [for no evil can befall me] unless my Lord so wills. My Lord embraces all things within His knowledge; will you not, then, reflect? And why should I fear anything you worship side by side with Him, when you are not afraid of associating with God partners without His ever giving you any warrant? Which of the two parties has a better right to feel secure, if you happen to know?'*" (Verses 80–1)

When human nature departs from the right path, it goes astray, and then it is automatically led further astray. The angle between its line and the right path becomes wider and wider, to make any return far more difficult. Abraham's people used to worship idols, planets and stars. They could not appreciate the great divide that separated them from Abraham after he had been helped by God and guided aright. In spite of the clear flimsiness of their concepts and beliefs, they came to him with their arguments.

Abraham, who could feel God within himself and in the universe around him, confronted them with decisiveness and reassurance: "*Do you argue with me about God, when it is He who has given me guidance?*" (Verse 80) He tells them that God Himself has helped him, opened his mind and shown him the right guidance. He has seen Him clearly, consciously in everything He has placed in the universe. How can they, then, argue with him about something he feels deep down within himself? The fact that God has guided him provides all the evidence and argument he needs.

"*I do not fear those beings you associate with Him.*" (Verse 80) This is both natural and logical. Having known God, what and whom would any person fear, when every power other than God's is of no consequence? However, with his strong faith, Abraham does not make any final statement without attaching it to God's free-will and perfect knowledge, "*[for no evil can befall me] unless my Lord so wills. My Lord embraces all things within His knowledge.*" (Verse 80) He, thus, entrusts himself to God's care, reassured of His protection. He declares that he fears nothing whatsoever from their deities, since he knows that nothing befalls him except by God's will and with God's knowledge.

"*And why should I fear anything you worship side by side with Him, when you are not afraid of associating with God partners without His ever giving you any warrant? Which of the two parties has a better right to feel secure, if you happen to know?*" (Verse 81) This is the logic of a believer who has a true understanding of the truth to be found in the universe. If anyone should entertain fear, that person is certainly not Abraham who believes in God and follows His guidance. How could he fear deities that are powerless, no matter what they are, even though they may wear the mask of tyrannical powers? After all, compared to God's power, theirs is insignificant. How could Abraham, then, fear such powerless deities while his people do not entertain fear as a result of having associated partners with God whom He has not sanctioned? Which party has a stronger claim to security: those who believe in God's oneness and reject the notion of Him having any partners, or a person who ascribes divinity to anything which has no power whatsoever? He tells them that they should answer him if they have any knowledge or true understanding.

But the answer is given by God who passes His verdict with absolute clarity: "*Those who believe and do not taint their faith with wrongdoing are the ones who will feel secure, as they follow the right path.*" (Verse 82) Those who believe and submit themselves purely to God, associating with Him no partners whom they obey or worship, are the ones who deserve security and receive guidance.

"*This was Our argument with which We furnished Abraham against his people. We raise whom We will, degree after degree.*" (Verse 83) This was the argument with which God inspired Abraham to refute all his people's arguments. He showed him how petty and worthless were their concepts and claims that their deities could harm him. It is clear that Abraham's people did not deny God's existence altogether, and did not deny that He had the ultimate power and authority in the universe. They only associated those partners with Him. Abraham confronted them with the fact that a person who submits himself totally to God does not fear anyone besides Him. On the other hand, a person who ascribes divinity to beings other than God is the one to experience fear. Thus, their arguments collapsed while Abraham's argument was triumphant. Abraham was thus raised above his people in rank, faith, argument and position. God thus raises in rank whomever He wills, in accordance with His knowledge and wisdom: "*Your Lord is Wise, All-Knowing.*" (Verse 83)

Before we move on to the next verses in this passage, let us reflect on the sort of life led by the Prophet's Companions as they were addressed by the Qur'ān. They certainly contemplated its meaning, appreciated its teachings and requirements, abiding by its instructions and committing themselves not to deviate from them. We cannot but admire their serious commitment which moulded their generation of believers in a way that enabled them to achieve, by God's will, and in a very short period of time, heights that were superior to anything humanity had ever known.

A report quoted by al-Ṭabarī on the authority of 'Abdullāh ibn Mas'ūd, says: "When this verse was revealed, speaking of '*Those who believe and do not taint their faith with wrongdoing*', the Prophet's Companions felt down-hearted and wondered: who of us does not wrong himself? God's Messenger told them: 'It is not as you think. This is a reference to what Luqmān said to his son: *Do not associate partners with God; for, to associate partners with God is serious wrongdoing.*'"[1]

Al-Ṭabarī also reports that after 'Umar ibn al-Khaṭṭāb once read, '*Those who believe and do not taint their faith with wrongdoing*', he was much alarmed. He went to Ubayy ibn Ka'b and asked him: "Who is safe after the revelation of this verse? Who of us does not wrong himself? Ubayy said: "May God forgive you. Have you not heard what God says: *To associate partners with God is indeed serious wrongdoing.* (31: 13) This verse means that true believers do not taint their faith by the association of partners with God".[2]

---

1. Al-Ṭabarī, *Jāmi' al-Bayān*, Dar al-Fikr, Beirut, 1984, Vol. 7, p. 255.
2. Ibid., Vol. 7, p. 257.

Al-Ṭabarī also reports that a man said to Salmān, one of the Prophet's Companions: "I am very scared by a Qur'ānic verse I read, saying: *Those who believe and do not taint their faith with wrongdoing.*" Salmān said: "It refers to associating partners with God." The man said: "To hear this from you is far more welcome to me than having twice as much of everything I own."[3]

These incidents give us an idea of how those people treated the Qur'ān very seriously. They took it as direct commandments which must be implemented and as a final judgement that could not be contested. If they felt that their limited ability could not cope with what was assigned to them, they were scared lest they should be held accountable for it. Their worry would not quieten until they were reassured by God and His Messenger. In their attitude we also recognize the nature of those people whom God has used to accomplish His will in human life.

The Bearers of Divine Guidance

The *sūrah* goes on to provide us with a glimpse of the procession of the faithful, led by the noble messengers, from the time of Noah and Abraham to the last of all prophets and messengers, Muhammad (peace be upon them all). This procession is shown to be continuous, uninterrupted, particularly since the time of Abraham and the prophets among his offspring. Those prophets are not given here in chronological order, which is the case elsewhere in the Qur'ān, because it is the fact that the procession has been a continuous one that is given importance here, not its historical order.

We bestowed on him Isaac and Jacob, and We guided each of them as We had guided Noah before them. Among his offspring were [the Prophets] David, Solomon, Job, Joseph, Moses and Aaron. Thus do We reward those who do good. And Zachariah, John, Jesus and Elijah; who were all righteous. And Ishmael, Elisha, Jonah and Lot. Every one of them did We favour above all people. And [We exalted likewise] some of their forefathers, their offspring and their brethren. We chose them and guided them to a straight path. Such is God's guidance; He bestows it on whomever He wills of His servants. Had they associated partners with Him, in vain would

---

3. Ibid., Vol. 7, p. 256.

certainly have been all that they ever did. On these did We bestow revelation, wisdom and prophethood. If this generation were to deny this truth, We have certainly entrusted it to others who will never deny it; those are the ones whom God has guided. Follow, then, their guidance, [and] say: "No reward do I ask of you for this. It is but an admonition to all mankind." (Verses 84–90)

These verses mention altogether seventeen messengers and prophets in addition to Noah and Abraham. There is also a reference to others among *'their forefathers, offspring and brethren'*. The verses which name these prophets are concluded with the comments, *"Thus do We reward those who do good."* (Verse 84) *"Every one of them did We favour above all people."* (Verse 86) *"We chose them and guided them to a straight path."* (Verse 87) All these comments endorse the nobility of this group of honourable prophets and the fact that they have been chosen by God and have been guided to the right path. All this, however, is made by way of an introduction to the three statements that follow.

"Such is God's guidance; He bestows it on whomever He wills of His servants. Had they associated partners with Him, in vain would certainly have been all that they ever did." (Verse 88) This first statement limits the sources of guidance in this world to what has been preached by God's messengers. The part of which we are absolutely certain and which we must follow is the Qur'ān, the single source which God Himself declares to be His guidance, and to which He guides whomever He wills of His servants. If those guided human beings deviate from the path of believing in God's oneness and change the source from which they receive their guidance, associating partners with God, in faith or worship, then they will see all their labours go to waste. The Arabic expression draws on an image of cattle grazing in a poisoned area: their bellies swell and then they die. This is the linguistic association of the expression used here for the wasting of their labours.

"On these did We bestow revelation, wisdom and prophethood. If this generation were to deny this truth, We have certainly entrusted it to others who will never deny it." (Verse 89) The first statement defines the source of guidance, limiting it to what has been given to God's messengers and conveyed by them. The second statement makes it clear that those messengers mentioned in the preceding verses were the ones to whom God has given the Book, wisdom, authority and prophethood. The Arabic word used for wisdom in this context also

connotes power and authority. Both aspects are acceptable within the context of this verse. Some of these messengers were given scriptures, such as the Torah given to Moses, the Psalms given to David and the Gospel given to Jesus. Others were given power, such as David and Solomon. All of them were given authority in the sense that their revelations detailed God's verdict, and the religion they preached outlined God's authority over their hearts and all affairs. God has sent His messengers to be obeyed and revealed His book to be implemented, as clearly stated in other verses.

All these prophets and messengers were also given wisdom and prophethood. They have been entrusted with God's message: to convey it to mankind and to supervise its implementation. If the Arab idolaters deny it, God has no need of them. Those prophets and the people who have followed them and believed in them are more than sufficient. This is an old fact that had established its roots and spread them wide. It is a long procession that continues uninterrupted. The same message has been conveyed by one messenger after another, accepted by those whom God has guided, knowing that they deserve His guidance.

This statement gives reassurance to the believers, although they may be few in number. Their community does not stand alone, isolated. It forms a branch of a huge tree with some roots and branches reaching to the sky. They are a group forming part of an honourable and noble procession that enjoys God's guidance. Every individual believer, everywhere on earth and in every generation is strong indeed and enjoys a noble position. He belongs to a community of believers that has continued for countless generations throughout human history.

"*Those are the ones whom God has guided. Follow, then, their guidance, [and] say: 'No reward do I ask of you for this. It is but an admonition to all mankind.'*" (Verse 90) Those noble leaders of the procession of faith are the ones who have been given God's guidance. What they received from God provides an example to be followed by God's Messenger, the Prophet Muḥammad, and those who follow him. He should follow only that guidance and submit only to its ruling. It is the only guidance which he preaches. As he does so, he says to those who are called on to believe in it: "*No reward do I ask of you for this. It is but an admonition to all mankind.*" (Verse 90) It is not the monopoly of any community, race or generation. It is God's guidance given to mankind in all ages and generations. The Messenger seeks no reward for his effort. His reward comes only from God.

Acknowledgement of God's Glory

The *sūrah* continues with the theme of God's messengers and their messages, and denounces those who deny the divine messages, describing them as having no true understanding of God, His wisdom, grace and justice. It states that the final message follows the same pattern of earlier messages, and that the Qur'ān, the last of the Books revealed by God, endorses earlier scriptures. All this fits beautifully with the procession of the faithful, led by the noble prophets, which was the subject matter of the preceding verses.

"*No true understanding of God have they when they say: 'God has never revealed anything to any human being.' Say: Who, then, revealed the Book which Moses brought to people as a light and a guidance? You transcribe it on sheets to show around, while you suppress much. You have been taught [by it] what neither you nor your forefathers had ever known. Say: God, and leave them to their play and foolish chatter. This is a blessed book which We have revealed, confirming what came before it, that you may warn the Mother City and all who dwell around it. Those who believe in the life to come do believe in it, and they are ever-mindful of their prayers.*" (Verses 91–2)

The unbelievers used to stubbornly argue that God had never sent a human messenger, nor had he ever revealed anything to a human being. They maintained this in spite of the fact that there lived alongside them in the Arabian Peninsula a number of Jewish communities. The Arab idolaters did not deny that the Jews had a revealed book or that the Torah was sent down to Moses (peace be upon him). Those Arabs made this argument in the midst of their stubborn refusal to accept the message given to the Prophet Muḥammad (peace be upon him). Hence, the Qur'ān denounces their claims and reminds them of Moses's scriptures.

"*No true understanding of God have they when they say: 'God has never revealed anything to any human being.'*" (Verse 91) This claim by the ignorant unbelievers in Makkah is reiterated by unbelievers in every period of history. It is even reiterated nowadays by those who claim that religions where invented by human beings and that they developed and became more sophisticated with the progress of human civilization. Such people make no distinction between man-made ideologies, such as idolatrous and pagan beliefs past and contemporary, which are indeed influenced by the stage of progress of their adherents, and divine religions preached by God's messengers. They ignore the fact that the main principles of these divine religions are the same, and that they are elaborated by every messenger. In each case, the divine religion was accepted by a community of believers and rejected by other people. As time passed, deviation occurred and distortion crept in. Thus, people reverted to their days of ignorance, awaiting the appearance of a new messenger to preach the divine faith.

This claim is reiterated in all ages by people who do not have any clear and true understanding of God and who are blind to God's grace, mercy and justice. They may say, as the Arabs at the time of the Prophet used to say, that God would not send a human messenger. Had He willed to send anyone, He would have chosen an angel for a messenger. Or they may say that the creator of this vast and great universe would not pay any attention to man, an insignificant creature in an exceedingly small planet called earth, to the extent of sending him messengers and revelations to guide him in his small world. This view was advanced by some philosophers in the past as also in modern times. Or they may say with the atheists that there is neither God nor a message to be revealed to anyone. They claim all this is the product of human fancies to enable some people to deceive others using the guise of religion.

All this betrays a shameful lack of understanding of God: His justice, mercy, wisdom, knowledge and grace. For it does not fit with God's grace to abandon man completely, when it is God who has created him and who knows his abilities and weaknesses. When it is God who knows his need for a proper standard by which to evaluate his concepts, notions, views, actions, traditions and systems, in order to choose what is right of all these and abandon what is bad or false. God also knows that the human mind is subjected to enormous pressures from a whole host of desires, whims and ambitions. Besides, man has been placed in charge of the earth, which God has made subservient to him. It is not his task to formulate an absolute concept of the universe or the essential principles of life. This is part of the domain of faith which God gives him so that he can formulate a proper concept of life and existence.

God does not abandon man to his own reason. Nor does He make his guidance to the truth dependent only on what He has planted in human nature of an innate yearning to know the true Lord. He does not leave him to reflect only on the fact that in times of great distress and hardship, man turns instinctively to God for help. Human nature may become distorted by internal and external pressures, and by the great variety of temptations. Therefore, God provides human beings with His revelations and sends them His messengers to put their nature back on a straight course and to keep their minds on the right track. It is part of the task assigned to God's messengers that they should remove all traces of distortion and delusion that may creep into human nature, whether of internal or external origin.

This is indeed what fits with God's grace, mercy, justice, wisdom and knowledge. He would not have abandoned human beings after having created them. Nor would He hold them to account on the Day of Judgement without first sending them a messenger: "*We would not have punished (people) without first sending (them) a messenger.*" (17: 15) Hence, a true understanding of God requires an acceptance that He has sent messengers to save mankind from a multitude of philosophies and pressures so that the mind remains free to contemplate and evaluate. It also requires that we believe that those messengers have been given the method of advocating faith and that some of them have been given scriptures to be maintained by their people for a period of time, as is the case with the scriptures of Moses, David and Jesus, or maintained for all time, as in the case of the Qur'ān.

Since the message of Moses and the people of earlier scriptures were known to the Arabs, God instructs His Messenger, Muḥammad (peace be upon him), to confront the unbelievers who denied revelation altogether with these facts. Thus, he asks them: "*Who, then, revealed the Book which Moses brought to people as a light and a guidance? You transcribe it on sheets to show around, while you suppress much. You have been taught [by it] what neither you nor your forefathers had ever known.*" (Verse 91)

One interpretation suggests that this particular verse was revealed in Madinah and was addressed to the Jews. Another interpretation, which the present author prefers,[4] maintains that this verse was, like the rest of the *sūrah*, revealed in Makkah. It addresses the unbelievers among the Arabs, telling them how the Jews used to play games with the Torah, showing only certain parts of it, which endorsed their treacherous methods and allowed them to change divine rulings. They suppressed much which censured their behaviour. The Arabs knew only a little of that, but God has told them in the Qur'ān much of what they did not

---

4. This view is expressed most clearly by Ibn Jarīr al-Ṭabarī, ibid., Vol. 7, pp. 268–9.

know. Although this reference is made in the form of an address, another authentically reported reading of it makes it in the form of a reported speech, which endorses the view we prefer.

Thus, the Prophet is instructed to ask the Arabs: '*Who revealed the Book which Moses brought to people as a light and a guidance?*' The Jews show of it only some parts but suppress others in order to achieve their own selfish ends. The Prophet is further instructed to remind them that God has taught them much that they did not know. It behoves them, then, to show their gratitude to God for revealing the Qur'ān, not to deny its truth by claiming that God has not sent down any revelations to His messengers.

They have not been given a chance to answer the question. God instructs His messenger to put a decisive end to this argument, in order not to allow it to become protracted. "*Say: God, and leave them to their play and foolish chatter.*" (Verse 91) It is God who has revealed it. The Prophet is instructed not to pay any attention to their arguments, described here as play and foolish chatter. This description implies a contemptuous look at their arguments and a serious threat. When foolishness is carried so far as to cause people to make such claims, the appropriate course of action is to make a final and decisive statement that leaves no room for any further argument.

Endorsement of Earlier Revelations

The *sūrah* now speaks of the new Book, the Qur'ān, whose revelation the unbelievers continue to deny. They are told that it is only a stage in a continuing chain. It is no new invention, but only one of the books God has revealed to His chosen messengers.

> *This is a blessed book which We have revealed, confirming what came before it, that you may warn the Mother City and all who dwell around it. Those who believe in the life to come do believe in it, and they are ever-mindful of their prayers.* (Verse 92)

That God should send messengers and give them revelations and scriptures is one of the laws He has set in this world. The new Book is blessed indeed, as God describes. It is blessed in its origin, since God has given it His blessings when He revealed it. It is also blessed in its destination, as it is engraved on Muḥammad's pure, large and noble heart. Furthermore, it is blessed in its size and contents. Compared to voluminous works written by human beings, it comprises a small number of pages; but its inspiration, impact, directives and meaning are far superior to those contained in scores of those books, each one of which is several times its size. A person who has been preoccupied with the art of expression and dealt with the relationship between words and meanings is better able to appreciate the fact that the Qur'ān, with its unique style, is blessed. It is simply impossible that human beings could express all the meanings, concepts and inspiration of the Qur'ān in a work which is a great many times its size. Many a single verse includes the meanings, facts and concepts that make it quotable in a variety of situations and for numerous purposes. This is a unique quality of the Qur'ān which has no parallel in the works of human beings.

The Qur'ān is also blessed in its effect. It addresses human nature and man as a whole, in a way which is remarkable, direct and gentle. It puts its facts before human nature in every direction, taking care of all its aspects. Its effect on it cannot be matched by the effect of anything else. The fact remains that it enjoys the authority of God. No other speech enjoys a similar authority.

We are constrained to go any further in describing the blessings of this Book. Whatever we say remains far short of the fact that God Himself describes it as a blessed Book. This is indeed the truth.

The next quality of the Qur'ān mentioned in this verse is that it confirms *what came before it*. It confirms all that has been revealed by God in its original, undistorted form. This confirmation is based on the fact that all those revelations established the basic truth about the question of faith. Apart from this, God has given every nation its own code and constitution within the framework of the basic belief in Him.

Those who write about Islam saying that it is the first religion to preach the whole faith of God's oneness, or the complete concept of the message and the Messenger, or the resurrection, reckoning and reward in the life to come, do so in an attempt to praise Islam. Yet these people do not read the Qur'ān. Had they read it carefully, they would have realized that God Himself states that all His messengers (peace be upon them all) preached the message of His absolute oneness, and that their messages, in all their forms, admitted no form or trace of polytheism whatsoever. All of them informed their communities, and mankind at large, that a messenger is a human being, like them.

He has no power to bring benefit or cause harm to them, or even to himself. He does not know what God has not informed mankind about, and cannot increase or reduce what God chooses to give to any one of His servants. They all warned their peoples about the resurrection and the life to come as well as the accountability, reward and punishment. The basic concept of faith, based on complete submission to God, has been preached by every messenger. The last message, the Qur'ān, confirms the Books revealed before it.

Those writers think that they are giving Islam a higher position when they claim that it is the most developed monotheistic faith. In this they are greatly influenced by European culture which claims that the human faith, including divine religions, have evolved and progressed in parallel with the evolution and progress of human communities. However, it is not permissible to defend Islam by undermining its fundamental concept, stated in the Qur'ān. Writers and readers alike should be cautious of such pitfalls.

The purpose of revealing this last message is so that the Prophet (peace be upon him) can use it to warn the people of Makkah, the Mother City, and its neighbouring areas: *"That you may warn the Mother City and all who dwell around it."* (Verse 92)

Makkah was called the Mother City because it is honoured by the first house ever to be built for mankind where they worship God alone, associating no partners with Him; a sanctuary where everyone enjoys peace. It is from that House that the universal call to every human being on earth was announced. It was never previously so universal. It is to that House that believers go on pilgrimage declaring their submission to God and honouring the House which is the birthplace of His call.

Some Orientalists who are hostile to Islam try to twist the meaning of this Qur'ānic statement in order to assert that the Islamic call was meant only for the people of Makkah and its surrounding area. They single out this statement to claim that in the early period, Muḥammad (peace be upon him) did not intend to address his message to anyone other than the people of Makkah and a few nearby towns. They claim that his ambition could not go beyond this area. They further say that he only broadened his scope to include the whole Arabian Peninsula, and then to carry it further, as a result of certain coincidences which he could not have envisaged at the outset. These coincidences only came about as a consequence of his migration to Madinah, where he established his state. All these claims are lies. In the Qur'ānic *sūrahs* revealed at Makkah, in the early period of Islam, we read statements addressed by God (limitless is He in His glory) to His Messenger asserting that his message is addressed to all mankind: "*We have sent you forth but as a blessing to mankind.*" (21: 107) "*We have sent you forth to all mankind, so that you may give them good news and forewarn them.*" (34: 28) When these verses were revealed, the Islamic call was still confined to small enclaves in Makkah where its advocates endured much persecution.

"*Those who believe in the life to come do believe in it, and they are ever-mindful of their prayers.*" (Verse 92) It is true that those who believe in the life to come, when people will have to account for their deeds and be rewarded or punished for them, also believe that God will no doubt send to mankind a messenger to convey to them His revelations. They have no problem in believing in this messenger. Indeed, they are inclined to believe in him.

Because they believe in the life to come and in the Qur'ān, they are always mindful of their prayer, so that they continue to maintain a close link with God and continue to demonstrate their obedience to Him. This is, then, all a part of human nature. When we believe in the hereafter, we accept that this Book, the Qur'ān, is revealed by God and we are keen to obey Him in order to enhance our closeness with Him. We need only to look at different types of human beings to be sure that all this is absolutely true.

The last two verses in this long passage portray a very vivid image of those wrongdoers, i.e. the unbelievers, who fabricate falsehood against God. Some of them go as far as to make blatantly false claims that they receive revelations from on high or that they can produce something similar to the Qur'ān. They are painted here when they are actually in the throes of death, with the angels coming to them, hands outstretched, to inflict their punishment, requiring them to yield up their souls. They face such a strong reproach when they leave everything behind them.

> *Who could be more wicked than one who invents a falsehood about God, or says: "This has been revealed to me", when nothing has been revealed to him? Or one who says, "I can reveal the like of what God has revealed"? If you could but see the wrongdoers when they are in the throes of death and the angels stretch out their hands*

[and say]: "Give up your souls!" Today you shall be rewarded with a humiliating punishment for having attributed to God something that is untrue and, in your arrogance, scorned His revelations. And now, indeed, you have come to Us individually, just as We created you in the first instance; and you have left behind all that We conferred on you. Nor do We see with you those intercessors of yours whom you had claimed to be partners in your affairs. Broken are the ties which bound you, and that which you have been asserting has failed you. (Verses 93–4)

A number of scholars like Qatādah and Ibn 'Abbās say that the first verse refers to Musaylamah, the Liar, his wife Sajāḥ bint al-Ḥārith and al-Aswad al-'Ansī. All three made claims during the Prophet's lifetime that they themselves were also prophets and that they received revelations from God. Another report attributed to Ibn 'Abbās suggests that the one who boasted that he would reveal something similar to God's revelations, or said that he received revelations himself, was 'Abdullāh ibn Sa'd ibn Abī Sarḥ. He had embraced Islam and the Prophet used to ask him to write down Qur'ānic revelations as he received them. He was once called in by the Prophet to write down some verses which are included in *Sūrah* 23, The Believers. *"Indeed, We create man out of the essence of clay, then We place him, a living germ, in a safe enclosure. Then We create out of this living germ a clot of congealed blood, and out of the clot We create an embryonic lump. Then We create within the embryonic lump bones, then We clothe the bones with flesh. We then bring this into being as another creation. Exalted be God, the best of creators."* (23: 12–14) When the Prophet dictated these verses, up to the phrase, *"We then bring this into being as another creation"*, 'Abdullāh marvelled at the details given in the Qur'ān about the creation of men. He said, "Exalted be God, the best of creators." The Prophet said to him: "This is exactly what has been revealed to me." This stirred up doubts in 'Abdullāh's mind. He thought: "If Muḥammad was truthful, I have received the same revelations, but if he was a liar, I have said the same as he did." He turned away from Islam and rejoined the unbelievers. According to this report, it is to him that reference is made by the sentence, *"Or one who says, 'I can reveal the like of what God has revealed.'"* (Verse 93)

The scene painted here of the punishment administered to those wrongdoers, i.e. the idolaters, fills us with awe and fear. The wrongdoers are shown when they are in the throes of death, totally overwhelmed, and angels stretching their hands out to punish them. They demand that they yield up their souls and reproach them for their misdeeds: "*If you could but see the wrongdoers when they are in the throes of death and the angels stretch out their hands [and say]: 'Give up your souls!' Today you shall be rewarded with a humiliating punishment for having attributed to God something that is untrue and, in your arrogance, scorned His revelations.*" (Verse 93) The humiliating punishment is a fitting reward for arrogance, and the public reproach answers their falsehood, which they invent against God. All this imparts to the scene shades of total misery and depression.

This is followed by a strong rebuke by God Himself about whom they asserted their fabrications. They stand in front of Him in a position of total misery: "*And now, indeed, you have come to Us individually, just as We created you in the first instance.*" (Verse 94)

You have nothing except your own selves, and you come as individuals, each one for himself. That is how you face your Lord, just as He created you: each is born alone, naked, helpless. You have left behind everything you have had; everybody else has deserted you; you have no power or authority over anything God had given to you: "*You have left behind all that We conferred on you.*" (Verse 94) All your wealth, children, prestige, position and power you have left behind because you could not bring them with you, even if you had so wished.

"*Nor do We see with you those intercessors of yours whom you had claimed to be partners in your affairs.*" (Verse 94) You used to claim that those beings would intercede on your behalf anytime you go through a hardship. You used to assign to them a portion of your lives and a share of your wealth, claiming that they would intercede for you with God. This is similar to their claim in defence of their idolatrous practices, when they said: "We only worship these (idols) so that they may bring us closer to God." These assumed intercessors may take different shapes and forms. They may be human, such as priests and people of power and authority, or they may be statues of stone, idols, *jinn*, angels, planets or indeed any being, which symbolized their gods. Yet they even went further than this, assigning to these beings a share of their lives, wealth and offspring, as will be explained later in this *sūrah*. (Verses 136–9)

Now that they have come to their Lord individually, each on his or her own, they are asked where have those partners and intercessors gone? The answer is given in the Qur'ānic verse in these terms: "*Broken are the ties which bound you.*" (Verse 94) Every link, and every tie has been broken. There is no longer anything to group them together in any way or form. "*And that which you have been asserting has failed you.*" (Verse 94) They used to make all sorts of assertions, including what they maintained about those beings whom they claimed to be partners with God or whom they alleged to be able to intercede with God. All these claims are now proven false. All trust they had put in anyone or anything has failed them. They are totally powerless.

This scene violently shakes the human heart as it holds out a vivid and awesome image, imparting its overtones to us so that we are able to contemplate its powerful message. This is just one example of the inimitable style of the Qur'ān.

12

The Miracle of Creation

It is God who splits the grain and the fruit-stone. He brings forth the living out of that which is dead and the dead out of that which is alive. Such is God. How, then, are you deluded away from the truth? (95)

﷽ إِنَّ ٱللَّهَ فَالِقُ ٱلْحَبِّ وَٱلنَّوَىٰ يُخْرِجُ ٱلْحَىَّ مِنَ ٱلْمَيِّتِ وَمُخْرِجُ ٱلْمَيِّتِ مِنَ ٱلْحَىِّ ذَٰلِكُمُ ٱللَّهُ فَأَنَّىٰ تُؤْفَكُونَ ﴿٩٥﴾

He is the One who causes the day to break. He has made the night to be [a source of stillness], and the sun and the moon for reckoning. All this is laid down by the will of the Almighty, the All-Knowing. (96)

فَالِقُ ٱلْإِصْبَاحِ وَجَعَلَ ٱلَّيْلَ سَكَنًا وَٱلشَّمْسَ وَٱلْقَمَرَ حُسْبَانًا ذَٰلِكَ تَقْدِيرُ ٱلْعَزِيزِ ٱلْعَلِيمِ ﴿٩٦﴾

It is He that has set up for you the stars, so that you may be guided by them in the deep darkness of land and sea. We have made Our revelations plain indeed to people who have knowledge. (97)

وَهُوَ ٱلَّذِى جَعَلَ لَكُمُ ٱلنُّجُومَ لِتَهْتَدُوا۟ بِهَا فِى ظُلُمَٰتِ ٱلْبَرِّ وَٱلْبَحْرِ قَدْ فَصَّلْنَا ٱلْءَايَٰتِ لِقَوْمٍ يَعْلَمُونَ ﴿٩٧﴾

He it is who has brought you all into being from a single soul and has given you a dwelling and a place of sojourn. We have made Our revelations plain indeed to people of understanding. (98)

وَهُوَ ٱلَّذِىٓ أَنشَأَكُم مِّن نَّفْسٍ وَٰحِدَةٍ فَمُسْتَقَرٌّ وَمُسْتَوْدَعٌ قَدْ فَصَّلْنَا ٱلْءَايَٰتِ لِقَوْمٍ يَفْقَهُونَ ﴿٩٨﴾

And He it is who sends down water from the sky with which We bring forth plants of every type and out of these We bring forth verdure from which We bring forth grain piled tight, packed on one another; and out of the spathe of the palm tree, dates in thick clusters; and gardens of vines; and the olive tree, and the pomegranate: all so alike, and yet so different. Behold their fruit when they come to fruition and ripen. Surely in these there are clear signs for people who truly believe. (99)

وَهُوَ ٱلَّذِىٓ أَنزَلَ مِنَ ٱلسَّمَآءِ مَآءً فَأَخْرَجْنَا بِهِۦ نَبَاتَ كُلِّ شَىْءٍ فَأَخْرَجْنَا مِنْهُ خَضِرًا نُّخْرِجُ مِنْهُ حَبًّا مُّتَرَاكِبًا وَمِنَ ٱلنَّخْلِ مِن طَلْعِهَا قِنْوَانٌ دَانِيَةٌ وَجَنَّـٰتٍ مِّنْ أَعْنَابٍ وَٱلزَّيْتُونَ وَٱلرُّمَّانَ مُشْتَبِهًا وَغَيْرَ مُتَشَـٰبِهٍ ٱنظُرُوٓا۟ إِلَىٰ ثَمَرِهِۦٓ إِذَآ أَثْمَرَ وَيَنْعِهِۦٓ إِنَّ فِى ذَٰلِكُمْ لَءَايَـٰتٍ لِّقَوْمٍ يُؤْمِنُونَ ﴿٩٩﴾

Yet they make the *jinn* equals with God, although He created them; and in their ignorance they invent for Him sons and daughters. Limitless is He in His glory, and sublimely exalted above all that which they attribute to Him. (100)

وَجَعَلُوا۟ لِلَّهِ شُرَكَآءَ ٱلْجِنَّ وَخَلَقَهُمْ وَخَرَقُوا۟ لَهُۥ بَنِينَ وَبَنَـٰتٍ بِغَيْرِ عِلْمٍ سُبْحَـٰنَهُۥ وَتَعَـٰلَىٰ عَمَّا يَصِفُونَ ﴿١٠٠﴾

He is the Originator of the heavens and the earth. How can He have a child when He has never had a consort? He has created everything and has full knowledge of all things. (101)

بَدِيعُ ٱلسَّمَـٰوَٰتِ وَٱلْأَرْضِ أَنَّىٰ يَكُونُ لَهُۥ وَلَدٌ وَلَمْ تَكُن لَّهُۥ صَـٰحِبَةٌ وَخَلَقَ كُلَّ شَىْءٍ وَهُوَ بِكُلِّ شَىْءٍ عَلِيمٌ ﴿١٠١﴾

Such is God, your Lord; there is no deity other than Him, the Creator of all things, so worship Him alone. He is the Guardian of everything. (102)

ذَٰلِكُمُ ٱللَّهُ رَبُّكُمْ لَآ إِلَـٰهَ إِلَّا هُوَ خَـٰلِقُ كُلِّ شَىْءٍ فَٱعْبُدُوهُ وَهُوَ عَلَىٰ كُلِّ شَىْءٍ وَكِيلٌ ﴿١٠٢﴾

No power of vision can encompass Him, whereas He encompasses all vision; He is above all comprehension, yet is all-aware. (103)

لَا تُدْرِكُهُ ٱلْأَبْصَرُ وَهُوَ يُدْرِكُ ٱلْأَبْصَرُ وَهُوَ ٱللَّطِيفُ ٱلْخَبِيرُ ۝

Means of insight have come to you from your Lord. Therefore, whoever chooses to see does so for his own good, and whoever chooses to remain blind only himself does he hurt. I am not your keeper. (104)

قَدْ جَآءَكُم بَصَآئِرُ مِن رَّبِّكُمْ فَمَنْ أَبْصَرَ فَلِنَفْسِهِ وَمَنْ عَمِيَ فَعَلَيْهَا وَمَآ أَنَا۠ عَلَيْكُم بِحَفِيظٍ ۝

Thus do We spell out Our revelations in diverse ways, that they may say, "You have studied this", and that We may make it clear to people of knowledge. (105)

وَكَذَٰلِكَ نُصَرِّفُ ٱلْأَيَٰتِ وَلِيَقُولُوا۟ دَرَسْتَ وَلِنُبَيِّنَهُۥ لِقَوْمٍ يَعْلَمُونَ ۝

Follow what has been revealed to you by your Lord, other than whom there is no deity, and turn your back on those who associate partners with God. (106)

ٱتَّبِعْ مَآ أُوحِىَ إِلَيْكَ مِن رَّبِّكَ لَآ إِلَٰهَ إِلَّا هُوَ وَأَعْرِضْ عَنِ ٱلْمُشْرِكِينَ ۝

Had God so willed, they would not have associated partners with Him. We have not made you their keeper, nor are you responsible for them. (107)

وَلَوْ شَآءَ ٱللَّهُ مَآ أَشْرَكُوا۟ وَمَا جَعَلْنَٰكَ عَلَيْهِمْ حَفِيظًا وَمَآ أَنتَ عَلَيْهِم بِوَكِيلٍ ۝

Do not revile those whom they invoke instead of God, lest they revile God out of spite, and in ignorance. Thus have We made the actions of every community seem goodly to them. Then to their Lord shall they all return, and He will explain to them all that they have been doing. (108)

وَلَا تَسُبُّوا ٱلَّذِينَ يَدْعُونَ مِن دُونِ ٱللَّهِ فَيَسُبُّوا ٱللَّهَ عَدْوًا بِغَيْرِ عِلْمٍ كَذَٰلِكَ زَيَّنَّا لِكُلِّ أُمَّةٍ عَمَلَهُمْ ثُمَّ إِلَىٰ رَبِّهِم مَّرْجِعُهُمْ فَيُنَبِّئُهُم بِمَا كَانُوا يَعْمَلُونَ ١٠٨

They swear by God most solemnly that if a miracle be shown to them they would believe in it. Say: "Miracles are in God's power." For all you know, even if one is shown to them, they may still not believe? (109)

وَأَقْسَمُوا بِٱللَّهِ جَهْدَ أَيْمَٰنِهِمْ لَئِن جَآءَتْهُمْ ءَايَةٌ لَّيُؤْمِنُنَّ بِهَا قُلْ إِنَّمَا ٱلْأَيَٰتُ عِندَ ٱللَّهِ وَمَا يُشْعِرُكُمْ أَنَّهَا إِذَا جَآءَتْ لَا يُؤْمِنُونَ ١٠٩

We will turn their hearts and eyes away since they did not believe in it the first time. We shall leave them to blunder about in their overweening arrogance. (110)

وَنُقَلِّبُ أَفْـِٔدَتَهُمْ وَأَبْصَٰرَهُمْ كَمَا لَمْ يُؤْمِنُوا بِهِ أَوَّلَ مَرَّةٍ وَنَذَرُهُمْ فِى طُغْيَٰنِهِمْ يَعْمَهُونَ ١١٠

Even if We were to send down angels to them, and if the dead were to speak to them, and even if We were to range all things before them, they would still not believe unless God so willed. Yet most of them are ignorant. (111)

وَلَوْ أَنَّنَا نَزَّلْنَا إِلَيْهِمُ ٱلْمَلَٰٓئِكَةَ وَكَلَّمَهُمُ ٱلْمَوْتَىٰ وَحَشَرْنَا عَلَيْهِمْ كُلَّ شَىْءٍ قُبُلًا مَّا كَانُوا لِيُؤْمِنُوا إِلَّا أَن يَشَآءَ ٱللَّهُ وَلَٰكِنَّ أَكْثَرَهُمْ يَجْهَلُونَ ١١١

Overview

We need to remind ourselves here of what we said in our Prologue to this *sūrah*. Most of all we need to remember how its waves follow close on the heels of each other in an endless flow, and how its scenes are portrayed in a breathtaking splendour, coupled with a superbly inspiring rhythm.

This *sūrah* tackles its subject matter in a unique way. At every turn, in every situation or scene, it brings out in sharp relief all the awesome splendour of what is being portrayed, keeping us spellbound, breathless. We follow its scenes and changing, powerful rhythm.

In its quick flow of scenes, inspirations, rhythms, images and shades, it resembles a fast, wide river flowing with white water. As one wave reaches its breaking place, the next one follows very closely, almost reaching out to the one that has just gone by. The flow remains continuous, unending.

In every one of these flowing and closely successive waves, the same rich splendour is there to see. And in all the scenes portrayed, we have superb harmony. Thus, we are absolutely enchanted; first by the splendid scenes, then their lively images, the powerful music, the inimitable expression, the flood of inspiring figures of speech. The *sūrah* addresses man's heart and mind from every angle and in every way possible.

All these features are seen at their clearest in this passage. The reader feels as though the scenes spring to life, with all their colour and brightness, jumping up in front of us just as the rhythm flows with the words that are recited, striking a note of perfect harmony. Each scene spreads itself before us like a bright spark appearing from the distance, and gradually exhibiting its full, captivating splendour before our very eyes. Another spark is then produced by the very expressions that are used, and its rhythm strikes harmony between the scenes portrayed and the meanings illustrated. Consistency is felt in the flow of expression and harmony is unmistakable in the brilliantly painted scenes.

Beauty is the main feature here: the *sūrah* attains its breathtaking climax, with scenes that are chosen for their beauty and wording and construction that are meticulously selected for their rhythm and power of expression. In addition, even the ideas floated here address the basic truth of the Islamic faith, with its infinitely rich meaning, and all from the angle of beauty. Thus, this truth appears to swim in a sea of absolute perfection.

The passage includes specific directives for us to appreciate the beauty which is all too visible in the flourish of life: *"Behold their fruit when it comes to fruition and ripens."* (Verse 99) This draws our attention directly to this splendid beauty, so that we may look and appreciate, but with open minds.

The beauty is brought to its perfect, enthralling climax at the end of those scenes which describe the universe and which reach out to the One beyond. In this way we behold the Originator of the heavens and earth who has placed all these wonderful things in the universe. The *sūrah* speaks of Him in images and expressions the beauty of which cannot be intimated except by the Qur'ānic text itself: *"No power of vision can encompass Him, whereas He encompasses all vision; He is above all comprehension, yet is all-aware."* (Verse 103)

In this passage we see the open book of the universe. People pass by it all the time without pausing for a moment to look at its miraculous features, its telling signs and wonderful features. The Qur'ān takes us on a tour of this universe, and we feel as if we see it for the first time. We want to look at its wonders, contemplate its beauty and enjoy its splendour.

It stops us in front of the miracle that occurs at every moment of the night and day: the miracle of life as it stirs in the midst of the dead world around it. How does it start? Where does it come from? It simply comes from God, and starts by His will. No human being can fathom its nature, let alone originate it.

It then stops us in front of the great, accurate movement of the cosmos. This is superior to all the miracles people demand. What is more is that it goes on at every moment without fail.

It then stops us again at the initiation of human life, from a single soul, and its procreation in the familiar way. We also stop at the origination of life in plants, rain pouring in torrents, growing plants of every type and colour, ripening fruits. All these give us a picture of the whole range of life which is so very worthy of reflection, if we could only see it all with open minds.

Then we look at the universe as a whole, and it is presented to us as if we are seeing it for the first time. It is alive, moving, interacting with us, remarkable in its effect on our senses and feelings, testifying to its Creator, displaying its features one by one all of which clearly point to God's great power.

As the *sūrah* places this rich and varied tapestry in front of unbelievers, the very concept of polytheism is felt to be infinitely absurd. Indeed, everyone who contemplates the great many signs pointing to the truth and indicating the source of guidance will find this concept too hideous to deserve even a moment's consideration. The whole argument of those unbelievers who associate partners with God falls to pieces.

In its presentation of the truth of God's existence and nature to mankind the Qur'ān demonstrates God's power which creates, provides and manages all matters, without partners, as the inspiring evidence to prove what it advocates. It simply calls on people to surrender themselves to God, purge their beliefs of any trace of polytheism, offer their worship to God alone and submit to His will. In this passage we are also required to offer all worship to God alone. This means that all Godhead belongs to Him alone, and that He is the ultimate arbiter in all affairs of human life.

In this passage we find an example of the linkage the Qur'ān makes between pure worship and recognizing that Godhead belongs only to God, the Creator and guardian of all: "*Such is God, your Lord; there is no deity other than Him, the Creator of all things, so worship Him alone. He is the Guardian of everything.*" (Verse 102)

At the end of the passage, the demand to produce miracles is shown to be stupid, and betrays the obstinate nature of the unbelievers. They do not reject the faith on the grounds of insufficient evidence of the truth. They reject it because of their twisted nature. Miraculous signs are everywhere in the universe, if they could only see them.

The Early Signs of Life

> *It is God who splits the grain and the fruit-stone. He brings forth the living out of that which is dead and the dead out of that which is alive. Such is God. How, then, are you deluded away from the truth?* (Verse 95)

This is the great miracle whose secret remains unknown to all creatures and which cannot be emulated by anyone. This is the miracle of life, its initiation and progress.[1] At every moment, a grain or seed splits open to produce a shoot of plant and a fruit-stone breaks open to begin the life of a tree. This life which remains latent in the seed, grain and the fruit-stone, and which is evident in plant and tree remains, is in both substance and source, a secret which is known only to God. Having observed all the various characteristics and stages of life, mankind remains today in the same position as the first man on earth. We know the outer aspects of life and its purpose, but its source and substance remain an unknown secret. Yet life goes on and the miracle of starting life occurs every second.

Right at the beginning, God brought forth the living out of the dead. The universe, or at least our planet earth, existed, but there was no life on it. Then life began after God originated it from something that was dead. How did He do that? We certainly do not know. Ever since that moment, life has been created out of what is dead. Dead particles are transformed every moment, through living creatures, into organic living substances that form part of living bodies. Although they are originally dead particles, they are transformed into living cells. The reverse also takes place. At every moment, living cells become dead particles, until one day a complete living entity becomes a dead body. *"He brings forth the living out of that which is dead and the dead out of that which is alive."* (Verse 95)

No one can do this other than God. It is God alone who can originate life from something that is dead, and it is He alone who gives a living entity the ability to transfer dead particles into living cells. Again, He alone can complete the cycle and transform the living cells into dead particles. No one has ever acquired certain knowledge of this cycle: when did it start and how does it proceed? We only have assumptions, theories and probabilities.

---

1. Atheists nowadays make a great fuss about man's ability to produce some substances which until recently could not have been produced except through interactions taking place within a living creature. They should know that there is a great difference between an organic substance and a living one. Moreover, this processed substance has been made out of material that has been created by God. Human beings will never be able to create it themselves. – Author's note.

This was written in the early 1960s, before the recent developments in various aspects of life study and the new techniques in genetic engineering. Still his view is valid, as none of these techniques attempts anything close to creation, not even cloning. These techniques rely on using what is created by God to modify the process of reproduction. – Editor's note.

Every attempt to explain the origination of life in any way other than its being created by God has ended in total failure. At one stage, Europeans ran away from the Church in a flight similar to the one described by the Qur'ān as a flight of those who wilfully turn away from divine guidance "*like terrified asses, fleeing from a lion.*" (74: 50–1) Ever since, they have been trying to find an explanation for the evolution of the universe and for life without having to admit that it is all God's work. All their attempts, however, have ended in miserable failure. In the twentieth century, there remained only a few lingering attempts, all totally devoid of sincerity. They all share a distinctive characteristic, namely, pigheadedness.

An increasing number of scientists admit that there is no way to explain the beginning and progress of life except by a clear acknowledgement that it is all God's work. What these scientists say is characteristic of the present attitude of modern science to this whole question. Nevertheless, some people in our part of the world continue to feed on the leftovers of eighteenth and nineteenth century Europeans. They turn away from religion because it speaks of 'imperceptibles', while they claim to be 'scientific'. Their assertions need no comment from us. What they really need to do is to refer to what scientists nowadays acknowledge and that is that the origins of life lie with God alone. We will select only a few quotations from some Western scientists.

Frank Allen, Professor of Biophysics at the University of Manitoba, Canada, says:

> If in the origin of life there was no design, then living matter must have arisen by chance. Now chance, or probability as it is termed, is a highly developed mathematical theory which applies to that vast range of objects of knowledge that are beyond absolute certainty. This theory puts us in possession of the soundest principles on which to discriminate truth from error, and to calculate the likelihood of the occurrence of any particular form of an event.

> Proteins are the essential constituents of all living cells, and they consist of the five elements, carbon, hydrogen, nitrogen, oxygen and sulphur, with possibly 40,000 atoms in the ponderous molecule. As there are 92 chemical elements in Nature, all distributed at random, the chance that these five elements may

come together to form the molecule, the quantity of matter that must be continually shaken up, and the length of time necessary to finish the task, can all be calculated. A Swiss mathematician, Charles Eugene Guye, has made the computation and finds that the odds against such an occurrence are 10^{160} to 1, or only one chance in 10^{160}, that is 10 multiplied by itself 160 times, a number too large to be expressed in words. The amount of matter to be shaken together to produce a single molecule of protein would be millions of times greater than that in the whole universe. For it to occur on the earth alone would require many, almost endless billions (10^{243}) of years.

Proteins are made from long chains called amino acids. The way those are put together matters enormously. If in the wrong way they will not sustain life and may be poisonous. Professor J.B. Leathes (England) has calculated that the links in the chain of quite a simple protein could be put together in millions of ways (10^{48}). It is impossible for all these chances to have coincided to build one molecule of protein.

But proteins as chemicals are without life. It is only when the mysterious life comes into them that they live. Only Infinite Mind,[2] that is God, could have foreseen that such a molecule could be the abode of life, could have constructed it, and made it live.[3]

Irving William Knobloch, Professor of the Natural Sciences at Michigan State University, says:

Science has no adequate explanation for the origin of the many sub-microscopic particles of matter known to exist. It cannot explain, solely upon the laws of chance, how atoms and molecules could have come together to form life. The theory which states dogmatically that all higher forms of life have evolved to their present state by chance mutations, recombinations, polyploidy

---

2. This is a philosophical expression used by the author as it is part of his culture. A Muslim does not refer to God Almighty except by the attributes He has outlined. – Author's note.

3. Frank Allen, "The Origin of the World – By Chance or Design?" in *The Evidence of God in an Expanding Universe*, (edited by John Clover Monsma), G.P. Putnam's Sons, New York, 1958, pp. 23–4.

or hybridization, requires an act of faith for adherence to it, an act of unreasoned acceptance.[4]

Albert McCombs Winchester, Chairman of the Department of Biology at Stetson University and former President of Florida Academy of Sciences, says:

> My field of study has been in the broad field known as biology, the science of the study of life. Of all the magnificent creations of God, there is none which can surpass the living things which inhabit our planet.
>
> Consider a small clover plant growing by the roadside. Where among all the marvellous man-made machines can we find its equal? Here we have a living "machine" which unobtrusively, but consistently, day in and day out, brings about thousands of complex chemical and physical reactions, all under the direction of protoplasm, the material of which all physical life is composed.
>
> From whence came this complex, living "machine"? God did not personally mould it with His own hands and shape every leaf and root on it. No – He has created life with the ability of self-perpetuation; the ability to continue the species down through the generations with all the characteristics which make it recognizable as a clover plant. To me, this is the most fascinating branch of biology and the greatest revelation of the majesty of God. Here we are dealing with a world of infinite smallness, because the pattern for the construction of a new clover plant must be contained within a portion of a single cell, so small that it can be seen only with a powerfully lensed microscope. Every vein, every hair, and every branch on the stems, roots and leaves have been formed under the direction of tiny engineers within the one cell from which the plant grew.[5]

There is a definite beauty in the way this Qur'ānic verse relates the operation of the life and death cycle to God alone. It first makes a clear statement: "*It is God who splits the grain and the fruit-stone. He brings forth the living out of that which is dead and the dead out of that which is alive.*" (Verse 95) It then attributes all to God: "*Such is God.*"

---

4. I.W. Knobloch, in *The Evidence of God in an Expanding Universe,* ibid., pp. 87–8.
5. A.M. Winchester, in *The Evidence of God in an Expanding Universe,* ibid., pp 165–6.

He is the originator of this ever-renewable miracle which remains covered with secrecy. He is the Creator and the Lord to whom everyone should submit themselves and obey without hesitation: "*Such is God. How, then, are you deluded away from the truth?*" (Verse 95) This is the truth which is clearly apparent to eyes, hearts and minds. How can anyone pretend not to see it or refuse to admit it?

The Qur'ān frequently mentions the miracle of bringing life out of that which is dead, as also the creation of the universe in order to turn our attentions to the nature of Godhead and the manifestations of the oneness of the Creator. The inevitable conclusion is that submission must be to God alone who is the only God and the only Lord. People must, then, address all their worship to Him alone and refer to Him in order to make their laws and formulate their code of living.

None of these aspects is mentioned in the Qur'ān in a form of an abstract, philosophical theory or religious dogma. This religion of Islam is too serious to allow people to waste their energies in such discussions. It aims to give people a proper concept, outlining true beliefs for them, so that they can enjoy a proper and sound life both in public and in private. This can only be achieved by freeing people from enslavement to other creatures so that they worship God alone and submit themselves only to Him in this life, in all its entirety. People will then refuse to acknowledge any authority claimed by usurpers who supposedly exercise the rights of Godhead, making their own laws and legislation for human life. Such people try to make of themselves false gods. By doing so, they undermine human life and cause people to be enslaved. Hence, this verse which begins with a wonderful description of the miracle of life concludes with this comment: "*Such is God. How, then, are you deluded away from the truth?*" (Verse 95)

Such is God who alone deserves to be acknowledged as the overall Lord who sustains life, provides guidance, exercises control and rules over the whole universe. Hence, no one else can be acknowledged as Lord.

Perfectionism at Its Best

He is the One who causes the day to break. He has made the night to be [a source of stillness], and the sun and the moon for reckoning. All this is laid down by the will of the Almighty, the All-Knowing. (Verse 96)

He who splits the grain and the fruit-stone is the One who causes the break of dawn. He has made the night a period of time when living things have their repose. Moreover, He has given the sun and the moon cycles that can be calculated with great accuracy. It is His power that controls everything in the universe. His knowledge overlooks nothing.

In the Arabic text the word used to denote the break of dawn is the same that describes the splitting of grains and fruit-stones. Life begins to spread as a result of dawn breaking in the same way as a plant shoots out of a grain that has been split. Aspects of vigour, liveliness and beauty are common to both phenomena. Moreover, there is an added link between these two phenomena and the stillness of the night. The cycles of morning and evening, activity and stillness in this planet have a direct bearing on plants and life. The fact that the earth revolves on its axis in front of the sun, the sizes given to the sun and the moon, the distances between them and the earth and the temperature of the sun are all determined by the Almighty who is in full control of all things and whose knowledge is faultless. Had these been different, life would not have sprung out of this earth in this fashion. We would not have had plants and trees sprouting forth from grains and fruit-stones.

Everything in the whole universe has been calculated and determined most accurately in order to determine the type and degree of life that exists in each part of it. There is simply no room for any coincidence in the universe. Indeed, even what some people call coincidence, or the result of chance, is subject to a definite law and is accurately calculated.

Some people say that life has been no more than a side affect in a small corner of the universe, to which the rest of the universe is blind or even hostile. They maintain that the fact that this type of life has taken place on a very small planet confirms the same. Indeed, some of them go further and say that the smallness of the earth suggests that had there been a god in control of the universe, he would not have bothered himself with this life. They assert such absurdities describing them at times as 'scientific logic' or 'philosophical theories', when they do not merit any discussion whatsoever.

Such people allow their prejudices to dictate their views. They do not pay heed to the results of their own scientific work which stares them in the face. When you read their writings you sense that they do everything in their power in order to evade a truism which they have already decided not to face. They see all the pointers asserting God's existence, His oneness and absolute power everywhere in the universe, but they flee from acknowledging these facts. Every time they take a route hoping to avoid such a confrontation and manage to reconcile themselves to the universal fact, they find that they come to the same end. Agitated and scared, they hurriedly try another route, but again they come to the same end. They find that they must acknowledge God's existence and His absolute power. Poor and helpless is what they are. One day they broke loose from the tyrannical rule of the Church, which was in the habit of imposing its fetters on people's minds and souls. In their flight, they behaved *"like terrified asses, fleeing from a lion."* (74: 50–1) But they continued in their flight until the early decades of the twentieth century, not daring to turn back and find out whether the Church was pursuing them, or whether it too was breathless like them.

They are indeed poor and helpless, because they have to face today the inescapable conclusions of their scientific work. Where can they flee?

Frank Allen, the Biophysicist whom we have already quoted, says in the same article:

> The adjustments of the earth for life are far too numerous to be accounted for by chance. First, the earth is a sphere freely poised in space ("He hangeth the earth upon nothing" – Job 26: 7), in daily rotation on its polar axis, giving the alternation of day and night, and in yearly revolution around the sun. These motions give stability to its orientation in space, and, coupled with the inclination (23 degrees) of the polar axis to the plane of its revolution (the ecliptic), affords regularity to the seasons, thus doubling the habitable area of the earth and providing a greater diversity of plant life than a stationary globe could sustain.

> Secondly, the atmosphere of life-supporting gases is sufficiently high (about 500 miles) and dense to blanket the earth against the deadly impact of twenty million meteors that daily enter it at speeds of about thirty miles per second. Among many other functions the atmosphere also maintains the temperature within safe limits for life; and carries the vital supply of fresh water-vapour far inland from the oceans to irrigate the earth, without

which it would become a lifeless desert. Thus the oceans, with the atmosphere, are the balance-wheel of Nature.[6]

Scientific evidence piles up in front of them and scientific facts support one another confirming that the theory of coincidence cannot give any plausible explanation for the origin of life. For life to begin, develop, progress, continue, be sustained and varied requires an endless number of balances and compatibilities in the design of the whole universe. Every scientist is aware of many of these in his own field, but beyond the total sum of these there are countless other balances and compatibilities that are required. How could they have come about except by the will and determination of the Almighty, the All-Knowing, who has given everything its shape and form, and guided it along its course of life, and who has created everything according to an established measure?

The *sūrah* continues with this awe-inspiring scene of the universe and relates it to human life and people's interests and concerns. The whole space, with its sun, moon and stars, is portrayed as directly relevant to people's lives: "*It is He that has set up for you the stars, so that you may be guided by them in the deep darkness of land and sea. We have made Our revelations plain indeed to people who have knowledge.*" (Verse 97)

On land and at sea people continue to find themselves lost at times and feel themselves to be in total darkness, and they continue to be guided by the stars. This used to be the case in ancient times, and it continues to be so today. Methods of being guided by stars may vary, and may indeed be wider in scope as a result of scientific discoveries, but the rule remains the same: these stars provide guidance out of darkness, whether the darkness be of the physical or mental type that affects people's thinking and colours their concepts. The Qurʾānic statement remains valid at all times. It addresses mankind in their primitive days, and they find its address true in their lives. It also addresses human beings after they have made great scientific advances and far-reaching discoveries relating to man and the universe. They continue to find the Qurʾānic statement true in their practical world.

---

6. Frank Allen, *Evidence of God in an Expanding Universe*, ibid., pp. 20–1.

The Qur'ānic method remains unique. As it addresses men, it does not portray universal facts in the form of a theory. It portrays them as they are, so that we see beyond them the work of the Creator: His elaborate design and His grace. It, thus, addresses people's hearts and minds, urging them to reflect and to make use of whatever knowledge they have in order to arrive at the great truth beyond. Hence, the verse which refers to the stars God has made to provide people with guidance in the darkness of land and sea is concluded with this inspiring comment: "*We have made Our revelations plain indeed to people who have knowledge.*" (Verse 97)

In order to be guided by the stars, people need to have knowledge of their positions, orbits and cycles as well as knowledge of how all these point to the Creator and His wisdom. As we have already said, the guidance is provided out of the physical darkness as well as the mental one. Those who make use of the stars to determine their route, without relating the information they receive from the stars to their Creator, do not receive their full benefit and do not have their full guidance. Such people overlook the relationship between the marvels of this universe and their definite pointer to the great Creator.

> *He it is who has brought you all into being from a single soul and has given you a dwelling and a place of sojourn. We have made Our revelations plain indeed to people of understanding.*" (Verse 98)

This time the *sūrah* provides a direct touch referring to the single human soul in which both the male and the female have one nature. With that single soul life begins its first step towards procreation with a fertilized cell. Thus we have a soul which provides a dwelling place for this cell in the body of the male and a soul which gives it its place of sojourn in the female's uterus. Life then begins its cycle of development, progress and procreation. The result is different races, tribes, nations, characteristics, colours and languages: countless patterns and widely different communities.

"*We have made Our revelations plain indeed to people of understanding.*" (Verse 98) A quality of understanding is necessary here in order to appreciate what God does with each single soul in order to bring out of it all those diverse communities and endless patterns. It also helps men to understand the remarkable compatibilities which are necessary to make conception the means for procreation and to always provide the appropriate numbers of human males and females, in order to establish the institution of marriage within which the process of conception and procreation operates. Marriage also provides the proper conditions for children to grow up within so that they, in turn, become fit to play their roles in promoting human life.

It is beyond the scope of this commentary to go deeper into this notion of necessary compatibilities. That would require a more specialized study. It is sufficient for our purposes here to mention that the sperm originates with male or female characteristics, and then the proper distribution dictated by God ensures that sufficient numbers of males and females are produced to sustain life and ensure its progress. We have mentioned earlier in this commentary that God's will, which is free and absolute, determines whether the fertilized egg produces a male or a female child.

As God operates His will every time a human conception takes place, giving whomever He wills of His servants daughters or giving them sons, He ensures that a permanent balance is maintained between the numbers of males and females in the whole world. There may be local or temporary variations, but at the level of humanity as a whole, the balance is never disturbed. Its function is not merely to ensure procreation, but it also serves for the establishment of stable marital life. Conception and procreation can take place with a minimum number of males. However, God does not wish to make the preservation of the human species the sole purpose of the union between the male and the female. The purpose which distinguishes human beings from animals is the creation of a stable marital life between a man and a woman. Such stability ensures the most important result of allowing young children to be taken care of by their parents within a family atmosphere. In this way, the parents do not merely provide food and physical protection for their offspring, as animals do, but they also prepare them for their human role which requires that the children stay a much longer time with their parents than young animals do.

Maintaining such a permanent balance is a sufficient indication of the Creator's elaborate planning and wisdom, provided people are endowed with understanding: "*We have made Our revelations plain indeed to people with understanding.*" (Verse 98) But the obstinate rejecters of the truth, particularly those who boast of their scientific approach and ridicule the notion of a world beyond, continue to persist in their obstinate rejection: "*Even though they may see every sign of the truth, they do not believe in it.*" (7: 146)

The Ever-Renewable Miracle of Creation

The *sūrah* now begins to draw our attention to scenes of life as they open up everywhere around us. We see life with our eyes and feel it as it springs out. As we contemplate it, we see the beauty of God's creation. The *sūrah* portrays these scenes as they actually are. It draws our attention to what they show of the various stages, shapes and forms of life. All this gives us a very distinct awareness of life as it grows and spreads, and also of the power that originates life. It also gives us a strong desire to look at and enjoy the beauty of life.

> *And He it is who sends down water from the sky with which We bring forth plants of every type and out of these We bring forth verdure from which We bring forth grain piled tight, packed on one another; and out of the spathe of the palm tree, dates in thick clusters; and gardens of vines; and the olive tree, and the pomegranate: all so alike, and yet so different. Behold their fruit when they come to fruition and ripen. Surely in these there are clear signs for people who truly believe.* (Verse 99)

Water is frequently mentioned in the Qur'ān within the context of life and vegetation: "*He it is who sends down water from the sky with which We bring forth plants of every type.*" (Verse 99) That water is necessary for the growth of every type of plant is something that all human beings know, whether they are primitive or civilized, illiterate or educated. Yet water plays a far greater and more important role than that, and the Qur'ān here reminds us of this. By God's will, water was instrumental in making the face of the earth of the type of soil we know, which is plant-supporting. (This assumes that the theory which suggests that the face of the earth burned for a period of time, before it solidified but could still not support plant life is correct. Then water and other atmospheric elements combined to transform it into soft soil) Water has then continued to play an important role in making this soil fertile by causing nitrogen to fall on it from the atmosphere. Every time there is lightning, the electric sparkle separates the nitrogen which dissolves in water. It thus falls with the rain to give the soil added fertility. Nitrogen is the main component of the fertilizers people now produce in the same way, learning from the laws of nature. Indeed, nitrogen is so essential for vegetation that without it the face of the earth would be completely barren.

"*And He it is who sends down water from the sky with which We bring forth plants of every type and out of these We bring forth verdure from which We bring forth grain piled tight, packed on one another; and out of the spathe of the palm tree, dates in thick clusters; and gardens of vines; and the olive tree, and the pomegranate: all so alike, and yet so different.*" (Verse 99) All plants begin green, but the Arabic text uses for the description for the colour of the plants a word which imparts a gentler and more familiar sense than would be understood by the word 'green'. Out of this green vegetation God brings forth grain piled tight, as we see in ears of wheat and corn which are "*packed on one another*". We then have an image of the palm tree and its spathe: "*Out of the spathe of the palm tree, dates in thick clusters.*" (Verse 99) Here the Qur'ān uses in its description a term which generally denotes a small branch, but in the palm tree it refers to the stick on which the dates grow. These sticks are described as bending down, bearing the clusters of dates to impart a sense of beauty and tranquillity. "*And gardens of vines, and the olive tree and the pomegranate*", (Verse 99), which are mentioned here as examples of different types and species of plants. All of them are "*so alike and yet so different*".

The Qur'ān invites us to look at these and attentively contemplate with open minds how God causes all of them to grow, adds to their beauty and watches over them when they come to fruition: "*Behold their fruit when they come to fruition and ripen.*" (Verse 99) We are not invited to eat of its fruit, but rather to contemplate the beauty of that ripening fruit because the emphasis here is on the splendid aspects of creation and on the perfection which is the essential characteristic of God's work.

"*Surely in these there are clear signs for people who truly believe.*" (Verse 99) It is faith which opens people's hearts and minds and alerts them to the close link between themselves and the universe. It then invites us to believe in God, the Creator of all. Yet numerous are the hearts which remain closed, the eyes which choose not to see and the natures which determine not to respond. They look at all this splendid creation and all these inspiring signs but they remain unresponsive. It is as the Qur'ān says: *"Only those that can hear will surely answer."* (Verse 36) These signs inspire only those who believe.

Once the *sūrah* has portrayed this universal scene with all its pointers to God's existence and His ability and perfect design, it then describes the beliefs of those who ascribe partners to God. Against this inspiring set up, these beliefs appear so singular. Their assertions are shown to be revolting delusions, and they are strongly denounced: *"Yet they make the jinn equals with God, although He created them; and in their ignorance they invent for him sons and daughters. Limitless is He in His glory, and sublimely exalted above all that which they attribute to Him."* (Verse 100)

Some of the Arabs in the pre-Islamic days of ignorance used to worship the *jinn* while not knowing exactly who those *jinn* were. These were merely the delusions of paganism. When a human being deviates from believing in the absolute oneness of God, even partially, he is bound to increase his deviation. At first, the point of diversion seems to be too small to notice, but then the gap grows wider and wider. Those ancient Arabs used to follow the faith preached by the Prophet Ishmael, which was based on the belief in God's oneness as preached by the Prophet Abraham. They subsequently deviated from this sound concept. Their deviation must have started in a small way, but then it went as far as to consider the *jinn* partners with God, when He Himself created them: *"Yet they make the jinn equals with God, although He created them."* (Verse 100)

Different forms of pagan communities were aware that there were evil beings, i.e. something similar to devils, and they feared those beings, whether they considered them evil spirits or evil creatures. Therefore, they used to provide offerings to them in order to circumvent their fury. Thereafter, they began to worship them. This form of paganism that prevailed in Arabia before Islam is just one of many forms in which such misconceptions flourished and led to the worship of the *jinn* describing them as God's partners. The *sūrah* uses a very simple sentence, conveyed in the Arabic text by just one word, to describe the stupidity of such beliefs: *"Although He created them"*. (Verse 100) The sarcasm here is very clear. If it is God, the Glorious who has created them, how is it, then, that they are His partners, sharing with Him the qualities of Godhead and Lordship of the universe?

Their misconceptions were not confined to this aspect alone. Once idolatry or polytheism takes root, deviation never stops and delusions become rife. Those idolaters used to allege that God – limitless is He in His glory – had sons and daughters: "*in their ignorance they invent for him sons and daughters.*" (Verse 100) It is all their inventions. The Qur'ān uses here a particularly expressive word to denote 'invention', one which gives an impression of physical and noisy fabrication.

Among those who have invented sons for God were the Jews who claimed that Ezra was so and for the Christians it was Jesus Christ. As for the pagan Arabs, they claimed that the angels were God's daughters, even though they had no way of knowing what gender, if any, the angels took. None of these claims is based on any measure of sound knowledge. They are all the product of total ignorance. Hence, the Qur'ānic comment: "*Limitless is He in His glory, and sublimely exalted above all that which they attribute to Him.*" (Verse 100)

A Clear Concept of the Creator

The *sūrah* puts these allegations face to face against the absolute truth of God. It makes its arguments against these misconceptions in such a way that reveals how hollow they are: "*He is the Originator of the heavens and the earth. How can He have a child when He has never had a consort? He has created everything and has full knowledge of all things.*" (Verse 101)

He who originates the whole universe out of nothing is in no need of a son. Offspring are needed by mortals as an extension of their existence and they are needed by the weak who want help and by the dull who can invent nothing. Moreover, those inventors were aware of how procreation takes place. Anyone who desires offspring must have a mate or a female consort from his own species. How, then, can God have a son when He has never had a consort, and when He is one, single, and has no similarities with anyone or anything? How can any offspring be born without a mate?

Here the *sūrah* makes use of a recognized fact in order to address their minds, giving them examples that are relevant to their own lives and what they see around them. Moreover, the *sūrah* gives special emphasis to the fact that all beings are created in order to disprove any suggestions of a multiplicity of gods. What is created can never be a partner to the Creator. The essence of the Creator and that of the created are totally different. The *sūrah* speaks of God's knowledge as absolute, while the unbelievers' knowledge is based on delusions and guesswork: "*He has created everything and has full knowledge of all things.*" (Verse 101)

The same truth of creation is re-emphasized in order to assert another aspect. It tells that the One who is worshipped and obeyed and to whom submission is made is the creator of all things. Hence, there is no deity save Him, the only Lord in the universe: "*Such is God, your Lord; there is no deity other than Him, the Creator of all things, so worship Him alone. He is the Guardian of everything.*" (Verse 102)

The fact that God, the Almighty, is the only Creator makes Him the only sovereign of the universe, and that, consequently, makes Him the only one who takes full care of His creation. As He is the Creator of all, He also provides sustenance to all using resources in which He has no partners. Whatever all creatures eat and whatever they enjoy in this life is part of what is the sole property of God. When it has been confirmed that God has all these qualities of creation, sovereignty and provision of sustenance, another fact is also established; that is, His Lordship of the universe. No one else shares with Him these qualities: He controls everything, His is the authority to which everything submits, and He operates the system by which He takes care of His servants. So He is the One to be worshipped in the full sense of the word, which denotes obedience and full submission.

In their days of ignorance, the Arabs did not deny that God was the Creator of the universe and human beings. Nor did they deny that He was the One who provided sustenance to all of them, or that there was no place or dominion other than His from where to obtain provisions and sustenance. Other deviant communities did not deny these facts either, apart from a few Greek philosophers who advocated materialism. The materialist creeds of today have spread much wider than those advanced by Greek philosophers. This meant that in Arabia Islam faced the sort of deviation which allowed worship to be offered to different deities, who were claimed to be God's partners, in the hope that they would intercede with God on behalf of those who worshipped them. It also faced the other form of deviation by which people received their legislation and traditions from other sources. In other words, Islam did not face in Arabia the sort of atheism which some people profess today. Such people deny the very existence of God, making boastful claims that have no basis in knowledge, and no guidance or revelation on which they are founded.

The truth remains that those who argue about the existence of God are few, and they will remain so. The basic deviation continues to be the same as that which prevailed in the days of pre-Islamic ignorance – that people receive legislations and laws concerning their lives from sources other than God. This is the traditional and basic form of idolatry that flourished in ignorant Arabia, and indeed in all *jāhiliyyah* communities.

The deviant minority which today disputes God's existence may boast about being scientific, but they have no scientific basis for their claims. Human knowledge cannot justify atheism or prove it, and cannot provide evidence for it based on science or the nature of the universe. It is all a misconception caused initially by the desire to break with the Church and its God whom it tried to impose on people and by means of which it subjugated them in a way that could not be approved of by faith. There is also the added reason of the nature of those who advance these arguments, which leads to a disuse of the basic functions of human beings.

The truth of creation and its deliberate design, as well as the truth of the origination of life, are not cited in the Qur'ān in order to prove God's existence. Arguments against His existence are too petty to merit any attention by the Qur'ān. Instead, these truths are given in order to help people return to the path of truth, so that they can implement in their lives what is entailed by the fact that God is the only God and the only Lord who has power and control over all things. This means that they have to submit to Him alone and worship Him alone, associating with Him no partners whatsoever. Nevertheless, the truths of creation and the origination of life provide irrefutable arguments against those who dispute God's existence. Confronted with this, they have no escape except through boastfulness and futile argument which borders on absolute stupidity.

We do not wish to refer such people who grope in the dark to the Qur'ān, nor do we wish to impose on them our logic which is guided by the Qur'ān. We refer them to some eminent scientists who make a serious and rational approach to this whole question based on human knowledge.

John Cleveland Cothran, Professor of Chemistry and Chairman of Science and Mathematics Division, Duluth Branch, University of Minnesota, says:

Can any informed and reasoning intellect possibly believe that insensible and mindless matter just chanced to originate itself and all this system, then chanced to impose the system upon itself, whereafter this system just chances to remain imposed? Surely the answer is "No!" When energy transforms into "new" matter, the transformation proceeds "according to law" and the resulting matter obeys the same laws that apply to the matter already existing.

Chemistry discloses that matter is ceasing to exist, some varieties exceedingly slowly, others exceedingly swiftly. Therefore the existence of matter is not eternal. Consequently matter must have had a beginning. Evidence from chemistry and other sciences indicates that this beginning was not slow and gradual; on the contrary, it was sudden, and the evidence even indicates the approximate time when it occurred. Thus at some rather definite time the material realm was *created* and ever since has been obeying *law*, not the dictates of chance.[7]

Now, the material realm not being able to create itself and its governing laws, the act of creation must have been performed by some non-material agent. The stupendous marvels accomplished in that act show that this agent must possess superlative intelligence, an attribute of *mind*. But to bring mind into action in the material realm, as, for example, in the practice of medicine and in the field of parapsychology, the exercise of *will* is required, and this can be exerted only by a *person*. Hence our logical and inescapable conclusion is not only that creation occurred but that it was brought about according to the plan and will of a Person endowed with supreme intelligence and knowledge (omniscience), and the power to bring it about and keep it running according to plan (omnipotence). That is to say, we accept unhesitatingly the fact of the existence of "the supreme spiritual Being, God, the Creator and Director of the universe," mentioned in the beginning of this chapter.

The advances that have occurred in science since Lord Kelvin's day would enable him to state more emphatically than ever: "If

---

7. We have already said that all conclusions made by science remain within the sphere of probability. We do not use these quotations to prove the truth of Islam. We only put them as a counter argument for those who rely only on science. – Author's note.

you think strongly enough, you will be forced by science to believe in God."[8]

A further quotation from biophysicist Frank Allen is also useful here:

It has often been made to appear that the material universe has not needed a Creator. It is undeniable, however, that the universe exists. Four solutions of its origin may be proposed: first, that it is an illusion – contrary to the preceding statement; second, that it spontaneously arose out of nothing; third, that it had no origin but has existed eternally; fourth, that it was created.

The first proposed solution asserts that there is no problem to solve except the metaphysical one of human consciousness, which has occasionally itself been considered an illusion! The hypothesis of illusion has been lately revived in physical science by Sir James Jeans[9] who states that from the concepts of modern physics "the universe cannot admit of material representation, and the reason, I think, is that it has become a mere mental concept." Accordingly, one may say that illusory trains apparently filled with imaginary passengers cross unreal rivers on immaterial bridges formed of mental concepts!

The second concept, that the world of matter and energy arose of itself out of nothing, is likewise too absurd a supposition for any consideration.

The third concept, that the universe existed eternally, has one element in common with the concept of creation: either inanimate matter with its incorporated energy, or a Personal Creator, is eternal. No greater intellectual difficulty exists in the one concept than in the other. But the laws of thermodynamics (heat) indicate that the universe is running down to a condition when all bodies will be at the same extremely low temperature and no energy will be available. Life would then be impossible. In infinite time this state of entropy would already have happened. The hot sun and stars, the earth with its wealth of life, are

---

8. J.C. Cothran, in *The Evidence of God in an Expanding Universe*, ibid., pp. 41–2.
9. James Jeans, *The Mysterious Universe*, Cambridge University Press, 1931, p. 169.

complete evidence that the origin of the universe has occurred in *time*, at a fixed point of time, and therefore the universe must have been *created*. A great First Cause, an eternal, all-knowing and all-powerful Creator must exist, and the universe is His handiwork.[10]

The fact that God is the Creator of all and that He is the only deity in the universe is the basic rule given in the Qur'ān for the need to worship and submit to God alone. It explains the fact that He is the Lord who controls everything and directs the whole universe: "*Such is God, your Lord; there is no deity other than Him, the Creator of all things, so worship Him alone. He is the Guardian of everything.*" (Verse 102) He not only controls human beings; rather, He controls everything, since He has created all things. This is the reason for stating this fact which the unbelievers do not deny. They simply do not recognize what it entails: submission to God, obedience of His laws and acknowledgement of His absolute authority.

The Choice to Remain Blind

The *sūrah* follows this with a description of God which is so powerful that it impresses man's whole being with connotations which I believe to be indescribable by any human language. Let us then allow these impressions to formulate as we behold the scene which allows God's reassuring attributes to be more prominent than His fear-inspiring attributes: "*No power of vision can encompass Him, whereas He encompasses all vision; He is above all comprehension, yet is all-aware.*" (Verse 103)

Those who demonstrate their naïvety by demanding to see God are the same as those who demonstrate their arrogance by demanding tangible evidence of His existence. Neither group understand what they say. The senses and mental faculties of human beings have been created so that they can interact with the world around them, fulfil their task of building human life on earth, and observe and understand what the world and the universe contain of pointers to God's existence and His work. As for the nature of God Himself, they have not been

---

10. Frank Allen, in *The Evidence of God in an Expanding Universe*, op. cit., pp. 19–20.

given the power to conceive of it, because a created mortal cannot comprehend what is ever present and immortal. Besides, such comprehension is not an essential requirement for them to fulfil their task on earth. They have, indeed, been given what they need for its fulfilment and are fully equipped for the same.

It may be possible to understand that ancient people were naïve, but the arrogance of later groups is totally unacceptable. They talk about the atom, electrons, protons and neutrons when none of them has ever seen any of these. It has not been possible yet to make a microscope powerful enough to allow scientists to see such infinitely small particles.[11] Nevertheless, those people accept their theoretic existence and determine the practical effect of their presence. When they see these effects, they declare with absolute certainty that such particles are present. They do so in spite of the fact that the ultimate conclusion to which their experiment leads is 'the possibility' of the presence of those particles. But when they are told of God's existence and are directed to the evidence of His presence, they dispute that fact, giving arguments that have no basis in scientific knowledge, proper guidance or revelation. They demand tangible evidence which they can see with their own eyes, as if this whole universe and all the wonders of life are not sufficient evidence.

The *sūrah* then comments on what it has already listed of signs and evidence available everywhere in the universe, and within the human soul itself. What follows serves also as a comment on the statement that concerns God's nature: "*No power of vision can encompass Him, whereas He encompasses all vision; He is above all comprehension, yet is all-aware.*" (Verse 103)

We have already said that no human language can explain or commentate on such a description. It imparts its own clear sense to our minds. However, it is followed by a significant comment: "*Means of insight have come to you from your Lord. Therefore, whoever chooses to see does so for his own good, and whoever chooses to remain blind only himself does he hurt. I am not your keeper.*" (Verse 104) What God has given us is indeed the means of insight which provides guidance and points to the right way. The choice is then left to every individual. He who chooses to see will find himself in the

---

11. The author wrote this in the early 1960s. – Editor's note.

light, equipped with guidance. Inevitably, the alternative is total blindness. No one deliberately persists in error after having seen these signs and received these insights except one who shuts out his senses, suppresses his feelings, stifles his conscience and remains blind. The Prophet is instructed to declare that he dissociates himself from them: "*I am not your keeper.*" (Verse 104)

Perhaps it is important to draw the readers' attention to the fact that in the Arabic text these verses use, in addition to their powerful rhythm, a few unmistakeable and beautiful stylistic elements, such as alliteration and the juxtaposition of opposites. Thus, their effect, as we read them in Arabic, is immeasurably enhanced.

The *sūrah* then addresses the Prophet, pointing out how revelations and signs of God's existence have been spelled out and explained in a way that could not fit with the Prophet's social environment or the fact that he could not read and write. For any open-minded person, this, in itself, is sufficient evidence to prove that these revelations were from God. But the idolaters did not wish to have such convincing evidence. Hence, they used to say that Muḥammad had studied these questions of faith and those aspects of the universe with a Christian or a Jewish scholar. They did not realize that no Christian or Jew could have attained the standard of knowledge which remotely approached what the Prophet said to them. Indeed, no one on earth today can hope to reach anywhere near this level, superior as it is to all human knowledge. Hence, the Prophet is instructed to follow what has been revealed to him and to turn away from the unbelievers: "*Thus do We spell out Our revelations in diverse ways, that they may say, 'You have studied this', and that We may make it clear to people of knowledge. Follow what has been revealed to you by your Lord, other than whom there is no deity, and turn your back on those who associate partners with God. Had God so willed, they would not have associated partners with Him. We have not made you their keeper, nor are you responsible for them.*" (Verses 105–7)

God spells out His revelations at a level that was totally unknown to the Arabs, because it did not originate from their social environment or indeed from any human environment. His explanation leads to two opposing results: those who accept and those who reject God's guidance. The latter who do not wish to learn or strive to know the truth will try to find some sort of argument to explain the superior excellence which characterizes the Prophet's address to them. They allege what they know to be false. They were aware of every detail in Muḥammad's life before he began to receive his message and after that. Nevertheless, they said to him: "Muḥammad, you have studied all this with Christian and Jewish scholars and learned it from them." No Christian or Jew had ever known anything like the Qur'ān. Their books are still available to us now. The gulf between what they have and the Qur'ān is very wide indeed. Now, all they have is merely a few inconsistent accounts of the histories of Prophets and Kings, mixed with legends and superstitions invented by unknown authors. This is the essence of what we find in the Old Testament.

As for the New Testament, it also contains some reports related by the disciples of Jesus Christ (peace be upon him), several decades after he was raised to heaven. Synods then introduced amendments and distortions of these. Even moral and spiritual teachings were subjected to distortions, amendments and omission. How does all this compare with the Glorious Qur'ān? In their ignorance, the Arab idolaters used to make such statements. What is most singular is that some ignorant people of our present day, including some Orientalists and some who claim to be Muslims, repeat such impudent claims. What is even more singular is that their claims are alleged to be the result of 'scientific study' or 'scholarly research', which only Orientalists are equipped to pursue!

As for those who have true knowledge, the spelling out of revelations in the Qur'ānic way allows them to realize the truth: "*That We may make it clear to people of knowledge.*" (Verse 105) As a result, the separation occurs between people endowed with knowledge and insight who know the truth, and people who are blind and ignorant.

Well-Defined Attitudes

This is followed by a divine order to the Prophet to follow what God has revealed to him and to turn away from pagan people who associate partners with Him. He is not to pay any attention to them or their petty arguments and not to worry about their stubborn rejection of his message. His task is to implement his message by moulding his life and the attitudes of his followers on the basis of the divine message. He is to care nothing for the unbelievers: "*Follow what has been revealed to you by your Lord, other than whom there is no deity, and turn your back on those who associate partners with God.*" (Verse 106)

Had God so willed, He would have imposed His guidance on them. He could, if He so willed, have created them knowing no way other than that of His guidance, in the same way as angels are bound always to obey Him. He, however, has created man with the ability to follow either right guidance or error. He has left him to choose his way and has held him accountable for his choice. All this is, of course, within the framework of God's absolute free will which governs everything that occurs in the universe, without imposing a choice on any human being. God has created man in this fashion for a purpose He knows. He has a role to play assigned to him by God, using his abilities and talents: "*Had God so willed, they would not have associated partners with Him.*" (Verse 107)

The Prophet is not responsible for their actions, and he has not been assigned as a watchdog over their hearts: "*We have not made you their keeper, nor are you responsible for them.*" (Verse 107) This instruction to the Prophet defines the area around which he should concentrate his efforts. The Prophet's successors and those who advocate his faith in every generation and every community are also made aware of their area of activity and its limits.

An advocate of God's message must not attach too much importance to, or pin his hopes on, those who turn their backs on His call and who do not respond to the pointers to faith and divine guidance. He should give top priority to, and concentrate his hopes on, those who listen and respond to his call. These are the ones who need to mould their whole existence on the basic rule of faith, which is the cornerstone of their religion. They also need to formulate a total concept of existence and life, and to regularize their moral values and conduct, and indeed all the affairs of their community, on the same basis. These tasks require and deserve all efforts the advocates of Islam can exert. Those who choose to remain in the opposing camp after having had God's message conveyed to them, deserve nothing but to be ignored. As the cause of the truth acquires strength, the rules God has set in operation complete their cycle when God hurls the truth at falsehood, and when the truth triumphs and falsehood is no more. What is extremely important is that the truth should exist in its completeness. When it does, falsehood has no sway: it just disappears, totally.

Moreover, the believers are instructed to adopt, as they turn away from the unbelievers, an attitude of propriety, decency and refinement which suits those who believe in God. They are instructed not to revile the idols or deities of the unbelievers so that the latter do not start to revile God, without knowing His true position and His majesty. Thus any abuse by the believers of their worthless deities would be taken as an excuse to abuse God, the Almighty: *"Do not revile those whom they invoke instead of God, lest they revile God out of spite, and in ignorance. Thus have We made the actions of every community seem goodly to them. Then to their Lord shall they all return, and He will explain to them all that they have been doing."* (Verse 108)

It is human nature that when a person does something, whether good or bad, he thinks that he has done well and he defends his actions. If he follows guidance, he finds it good; and if he is in error, he still believes that his error is good. The unbelievers ascribed partners to God and appealed to them instead of appealing to Him; yet they accepted that God is the One who creates and provides sustenance. If the Muslims had reviled the unbelievers' deities, the latter would have disregarded what they believed of God's position and abused God Himself in order to defend their concepts and worship of other deities. Hence, the believers are required to let them alone: *"Then to their Lord shall they all return, and He will explain to them all that they have been doing."* (Verse 108)

This is the sort of decent attitude which is worthy of a believer who is sure that the faith he follows is that of the truth and who does not indulge in what is useless or unbecoming. Abusing the deities worshipped by unbelievers will not put those unbelievers on the course of guidance. Instead, it will only add to their stubbornness. Why, then, should believers engage in what is useless, when it could lead them to hearing what they do not like, as the unbelievers begin to retaliate by abusing God?

The passage concludes by mentioning those unbelievers who used to swear most solemnly that if only a miracle, like those given to earlier prophets and messengers, were shown them they would certainly believe. On hearing such assurances, some Muslims suggested to the Prophet (peace be upon him) that he should pray to God to show them such a miracle. Here they are given a clear answer, which shows the nature of those people and their obstinate rejection of the divine faith: *"They swear by God most solemnly that if a miracle be shown to them they would believe in it. Say: 'Miracles are in God's power'. For all you know, even if one is shown to them, they may still not believe? We will turn their hearts and eyes away since they did not believe in it the first time. We shall leave them to blunder about in their overweening arrogance. Even if We were to send down angels to them, and if the dead were to speak to them, and even if We were to range all things before them, they would still not believe unless God so willed. Yet most of them are ignorant."* (Verses 109–11)

A person who does not believe when his attention has been drawn to the miraculous nature of creation and to all the pointers in the world around him directing him to faith adopts a very strange attitude. A person who looks at all the signs and indicators that he sees within himself and everywhere around him and still does not turn to his Lord and declare his belief in Him is one who follows a twisted logic. What hinders such people from believing in the truth in the first instance will certainly stop them from accepting the faith after a miracle has been shown to them. How could Muslims who suggested showing them a miracle tell that it could be otherwise? It is God alone who knows the nature of those people. He leaves them to blunder about in their arrogance, because He knows that they will not respond. They actually deserve the punishment their rejection of the faith incurs. God knows that they would not believe even if He did send down the angels or resurrect the dead to speak to them, in response to their suggestions. Nor would they believe even if He ranged everything in the universe in front of them to call on them to accept the faith. They do not believe unless God wills, and He does not will that because they do not strive to find guidance. This fact describes in a nutshell the nature of their hearts and minds. What those who stubbornly follow error and turn away from faith lack is not a proof or a sign. They are simply sick at heart, having shut down their natural responses and stifled their consciences. Guidance is a reward deserved only by those who strive for it.

Basic Facts on Faith and God's Power

Moreover, these verses outline certain basic facts that we must consider. The first of these facts is that to accept the faith or to deny it, to follow the right guidance or to remain in error, does not depend on the provision of proofs and evidence of the truth. The truth is its own proof and it can easily prevail over the human mind to accept it and submit to it with reassurance. There are impediments that may prevent a person from accepting the truth. Indeed, God refers to these as He addresses the believers: "*For all you know, even if one [i.e. a miracle] is shown to them, they may still not believe? We will turn their hearts and eyes away since they did not believe in it the first time. We shall leave them to blunder about in their overweening arrogance.*" (Verses 109–10) What prevented them the first time round from accepting divine guidance could happen again even after a miracle is shown them, and they could, thus, continue to go astray and reject guidance.

The pointers to faith are latent within man himself and are inherent within the truth itself. They do not relate to any external factor. It is imperative, therefore, that man's heart is purged of all external factors impeding its acceptance of the faith.

The second fact is that God's will is the ultimate factor which determines who follows guidance and who goes astray. God has willed that human beings be tested, allowing us the freedom of choice to determine which course we follow. Anyone who utilizes this freedom in order to seek guidance with the intention of following it once it is received, though he may not know at that moment where he stands, will find that God, by His will, is helping him and showing him the right way. Conversely, a person who uses this freedom of choice to turn away from guidance and the pointers to faith, will find himself further away from the truth, because God's will has determined that he should drift further astray and continue to grope in the dark. God's will prevails over human beings in all situations. It is He who determines everything in the end.

It is to this fact that the passage we are discussing refers: "*We will turn their hearts and eyes away since they did not believe in it the first time. We shall leave them to blunder about in their overweening arrogance. Even if We were to send down angels to them, and if the dead were to speak to them, and even if We were to range all things before them, they would still not believe unless God so willed. Yet most of them are ignorant."* (Verses 110–11) Indeed, two earlier verses in this passage also refer to this fact: *"Follow what has been revealed to you by your Lord, other than whom there is no deity, and turn your back on those who associate partners with God. Had God so willed, they would not have associated partners with Him. We have not made you their keeper, nor are you responsible for them."* (Verses 106–7)

A further reference to this fact is provided in the verse that begins the next passage: *"Thus We have set up against every prophet enemies: the evil ones among human beings and the jinn, who inspire each other with varnished and deluding falsehood. Had your Lord willed otherwise, they would not have done it. Therefore, leave them to their own inventions."* (Verse 112)

Everything is thus left to God's will. It is He who has willed not to guide them, because they did not take the necessary measures to seek and follow His guidance. He has also willed to allow them this measure of freedom to test them. It is He who guides them if they strive for guidance and leaves them to go astray if they choose to do so. According to the Islamic concept, there is no contradiction between the fact that God's will is absolutely free and that He has allowed human beings this measure of freedom to test them.

The third fact is that those who obey God and those who disobey Him are equally subject to His power; He controls everyone's destiny. They cannot do anything except in accordance with God's will which has determined the laws that govern human life. In the area of choice left for man, a believer achieves harmony between the fact that he is inevitably subject to God's authority in the way he is made, his physical and spiritual constitution, the function of every part of his body, etc. and his willing submission to God as the natural result of choosing to follow God's guidance. Thus, a believer lives at peace with himself because what is inevitable and what is the result of free choice in his life follow the same law and submit to the same authority. The unbelievers cannot break away from God's law which governs their constitution and their natural needs. They have to submit to God's law. However, where they have freedom of choice, they rebel against God's authority and refuse to implement His law and constitution. This conflict leaves them miserable. Ultimately, they remain within God's power and He controls their destinies. They indeed cannot do anything without His will.

This last fact is particularly relevant to the issues which will be presented in the remaining part of this *sūrah*. Hence, it is going to be repeated in different forms. The rest of the *sūrah* tackles the question of God's authority over people's lives and the law they implement. Hence, the *sūrah* repeatedly emphasizes that all authority belongs to God who continues to govern the destiny of those who disobey Him and turn away from His constitution. These people cannot do any harm to believers, unless God so wills. Indeed, they are too weak to have any authority over themselves, let alone over believers. What takes place in life is simply the fulfilment of God's will as it relates to both those who obey Him and those who refuse to do so.

"Even if We were to send down angels to them, and if the dead were to speak to them, and even if We were to range all things before them, they would still not believe unless God so willed. Yet most of them are ignorant." (Verse 111) Al-Ṭabarī, a famous scholar and commentator on the Qur'ān says of this verse: "God says to His Messenger (peace be upon him): Muḥammad, you should give up any hope of success for those who equate idols with their Lord and who claim that they would believe if they are given a sign. Even though We would send the angels down to them so that they may see them with their own eyes, and if we cause the dead to come back to life and speak to them supporting you and confirming your prophethood and assuring them that your message is the truth, and even if we would range everything in front of them testifying to your message, they would still refuse to believe in you and would continue to deny your message, unless God wills otherwise. Most of those unbelievers are ignorant of this fact. They think that accepting the faith or denying it is their prerogative. This is not true. It is all within My power. Only those I guide to success accept the faith, and those I turn away deny it."

What al-Ṭabarī says here is true, but it requires the clarification that we have given, taking into account the import of all Qur'ānic statements relevant to guidance, error, God's will and man's endeavour. To accept the faith is an event, and so is rejecting it. No event takes place in the universe except by God's will: *"Indeed, We have created everything in due measure and proportion."* (54: 49)

The law which operates God's will, so that one person becomes a believer and one rejects the faith, is explained by the total sum of the relevant Qur'ānic statements. Every man is tested with a measure of free choice which determines his direction. If he sets himself on the route to guidance and strives to achieve it, he will certainly be guided by God's will. If he chooses the other way and turns away from guidance, God will send him further astray. In this respect, both following God's guidance and turning away from it are accomplished by God's will. Man remains within God's power and his life continues according to God's will, which is free, absolute and unrestrained.

13

On Permissibility and Prohibition

Thus We have set up against every prophet enemies: the evil ones among human beings and the *jinn*, who inspire each other with varnished and deluding falsehood. Had your Lord willed otherwise, they would not have done it. Therefore, leave them to their own inventions, (112)

وَكَذَٰلِكَ جَعَلْنَا لِكُلِّ نَبِيٍّ عَدُوًّا شَيَٰطِينَ ٱلْإِنسِ وَٱلْجِنِّ يُوحِى بَعْضُهُمْ إِلَىٰ بَعْضٍ زُخْرُفَ ٱلْقَوْلِ غُرُورًا وَلَوْ شَآءَ رَبُّكَ مَا فَعَلُوهُ فَذَرْهُمْ وَمَا يَفْتَرُونَ ۝

so that the hearts of those who do not believe in the life to come may be inclined to what they say and, being pleased with it, persist in their erring ways. (113)

وَلِتَصْغَىٰ إِلَيْهِ أَفْـِٔدَةُ ٱلَّذِينَ لَا يُؤْمِنُونَ بِٱلْآخِرَةِ وَلِيَرْضَوْهُ وَلِيَقْتَرِفُوا۟ مَا هُم مُّقْتَرِفُونَ ۝

Am I to seek for judge anyone other than God, when it is He who has revealed the Book to you, clearly spelling out the truth. Those to whom We previously gave revelations know that it is the truth revealed by your Lord. So, do not be among the doubters. (114)

أَفَغَيْرَ ٱللَّهِ أَبْتَغِى حَكَمًا وَهُوَ ٱلَّذِى أَنزَلَ إِلَيْكُمُ ٱلْكِتَٰبَ مُفَصَّلًا وَٱلَّذِينَ ءَاتَيْنَٰهُمُ ٱلْكِتَٰبَ يَعْلَمُونَ أَنَّهُۥ مُنَزَّلٌ مِّن رَّبِّكَ بِٱلْحَقِّ فَلَا تَكُونَنَّ مِنَ ٱلْمُمْتَرِينَ ۝

Perfected are the words of your Lord in truth and justice. No one can change His words. He hears all and knows all. (115)

وَتَمَّتْ كَلِمَتُ رَبِّكَ صِدْقًا وَعَدْلًا لَّا مُبَدِّلَ لِكَلِمَٰتِهِۦ وَهُوَ ٱلسَّمِيعُ ٱلْعَلِيمُ ١١٥

If you were to pay heed to the greater part of those on earth, they would lead you away from God's path. They follow nothing but conjecture and they do nothing but guess. (116)

وَإِن تُطِعْ أَكْثَرَ مَن فِى ٱلْأَرْضِ يُضِلُّوكَ عَن سَبِيلِ ٱللَّهِ إِن يَتَّبِعُونَ إِلَّا ٱلظَّنَّ وَإِنْ هُمْ إِلَّا يَخْرُصُونَ ١١٦

Your Lord surely knows best who strays from His path, and best knows He those who are right-guided. (117)

إِنَّ رَبَّكَ هُوَ أَعْلَمُ مَن يَضِلُّ عَن سَبِيلِهِۦ وَهُوَ أَعْلَمُ بِٱلْمُهْتَدِينَ ١١٧

Eat, then, of that over which God's name has been pronounced, if you truly believe in His revelations. (118)

فَكُلُوا۟ مِمَّا ذُكِرَ ٱسْمُ ٱللَّهِ عَلَيْهِ إِن كُنتُم بِـَٔايَٰتِهِۦ مُؤْمِنِينَ ١١٨

And why should you not eat of that over which God's name has been pronounced when He has clearly spelled out to you what He has forbidden you (to eat) unless you are driven to do so by sheer necessity? Many people lead others astray by their errant views and lack of knowledge. Your Lord is fully aware of those who transgress. (119)

وَمَا لَكُمْ أَلَّا تَأْكُلُوا۟ مِمَّا ذُكِرَ ٱسْمُ ٱللَّهِ عَلَيْهِ وَقَدْ فَصَّلَ لَكُم مَّا حَرَّمَ عَلَيْكُمْ إِلَّا مَا ٱضْطُرِرْتُمْ إِلَيْهِ وَإِنَّ كَثِيرًا لَّيُضِلُّونَ بِأَهْوَآئِهِم بِغَيْرِ عِلْمٍ إِنَّ رَبَّكَ هُوَ أَعْلَمُ بِٱلْمُعْتَدِينَ ١١٩

Abstain from all sin, be it open or secret. Those who commit sins will be requited for what they have committed. (120)

وَذَرُواْ ظَـٰهِرَ ٱلْإِثْمِ وَبَاطِنَهُۥٓ إِنَّ ٱلَّذِينَ يَكْسِبُونَ ٱلْإِثْمَ سَيُجْزَوْنَ بِمَا كَانُواْ يَقْتَرِفُونَ ١٢٠

Hence, do not eat of that over which God's name has not been pronounced; for that is sinful. The evil ones do whisper to their friends to argue with you. Should you pay heed to them, you will end up associating partners with God. (121)

وَلَا تَأْكُلُواْ مِمَّا لَمْ يُذْكَرِ ٱسْمُ ٱللَّهِ عَلَيْهِ وَإِنَّهُۥ لَفِسْقٌ وَإِنَّ ٱلشَّيَـٰطِينَ لَيُوحُونَ إِلَىٰٓ أَوْلِيَآئِهِمْ لِيُجَـٰدِلُوكُمْ وَإِنْ أَطَعْتُمُوهُمْ إِنَّكُمْ لَمُشْرِكُونَ ١٢١

Is he who was dead and whom We have raised to life, and for whom We set up a light to see his way among men, to be compared to one who is in deep darkness out of which he cannot emerge? Thus do their deeds seem goodly to the unbelievers. (122)

أَوَمَن كَانَ مَيْتًا فَأَحْيَيْنَـٰهُ وَجَعَلْنَا لَهُۥ نُورًا يَمْشِى بِهِۦ فِى ٱلنَّاسِ كَمَن مَّثَلُهُۥ فِى ٱلظُّلُمَـٰتِ لَيْسَ بِخَارِجٍ مِّنْهَا كَذَٰلِكَ زُيِّنَ لِلْكَـٰفِرِينَ مَا كَانُواْ يَعْمَلُونَ ١٢٢

And thus in every city have We placed arch-criminals so that they weave their schemes there. But it is only against themselves that they scheme, though they do not perceive it. (123)

وَكَذَٰلِكَ جَعَلْنَا فِى كُلِّ قَرْيَةٍ أَكَـٰبِرَ مُجْرِمِيهَا لِيَمْكُرُواْ فِيهَا وَمَا يَمْكُرُونَ إِلَّا بِأَنفُسِهِمْ وَمَا يَشْعُرُونَ ١٢٣

When a sign comes to them, they say: "We shall not believe unless we are given the same as God's messengers were given." But God knows best whom to entrust with His message. Humiliation before God and severe suffering will befall those guilty of evildoing for all their scheming. (124)

وَإِذَا جَآءَتْهُمْ ءَايَةٌ قَالُوا۟ لَن نُّؤْمِنَ حَتَّىٰ نُؤْتَىٰ مِثْلَ مَآ أُوتِىَ رُسُلُ ٱللَّهِ ٱللَّهُ أَعْلَمُ حَيْثُ يَجْعَلُ رِسَالَتَهُۥ سَيُصِيبُ ٱلَّذِينَ أَجْرَمُوا۟ صَغَارٌ عِندَ ٱللَّهِ وَعَذَابٌ شَدِيدٌ بِمَا كَانُوا۟ يَمْكُرُونَ ﴿١٢٤﴾

Whomever God wills to guide, He makes his bosom open wide with willingness towards self-surrender (to Him); and whomever He wills to let go astray, He causes his bosom to be tight and constricted, as if he were climbing up into the skies. Thus does God lay the scourge on the unbelievers. (125)

فَمَن يُرِدِ ٱللَّهُ أَن يَهْدِيَهُۥ يَشْرَحْ صَدْرَهُۥ لِلْإِسْلَٰمِ وَمَن يُرِدْ أَن يُضِلَّهُۥ يَجْعَلْ صَدْرَهُۥ ضَيِّقًا حَرَجًا كَأَنَّمَا يَصَّعَّدُ فِى ٱلسَّمَآءِ كَذَٰلِكَ يَجْعَلُ ٱللَّهُ ٱلرِّجْسَ عَلَى ٱلَّذِينَ لَا يُؤْمِنُونَ ﴿١٢٥﴾

Such is the path of your Lord, a straight path. We have made Our revelations plain for people who reflect. (126)

وَهَٰذَا صِرَٰطُ رَبِّكَ مُسْتَقِيمًا قَدْ فَصَّلْنَا ٱلْآيَٰتِ لِقَوْمٍ يَذَّكَّرُونَ ﴿١٢٦﴾

Theirs shall be an abode of peace with their Lord. He will be their patron in reward for what they have been doing. (127)

۞ لَهُمْ دَارُ ٱلسَّلَٰمِ عِندَ رَبِّهِمْ وَهُوَ وَلِيُّهُم بِمَا كَانُوا۟ يَعْمَلُونَ ﴿١٢٧﴾

Overview

With this passage we begin discussion of the great issue treated in the remainder of this *sūrah*. The groundwork for this discussion has been prepared throughout the *sūrah*, including the discussion of major faith concepts. Further preparation is given in the first two verses of this passage which speak of the continuing battle launched against every prophet by the evil ones among human beings and the *jinn*, and how this battle is resolved. The preparation may also be seen in earlier references to the rules that govern divine guidance and how people react to it.

Now the *sūrah* dwells on the issue of what is lawful or forbidden of slaughtered animals, and whether God's name is invoked at the time of their slaughter or not. This theme reiterates the basic Islamic concept acknowledging God's absolute authority over everything in the universe, and His unquestionable sovereignty and right to legislate. Human beings are denied any share of this authority and sovereignty. Within the framework of this concept, every violation, large or small, acquires the same degree of importance. A ruling may relate to a very simple issue such as the definition of which slaughtered animals to eat from, or it may be very serious, relating to the state, the system of government and social relations. Within the light of the basic principle, both equally concern the recognition or rejection of God's absolute authority and His Lordship over the universe.

The Qur'ān emphasizes this principle on every occasion. It is reiterated when any new legislation is outlined. This is because this principle is central to faith and submission to God. Once this principle is settled, what remains is its implementation in matters of detail.

We will see in this passage, and in the rest of the *sūrah*, that this principle is repeated in various ways, as the *sūrah* refers to some of the laws and traditions of pre-Islamic society. The relationship between these laws and traditions on the one hand and a rejection of Islam on the other is made clear by virtue of the fact that their enactment and practice is possible only when Godhead is attributed to an entity other than God Almighty. Hence, the Qur'ān launches a sustained attack on them, using different ways and methods, but always linking its campaign to the basic issue of faith and submission to God alone.

Enemies of the Prophets

The first two verses complement the passage discussed in the previous chapter. They also serve as a prelude to the important issues that relate to authority, law and sovereignty which take up the remaining part of this *sūrah*.

> *Thus We have set up against every prophet enemies: the evil ones among human beings and the jinn, who inspire each other with varnished and deluding falsehood. Had your Lord willed otherwise, they would not have done it. Therefore, leave them to their own inventions, so that the hearts of those who do not believe in the life to come may be inclined to what they say and, being pleased with it, persist in their erring ways.* (Verses 112–13)

The first word here reminds us that God has ruled that those unbelievers who demand miracles in order to believe and who turn away from the pointers to faith which are present everywhere around them do not actually ever come to accept the faith, even though they may be shown every miracle they can possibly imagine. By God's same free-will, He has assigned to every prophet enemies who are the evil ones among human beings and the *jinn*. Those evil ones inspire each other with varnished falsehoods, half-truths and delusive whispers in order to resist God's guidance and combat His messengers. It is God's will also that those who do not believe in the hereafter shall listen attentively to such deceptive falsehood and half-truths and be pleased with what they hear. This enables them to continue with their opposition to God's messengers and the truth they preach, endeavouring to spread corruption on earth.

All this occurs as God has determined and according to His free-will. Had he willed otherwise, they would not have done so. His will is accomplished in the manner which pleases Him, leading to different results. In a nutshell, nothing of what happens in the universe comes about as mere coincidence, or through human power or authority. When we realize that everything that takes place on earth actually happens according to God's will, including the unabating fight between truth and falsehood, God's messengers and evil forces, then we should try to understand God's purpose in so letting it take place: "*Thus We have set up against every prophet enemies: the evil ones among human beings and the jinn, who inspire each other with varnished and deluding falsehood.*" (Verse 112)

It was God's will and planning that every prophet faced enemies, and that those enemies were the evil ones among the human race and *jinn*. The Arabic term used here for 'the evil ones' is 'satans'. From a linguistic point of view, to be a satan is to rebel, to follow every error and to give oneself up completely to evil. This can be true of human beings as well as the *jinn*. If such rebellion and dedication to evil by anyone from the *jinn* makes him a satan, the same title is given to any human being who does likewise. Indeed, this description can be applied to an uncontrollable animal that causes endless harm. It is said in Arabic: "The black dog is a satan."

Those satans, be they human or *jinn*, whom God has made enemies to every prophet, deceive one another by falsehood that is given a bright and unreal glitter. Thus, they urge one another to continue in their rebellion, evil and disobedience to God.

Evil human beings are easily identifiable; and their work is familiar. All the different patterns of their hostility towards prophets, the truth they preach and to the believers who follow them are well known. The satans among the *jinn,* and indeed all the *jinn,* are creatures about whom we know only what God, who knows all, has chosen to tell us. In principle, we accept without hesitation what God has told us about the existence of creatures other than man and the living species known to man. We accept God's statement as it is, within the limits He has set for it. Those who claim to follow a scientific approach and who use this in order to deny what God has stated in this regard do not base their argument on any solid foundation. They do not claim that their knowledge is aware of every type of living species on this planet, let alone what exists on other planets. All that human science can assume is that the type of life which exists on earth may or may not exist on other planets and stars. Even if these assumptions prove to be true, they cannot preclude the possibility that other types of life and beings may inhabit other parts of the universe which remain totally unknown to man. Therefore, it is far too arrogant for anyone to deny the existence of such a living world on the basis of human knowledge or science.

The nature of the *jinn*, some of whom like *Iblīs* and his offspring give themselves up totally to evil, remains unknown to us except in as far as God tells us in the Qur'ān and His Messenger in the *ḥadīth*. On the basis of these accurate statements we know that the *jinn* have been created out of fire and that they are able to live on the face of the earth, inside it or even outside it. They can move much more swiftly than human beings. They include some who are good believers and some who reject the faith totally. They can see human beings, while human beings cannot see them in their original form. This is not surprising, because there are numerous species that see man while man does not see them. We know also that satans have access to human beings and that they tempt them to stray. We do not know how this is done, but we know that these satans have no power over true believers. A satan constantly remains with a believer: when the believer remembers God, the satan shrinks and disappears, but when the believer is absorbed with worldly matters, the satan tries to tempt him. All satanic scheming is hollow and weak if the believer continues to remind himself of God. The *jinn* will also be resurrected at the same time as human beings, and all will be held to account. The *jinn* will either be rewarded with heaven or punished in hell, in the same way as human beings. Compared to angels, the *jinn* are very weak and powerless.

From this verse we learn that God has set up enemies for every prophet from among the evil ones, human and *jinn* alike. Had it been God's will, they would have done nothing of this. They would not have rebelled, given themselves up to evil, fought against the prophets, harmed the believers and tried to turn people away from God's path. God could have compelled them to follow His guidance, or made it easy for them to follow it, should they have shown the inclination to do so. Furthermore, He could have made them totally incapable of standing up to the prophets and the believers. He has, however, left them this measure of free choice, and enabled them to cause His servants harm in order to test them. Likewise, He tests His enemies by the choice He has given them. They certainly can cause no servant of God any harm beyond what God has willed. "*Had your Lord willed otherwise, they would not have done it.*" (Verse 112)

The Limits of Evil Power

What conclusions can we draw from the statements made in this verse? The first is that those who are hostile to every prophet and who try to cause harm to those who follow the prophets are evil whether they belong to the human race or to the *jinn*. They all work for the same end. Some of them may deceive others, but they all rebel against God's guidance, follow evil ways and maintain their hostility towards the believers.

Second, these devils cannot do any of this through any inherent ability of their own. They are subject to God's will. He uses them to test those who believe in Him for a definite purpose of His own. He puts the believers to such a test so that they may show how determined they are to defend the truth entrusted to them. He also wants their hearts to be purged of anything that is unacceptable to Him. When they come through the test with their heads raised high, He stops their enemies from harming them any further. These enemies, who are indeed God's own enemies, find themselves powerless, humiliated, shouldering their heavy burdens and lacking the support of others.

Third, it is God's wisdom that has allowed these evil ones to give themselves up totally to evil. God tests them within the limits of the ability and choice He has allowed them, and He leaves them, for a while at least, with some ability to harm the believers. By the same process, He tests believers so that they show their perseverance and dedication to the cause of the truth they serve. When falsehood seems to have complete power over them, are they able to show that they have completely dedicated themselves to God and that they are willing to sacrifice their all for His cause? Those who persevere in times of both hardship and ease can thus distinguish themselves. All this is part of God's purpose. Otherwise, He is always able to prevent anything from happening.

Lastly, those devils, be they human or *jinn,* and the scheming and harm they cause are not to be given any great importance. They have no independent power of their own. Indeed, they cannot exceed the limits God has allowed them. When a believer realizes that it is his Lord who has all the power and who determines everything according to a definite measure, he should look down upon the devils who set themselves up in hostility to Him whatever power and authority they claim to command. Hence, the divine instruction to God's Messenger (peace be upon him): "*Therefore, leave them to their own inventions.*" (Verse 112) Let them do whatever they want, because I, the Lord of the universe, am able to smite them whenever I wish. Their retribution is kept in store for them.

There is another purpose for this enmity, which differs from testing both the believers and the evil ones. This is stated clearly in the second verse in this passage: "*So that the hearts of those who do not believe in the life to come may be inclined to what they say and, being pleased with it, persist in their erring ways.*" (Verse 113) This means that those who

285

do not believe in the hereafter will listen to such glittering and deluding falsehood. Such people attach all importance to the life of this world. As they see the devils standing up to every prophet, inflicting harm and hardship on their followers and deluding one another with sweet words and deceptive action, they are ready to follow these devils wherever they lead them. They admire their power, unreal as it is, and they are impressed by their deception. They thus commit sin and error, and indulge in disobedience and corruption.

This is also something that God has willed and has allowed to happen because of what it involves of testing people. Thus, everyone has a chance to prove himself, do what he likes and earn his reward or punishment in all fairness. Human life is thus maintained, the truth is shown distinctly, and goodness is identified through perseverance in times of hardship. The evil ones will shoulder all their burdens on the Day of Judgement. Everything takes place in accordance with God's will whether it is a matter that relates to God's enemies or to His obedient servants.

The scene painted in the Qur'ān showing the battle between the evil ones, human and *jinn,* on the one side and the prophets and their followers on the other, as well as God's overpowering will, is certainly worth contemplating. It is a battle in which the universal forces of evil combine, with determined cooperation and coordination, to achieve a definite objective. Their uniting force is their enmity to the truth, which is represented by the messages God has sent down through His prophets. To achieve their objective, they have a well-defined plan in which they employ specific methods: they "*inspire each other with varnished and deluding falsehood.*" (Verse 112) They supply one another with the means of temptation, and at the same time they try to cause one another to yield to temptation. This phenomenon applies to every evil force which aims to suppress the truth and subdue its advocates. The evil ones cooperate among themselves and they help one another to persist in error. They never try to guide one another to the truth. Indeed, they always counsel each other to persist with their hostility to the truth.

But nothing of this scheming is free of restraints. It remains within the realm of God's will. The evil ones cannot accomplish any part of it beyond the extent that God's will allows. Great and overpowering as their scheming may seem, mustering the combined forces of evil, it remains constrained, unable to have a free rein. It cannot help anyone, nor can it escape questioning or being held to account. Indeed, dictators and tyrants try to convince their subjects that they are not accountable to anyone so that their subjects remain submissive towards them. This, however, is false. These tyrants' will and power are indeed subject to God's will and can operate only within the limits God has allowed them. They cannot cause any of God's servants any harm except within the limits God has allowed them in order to test that servant. Eventually, all power belongs to God.

The advocates of the truth are well advised to look carefully at the scene which portrays the evil ones working together to carry out a unified plan, so that they can realize the nature of that plan and its method. They also should contemplate that scene which portrays God's controlling power and His overpowering will because this should give them confidence and reassurance. They should always look up to God's will, which cannot be resisted, and His authority to which the whole universe submits. When they do so, they will not care for what the evil ones desire. The believers will then be able to continue along the way God has chosen for them. They continue to establish the truth in their everyday life after having established it in their hearts. The hostility of the evil ones does not worry them, because they leave it all to God who will certainly take care of it: *"Had your Lord willed otherwise, they would not have done it. Therefore, leave them to their own inventions."* (Verse 112)

A Revelation to Explain All Issues

The passage then emphasizes once more that the authority to legislate in all matters that relate to human life belongs to God alone. This is preliminary to stating that it is God who determines which slaughtered animals are lawful to eat and which are forbidden. Those who associate partners with God often exercise this authority in blatant aggression against God and His sovereignty. We note that a long prelude is included here before the issue is clearly tackled: *"Am I to seek for judge anyone other than God, when it is He who has revealed the Book to you, clearly spelling out the truth. Those to whom We previously gave revelations know that it is the truth revealed by your Lord. So, do not be among the doubters. Perfected are the words of your Lord in truth and justice. No one can change His words. He hears all and knows all. If you were to pay heed to the greater part of those on earth, they would lead you away from God's path. They follow nothing but conjecture and they do nothing but guess. Your Lord surely knows best who strays from His path, and best knows He those who are right-guided."* (Verses 114–17)

These four verses serve as a long preamble, introducing the main subject and closely relating it to the central issue of acceptance or denial of the faith: *"Eat, then, of that over which God's name has been pronounced, if you truly believe in His revelations. And why should you not eat of that over which God's name has been pronounced when He has clearly spelled out to you what He has forbidden you (to eat) unless you are driven to do so by sheer necessity?"* (Verses 118–19)

Before the discussion of the question of permissibility and prohibition is completed, the *sūrah* gives a number of instructions with strong overtones of authority and warning: *"Many people lead others astray by their errant views and lack of knowledge. Your Lord is fully aware of those who transgress. Abstain from all sin, be it open or secret. Those who commit sins will be requited for what they have committed."* (Verses 119–20)

The question of permissibility and prohibition is then resumed and linked directly to the question of submission to God alone, as opposed to associating partners with Him: *"Hence, do not eat of that over which God's name has not been pronounced; for that is sinful. The evil ones do whisper to their friends to argue with you. Should you pay heed to them, you will end up associating partners with God."* (Verse 121)

This is followed by further discussion on the nature of faith and disbelief, which too serves as a comment on the question of permissibility and prohibition. Such emphasis and re-emphasis as well as the links between matters of detail and major issues serves to outline how Islam views the basic issue of legislation for matters of ordinary day-to-day life.

"Am I to seek for judge anyone other than God, when it is He who has revealed the Book to you, clearly spelling out the truth. Those to whom We previously gave revelations know that it is the truth revealed by your Lord. So, do not be among the doubters." (Verse 114) This verse comes in the form of a question asked by God's Messenger, denouncing the very idea of seeking anyone other than God for judgement in any matter whatsoever. It follows this with stating that the authority to legislate in all matters belongs indisputably to God alone. There is simply no one other than God to turn to for judgement in any matter of human life:

"Am I to seek for judge anyone other than God?" (Verse 114) This initial rhetorical question is supplemented by an outline of the factors which make turning to someone other than God for judgement an extremely singular attitude. God has explained all things, leaving nothing obscure or confusing. There is absolutely no need for human beings to turn to any other authority to judge over any matter or question: *"It is He who has revealed the Book to you, clearly spelling out the truth."* (Verse 114)

This Book has been revealed in order to settle human disputes in all fairness. It outlines God's authority to legislate and explains what Godhead means practically. Moreover, this Book sets forth, in detail, the basic principles which serve as the foundation for the Islamic constitution regarding human life. It also includes detailed rulings for those questions which God wants to settle, regardless of the economic and scientific progress of any human community. Together, these give the revealed Book its status, removing any need to refer to anyone other than God for judgement on any matter of life. This is what God states in His Book. Let anyone, then, claim that during a particular stage of development, mankind does not find this Book sufficient for their purposes. But he should also say in conjunction with this claim that he does not believe in this religion, and that he rejects what the Lord of this universe states.

There is another factor which makes any attempt to seek a judgement other than God's ruling, on any matter, exceedingly strange. Those who were given divine revelations in the past recognize that this Book, the Qur'ān, is revealed by God. They should know, since they were also given scriptures: *"Those to whom We previously gave revelations know that it is the truth revealed by your Lord."* (Verse 114) This factor was present in Makkah and the Arabian Peninsula. Hence, God mentions it to the unbelievers, whether the people of earlier revelations acknowledge it or not. Indeed, some of them did acknowledge it and these were guided to the truth of Islam. Others denied it. However, the truth of this Book has been established by the fact that God tells us that the people who received earlier revelations know that the Qur'ān is revealed by God with the truth. Indeed, the truth is its subject matter and it is revealed by God simply to explain that truth.

The fact is that the people of earlier revelations continue to realize that the Qur'ān is revealed by God and that the strength of Islam comes from the fact that there is nothing in the Qur'ān but the truth. Knowing all this, they continue in their unabating war against this religion and its Book. This war is most determined when it comes to the attempt to usurp God's authority to legislate by abandoning the law of the Qur'ān and replacing it with man-made laws. In this way, someone other than God is called upon for judgement. The end result is that God's Book is not implemented and faith disappears. It is to this end that the people of earlier revelations, be they Crusaders or Zionists, support every system and government which aims to change the character of the land of Islam, distinguished by its people's submission to God alone and their implementation of the law outlined in His Book.

The *sūrah* then addresses God's Messenger and, by implication, those who believe in His message, telling them not to take to heart the determined opposition they encounter from those who disbelieve or the suppression of the truth by some of the people of earlier revelations: "*So, do not be among the doubters.*" (Verse 114) The truth is that God's Messenger has never entertained any doubt. An authentic report states: "When God revealed to him the verse which says, '*If you are in doubt concerning what We have sent down to you, ask those who have read the Scriptures before you. It is surely the truth that has come to you from your Lord. Do not, then, be among the doubters*'. (10: 94) God's Messenger said, 'I do not doubt, and I am not going to ask anyone.'"

This directive, however, and similar ones in the Qur'ān which aim to strengthen the Prophet's resolve to advocate the truth, give us an impression of the size of the opposition, denial and scheming the Prophet and the early Muslim community had to put up with. They also show how kind God was to them, constantly giving them this reassurance.

The *sūrah* then tells us that God's decisive word has been passed and it cannot be altered by human efforts, no matter what means they employ: "*Perfected are the words of your Lord in truth and justice. No one can change His words. He hears all and knows all.*" (Verse 115) Indeed, God's word is perfect. Whatever He says is the truth and whatever ruling or legislation He pronounces is just. Hence, no one else may say anything different whether it relates to faith, concepts, principles, values, law, custom or tradition. No one may amend His rulings or revise them. Indeed, He hears everything His servants say and He knows their every intention. He knows what is good for them and what establishes their life on the right basis: "*He hears all and knows all.*" (Verse 115)

All Erring Ways to be Abandoned

Having stated that the truth is simply what is contained in the Book revealed by God, the *sūrah* states that what human beings legislate is the result of following conjecture which is devoid of all certainty. To follow it leads to one clear outcome: error. It also explains that human beings cannot be certain of the truth and cannot follow it unless they receive it from its only source. The *sūrah* also warns God's Messenger (peace be upon him) against obeying people in what they say or advocate, no matter how great their number may be. Ignorance remains the same even though it gathers a very large following: "*If you were to pay heed to the greater part of those on earth, they would lead you away from God's path. They follow nothing but conjecture and they do nothing but guess.*" (Verse 116)

At the time when the Qur'ān was revealed, most people on earth belonged to the world of *jāhiliyyah*, as is certainly the case today. They did not refer to God for judgement in all their affairs. Nor did they make the divine law contained in His revealed Book the law which they implemented. Nor did they derive their concepts, ideas, thoughts and code of living from God's guidance. Hence, they followed the way of ignorance, as they certainly do today. They could not formulate any opinion or advocate any ruling based on the truth, and they could not lead anyone who followed them except into error. Just as people do today, they abandoned certitude in order to follow conjecture and guesswork. Hence, God warns His Messenger and his followers against obeying them so that they do not stray from His path. This warning has a general import, although it is given in connection with the prohibition of certain types of slaughtered animals and permitting others, as is later explained.

The Qur'ān then states that it is God alone who decides which of His servants follow right guidance and which go astray. It is God alone who knows what is in people's inmost hearts, and it is He who determines what constitutes proper guidance and what takes people away from it: "*Your Lord surely knows best who strays from His path, and best knows He those who are right-guided.*" (Verse 117)

It is necessary, then, to have a proper rule to evaluate people's beliefs, concepts, values, standards, activities and actions. This rule will determine what is true and what is false, so that nothing of it is judged according to people's changing desires or ill-founded criteria. It is also necessary that a sovereign authority establishes standards to evaluate all these matters so that people may refer to it for verdicts.

Here God declares that He alone has that authority as well as the authority to judge people as to whether they follow guidance or error. It is not 'human society' that is empowered to issue such verdicts according to its changeable values. Society changes its forms and material foundations, and such changes are bound to lead to an amendment of its values and verdicts. Human beings have held different values and moral standards depending on whether society is based on agricultural, industrial, capitalist, socialist or communist lines. The criteria to judge people and their actions differ in accordance with the different bases adopted by these societies.

But Islam does not recognize this at all. Islam establishes its own values which are determined by God and which remain constant despite the different forms human society may take. Any society which abandons these has its own title according to Islamic terminology: it is un-Islamic, *jāhilī*, unbelieving because it allows human beings to establish criteria, values, concepts, systems and situations other than those established by God. This is the only classification of societies, values and moral standards Islam acknowledges. These can be either Islamic or *jāhiliyyah*, regardless of their shape or form.

Having made this long factual introduction, the *sūrah* moves on to discuss the question of slaughtered animals based on the fundamental principle: "*Eat, then, of that over which God's name has been pronounced, if you truly believe in His revelations. And why should you not eat of that over which God's name has been pronounced when He has clearly spelled out to you what He has forbidden you (to eat) unless you are driven to do so by sheer necessity?*" (Verses 118–19) Before discussing the details of the legislation contained in these verses, we should point out the basic principles of faith to which these verses refer.

There is first an order to eat of animals over which God's name has been pronounced at the time of their slaughter. Such a pronouncement determines people's direction and highlights the relationship between accepting the faith and obeying this directive given to them by God: "*Eat, then, of that over which God's name has been pronounced, if you truly believe in His revelations.*" (Verse 118) They are then asked why they should not eat of such animals over which God's name has been mentioned. They are reminded that God has detailed for them what He has forbidden them, unless they are compelled to eat it out of necessity. With such explanation, every argument concerning the permissibility or prohibition of meat is over: "*And why should you not eat of that over which God's name has been pronounced when He has clearly spelled out to you what He has forbidden you (to eat), unless you are driven to do so by sheer necessity?*" (Verse 119)

These statements directly addressed a major issue in Arabian society. The unbelievers used to forbid themselves the eating of certain animals which God had made lawful, and they made lawful certain animals which God had forbidden. They claimed that their action relied on God's legislation. Hence, the *sūrah* gives its verdict concerning those who made false claims and who sought to exercise an authority that belongs to God alone. It states that what they legislated was a manifestation of their own vain desires, one based on total ignorance. They led people astray by the laws they issued and usurped God's authority to legislate: "*Many people lead others astray by their errant views and lack of knowledge. Your Lord is fully aware of those who transgress.*" (Verse 119)

They are then commanded to abandon all sin, whether open or secret. Part of that sin was to lead people astray with vain desires and errant views, all totally baseless. They actually compelled them to implement laws that God had not promulgated, falsely claiming that these were divine laws. They are, therefore, warned against this grave sin: "*Abstain from all sin, be it open or secret. Those who commit sins will be requited for what they have committed.*" (Verse 120)

Eating Meat with God's Permission

This is followed by a strict order not to eat from any slaughtered animal over which God's name has not been pronounced at the time of slaughter. The Arabs in pre-Islamic days used to pronounce the names of some of their idols when they slaughtered animals for eating, or when they slaughtered them for gambling or drawing lots. This prohibition covers the eating of carrion, which refers to animals that die naturally. The unbelievers used to argue with the Muslims about this prohibition, claiming that such animals had been killed by God. Thus, they wondered that the Muslims would eat of what they themselves slaughtered but would not eat of what God had slaughtered. This is just one of the infinitely stupid arguments that people of ignorance may advance, prompted by the evil ones among them and the *jinn*. Hence, the command given in this verse is coupled with a warning: "*Hence, do not eat of that over which God's name has not been pronounced; for that is sinful. The evil ones do whisper to their friends to argue with you. Should you pay heed to them, you will end up associating partners with God.*" (Verse 121)

This statement requires some reflection, for it is decisive in its reference to the authority every Muslim should obey. It clearly demonstrates that even in matters of detail, obedience by a Muslim to anyone who orders him to do something which is at variance with God's law and which does not recognize God's sovereignty and authority to legislate takes that Muslim out of Islam and leads him to associate partners with God.

In discussing the statement, "*should you pay heed to them, you will end up associating partners with God*" Ibn Kathīr says: This means that when you have abandoned God's law, disregarded His commandments and preferred someone else's law, then you are guilty of associating partners with Him. This is comparable to God's description of the followers of earlier religions: "*They have taken their rabbis and their monks for their lords beside God.*" (9: 31) In his interpretation of this verse, al-Tirmidhī reports that 'Adī ibn Ḥātim said to the Prophet: "Messenger of God, they did not worship them." The Prophet said: "Yes, indeed. They (meaning the rabbis and monks) made lawful to them what God has made unlawful, and they have forbidden them what God has made lawful, and they (meaning the followers of those religions) followed them. That is indeed their worship of them."

Similarly, Ibn Kathīr quotes al-Suddī in his commentary on the Qur'ānic statement, '*They have taken their rabbis and monks for lords beside God.*' Al-Suddī says: "They have taken the views of human beings, abandoning God's Book and His law. Hence, God follows this with the statement, '*they have been ordered only to worship the one God*', (9: 31) referring to the One who has the authority to forbid and make lawful and who must be obeyed whatever He legislates."[1]

Both distinguished scholars, al-Suddī and Ibn Kathīr, state with total clarity, that whoever obeys any man-made law which is at variance with God's law, even in a matter of detail, associates partners with

---

1. Ibn Kathīr, *Tafsīr al-Qur'ān al-'Aẓīm*, Vol. 2, p. 159.

God. If he is a Muslim yet continues to do so, he actually leaves the fold of Islam altogether, even though he declares verbally that he believes in God's oneness. This is because he receives his laws from an authority other than God's. When we look everywhere on earth today, we find ignorance and the association of partners with God among all peoples, with the exception of those God has guided to His path. These are the ones who refuse to accept the claims of all deities to any of the attributes of Godhead. They reject all such laws and legislation, except when they are compelled to accept them by force.

Let us now consider the implication of the divine statement, *"Do not eat of that over which God's name has not been pronounced; for that is sinful."* (Verse 121) We need to learn from this statement which animals are lawful to eat and which are not, and whether God's name is pronounced or omitted at the time of slaughter. Ibn Kathīr sums up the various views of a large number of scholars as follows:

> This Qur'ānic verse provides the evidence supporting the view that when God's name is not pronounced at the time of the slaughtering of any animal, it becomes unlawful to eat, even though the man carrying out the slaughter is a Muslim. Leading scholars have three different views in this respect. The first view is that such an animal is unlawful to eat, whether the omission of pronouncing God's name at its slaughter has been deliberate or out of forgetfulness. This view is supported by 'Abdullāh ibn 'Umar, Nāfi', 'Āmir al-Sha'bī and Muḥammad ibn Sīrīn. It is also reported to be one view held by Imāms Mālik and Aḥmad ibn Ḥanbal. Some early and later scholars of the Ḥanbalī school support this view. It is also supported by Abū Thawr and Dāwūd al-Zāhirī. It is the preferred view of Muḥammad al-Ṭā'ī, of the Shāfi'ī school in his book, *Al-Arba'īn*. These scholars support their view with this verse and the verse concerned with the permissibility of hunted animals which states: *"you may eat of what they catch for you. But mention God's name over it."* (5: 4) This prohibition is further confirmed by the statement, *"for that is sinful."* (Verse 121) The pronoun, 'that', is understood to refer either to the eating or the slaughtering without pronouncing God's name. This view is also supported by the *aḥādīth* ordering the pronouncement of God's name at slaughter and hunting, such as: "If you set your trained dog and mention God's name, you may

eat of what it catches for you." (Related by al-Bukhārī and Muslim.) "You may eat of animals whose blood is spilled and over which God's name has been pronounced." (Related by al-Bukhārī and Muslim.)

The second view is that the pronouncement of God's name at the time of slaughter is recommended, and not obligatory. If it is omitted, whether deliberately or through forgetfulness, it does not affect the fact that the animal is permissible to eat. This is the view of Imām al-Shāfi'ī and all his disciples. It is also reported to have been expressed by Imāms Aḥmad and Mālik, as well as Ibn 'Abbās, Abū Hurayrah and 'Aṭā'. As for the Qur'ānic statement, *"Do not eat of that over which God's name has not been pronounced; for that is sinful,"* (Verse 121), al-Shāfi'ī interprets this as referring to animals dedicated to deities or beings other than God. Imām al-Shāfi'ī's view is considered to be strongly supported. A report attributed to Ibn 'Abbās suggests that the statement, *'Do not eat of that over which God's name has not been pronounced',* refers to carrion. A *ḥadīth* related by Abū Dāwūd quotes the Prophet as saying: "An animal slaughtered by a Muslim is permissible to eat, whether he pronounces God's name or not, because if he is to mention any name, he would pronounce only God's name." This ḥadīth is not strongly authentic, but it is endorsed by one related by al-Dāraquṭnī who quotes Ibn 'Abbās as saying: "If a Muslim slaughters an animal without pronouncing God's name, he may eat of it, because a Muslim bears a name of God."

The third view makes it clear that if the pronouncement of God's name is omitted out of forgetfulness, the animal is lawful to eat; while if it is omitted deliberately, the slaughtered animal is unlawful. This is the view most commonly associated with the Mālikī and Ḥanbalī schools. It is the one to which Imām Abū Ḥanīfah and his school subscribe. It is supported by many other scholars, such as Isḥāq ibn Rāhawayh, 'Alī, Ibn 'Abbās, Sa'īd ibn al-Musayyib, 'Aṭā', Ṭāwūs, al-Ḥasan al-Baṣrī, Abū Mālik, Ibn Abī Laylā, Ja'far al-Ṣādiq, and Rabī'ah ibn 'Abd al-Raḥmān.

Ibn Jarīr al-Ṭabarī mentions that scholars hold different views with regard to whether any part of the rulings in this verse have been abrogated. Some of them say that no abrogation has taken place; its import is certainly clear. This is the view of Mujāhid and most scholars.[2] However, 'Ikrimah and al-Ḥasan al-Baṣrī, two prominent scholars, refer to the verses in this *sūrah*: "*Eat, then, of that over which God's name has been pronounced, if you truly believe in His revelations.*" (Verse 118) "*Hence, do not eat of that over which God's name has not been pronounced; for that is sinful.*" (Verse 121) They also refer to a verse in another *sūrah*: "*The food of those who were given revelations is lawful to you, and your food is lawful to them.*" (5: 5) These scholars quote Makḥūl as saying: "God revealed in the Qur'ān, '*Do not eat of that over which God's name has not been pronounced*'. Then God abrogated it out of mercy shown to Muslims, saying: '*Today, all the good things of life have been made lawful to you. The food of those who were given revelations is lawful to you, and your food is lawful to them*'. (5: 5) Thus, the abrogation of the first verse is effected as God has made the animals slaughtered by people of earlier revelations lawful for Muslims to eat." Al-Ṭabarī adds: "The fact is that there is no conflict between making the food of the people of earlier revelations lawful and prohibiting the meat of animals over which God's name has not been pronounced." His view is certainly right. Those early scholars who say that the earlier ruling has been abrogated actually mean that it has been qualified.[3]

Incomparable Situations

Next we have a full treatment of the nature of both faith and disbelief. The following verses speak of God's will that manifests itself in every community, even where the most hardened of criminals scheme and give themselves airs. Their arrogance prevents them from accepting the faith. This concludes with a splendid image portraying the faith that opens people's hearts and minds, contrasting it with the oppressive situation of disbelief, which weighs heavily on people's minds. The whole passage relates to the question of prohibition and permissibility concerning slaughtered animals, in the same way as a basic rule is related to a detailed application.

---

2. Al-Ṭabarī, *Jāmi' al-Bayān*, Dār al-Fikr, Beirut, 1984, Vol. 8, p. 21.
3. Ibn Kathīr, op. cit., Vol. 2, pp. 157–8.

Is he who was dead and whom We have raised to life, and for whom We set up a light to see his way among men, to be compared to one who is in deep darkness out of which he cannot emerge? Thus do their deeds seem goodly to the unbelievers. And thus in every city have We placed arch-criminals so that they weave their schemes there. But it is only against themselves that they scheme, though they do not perceive it. When a sign comes to them, they say: "We shall not believe unless we are given the same as God's messengers were given." But God knows best whom to entrust with His message. Humiliation before God and severe suffering will befall those guilty of evildoing for all their scheming. Whomever God wills to guide, He makes his bosom open wide with willingness towards self-surrender (to Him); and whomever He wills to let go astray, He causes his bosom to be tight and constricted, as if he were climbing up into the skies. Thus does God lay the scourge on the unbelievers. (Verses 122–5)

These verses delineate the nature of faith and divine guidance in a factual statement describing a true fact. The apparent allegory magnifies this in an inspiring way, but the statement itself expresses a practical fact. Indeed, the nature of that fact requires the use of such splendid images. We are speaking here of a spiritual and intellectual fact, one which can only be appreciated when experienced. Its description brings this whole experience into full relief, particularly to those who have actually gone through it.

It is true that faith revives people's hearts after they have been dead and gives them light to bring them out of darkness. Their new life enables them to appreciate and evaluate all things in a new light and according to a new measure they did not previously know. The light they are given makes everything appear new. It is as if it has never been seen by those hearts that now bask in the light of faith.

This experience cannot be described in words, because it is known only to those who have actually gone through it. The Qur'ānic statement is the strongest that can express for us the nature of this experience, because it depicts it in its true colours.

Rejection of the divine faith is indeed a break with the true life which is ever present, eternal. It is a self-imposed isolation from the effective power that influences the whole of existence, and a breakdown of all natural systems of reception and response. Hence, it is an effective death. Faith, on the other hand, is a real bond of communication and response. As such, it is life.

Denial of the divine truth is a cover that prevents the soul from looking around, a screen over human powers and feelings, and a state of complete loss. Hence, it is darkness. Faith, on the other hand, means opening up, looking around, appreciating and understanding. As such, it is the true light.

Disbelief means shrinking within oneself, so it signifies narrowness. It is a deviation from the natural, easy method; hence, it signifies difficulty and affliction. It is a deprivation of security and reassurance; hence, it signifies worry. Faith, on the other hand, signifies openness, ease and reassurance.

How do we describe an unbeliever? He is no more than a parasitic growth that has no real roots in the soil of this universe. He is an isolated individual who has no tie with the Creator of the universe. Consequently, his ties with the universe are very flimsy, extending only within the limitations of his own existence. In other words, unbelievers are confined to the limitations placed on the physical world of animals.

When a believer establishes his bond with the Creator and makes faith the basis of all his ties with other people, he actually reaches out, within his short life, to that existence which was there before the beginning of time and to immortality which has no end. He also establishes firm ties with the universe and with all aspects of life. He also establishes ties with the procession of the faithful who constitute a single nation whose history stretches back to time immemorial and extends far into the future, indeed for as long as human life continues. Thus, a believer has a great treasure of ties going well beyond his own limited lifetime.

As a believer feels the light in his heart, he begins to discover the basic facts of this religion and its method of action. The scene that extends before man's eyes is breathtaking because it portrays the unique harmony in the nature and the details of this religion and the elaborate complementarity of its method of action. The believer then begins to look at this religion, not as a set of beliefs, acts of worship, laws and directives but as a complete whole which is alive, interacting with nature like an intimate and loving friend.

With this light in his heart, a believer begins to discover the facts behind existence, life, people and the facts of the events that take place on earth and in the universe. Again, within this wonderful scene he sees the perfect divine laws that relate starting premises to their natural conclusions in an elaborate, but natural and easy system. He sees how God's free-will determines the law and its operation, while continuing to be free, absolute. He sees that people and events react to natural laws which remain subject to God's will.

This light also gives man complete clarity in all matters and events. He is clear about the thoughts and intentions he entertains and the actions he plans. He sees with absolute clarity the events that take place around him, whether they are the result of the laws of nature or of people's actions and plans. To him, the whole history of mankind and the universe becomes an open book that he reads with absolute transparency. His thoughts and feelings become bright; he has no worry about his existence or his future; events and happenings take place and he is relaxed, reassured.

The Qur'ān describes all this with inspiring touches: "*Is he who was dead and whom We have raised to life, and for whom We set up a light to see his way among men, to be compared to one who is in deep darkness out of which he cannot emerge?*" (Verse 122)

This verse describes the situation of Muslims before they came to believe in this religion, and before faith breathed life into their souls to release within them their great store of ability, action and forward-looking qualities. Their hearts were dead, and their spirits were in darkness, but when faith touched their hearts they quickened and light brightened their souls. Thus they were able to bring guidance, reassurance and freedom to mankind, showing them the way and making an all-important declaration that man has been reborn. With faith, man is liberated, enlightened, submitting to no authority other than that of God's.

Can they be compared: the one in whom God has breathed life and to whom He has given light, and the one who lingers in darkness, knowing no way out of it? The two worlds are set widely apart. Why do people, then, linger in darkness when the light is bright all around them? "*Thus do their deeds seem goodly to the unbelievers.*" (Verse 122)

This is the secret then. Disbelief, darkness and even death have been made to seem good to the unbelievers. This is part of God's will which has made men, by nature, susceptible to the dual lure of light and darkness. Thus, man is put to a test to find out whether he chooses darkness or light. When he chooses darkness, it is made to look good to him so that he goes deeper and deeper into it. Additionally, the evil ones among both human beings and *jinn* continue to inspire each other with fabricated falsehoods and continue to make their actions seem goodly to the unbelievers. A heart that has been cut off from life, faith and light listens to evil whispers in the dark, because it cannot see or feel or distinguish guidance from error. How can it make such a distinction in the depth of the darkness into which it has sunk?

Who May be Entrusted with a Divine Message?

By the same token and for the same reasons, God has placed in every land criminals who enjoy a position of power so that they can scheme and plot. Their scheming allows the test to be completed, and God's will to take effect. Everyone is thus able to follow the path made easy and reap his reward at the end of the day: "*And thus in every city have We placed arch-criminals so that they weave their schemes there. But it is only against themselves that they scheme, though they do not perceive it.*" (Verse 123)

It is an aspect of the law God has set in operation that in every main or capital city, a group of those who have power and are hardened in sin take a very hostile attitude towards divine faith. This is due to the fact that divine faith begins by depriving such people of the power which enables them to establish their authority over others, making them subservient and for whom they claim they have the power to legislate. It re-establishes God's authority as He is indeed the Lord, King and God of mankind. It is part of the laws of human nature that God sends His messengers with the truth which deprives those who claim Godhead of every aspect of lordship and authority over mankind. Hence, such people declare their opposition to the divine faith and to God's messengers. They weave their schemes and try to inspire one another with deceptive falsehoods, cooperating with the evil ones among the *jinn* to try to win their battle against the truth and divine guidance. Thus they work hard spreading falsehood and error, deceiving people with their scheming.

The fight is inevitable because it is caused by the inherent and complete opposition between the basic principle of faith, which declares that all sovereignty belongs to God, and the ambitions of those criminals occupying positions of power. Every prophet will inevitably fight this battle because he cannot avoid it. Similarly, those who believe in a prophet will inevitably be engaged in this battle to the end. God reassures the believers that no matter how great and powerful the scheming of these criminals may appear to be, it will inevitably turn against them in the end. The believers are not alone in this battle, because God is their patron. That is sufficient for them, because it is He who makes the scheming of the criminals turn against them: "*But it is only against themselves that they scheme, though they do not perceive it.*" (Verse 123) Let the believers then be reassured.

The *sūrah* then reveals the arrogant nature of those who are hostile towards God's messengers and His religion. It is their arrogance which prevents them from surrendering themselves to God because that would place them on the same level as the rest of God's servants. They want a place of distinction to preserve their positions among their followers. They feel that it is beneath them to believe in the Prophet after having enjoyed a position of lordship over others. Hence, they come out with their singularly stupid declaration: "*When a sign comes to them, they say: 'We shall not believe unless we are given the same as God's messengers were given.'*" (Verse 124)

Al-Walīd ibn al-Mughīrah, one of the tribal chiefs of the Quraysh, said to the Prophet: "Had prophethood been true, I would have been more entitled to it than you, because I am older and richer than you." Abū Jahl, the most hardened opponent of Islam among the Quraysh said: "By God, we shall never accept or follow Muḥammad, unless we are given revelations just as he receives."

It is clear that their self-esteem and the special position they enjoyed among their followers and the fact that their orders were obeyed were the real reasons to justify their opposition and hostility to God's messengers and the divine faith. God replies to their singular statement by making it clear first that the question of choosing messengers to be entrusted with His message is something that He determines in accordance with His knowledge of who may be trusted with it. He then warns them that they will suffer great humiliation: "*God knows best whom to entrust with His message. Humiliation before God and severe suffering will befall those guilty of evildoing for all their scheming.*" (Verse 124)

The divine message is something very serious because it provides a link between God's will and a single one of His servants, and between the supreme society and the limited world of human beings. Through the message a linkage is made between heaven and earth, this life and the life to come. The eternal truth is placed in human hearts and implemented in human society and becomes the initiator of historical events. A human being is purged of every trace of self-interest so that he or she may be totally dedicated to God, not only in intention, purpose and action, but in their whole being. Thus, God's Messenger (peace be upon him) has a direct link with this truth and its source. Such a direct link can only be established with a soul that is worthy of this honour, of receiving the truth directly without impediments. God alone knows whom to entrust with His message. He chooses that person from among billions of people, and assigns to him his mission.

Those who aspire to be given that honour or demand that they be given similar revelations are unsuitable by their very nature for this task, because they think themselves to be the pivot around which the whole universe turns. Messengers are of a totally different nature, because they receive their message with complete surrender, dedicate themselves to it and have no aspirations or ambitions of their own: "*You could never aspire to that this Book would be offered to you, but it [came to you] only by the grace of your Lord.*" (28: 86) Moreover, such people are ignorant of the seriousness of the divine message and do not know that it is God alone who chooses His messengers. Hence, God gives them His decisive answer: "*God knows best whom to entrust with His message.*" (Verse 124) He certainly chose for it the noblest souls among His creation and the most dedicated of them. These were the messengers of whom Muḥammad was the last.

This is followed with a warning that humiliation and severe suffering awaits those criminals: "*Humiliation before God and severe suffering will befall those guilty of evildoing for all their scheming.*" (Verse 124) The humiliation is an answer to their arrogance and their impudent aspiration to be given divine messages. Their severe suffering is a fitting retribution for their scheming and hostility towards God's messengers and the believers.

Choosing Divine Guidance

The whole passage concludes with a description of the state that ensues when divine guidance is followed, when the faith is accepted and the effect it has on people's hearts. "*Whomever God wills to guide, He makes his bosom open wide with willingness towards self-surrender (to Him); and whomever He wills to let go astray, He causes his bosom to be tight and constricted, as if he were climbing up into the skies. Thus does God lay the scourge on the unbelievers."* (Verse 125)

God has set in operation a law that ensures guidance for everyone who wishes to be guided and who takes the necessary action to achieve that guidance. All this remains within the limits of choice given to human beings by way of a test. Within this law, when God wishes to guide a person, *"He makes his bosom open wide with willingness towards self-surrender (to God)."* (Verse 125) He thus receives the concept of surrendering himself to God with willingness and reassurance. Again, in accordance with God's law that He leaves anyone who turns his back on guidance and closes his mind to it to his own devices, it is said of God that: *"He causes his bosom to be tight and constricted."* (Verse 125) His mind is shut and he finds difficulty in accepting God's guidance. He is just like one who *"is climbing up into the skies."* (Verse 125) This is a mental state described in terms of a physical condition which combines difficult breathing, stress and the exhaustion which accompanies climbing up stage after stage into the skies. The very word chosen here to denote 'climbing up' imparts a sense of difficulty and strenuous physical effort. Thus, the whole scene is in perfect harmony both with the physical condition and the verbal expression describing it.

The scene is concluded with a fitting comment: *"Thus does God lay the scourge on the unbelievers."* (Verse 125) Just as it is God's will to cause the bosom of a person who wishes to be guided to open wide with willingness to surrender himself to God, and causes the one who chooses to go astray to find things hard and difficult, so does God lay a scourge on those who do not believe. The Arabic term which is rendered here as 'scourge' has a variety of meanings. It denotes 'suffering, blight, ignominy, etc.' Together, its nuances give us a picture of a person who is completely incapable of rescuing himself. He continues to endure most severe suffering without any hope of salvation.

We need to say something further about this verse: *"Whomever God wills to guide, He makes his bosom open wide with willingness towards self-surrender (to Him); and whomever He wills to let go astray, He causes his bosom to be tight and constricted, as if he were climbing up into the skies. Thus does God lay the scourge on the unbelievers."* (Verse 125)

This verse and similar ones in the Qur'ān refer to the essential relationship between God's will and people's choices, and what befalls them of either being guided or going astray and the consequent reward or punishment they receive. To fully appreciate the facts such verses describe requires a level of human understanding different from that of intellectual logic. All the controversy that has taken place around this issue over the years, in the history of Islamic thought, particularly between the Mu'tazilah, the Murji'ah and the mainstream Sunnīs, and in the history of divinity and philosophy, and all that has been written about it have a distinct intellectual drift.

But as we have said, this whole question requires the use of a different level of understanding. It also requires us to deal with practical facts, not intellectual arguments. The Qur'ān describes the true facts within the human self and the universe at large. These portray distinctly the close interrelation between what God determines and man's choice and action in a way that cannot be properly appreciated by intellectual logic.

To say that God's will pushes man into taking one of two ways, either guidance or error, is not compatible with practical reality. Nor is this reality compatible with saying that man's will determines his destiny. Instead, the practical reality is made up of an elaborate mixture which combines the freedom and authority of God's will on the one hand and man's free choice on the other, without these being in conflict with each other.

As has already been stated, understanding this reality cannot be done within the confines of intellectual logic or argument. It is the nature of a certain reality that determines how it should be approached and expressed. Understanding this reality as it is also requires going through a complete spiritual and psychological experience. When people move towards surrendering themselves to God, they find that their hearts open up warmly to such surrender. This is certainly of God's own doing. To feel inclined to something takes place only by God's will. On the other hand, a person who prefers the path which leads astray feels his bosom tightening and constricted. This is again of God's own doing, because it is an event that cannot come about unless God wills it to be. But this is not the will of force. It is the will that has set a particular law in operation so that man is tested with the measure of choice he has been given. Moreover, it is God's will to determine the consequences of the type of choice man makes and whether he follows guidance or error.

When one intellectual issue is set against another, and when the benefit of practical experience of how to deal with these intellectual issues is not made use of, we cannot have a complete and accurate understanding of the practical reality involved. This is the shortcoming of all intellectual arguments on these issues, whether we find them in Islamic philosophy or elsewhere. Hence, a different approach is needed.

Let us now pick up the thread of our commentary on this passage, which is stated as a comment on the question of which slaughtered animals it is permissible to eat. All these issues form a single unit in the Qur'ān, in a Muslim's mind and in the structure of the Islamic faith. The question of which meat is lawful is a question of legislation, and this is a question of authority, which is, in turn, a question of faith. This means that this approach to faith is the right one, given in the right place.

The final comment in this passage provides the last link between the issues of faith and legislation. Together they form God's straight path. To violate either of them is to abandon the path set by God. To stick to them both is to follow the path which leads to the abode of peace and ensures God's patronage to those who do well: *"Such is the path of your Lord, a straight path. We have made Our revelations plain for people who reflect. Theirs shall be an abode of peace with their Lord. He will be their patron in reward for what they have been doing."* (Verses 126–7)

The path is described as 'the path of your Lord' to add a sense of reassurance about the outcome. His law governing guidance and error has been outlined, and His legislation concerning permissibility and prohibition has been spelled out. Both enjoy equal importance in God's sight. Both are approached in the same way in His Book, the Qur'ān.

God has made plain His revelations, but it is those who take heed and do not overlook these revelations that benefit by such a detailed statement. A believer's heart is always alert, wide open, happy, alive, responsive. Those who reflect and take heed will enjoy the abode of peace with their Lord. Their reward will not fail to come. God will grant them His support as He takes good care of them to reward them for what they have been doing. They have passed the test well and their reward is generous indeed.

Once more we find ourselves looking at one of the fundamental issues of this faith, showing God's straight path to reflect the recognition of His sovereignty and the following of His code. Beyond both lies faith. Together they define the nature of the Islamic faith as stated by the Lord of the universe.

14

Judgement According to Deeds

On the day when He shall gather them all together, (He will say): "O you company of *jinn*! A great many human beings have you seduced." Those who were their close friends among human beings will say: "Our Lord, we have enjoyed each other's fellowship, and we have now reached the end of our term which You have appointed for us." He will say: "The fire shall be your abode, where you shall remain, unless God wills it otherwise." Indeed, your Lord is wise, all-knowing. (128)

In this manner do We cause the wrongdoers to be close allies of one another, because of that which they do. (129)

"O you company of *jinn* and humans! Have there not come to you messengers from among yourselves who related to you My revelations and warned you of the coming of this your day?"

يَوۡمَ يَحۡشُرُهُمۡ جَمِيعٗا يَٰمَعۡشَرَ
ٱلۡجِنِّ قَدِ ٱسۡتَكۡثَرۡتُم مِّنَ ٱلۡإِنسِ
وَقَالَ أَوۡلِيَآؤُهُم مِّنَ ٱلۡإِنسِ رَبَّنَا
ٱسۡتَمۡتَعَ بَعۡضُنَا بِبَعۡضٖ وَبَلَغۡنَآ
أَجَلَنَا ٱلَّذِيٓ أَجَّلۡتَ لَنَاۚ قَالَ ٱلنَّارُ
مَثۡوَىٰكُمۡ خَٰلِدِينَ فِيهَآ إِلَّا مَا شَآءَ
ٱللَّهُۚ إِنَّ رَبَّكَ حَكِيمٌ عَلِيمٞ ۝١٢٨

وَكَذَٰلِكَ نُوَلِّي بَعۡضَ ٱلظَّٰلِمِينَ بَعۡضَۢا
بِمَا كَانُواْ يَكۡسِبُونَ ۝١٢٩

يَٰمَعۡشَرَ ٱلۡجِنِّ وَٱلۡإِنسِ أَلَمۡ يَأۡتِكُمۡ
رُسُلٞ مِّنكُمۡ يَقُصُّونَ عَلَيۡكُمۡ ءَايَٰتِي
وَيُنذِرُونَكُمۡ لِقَآءَ يَوۡمِكُمۡ هَٰذَاۚ قَالُواْ

They will reply: "We bear witness against ourselves." The life of this world has beguiled them. So they will bear witness against themselves that they were unbelievers. (130)

شَهِدْنَا عَلَىٰ أَنفُسِنَا وَغَرَّتْهُمُ الْحَيَوٰةُ الدُّنْيَا وَشَهِدُواْ عَلَىٰ أَنفُسِهِمْ أَنَّهُمْ كَانُواْ كَٰفِرِينَ ﴿١٣٠﴾

And so it is that your Lord would never destroy a community for its wrongdoing, while they remain unaware. (131)

ذَٰلِكَ أَن لَّمْ يَكُن رَّبُّكَ مُهْلِكَ الْقُرَىٰ بِظُلْمٍ وَأَهْلُهَا غَٰفِلُونَ ﴿١٣١﴾

They all shall have their grades in accordance with their deeds. Your Lord is not unaware of what they do. (132)

وَلِكُلٍّ دَرَجَٰتٌ مِّمَّا عَمِلُواْ وَمَا رَبُّكَ بِغَٰفِلٍ عَمَّا يَعْمَلُونَ ﴿١٣٢﴾

Your Lord is the self-sufficient One, the Merciful. If He so wills, He may remove you altogether and cause whom He wills to succeed you, just as He brought you into being out of other people's seed. (133)

وَرَبُّكَ الْغَنِيُّ ذُو الرَّحْمَةِ إِن يَشَأْ يُذْهِبْكُمْ وَيَسْتَخْلِفْ مِنۢ بَعْدِكُم مَّا يَشَآءُ كَمَا أَنشَأَكُم مِّن ذُرِّيَّةِ قَوْمٍ ءَاخَرِينَ ﴿١٣٣﴾

That which you are promised will inevitably come, and you cannot elude it. (134)

إِنَّ مَا تُوعَدُونَ لَءَاتٍ وَمَا أَنتُم بِمُعْجِزِينَ ﴿١٣٤﴾

Say: "My people! Do all that may be in your power, and I will do what I can. You shall come to know to whom the future belongs. Never will the wrongdoers attain success. (135)

قُلْ يَٰقَوْمِ اعْمَلُواْ عَلَىٰ مَكَانَتِكُمْ إِنِّي عَامِلٌ فَسَوْفَ تَعْلَمُونَ مَن تَكُونُ لَهُۥ عَٰقِبَةُ الدَّارِ إِنَّهُۥ لَا يُفْلِحُ الظَّٰلِمُونَ ﴿١٣٥﴾

Overview

This whole passage is a continuation of the previous one. Since the *sūrah* previously outlined the destiny of those who follow the path acceptable to God, it now outlines the fate of satans, be they human or *jinn*. On the other hand, it continues to tackle the great issue of faith and its rejection, which is mentioned here within the framework of God's sovereignty and authority to legislate. It links the issue of sovereignty with the main issues of the Islamic faith, including that of reward in the life to come for what people do in this present life. Other issues linked with this are God's ability to remove all satans, their friends and all mankind, and to replace them with others, as also mankind's weakness in the face of God's irresistible power. All these faith issues are mentioned here within the context of the prohibition and permissibility of animal food, which has already been discussed, and the forthcoming discussion of offerings of crops, animals and offspring, as well as other ignorant traditions and *jāhiliyyah* concepts. Thus all these issues appear to be closely related. They are seen in their appropriate positions as designated by Islam. That is, they are all faith questions, equally treated according to God's measures established in His revealed Book.

The Power of the Wicked

The previous passage of the *sūrah* contained a full discussion of the situation of those whose hearts God opens up to receive the message of surrender to Him. They remain conscious of God and continue to watch Him in all their actions, move towards a life of peace, assured that they will have the patronage of their Lord. As it is customary in the Qur'ān for contrasting scenes of the Day of Judgement to be portrayed, we now have a sketch showing the lot of the evil ones among humans and *jinn*. These spend their lives inspiring one another with deceptive falsehood, supporting one another in their hostility to every prophet and messenger and pointing out to each other what arguments to use with the believers in order to raise doubts in their minds about what God has made lawful and what He has forbidden. All this is portrayed in a very vivid sketch, characterized by dialogue, confession and reproach.

> *On the day when He shall gather them all together, (He will say): "O you company of jinn! A great many human beings have you seduced." Those who were their close friends among human beings*

will say: "Our Lord, we have enjoyed each other's fellowship, and we have now reached the end of our term which You have appointed for us." He will say: "The fire shall be your abode, where you shall remain, unless God wills it otherwise." Indeed, your Lord is wise, all-knowing. In this manner do We cause the wrongdoers to be close allies of one another, because of that which they do. "O you company of jinn and humans! Have there not come to you messengers from among yourselves who related to you My revelations and warned you of the coming of this your day?" They will reply: "We bear witness against ourselves." The life of this world has beguiled them. So they will bear witness against themselves that they were unbelievers." (Verses 128–30)

Full of life, the scene is shown first to be one of the future, when all creation will be gathered before God. Yet it soon becomes a scene of the present, held in front of the eyes of every listener. This is achieved by the omission of one Arabic word which means in English, "He will say", included in the translation between brackets for clarity. The omission of this phrase, expressed in a single Arabic word, brings the whole scene right into the present so as not to speak of something to be awaited in future but of something that is taking place now. This method is characteristic of the inimitable style of the Qur'ān.

Let us now look at what is sketched out in this scene. It begins with an address to the *jinn*: "*On the day when He shall gather them all together, (He will say): 'O you company of jinn! A great many human beings have you seduced.'*" (Verse 128) You have managed to gather a large following from among human beings who listen to your inspiration, follow in your footsteps and obey your suggestions. Although this is given in the form of a factual statement, it is not meant to merely impart information. The *jinn* know what they have done. Rather, the statement is intended to record the crime of leading such a large number of humans astray and to reproach the *jinn* for so doing. In this gathering of all humans and *jinn* on the Day of Judgement, all evidence of the crime is shown. Therefore, the *jinn* do not make any reply. However, the imbeciles among human beings who take satanic inspiration lightly are the ones to answer: "*Those who were their close friends among human beings will say: 'Our Lord, we have enjoyed each other's fellowship, and we have now reached the end of our term which You have appointed for us.'*" (Verse 128)

The answer betrays their lack of awareness, and demonstrates to them how Satan finds his way into their thinking. They used to enjoy the ideas, the lack of discipline, the pleasures and the sinful ways which the *jinn* portrayed to them in attractive colours. It was their keenness to enjoy themselves that provided Satan with the opportunity to lure and play tricks on them. Thus were they made to work for the fulfilment of Satan's goal.

Yet those imbeciles also used to think that the enjoyment was mutual and that they were giving as much pleasure as they were receiving. Hence they state in their answer: "*Our Lord, we have enjoyed each other's fellowship.*" (Verse 128) That enjoyment lasted for the duration of their life on earth. On the day when they are gathered, they will know that they have always been subject to God's power and that it was He who gave them this span of time to reflect and respond: "*We have now reached the end of our term which You have appointed for us.*" (Verse 128) With that knowledge, the judgement is made so that they receive their fair punishment: "*He will say: 'The fire shall be your abode, where you shall remain, unless God wills it otherwise.'*" (Verse 128)

The fire is, then, their abode. Abodes are meant for continuity. But the qualification is added, "*unless God wills it otherwise.*" (Verse 128) This qualification is in line with the fact that God's will is free, subject to no restraining factor. Indeed, it is not subject even to what it has determined. This is a basic principle of the Islamic faith.

"*Indeed, your Lord is wise, all-knowing.*" What He determines for people is based on His unflawed and perfect knowledge.

A comment on this part of the scene is inserted here before the dialogue is resumed to complete it: "*In this manner do We cause the wrongdoers to be close allies of one another, because of that which they do.*" (Verse 129)

It is in the manner that established the fellowship between the *jinn* and the human beings and the ultimate end to which this fellowship has come that wrongdoers get to be closely allied, on account of what they do. The similarity of their nature, the unity of their direction and goal, and the fact that their end will be the same establishes an alliance between them. This is a statement that goes beyond its immediate occasion. It speaks of the nature of the fellowship between all evil ones, *jinn* and human. The wrongdoers who associate partners with God in one form or another gather together in one camp to oppose the truth and divine guidance. They establish a relationship of mutual support against every prophet and those who believe in Him. It is not only that they share the same nature, despite their different appearances, but they also have the same interest which can only be served by usurping the rights of Lordship over mankind and giving unrestrained rein to their desires.

Indeed, we see them in every age supporting one another in every fight against faith and believers, despite their own internal rivalry and differences. Hence, their common nature and common objectives help to establish their alliance. The evil they do and the sins they commit determine that they will suffer the same fate in the hereafter, as is portrayed in this scene.

In our present day we see a grand alliance of evil, in which Zionists, Crusaders, pagans and Communists work together despite their great differences. This alliance has been going on for centuries, united by its hostility to Islam and its determination to crush Islamic revivalist movements wherever they function. It is, indeed, a mighty alliance. It benefits from its experience of long centuries of combat against the principle of submission to God. Furthermore, it mobilizes material and cultural forces and makes use of systems and machinery available within the Muslim world to serve its evil plans. It is a confirmation of God's own words: "*In this manner do We cause the wrongdoers to be close allies of one another, because of that which they do.*" (Verse 129)

But the reassurance given by God to His Messenger also applies here: "*Had your Lord willed otherwise, they would not have done it. Therefore, leave them to their own inventions.*" (Verse 112) This reassurance, however, requires that the community of believers continues to follow in the footsteps of God's Messenger recognizing that they have to hold the banner and defend the cause of Islam and Muslims, whatever sacrifice they may have to make.

Let us consider now the last part of this scene: "*'O you company of jinn and humans! Have there not come to you messengers from among yourselves who related to you My revelations and warned you of the coming of this your day?' They will reply: 'We bear witness against ourselves.' The life of this world has beguiled them. So they will bear witness against themselves that they were unbelievers.*" (Verse 130)

The question here is not meant to seek information but to provide it and record the facts as they took place. God who is infinite in His Glory knows what their situation in this life was. Their answer to this question is simply an acknowledgement on their part that they deserve the punishment of the hereafter.

This question is addressed to the *jinn* as well as humans. Does this mean that God has sent messengers to the *jinn* from among themselves, in the same way as He sent messengers to human beings? God alone knows the nature of this species of His creation, the *jinn,* who remain unknown to us human beings. However, the Qur'ānic statement may be interpreted to mean that the *jinn* have been able to listen to the revelations sent down to God's Messenger and to convey it to their people, warning them against continuing in their disbelief. An example of this is reported in *Sūrah* 46, The Sand Dunes, or *al-Aḥqāf*:

> *Tell how We sent to you a band of jinn who, when they came and listened to the Qur'ān, said to each other: "Listen attentively." As soon as its recitation was ended, they betook themselves to their people and gave them warning. "Our people", they said, "We have just been listening to a revelation bestowed from on high after that of Moses, confirming what was revealed before it, and guiding to the truth and to a straight path. Our people, answer the call of the one who summons unto God and believe in Him! He will forgive you your sins and deliver you from a woeful scourge. Those that give no heed to the one who calls unto God can never elude Him on earth, nor can they have any to protect them besides Him. Surely they are in evident error." (46: 29–32)*

It is probable that the question put by the *jinn* and human beings and the answer they receive are based on this fact. The whole matter is part of the knowledge God has kept for Himself. It is useless to try to go any further in establishing any clear answer on this point.

Anyhow, those of the *jinn* and humans who are addressed in this way recognize that the question is not meant to solicit information but to record it and to add an element of reproach for their attitude. Therefore, they make a full confession and state that they deserve the punishment they are bound to receive: "*They will reply: 'We bear witness against ourselves.'*" (Verse 130) At this point we have a comment to make: "*The life of this world has beguiled them. So they will bear witness against themselves that they were unbelievers.*" (Verse 130) This comment describes their situation in this life, lured on by pleasures, with an arrogance that has led them to be unbelievers. On the Day of

Judgement, they testify against themselves because they realize that denial is of no use. Can there be any situation more miserable than to find oneself in a fix where one cannot say in one's own defence even a word of denial, let alone a word of justification?

Let us reflect for a moment on the remarkable Qur'ānic style which paints future events so that we can visualise them now, as if they were taking place in front of our very eyes. The Qur'ān is revealed so that it is read to people in this life, in their own surroundings. But it portrays the scenes of the life to come as if they are taking place now, while scenes of this life belong to an era which has long since passed. In this way, we forget that the Day of Judgement is still to come. We feel that it is here, now. This is only made possible by the remarkable style of the Qur'ān: "*The life of this world has beguiled them. So they will bear witness against themselves that they were unbelievers.*" (Verse 130)

When the scene is complete, the address is made to God's Messenger (peace be upon him), his followers and to mankind generally. The address includes a comment on the judgement made against evil human beings and *jinn* and the fact that such a great multitude are condemned to the fire. Their fate is sealed only after they have testified against themselves that they continued to disbelieve despite receiving messengers who related to them God's revelations and warned them against what awaited them of God's punishment if they continued to reject the faith. The comment here makes it clear that God's punishment does not befall anyone without warning. God does not hold people accountable and does not punish them for their disbelief until after they have been shown the fact and received warnings from God's messengers who relate His revelations to them: "*And so it is that your Lord would never destroy a community for its wrongdoing, while they remain unaware.*" (Verse 131)

God's grace is such that in spite of the fact that He has shaped human nature in a way which makes it always keen to seek its Lord, and the fact that He has given human beings intelligence and understanding, He does not punish them for their disbelief until He sends them messengers to warn them. Their nature may deviate and their intellect may be lured away. Indeed, all human responses may be defective despite all the signs and indicators man sees in the world around him. Hence, God has assigned to His messengers the task of saving human nature and intellect from deviation and of making their receptive qualities open to what He has placed of indicators so that they can give the right responses. Punishment only comes after deliberate denial and rejection of the faith despite God's warnings and messages.

So man's nature and intellect do not provide immunity from error nor do they guarantee guidance to the truth and resistance to desire. Rather, all these must be supported by faith.

Another rule is stated concerning reward and punishment. It is applicable to believers and evil ones in equal measure: *"They all shall have their grades in accordance with their deeds. Your Lord is not unaware of what they do."* (Verse 132) The believers have their grades, one above the other, while the evil ones have their own grades, one sinking below the other. They attain or sink into their grades according to their deeds which have been monitored to the finest detail: *"Your Lord is not unaware of what they do."* (Verse 132)

Emphasis on Practical Details

God sends His messengers to human beings as a gesture of His grace. He Himself has no need of them, their worship or even their belief in Him. When they do well, they only benefit themselves both in this life and in the life to come. His grace is also seen in the fact that He grants a chance to the disobedient generation which continues to do wrong and to deny Him altogether, while He is able to destroy it completely and bring in its place a different generation: *"Your Lord is the self-sufficient One, the Merciful. If He so wills, He may remove you altogether and cause whom He wills to succeed you, just as He brought you into being out of other people's seed."* (Verse 133) Therefore, human beings must never forget that they survive only by God's grace, and that their existence depends on His will. Whatever power they enjoy, has been given to them by God. Theirs is not an intrinsic power or a self-determined existence. No one has any choice with regard to their coming into being, and no one determines what sort of power he can exercise. To remove them altogether and to bring another community in their place is very easy for God. After all, it is He who has brought them into being from the seed of a past generation so that they succeed that generation by His will.

This verse shakes the hearts of those wrongdoers who scheme, exceed their bounds, claim for themselves the authority to forbid things and make others lawful, and who argue about the validity of God's law. Yet they remain all the time within God's grasp. He can let them be or remove them altogether when He wills, and bring about whomever He pleases to succeed them. At the same time, these strong tones reassure the Muslim community of the rightness of its course of action, at a time when it faces the wicked designs, power and hostility of those who are evil. All are powerless when it comes to resisting God's will.

This is followed by another strong warning note: "*That which you are promised will inevitably come, and you cannot elude it.*" (Verse 134) You are all the time within God's grasp and subject to His will. It is He who determines your fate, and you cannot resist Him or escape from your fate. The Day of Resurrection, a scene from which has just been painted, awaits you. It will inevitably come. When it does, nothing will avail you against God Almighty.

The final comment includes an implicit, but highly effective warning: "*Say: My people! Do all that may be in your power, and I will do what I can. You shall come to know to whom the future belongs. Never will the wrongdoers attain success.*" (Verse 135)

This is a warning made by one who is certain that he follows the truth and who has complete trust in the power of the truth, and of the great power that supports the truth. The warning is made by God's Messenger (peace be upon him) who says that he is disclaiming any responsibility for them, confident that what he has is the truth, absolutely certain of his way. He is also certain that what they follow is error and their prospects are very gloomy indeed: "*Never will the wrongdoers attain success.*" (Verse 135) This is an unfailing rule. Those who associate partners with God will never be successful, because success is granted only by God. Those who do not follow His guidance are in deep error and will end up as miserable losers.

Why the Method of Slaughter is Important

This passage falls between two passages which differ greatly: the first speaks of slaughtered animals and the need to mention God's name at the time of slaughter, while the next passage speaks about fruit, cattle and children which are pledged for charity or made as offerings. This middle passage includes a number of facts which relate to pure faith and a number of scenes and statements that relate to the nature of believing in God or denying Him. It also speaks of the battle between those who are evil on the one side and the prophets and those who follow them on the other. It also contains a large number of inspirational elements similar to those included earlier in the *sūrah* when it spoke of the basic principles of faith.

It is worth our while to reflect on the fact that the Qur'ān attaches such importance to practical details of human life and how they are brought in line with God's law. It also emphasizes that they must always be based on the fundamental principle that the authority to legislate, or indeed the overall lordship in the universe, belongs only to God. It is pertinent perhaps to ask here why the Qur'ān gives such importance to this question.

The answer from the Islamic point of view, is that it is the summing-up of the question of faith and religion. In Islam, the central principle is belief in God's oneness: He is certainly the only God in the universe. When a Muslim declares that he believes that there is no deity other than God, he purges his mind of all traces of any concept that assigns Godhead to anyone other than God Almighty. Consequently, he is absolutely clear that all sovereignty and the authority to legislate belong solely to God. Making laws and regulations on matters of detail is the same as making them on larger issues: it is an exercise of the authority to legislate, which means that it is an exercise of Godhead. A Muslim can never accept this. Religion in the Islamic lexicon means that people submit in their practical life, as well as in their faith, to God alone. They accept no submission to anyone else. If issuing legislation is an exercise of Godhead, accepting such legislation is submission to that Godhead. A Muslim cannot attain the status of a believer, unless he submits to God alone in all matters, and rejects all submission to anyone else.

It is in this light that we should view the emphasis given in the Qur'ān to these principles of faith. We see an example of this emphasis in this *sūrah* which was revealed in Makkah, before the Prophet's migration to Madinah. As we have already said, the parts of the Qur'ān which were revealed in the Makkan period did not tackle the question of the Islamic system of government or the laws that govern the life of the Muslim community. They simply tackled the question of faith. Nevertheless, the *sūrah* attaches such great importance to the establishment of this basic principle concerning God's sovereignty and His authority to legislate for human life. This is profoundly significant in itself.

15

Intertwining Laws and Concepts

Out of the produce and the cattle He has created, they assign a portion to God, saying: "This is for God" – or so they pretend – "and this is for the partners we associate [with Him]". Whatever they assign to their partners never reaches God, but that which is assigned to God does reach their partners. How ill they judge! (136)

وَجَعَلُوا۟ لِلَّهِ مِمَّا ذَرَأَ مِنَ ٱلْحَرْثِ وَٱلْأَنْعَـٰمِ نَصِيبًا فَقَالُوا۟ هَـٰذَا لِلَّهِ بِزَعْمِهِمْ وَهَـٰذَا لِشُرَكَآئِنَا فَمَا كَانَ لِشُرَكَآئِهِمْ فَلَا يَصِلُ إِلَى ٱللَّهِ وَمَا كَانَ لِلَّهِ فَهُوَ يَصِلُ إِلَىٰ شُرَكَآئِهِمْ سَآءَ مَا يَحْكُمُونَ ۝

Thus have the partners they associate [with God] made the killing of their own children seem goodly to many idolaters, seeking to bring them to ruin and to confuse them in their faith. Had God willed otherwise, they would not have done so. Leave them, then, to their false inventions. (137)

وَكَذَٰلِكَ زَيَّنَ لِكَثِيرٍ مِّنَ ٱلْمُشْرِكِينَ قَتْلَ أَوْلَـٰدِهِمْ شُرَكَآؤُهُمْ لِيُرْدُوهُمْ وَلِيَلْبِسُوا۟ عَلَيْهِمْ دِينَهُمْ وَلَوْ شَآءَ ٱللَّهُ مَا فَعَلُوهُ فَذَرْهُمْ وَمَا يَفْتَرُونَ ۝

They say: "Such cattle and crops are forbidden. None may eat of them save those whom we permit" – so they falsely claim. Other cattle they declare to be forbidden to burden their backs; and there are cattle over which they do not pronounce God's name, inventing [in all this] a lie against Him. He will surely requite them for their inventions. (138)

وَقَالُوا۟ هَٰذِهِۦٓ أَنْعَٰمٌ وَحَرْثٌ حِجْرٌ لَّا يَطْعَمُهَآ إِلَّا مَن نَّشَآءُ بِزَعْمِهِمْ وَأَنْعَٰمٌ حُرِّمَتْ ظُهُورُهَا وَأَنْعَٰمٌ لَّا يَذْكُرُونَ ٱسْمَ ٱللَّهِ عَلَيْهَا ٱفْتِرَآءً عَلَيْهِ ۚ سَيَجْزِيهِم بِمَا كَانُوا۟ يَفْتَرُونَ ﴿١٣٨﴾

They also say: "That which is in the wombs of these cattle is reserved to our males and forbidden to our women." But if it be stillborn, they all partake of it. He will requite them for all their false assertions. He is wise, all-knowing. (139)

وَقَالُوا۟ مَا فِى بُطُونِ هَٰذِهِ ٱلْأَنْعَٰمِ خَالِصَةٌ لِّذُكُورِنَا وَمُحَرَّمٌ عَلَىٰٓ أَزْوَٰجِنَا ۖ وَإِن يَكُن مَّيْتَةً فَهُمْ فِيهِ شُرَكَآءُ ۚ سَيَجْزِيهِمْ وَصْفَهُمْ ۚ إِنَّهُۥ حَكِيمٌ عَلِيمٌ ﴿١٣٩﴾

Losers indeed are those who, in their ignorance, foolishly kill their children and declare as forbidden what God has provided for them as sustenance, falsely attributing such prohibitions to God. They have gone astray and they have no guidance. (140)

قَدْ خَسِرَ ٱلَّذِينَ قَتَلُوٓا۟ أَوْلَٰدَهُمْ سَفَهًۢا بِغَيْرِ عِلْمٍ وَحَرَّمُوا۟ مَا رَزَقَهُمُ ٱللَّهُ ٱفْتِرَآءً عَلَى ٱللَّهِ ۚ قَدْ ضَلُّوا۟ وَمَا كَانُوا۟ مُهْتَدِينَ ﴿١٤٠﴾

It is He who has brought into being gardens – both of the cultivated type and those growing wild – and the date-palm, and fields bearing different produce, and the olive

وَهُوَ ٱلَّذِىٓ أَنشَأَ جَنَّٰتٍ مَّعْرُوشَٰتٍ وَغَيْرَ مَعْرُوشَٰتٍ وَٱلنَّخْلَ وَٱلزَّرْعَ مُخْتَلِفًا أُكُلُهُ

tree, and the pomegranates, all resembling one another and yet so different. Eat of their fruit when they come to fruition, and give (to the poor) what is due to them on harvest day. But do not waste, for He does not love the wasteful. (141)

وَٱلزَّيْتُونَ وَٱلرُّمَّانَ مُتَشَٰبِهًا وَغَيْرَ مُتَشَٰبِهٍ كُلُواْ مِن ثَمَرِهِۦٓ إِذَآ أَثْمَرَ وَءَاتُواْ حَقَّهُۥ يَوْمَ حَصَادِهِۦ وَلَا تُسْرِفُوٓاْ إِنَّهُۥ لَا يُحِبُّ ٱلْمُسْرِفِينَ ۞

And of the cattle some are reared for work and others for food. Eat of that which God has provided for you as sustenance and do not follow Satan's footsteps; he is your open foe. (142)

وَمِنَ ٱلْأَنْعَٰمِ حَمُولَةً وَفَرْشًا كُلُواْ مِمَّا رَزَقَكُمُ ٱللَّهُ وَلَا تَتَّبِعُواْ خُطُوَٰتِ ٱلشَّيْطَٰنِ إِنَّهُۥ لَكُمْ عَدُوٌّ مُّبِينٌ ۞

Of cattle you have eight in [four] pairs: a pair of the sheep and a pair of the goats. Say: Is it the two males that He has forbidden, or the two females, or that which the wombs of the two females may contain? Tell me plainly if you are men of truth. (143)

ثَمَٰنِيَةَ أَزْوَٰجٍ مِّنَ ٱلضَّأْنِ ٱثْنَيْنِ وَمِنَ ٱلْمَعْزِ ٱثْنَيْنِ قُلْ ءَآلذَّكَرَيْنِ حَرَّمَ أَمِ ٱلْأُنثَيَيْنِ أَمَّا ٱشْتَمَلَتْ عَلَيْهِ أَرْحَامُ ٱلْأُنثَيَيْنِ نَبِّـُٔونِي بِعِلْمٍ إِن كُنتُمْ صَٰدِقِينَ ۞

And, likewise, a pair of camels and a pair of oxen. Say: Is it the two males that He has forbidden, or the two females, or that which the wombs of the two females may contain? Is it, perchance, that you were witnesses when God gave you

وَمِنَ ٱلْإِبِلِ ٱثْنَيْنِ وَمِنَ ٱلْبَقَرِ ٱثْنَيْنِ قُلْ ءَآلذَّكَرَيْنِ حَرَّمَ أَمِ ٱلْأُنثَيَيْنِ أَمَّا ٱشْتَمَلَتْ عَلَيْهِ أَرْحَامُ ٱلْأُنثَيَيْنِ أَمْ كُنتُمْ شُهَدَآءَ إِذْ وَصَّىٰكُمُ ٱللَّهُ بِهَٰذَا فَمَنْ أَظْلَمُ مِمَّنِ ٱفْتَرَىٰ

these commandments? Who could be more wicked than one who, without any real knowledge, invents lies about God in order to lead people astray? God does not guide the wrongdoers. (144)

عَلَى ٱللَّهِ كَذِبًا لِّيُضِلَّ ٱلنَّاسَ بِغَيْرِ عِلْمٍ إِنَّ ٱللَّهَ لَا يَهْدِى ٱلْقَوْمَ ٱلظَّـٰلِمِينَ ﴿١٤٤﴾

Say: In all that has been revealed to me, I do not find anything forbidden to eat, if one wishes to eat thereof, unless it be carrion, or blood poured forth, or the flesh of swine for all that is unclean – or a sinful offering over which any name other than God's has been invoked. But if one is driven by necessity, neither intending disobedience nor exceeding his bare need, then know that your Lord is much-forgiving, merciful. (145)

قُل لَّآ أَجِدُ فِى مَآ أُوحِىَ إِلَىَّ مُحَرَّمًا عَلَىٰ طَاعِمٍ يَطْعَمُهُ إِلَّآ أَن يَكُونَ مَيْتَةً أَوْ دَمًا مَّسْفُوحًا أَوْ لَحْمَ خِنزِيرٍ فَإِنَّهُ رِجْسٌ أَوْ فِسْقًا أُهِلَّ لِغَيْرِ ٱللَّهِ بِهِۦ فَمَنِ ٱضْطُرَّ غَيْرَ بَاغٍ وَلَا عَادٍ فَإِنَّ رَبَّكَ غَفُورٌ رَّحِيمٌ ﴿١٤٥﴾

To those who followed the Jewish faith did We forbid all animals that have claws; and We forbade them the fat of both oxen and sheep, except that which is in their backs and entrails and what is mixed with their bones. Thus did We requite them for their wrongdoing. We are certainly true to Our word. (146)

وَعَلَى ٱلَّذِينَ هَادُواْ حَرَّمْنَا كُلَّ ذِى ظُفُرٍ وَمِنَ ٱلْبَقَرِ وَٱلْغَنَمِ حَرَّمْنَا عَلَيْهِمْ شُحُومَهُمَآ إِلَّا مَا حَمَلَتْ ظُهُورُهُمَآ أَوِ ٱلْحَوَايَآ أَوْ مَا ٱخْتَلَطَ بِعَظْمٍ ذَٰلِكَ جَزَيْنَٰهُم بِبَغْيِهِمْ وَإِنَّا لَصَٰدِقُونَ ﴿١٤٦﴾

If they accuse you of lying, then say: Limitless is your Lord in His grace; but His punishment shall not be warded off from evildoing folk. (147)

فَإِن كَذَّبُوكَ فَقُل رَّبُّكُمْ ذُو رَحْمَةٍ وَسِعَةٍ وَلَا يُرَدُّ بَأْسُهُۥ عَنِ ٱلْقَوْمِ ٱلْمُجْرِمِينَ ۝

Those who associate partners with God will say: Had God so willed, neither we nor our fathers would have associated any partners with Him; nor would we have declared anything as forbidden. In like manner did those who have lived before them deny the truth, until they came to taste Our punishment. Say: Have you any certain knowledge which you can put before us? You follow nothing but conjecture, and you do nothing but guess. (148)

سَيَقُولُ ٱلَّذِينَ أَشْرَكُوا لَوْ شَاءَ ٱللَّهُ مَا أَشْرَكْنَا وَلَا ءَابَآؤُنَا وَلَا حَرَّمْنَا مِن شَىْءٍ كَذَٰلِكَ كَذَّبَ ٱلَّذِينَ مِن قَبْلِهِمْ حَتَّىٰ ذَاقُوا بَأْسَنَا قُلْ هَلْ عِندَكُم مِّنْ عِلْمٍ فَتُخْرِجُوهُ لَنَا إِن تَتَّبِعُونَ إِلَّا ٱلظَّنَّ وَإِنْ أَنتُمْ إِلَّا تَخْرُصُونَ ۝

Say: With God alone rests the final evidence. Had He so willed, He would have guided you all aright. (149)

قُلْ فَلِلَّهِ ٱلْحُجَّةُ ٱلْبَٰلِغَةُ فَلَوْ شَاءَ لَهَدَىٰكُمْ أَجْمَعِينَ ۝

Say: Bring forward your witnesses who will testify that God has forbidden this. If they so testify, do not you testify with them; and do not follow the wishes of those who deny Our revelations, and those who do not believe in the life to come and who consider others as equal to their Lord. (150)

قُلْ هَلُمَّ شُهَدَآءَكُمُ ٱلَّذِينَ يَشْهَدُونَ أَنَّ ٱللَّهَ حَرَّمَ هَٰذَا فَإِن شَهِدُوا فَلَا تَشْهَدْ مَعَهُمْ وَلَا تَتَّبِعْ أَهْوَآءَ ٱلَّذِينَ كَذَّبُوا بِـَٔايَٰتِنَا وَٱلَّذِينَ لَا يُؤْمِنُونَ بِٱلْءَاخِرَةِ وَهُم بِرَبِّهِمْ يَعْدِلُونَ ۝

323

Say: Come, let me tell you what your Lord has forbidden to you: Do not associate partners with Him; [do not offend against but, rather,] be kind to your parents; do not kill your children because of your poverty – We provide for you and for them; do not commit any shameful deed, whether open or secret; do not take any human being's life – which God has made sacred, except in the course of justice. This He has enjoined upon you so that you may use your reason. (151)

بِسْمِ ٱللَّهِ قُل تَعَالَوْاْ أَتْلُ مَا حَرَّمَ رَبُّكُمْ عَلَيْكُمْ أَلَّا تُشْرِكُواْ بِهِ شَيْئاً وَبِٱلْوَٰلِدَيْنِ إِحْسَٰناً وَلَا تَقْتُلُوٓاْ أَوْلَٰدَكُم مِّنْ إِمْلَٰقٍ نَّحْنُ نَرْزُقُكُمْ وَإِيَّاهُمْ وَلَا تَقْرَبُواْ ٱلْفَوَٰحِشَ مَا ظَهَرَ مِنْهَا وَمَا بَطَنَ وَلَا تَقْتُلُواْ ٱلنَّفْسَ ٱلَّتِي حَرَّمَ ٱللَّهُ إِلَّا بِٱلْحَقِّ ذَٰلِكُمْ وَصَّىٰكُم بِهِ لَعَلَّكُمْ تَعْقِلُونَ ﴿١٥١﴾

Do not touch the property of an orphan before he comes of age, except to improve it. Give just weight and full measure. We do not charge a soul with more than it can bear. When you speak, be just, even though it be against one of your close relatives. Be true to your covenant with God. This He has enjoined upon you so that you may bear it in mind. (152)

وَلَا تَقْرَبُواْ مَالَ ٱلْيَتِيمِ إِلَّا بِٱلَّتِي هِيَ أَحْسَنُ حَتَّىٰ يَبْلُغَ أَشُدَّهُ وَأَوْفُواْ ٱلْكَيْلَ وَٱلْمِيزَانَ بِٱلْقِسْطِ لَا نُكَلِّفُ نَفْساً إِلَّا وُسْعَهَا وَإِذَا قُلْتُمْ فَٱعْدِلُواْ وَلَوْ كَانَ ذَا قُرْبَىٰ وَبِعَهْدِ ٱللَّهِ أَوْفُواْ ذَٰلِكُمْ وَصَّىٰكُم بِهِ لَعَلَّكُمْ تَذَكَّرُونَ ﴿١٥٢﴾

Know that this is the way leading to Me, a straight path. Follow it, then, and do not follow other ways, for they cause you to deviate from His way. All this He has enjoined upon you so that you may remain God-fearing. (153)

وَأَنَّ هَٰذَا صِرَٰطِي مُسْتَقِيماً فَٱتَّبِعُوهُ وَلَا تَتَّبِعُواْ ٱلسُّبُلَ فَتَفَرَّقَ بِكُمْ عَن سَبِيلِهِ ذَٰلِكُمْ وَصَّىٰكُم بِهِ لَعَلَّكُمْ تَتَّقُونَ ﴿١٥٣﴾

Overview

This long passage speaks of legislation and the authority to promulgate laws and regulations. What is surprising about this passage, together with the two preceding it and the comments interspersed within them, is that they are included in a *sūrah* revealed in Makkah, when the subject matter of all Qur'ānic revelation was faith. Indeed, portions of the Qur'ān revealed in Makkah do not tackle any Islamic laws, except to establish the ideological basis of such legislation. This was due to the fact that there was no Islamic government to implement Islamic law. Hence, God did not wish that His law become a matter of theoretical discourse or academic study before the establishment of a society that submitted to God alone and which worshipped Him by obeying His law, or before the existence of a sovereign state to implement that law in everyday life. Thus, outlining the legal details was linked to people's practical ability to implement them. This is just one aspect of the serious and yet practical nature of the Islamic faith.

The fact that this long passage of detailed legislation occurs in a Makkan *sūrah* is indicative of the nature of this question. It is indeed a question of faith, one which acquires added seriousness in the general outlook of this religion of Islam. It is indeed its principal issue. However, before we comment on this passage and its provisions in detail, we would like to provide a general overview of its contents and a foretaste of its import.

The passage begins with a brief reference to a host of concepts that prevailed in *jāhiliyyah* days, and the pagan practices of the Arabs concerning their agricultural produce, livestock and children. In other words, these practices related to their economic and social set-up. The following are given by way of example:

1. They divided the provisions of sustenance God gave them, their crops and cattle into two portions, assigning one to God and claiming that they did this in accordance with God's law. They assigned the other portion to the deities they invented and who they considered as partners with God, having power over their lives, wealth and children: "*Out of the produce and the cattle He has created, they assign a portion to God, saying: 'This is for God' – or so they pretend – 'and this is for the partners we associate [with Him].'*" (Verse 136)

2. Having done so, they deal unfairly with the portion they assigned to God. They add a part of it to the portion assigned to their other deities or partners and never do the same with the other portion: *"Whatever they assign to their partners never reaches God, but that which is assigned to God does reach their partners."* (Verse 136)

3. They willingly kill their children, having been induced to do so by their partners. The partners in this case are their priests and lawmakers who initiate traditions which acquire a force of their own, relying on social pressure and ancient legends with their religious overtones. Such killing of children claimed the lives of their daughters in the first place for fear of poverty and shame. Occasionally, it claimed the life of a son, particularly when the slaughter of a son was made in the form of a religious offering. An example of this was the pledge made by 'Abd al-Muṭṭalib, the Prophet's grandfather, that should God give him ten sons to protect him, he would slay one of them as an offering to the gods: *"Thus have the partners they associate [with God] made the killing of their own children seem goodly to many idolaters, seeking to bring them to ruin and to confuse them in their faith."* (Verse 137)

4. They consecrated certain portions of their livestock and certain types of produce, falsely claiming that they could not be eaten without special permission from God. They also made certain animals unlawful to ride, and prohibited that God's name be mentioned over them at the time of slaughter or riding. They also prohibited such animals from being ridden at pilgrimage time, because pilgrimage involved glorifying God. They further claimed that all these restrictions had been ordered by God Himself: *"They say: 'Such cattle and crops are forbidden. None may eat of them save those whom we permit' – so they falsely claim. Other cattle they declare to be forbidden to burden their backs; and there are cattle over which they do not pronounce God's name, inventing [in all this] a lie against Him."* (Verse 138)

5. They also consecrated what was in the bellies of their cattle to their men, prohibiting them to their women. However, if it happened to be stillborn, they would allow both males and females to partake of it. They attributed such absurdities to

God: *"They also say: "That which is in the wombs of these cattle is reserved to our males and forbidden to our women." But if it be stillborn, they all partake of it. He will requite them for all their false assertions. He is wise, all-knowing."* (Verse 139)

Such were the concepts and traditions which characterized Arabian society in ignorant, pre-Islamic days. This long passage, occurring in a Makkan *sūrah*, seeks to put an end to them and to purge people's hearts and souls of their effects. The Qur'ān follows a deliberate, slow and detailed approach in order to achieve its purpose.

It begins first by declaring that those who in their ignorance kill their children and forbid themselves what God has provided for them are indeed losers. These concepts they attribute to God are declared to be both absurd and erroneous.

The Qur'ān then draws their attention to the fact that it is God who has given them their wealth which they misuse. It is He who has given them gardens, both of the cultivated and wild types. It is He who has created their cattle for them. The one who provides sustenance in this way is the one who exercises control and promulgates laws concerning the use of what He has provided. The Qur'ān uses here a host of images, such as scenes of produce, fruits as well as cultivated and wild gardens. It also reminds them of the cattle God has created, making some for riding and carrying goods and others for eating, with their hide, wool and hair usable in various ways. The Qur'ān refers to the life-long enmity between human beings and Satan. How is it, then, that they follow the footsteps of Satan and fulfil his bidding when he is their declared enemy?

The *sūrah* then speaks in full detail of the absurdity of their concepts concerning their cattle. These concepts are made to appear hollow, stupid and inconsistent. It concludes by asking them what basis they have for such absurd laws: *"Is it, perchance, that you were witnesses when God gave you these commandments?"* (Verse 144) Was it, then, a secret that you have been let into, or a commandment given specially to you? It follows this by describing the ghastly nature of the crime of inventing falsehood against God and trying to lead people astray. This condemnation is one of the most effective aspects of the Qur'ānic method.

The Qur'ān then states clearly who has the authority to legislate, outlining what this authority has actually made forbidden to Muslims.

It also mentions what God forbade the Jews in particular, while making it lawful to Muslims.

It then discusses how the Arab idolaters used to attribute to God's will the fact that they lived in ignorance, evidenced by their association of partners with God and the forbidding of what God had made lawful. Both actions carry the same legal status in God's view. It quotes their statements: "*Had God so willed, neither we nor our fathers would have associated any partners with Him; nor would we have declared anything as forbidden.*" (Verse 148) The *sūrah* makes it clear that such a statement can only be made by an unbeliever who denies the truth. Earlier generations of unbelievers maintained the same assertions until they were struck with God's might: "*In like manner did those who have lived before them deny the truth, until they came to taste Our punishment.*" (Verse 148) To associate partners with God is the same as the unauthorized declaration of anything as forbidden. Both are done by those who deny God's revelations. A rhetorical question is put to them concerning the basis of their assertions: "*Say: Have you any certain knowledge which you can put before us? You follow nothing but conjecture, and you do nothing but guess.*" (Verse 148)

The discussion is brought to a conclusion by inviting them to make an unequivocal declaration and clear testimony of their stand. This is the same invitation as the one made at the beginning of the *sūrah* concerning the very basis of faith. In both cases, the same expression, indeed the same terminology is used in order to indicate that the two aspects are the same: associating partners with God and legislating without His permission: "*Say: Bring forward your witnesses who will testify that God has forbidden this. If they so testify, do not you testify with them; and do not follow the wishes of those who deny Our revelations, and those who do not believe in the life to come and who consider others as equal to their Lord.*" (Verse 150) This verse makes it clear that those who promulgate these legislations are indeed the ones who follow their own desires, deny God's revelations and disbelieve in the life to come. Had they believed in what God has revealed and in the Day of Judgement, and had they followed God's guidance, they would not have legislated for themselves or for mankind anything that God has not permitted. Nor would they have described things as lawful or unlawful without God's permission.

The *sūrah* goes on to outline what God has actually forbidden. Here we have a collection of the basic principles of social life, beginning with the belief in God's oneness. Some of these principles include certain orders, but the prohibitions form the larger part. Therefore, they provide the overall title.

God has forbidden that divinity be ascribed to anyone other than Him. He has commanded all people to be kind to their parents and He has forbidden the killing of children out of poverty, reassuring people that He provides for them. He has also forbidden all types of indecency and shameful sin, whether committed in the open or in secret, as well as the killing of other human beings except in a just cause. He has also forbidden any tampering with the property of an orphan, except to improve it, until he has come of age. He has ordered that people should deal in fair weights and measures and ordered that justice be maintained in all types of statements and testimony. He has further ordered that people should fulfil their covenants with God. All this has been enjoined by God on people. Hence, they are reminded that it is their duty to fulfil it.

The passage as a whole gives prominence to the basic concept of faith and to the principles of Islamic legislation. The two aspects are closely intertwined in a perfectly consistent exposition, the significance of which is made clear to everyone who understands the Qur'ānic approach and what it drives at. At the end of this passage, with all that it has to say about faith and legislation, God's statement is absolutely clear: "*Know that this is the way leading to Me, a straight path. Follow it, then, and do not follow other ways, for they cause you to deviate from His way. All this He has enjoined upon you so that you may remain God-fearing.*" (Verse 153) The import of this whole passage is thus highlighted in a single statement which combines clarity with decisiveness.

Islamic law is just the same as Islamic faith with regard to describing a person or a situation as pagan or Islamic. Indeed, the law is part of the faith in this respect, or indeed it is the faith, since it is concerned with its practical implementation. This is a basic fact that is made clear in several Qur'ānic statements.

The concept of faith in the minds of those who believe in this religion of Islam has consistently moved away from this basic fact over a period of centuries. A great variety of evil means and methods have been used for this purpose. The result is that a great number of those who enthusiastically believe in this religion, let alone its opponents and those who are careless about religion altogether, have come to consider the question of legislation as separate from that of faith. Hence, their hearts do not warm to the question of legislation as they do to faith. Nor do they consider its cancellation or abrogation a departure from faith in the same way as the cancellation of a certain belief or a certain act of worship. This religion of Islam does not recognize any separation between faith, worship and law. What we see today is the result of a progressive departure induced by well-trained forces over a number of centuries. Their aim has always been to reduce the importance of the question of law and make it fade away in the minds of even those who are enthusiastic supporters of Islam. This is the central question in this Makkan *sūrah*, which is not meant to discuss the Islamic system or Islamic law, but rather devote itself to the discussion of the Islamic faith. The *sūrah* employs all manner of literary and linguistic stylistics and makes all sorts of statements when discussing a matter of detail concerned with social traditions. The reason is that this small matter is related to the much wider question of sovereignty which, in turn, has a direct bearing on the very basis of this religion and its very existence.

Those who describe idolaters as pagan and do not give the same description to those who receive their legislation from any oppressive authority, or claim that this description applies to the first but not to the second, neither read the Qur'ān properly nor understand the nature of Islam. They need to read the Qur'ān as it has been revealed and to take seriously what God states clearly: "*Should you pay heed to them, you will end up associating partners with God.*" (Verse 121)

Some of those of who try to defend Islam with zeal and vigour make much ado about whether a particular law, regulation or even statement is in harmony with the divine law or in conflict with it. They are aggrieved when they see some offences being committed here and there. Their attitude suggests that Islam is actually being implemented, but its application needs some improvement by preventing such offences. Enthusiastic and committed to Islam as these people are, they unwittingly do Islam a disservice, damaging its cause by concentrating on such petty preoccupations. What they actually do is to divert the power of faith that remains in society, concentrating it on such side issues. By so doing, they implicitly endorse the prevailing *jāhiliyyah* systems suggesting that they have an Islamic character and that they only need to make certain modifications or take some corrective measures in order to be fully

Islamic. The fact is that in such societies, the Islamic faith is non-existent since it does not express itself in a set-up that gives sovereignty to God alone.

For Islam to come into existence requires that sovereignty belongs to God alone. If this basic rule does not exist in practice, then the entire religion of Islam is non-existent. The problem which Islam faces today is the fact that certain tyrannical powers usurp God's authority and give themselves the right to promulgate laws, making certain allowances and restrictions concerning people's lives, fortunes, wealth and children. It is indeed the same problem the Qur'ān addresses with such clear and decisive statements, establishing a direct link between it and the concept of Godhead and people's submission to God. It is the issue that separates Islam from *jāhiliyyah*.

The main battle which Islam fought in order to establish itself was not against atheism, nor did it aim at the mere adoption of certain Islamic practices. Furthermore, the fight was not against social or moral corruption. These battles came later, after the battle seeking to establish the very existence of faith had been won. The main battle Islam fought in order to establish itself was over sovereignty and to whom it belonged. This was indeed the battle fought in Makkah, when Islam was striving to establish the faith, making no reference to its law or social system. The aim of that effort was to establish in people's minds that sovereignty cannot be claimed by a Muslim, nor can a Muslim accept that it belongs to anyone other than God. When this basic concept of faith was truly established in the minds of the small Muslim community in Makkah, God facilitated for them its implementation when they migrated to Madinah. Let those enthusiastic advocates of Islam today take another look at what they do and what they should do, after they properly understand the true meaning of Islam.

Let us now consider the verses of this passage in detail.

Temptation on the Way to Ruin

> *Out of the produce and the cattle He has created, they assign a portion to God, saying: "This is for God" – or so they pretend – "and this is for the partners we associate [with Him]". Whatever they assign to their partners never reaches God, but that which is assigned to God does reach their partners. How ill they judge!"* (Verse 136)

In discussing the concepts and traditions of ignorant Arabian society in relation to agricultural produce and cattle, the *surah* states clearly that it is God who creates crops and cattle. No one other than God provides sustenance for people, whether originating in the earth or emanating from the sky. The *surah* then follows this with a reference to their practices in respect of what God has provided for them. They divided it into parts, assigning a portion to God and another portion for the idols and deities they associated with Him. Needless to say, that portion ended up in the homes of the guards or the custodians attending those deities. Yet they deal unfairly with the portion they assign to God, as the Qur'ānic verse explains.

Ibn 'Abbās, the Prophet's cousin and Companion, reports: "When those people have taken stock of the food they have, they make it in lots, assigning a portion of it to God and another portion to their deities. If the wind blows from the side of the portion they have assigned to their deities so as to carry some of it and place it on top of what they have assigned to God, they take it back and put it where it was. However, if the wind blows in the other direction, they take no action, leaving what has been carried by the wind from God's portion to the portion of their deities where it landed. That is why God says about their action: *"How ill they judge!"* (Verse 136)

Mujāhid reports: "They used to set aside a portion of their crops for God, and another portion for the partners they associated with Him. If the wind took something from the first portion to land it on the portion of their partners, they left it there. On the other hand, if something of the portion of their partners was transferred by wind to God's portion, they took it back. They justified their action by saying that God was in no need of this."

Qatādah reports: Some ignorant people in the days of *jāhiliyyah* used to assign a portion of their crops and cattle to God, and a portion to the partners they associated with Him. If a part of what they kept to God was transferred accidentally to the portion they gave to their partners, they left it there. It the reverse happened, they would take back what came by accident to God's portion. If they suffered a drought or shortage of crops, they would not touch what they assigned to their partners, but they would use up what they assigned to God. Hence God says: *"How ill they judge!"* (Verse 136)

Al-Suddī reports: They used to give a portion of their property to God and assign to Him a certain area of their agricultural land and a similar one to their deities. Whatever crops were yielded in the portion of their deities was spent on those deities, and what was yielded in the portion left to God was given to charity. Should the portion given to their deities be used up or give a small yield, while the one going to God gave abundant yield, they would say: our deities need to be properly served and that requires funds. Therefore, they would take what they had assigned to God and spend it on their deities. On the other hand, if the land assigned to God delivered a poor yield, while the one given to their deities gave in abundance, they would say: had God so willed, He would have made His land yield more. They would not transfer to Him anything of what had been yielded to their deities. God says that had they been honest in their division, they would not have judged ill. How is it that they take from Me but they do not give to Me? That is the meaning of the concluding comment in this verse: *"How ill they judge!"* (Verse 136)[1]

Ibn Jarīr says: "The comment at the end of this verse, *'How ill they judge'*, is a description by God of what those unbelievers did. God the Almighty says that they have judged ill, since they take from His portion to give to their partners, and do not give Him any part of their partners' share. Thus God denounces them for their ignorance and lack of fairness. They not only set up partners which they claimed to be equal to the One who created them, but they also provided them with sustenance and bestowed His grace on them. Those deities which they claimed to be equal to Him can cause them no harm or benefit. Nevertheless, they give preference to them in what they assign".[2]

It is such absurdities that evil human beings and *jinn* referred to so that they could argue with the believers concerning their cattle and crops. It is evident that these practices served only their evil interests. For example, pagan priests and custodians of those deities and other chiefs, have vested interests in maintaining their influence on their followers, so as to make them adhere to false concepts and beliefs. They also have their own personal interests to serve. As a result of what they implant in their followers' minds, they are able to take to themselves what the unthinking masses assign to their deities. On the other hand, the evil *jinn* have a vested interest in leading human beings astray so that they bring them to ruin and confuse them in their faith.

---

1. All four reports are quoted by Al-Ṭabarī, *Jāmi' al-Bayān*, Dār al-Fikr, Beirut, 1984, Vol. 8, pp. 40–1.

2. Al-Ṭabarī, ibid., Vol. 8, p. 42.

In this way, they lead human beings to ruin in this life and to hell in the life to come.

Such practices prevailed in the ignorant Arabian society, but similar practices prevailed in other *jāhiliyyah* societies in Greece, Persia and Byzantium. Similar ones continue to be practised in Africa, India and a number of Asian countries. All these are simply methods of using one's property in a way that God does not sanction. Since such practices continue to be followed in today's *jāhiliyyah* societies, these latter ones are the same in their polytheism as the old ones. Ignorance is the basis of any situation which allows people's affairs to be conducted in conflict with what God has legislated. What form the conducting of such affairs takes is immaterial. The essence is the same although forms and appearances may differ.

> *Thus have the partners they associate [with God] made the killing of their own children seem goodly to many idolaters, seeking to bring them to ruin and to confuse them in their faith. Had God willed otherwise, they would not have done so. Leave them, then, to their false inventions.* (Verse 137)

The *sūrah* says that in the same way as the evil ones made it acceptable for people to assign part of their crops and cattle in a particular fashion, they also made the killing of their own children seem goodly to them. This is a reference to what people in Arabia used to do, when they buried their daughters alive for fear of poverty or shame. They even went beyond this and killed some of their sons in fulfilment of pledges they made to their deities. It is well known that 'Abd al-Muṭṭalib, the Prophet's grandfather, pledged to slaughter one of his sons, if God would favour him with ten sons.

It is clear that all these practices were accepted as normal in the ignorant society of Arabia. These were traditions established by human beings and followed by human beings. The partners mentioned in this verse are the evil ones among human beings and *jinn*, including the priests, the guards of temples and tribal chiefs as well as the evil ones among the *jinn* who whisper to their partners. The *sūrah* makes the purpose of all this deception very clear: "*Seeking to bring them to ruin and to confuse them in their faith.*" (Verse 137) Thus, they not only bring them to ruin but they also place them in utter confusion with regard to their faith, so that they lack a clear concept.

The ruin is evident. They kill their own children and they corrupt their own social life. As a result, people become like animals led by corrupt shepherds in whichever way those shepherds find their interest. The evil ones are thus able to exercise complete authority over the lives, the children and the property of the masses, killing and ruling them, while the masses are forced to submit with humility. This is the result of the mutual effects produced by confused concepts of faith and their influence on human beings and the prevalent social traditions. Together those concepts and traditions exercise enormous pressure to which people have to submit, unless they seek protection in a clearly outlined faith and unless they place all their affairs within a consistent standard.

False Absurdity or Absurd Falsehood?

Such blurred, confused concepts and the social traditions they establish to weigh heavily on the masses are not limited to the types known in bygone ignorant or *jāhiliyyah* societies. We find clearer versions of them in modern societies, in the form of customs and traditions which people feel to be inescapable, even though they are very hard to observe. Take, for example, the case of fashion and other observances which impose themselves on people, costing them at times what they cannot afford, taking a high position on their list of concerns and ultimately corrupting their moral values and whole lives. Nevertheless, people feel that they must comply with all these dictates: a particular fashion for morning, another for afternoon, and a different one for evening. One fashion imposes short dress, another dictates tight clothes, and a third makes people wear that which is ridiculous. In addition, there is an endless variety of cosmetics, and hair styles, etc. Who imposes all this humiliating subjugation and who lends it support and backing? When we look for the facts we find that it is backed by the major fashion houses, manufacturers and dressmakers, as well as the usurious banks and finance companies who lend money to the industry in order that they themselves win a large share of the profits. It is also supported by the Zionists who work hard to weaken all mankind so that they become the masters of the world. They do not give their support in the shape of heavy armour and military prowess. They support it by the concepts and values they initiate and then formulate in the shape of theories and cultural beliefs. Then they help to translate these into a code of social behaviour. They realize that theories are of little effect unless they are seen in practice in the shape of systems of government, a social structure and an unambiguous social code that people accept without question because its roots and branches are irretrievably interlinked.

It is all perpetrated by evil human beings and the *jinn*. The result is different forms and shapes of *jāhiliyyah*, but they all have the same roots and origins.

We certainly do not give the Qur'ān its due position if we read and understand it as a reference only to ancient forms of *jāhiliyyah*. It, indeed, refers to its countless forms in all periods of human life. It confronts every deviant situation, trying to put it back on the straight path defined by God.

Wicked as their schemes against the divine message are, and heavy as the pressures on it are, the Qur'ān makes little of the might of *jāhiliyyah*. It exposes its reality, something which could easily be overlooked because of its apparent strength. The fact remains that these evil ones and their patrons and supporters are within God's grasp and subject to His authority. They have no power of their own to enable them to do what they want. They can only do it because God has enabled them to play their game for a while in order to accomplish His purpose in putting His servants to a test. Had God willed otherwise, they would not have been able to do or achieve anything. Hence, the Prophet and the believers should pay little attention to those evil ones and should pursue their own objectives. As for the evil ones, the believers should leave them to God to punish them for their invented falsehood: "*Had God willed otherwise, they would not have done so. Leave them, then, to their false inventions.*" (Verse 137)

We need to mention here that they dare not admit that they originated these concepts and practices. Instead, they lie to God, alleging that He originated them, asserting that these concepts and practices were derived from the religion preached by the Prophets Abraham and Ishmael.

The evil ones in modern *jāhiliyyah* do the same. The vast majority of them feel unable to deny God publicly and denounce His faith as atheist Communists do. They resort instead to the same old tactics of the evil ones in ignorant Arabia, asserting that they respect religion, and alleging that their own legislation is based on that religion. This approach is all the more wicked because it blurs religious feelings in people's hearts. It must be re-emphasized that these feelings do not represent Islam, because Islam is a clear, practical code of living which must be implemented in real life. It is not an ambiguous emotion. By their wicked approach, evil people these days channel other's intrinsic religious zeal into non-Islamic structures.

With all this we find that people who are most enthusiastically religious concentrate all their power and efforts on the denunciation of some practical details which are largely marginal. They find these details highly objectionable, not realizing that the whole set-up is a non-Islamic one, totally usurping God's authority and denying His Godhead. By their naïve enthusiasm they actually promote these non-Islamic set-ups, imparting to them an Islamic colour. They, thus, implicitly endorse them as having a religious basis, although they deviate from religion in such matters of detail. Those enthusiastic people, then, play their part in strengthening those systems, serving in the same capacity as official religious institutions which claim to speak for Islam. It is well known that the religion of Islam has no clerical order and has no official spokesmen who wear the guise of priests, monks, or indeed any other guise.

> They say: "Such cattle and crops are forbidden. None may eat of them save those whom we permit" – so they falsely claim. Other cattle they declare to be forbidden to burden their backs; and there are cattle over which they do not pronounce God's name, inventing [in all this] a lie against Him. He will surely requite them for their inventions. (Verse 138)

Al-Ṭabarī, a leading commentator on the Qur'ān, says: "Here God Himself, limitless is He in His Glory, is telling us that those idolaters used to forbid certain things and make others lawful, at their own behest, without referring to any authority or permission from God."[3]

As has already been mentioned, those usurpers of God's authority who claimed to derive their legislation from God's law, assigned certain portions of their agricultural produce and cattle, dedicating them to the partners they associated with God. Then they said that such assigned cattle and produce were forbidden to them to eat. Indeed, they asserted that none would be permitted to eat from them except those which God permitted. Needless to say that the decision in such matters was

---

3. Al-Ṭabarī, ibid., Vol. 8, p. 44.

usually left to priests, clerics and chiefs. They also assigned certain types of cattle and determined that they were forbidden to ride. It is said that those were mentioned in the previous *sūrah* and given the Arabic titles *Baḥīrah, Sā'ibah, Waṣīlah* and *Ḥāmī*. They also assigned other cattle and prohibited God's name from being mentioned over them when they were ridden, milked or slaughtered. This is because they consecrated these to partners they associated with God and whose names they did mention. All these claims were lies they had fabricated against God.

Al-Ṭabarī says: "God describes their action saying that by their practices, they invent a lie against God. This means that when they outlined their prohibitions and made their claims, they were simply lying to God and asserting falsehoods against Him. This is because they attributed their prohibitions, as described in God's Book, to His own authority, claiming that it is He Who had forbidden them. God denies this, making their lies appear as they are, and telling His Messenger and the believers of their false claims."[4]

The Absolute Losers

Once again we find here a repeated example of the people of ignorance and their thoughts, some arrogantly boasting that life is matter, with others, unable to deny God altogether, claiming that faith is merely a matter of beliefs and has nothing to do with social, economic or political systems.

We should always be aware, however, that ignorant societies like these which establish a system giving sovereignty and the authority to legislate to human beings, rather than to God, claim at the same time that they respect religion and derive their system from it. Theirs is a very sly and wicked approach. International Zionist and Christian forces hostile to Islam have adopted this method in areas that used to be the home of the Islamic faith where God's law was implemented. These forces have now realized that their experience in Turkey, carried out by the false hero they created, has ended in failure. Nonetheless, their efforts played an important part in destroying the Islamic Caliphate, the last symbol of Islamic unity. But the experience, adopting an open

---

4. Al-Ṭabarī, ibid., Vol. 8, p. 47.

secular stand as it did, failed to provide a model system to be emulated by other countries in the region. By wrenching itself totally from religion, it gave itself an alien colour which was too hard for people still entertaining some religious sentiments to accept. Hence, in their subsequent attempts to achieve the same goal, international Zionist and Christian forces hostile to Islam tried not to repeat the mistake they made with Kemal Ataturk. They began to dress their new experiments around a religious mask. They allowed their new heroes to establish institutions with a superficially religious character. They stressed that in two ways: by direct, straightforward propaganda or by allowing these institutions to denounce some unimportant details so as to give the impression that the system's major aspects were religiously sound.

These Christian and Zionist institutions which we see mobilizing their forces, harnessing their alliance and benefiting from their past experience, continue to try to repair the damage which followed the Turkish experience. They claim that Ataturk's initiative was essentially an Islamic revivalist movement, that it was not secular in nature and, therefore, could not be said to have nothing to do with religion.

Orientalists, who provide intellectual support to Christian and Zionist imperialism, continue to exert strenuous efforts in order to show that Kemal Ataturk's experience was not an atheist one. But once we expose the Kemalist experience as essentially atheistic we curtail its role, confining it to its destruction of the last vestige of Islamic unity. This is certainly important, but Ataturk's efforts failed to produce anything further unlike other experiments in the region which aimed at channelling religious concepts and enthusiasm into endorsing un-Islamic systems and situations. These later experiments sought to change the very essence of Islam while at the same time claiming to be Islamic. They wanted to corrupt sound, well-established values in the name of Islam. Indeed, they wanted to impart an Islamic colour to *jāhiliyyah* itself, so that it could fulfil its task wherever ill-defined religious sentiments provided the necessary driving force. In this way, they offer a false leadership which seeks to drive the Muslim world astray and eventually deliver it to Zionist and Christian forces. Thus they hope to achieve the same goal which past Crusading and Zionist efforts, launched over a period of 1300 years, failed to achieve.

"They also say: That which is in the wombs of these cattle is reserved to our males and forbidden to our women. But if it be stillborn, they all

partake of it. He will requite them for all their false assertions. He is wise, all-knowing." (Verse 139) They had gone too far in adopting false concepts and misguided practices based on polytheism and idolatry. They had gone even further in giving human beings the authority to make certain types of cattle lawful and others forbidden, claiming that what they did was sanctioned by God. Thus they claimed that what was in the wombs of those cattle should be given to their men and forbidden for their women. However, if any of these were stillborn, it was shared out by all. Try as you may to find a reason or justification for this, you are bound to find nothing. It is merely the whims of those who invent a confused sort of religion.

The Qur'ānic comment here gives an implicit warning to those who have enacted these laws and falsely claimed that they form a part of divine faith: "*He will requite them for all their false assertions. He is wise, all-knowing.*" (Verse 139) He knows the facts as they are, and deals with them in accordance with His infallible wisdom.

When we look at these practices and the losses and sacrifices made willingly by those who adopted them, we wonder at the costs people are prepared to incur when they deviate from the straight path established by God. We wonder at the heavy burden imposed by superstition and the delusions of those who have gone astray. How can people accept to fetter themselves with false beliefs? How is it that they can accept that these beliefs claim the lives of their own children and create endless complications in their own lives? How is it that they accept such deviant beliefs when they have in front of their eyes the surety of faith and God's Oneness; a faith to release human minds from the chains of delusion, superstition and blind imitation. It releases human society from ignorance and its imposed burden. It liberates men from servitude to other creatures in the form of man-made laws and man-made values and standards. In place of all this, it establishes a well-defined, clearly understood, logical and disciplined faith and a practical code of living. It provides a clear vision of the truth of existence and human life. It not only liberates man from subservience to other creatures but it elevates him to the position of God's servant. That is the summit only prophets can achieve.

When humanity deviates from the straight path provided by God and sinks into ignorance, accepting subservience to false gods, it suffers a great loss here in this life, before the one it incurs in the life to come: "*Losers indeed are those who, in their ignorance, foolishly kill their children and declare as forbidden what God has provided for them as sustenance, falsely attributing such prohibitions to God. They have gone astray and they have no guidance."* (Verse 140)

They are absolute losers, because they have lost both this life and the life to come. They have lost their children, their own souls and minds and the position of dignity which God gave them when He released them from subservience to beings other than Himself. Instead, they willingly submit themselves to other deities which are themselves subject to God's power. Above all, they lost God's guidance when they lost His faith. Their loss is doubly confirmed and now they can hope for no guidance whatsoever: *"They have gone astray and they have no guidance."* (Verse 140)

The Originator of All Creation

The *sūrah* then puts them face to face with the eternal truth that they strayed away from. It has already referred to it when speaking of how the Arabs assigned a portion of their agricultural produce and cattle to God and another portion to the false deities which they associated with Him. Now the *sūrah* states clearly to them that although they dispense of such produce and cattle in ways suggested by evil beings, human and *jinn*, these have had no say whatsoever in their creation. It is God who created them all so that people could benefit from them and praise God for what He has created and worship Him alone. It must be stated here that God does not need their praise or worship, for He has no need of anything or anyone. He is compassionate and He knows that through praising and worshipping Him alone, people achieve what sets their world on the right course as they adopt the right faith. How is it then that they allow those who have created nothing to rule over the produce and cattle God has created? How is it that they give a portion of these to God and another portion to other beings, and even cheat with the portion they assign to God?

The Creator who gives sustenance is the Lord who owns all. Hence, it is not permissible for anyone to have any authority over the use of what He has created except by His permission stipulated in the law He has laid down. This law is fully explained in the message conveyed by His Messenger, not in what is claimed by those deities trying to usurp God's authority: *"It is He who has brought into being gardens – both of the cultivated type and those growing wild – and the date-palm, and fields bearing different produce, and the olive tree, and the pomegranates, all resembling one another and yet so different. Eat of their fruit when they come to fruition, and give (to the poor) what is due to them on harvest day. But do not waste, for He does not love the wasteful. And of the cattle some are reared for work and others for food. Eat of that which God has provided for you as sustenance and do not follow Satan's footsteps; he is your open foe.*" (Verses 141–2)

All praise is due to God who has created all those gardens, bringing life out of what is dead. Some of these gardens are of the cultivated type which human beings tend and support with trellis, posts and weed killing, and some are of the wild type that requires little or no attention or help from man. God has also made the palm tree and other types of cultivation, giving them different colours, tastes and shapes. It is God who has created the olives and the pomegranates with a wide range of varieties and yet all so similar. Furthermore, God has created the cattle and made some of them stand on high legs so that they can carry large loads and made others of shorter height and supplied them with wool or hair which can be used for making clothes.

It is God who has originated life on earth and given it such wide variety so as to satisfy the needs of human beings in their life on earth. In spite of these clear facts of creation, people still refer to beings other than God for rulings over the distribution of crops, cattle and wealth.

We often find references in the Qur'ān to the fact that it is God alone who provides the means of sustenance for people. This fact is often given as an argument in support of the principle that people should refer to God alone to determine how they conduct their affairs. The Creator who alone provides sustenance is, without question, the One who alone combines the overall Lordship of human life with total sovereignty, including the full authority to rule and legislate.

At this point, we are given a variety of scenes showing growing plants, the yielding of fruits, cattle and what God has provided for us in them all. These are given in order to add strength to the Islamic point of view concerning the authority to legislate just as they are also used to support the fact that Godhead belongs to God alone. In this way, both questions are made to appear a complete unit, as indeed they are in the Islamic faith. When plants and fruits are mentioned, God says: "*Eat of their fruit when they come to fruition, and give (to the poor) what is due to them on harvest day. But do not waste, for He does not love the wasteful.*" (Verse 141) The order to give to the poor what is due to them on harvest day is perhaps the reason why some reports suggest that this verse was revealed in Madinah. We have said in the Prologue to this *sūrah*, however, that this verse was also revealed in Makkah, because it is not possible that the Makkan parts of the *sūrah* could have been revealed without this verse. Had it been delayed until revelation was given in Madinah, there would be a gap in the passage. The order to give to the poor what is their due on harvest day does not necessarily refer to *zakāt*. Some reports suggest that this simply refers to charity which is not specified. *Zakāt*, however, and its specified measures were outlined in the second year after the Prophet's settlement in Madinah.

The Qur'ānic statement: "*Do not waste, for He does not love the wasteful*", can be construed as referring to charitable donations or to eating and personal use. It has been suggested that the early Muslims competed in giving to charity to a degree which made their action wasteful. Hence God orders them not to be prodigal.

Referring to cattle, God says to them: "*Eat of that which God has provided for you as sustenance and do not follow Satan's footsteps; he is your open foe.*" (Verse 142) Thus God reminds them that all the sustenance they have been given is provided by Him, the Creator of all. Satan has created nothing. How is it, then, that people follow Satan's dictates on how they should use what God has provided for them? He follows this with a reminder that Satan is their manifest enemy. How, then, can they follow Satan' s footsteps?

The *sūrah* then sheds ample light on the points around which ignorant misconceptions concentrate. These are examined in detail in order to expose their unjustifiable and indefensible absurdity. They realize that with regard to such misconceptions they have no leg to stand on: "*Of cattle you have eight in [four] pairs: a pair of the sheep and a pair of the goats. Say: Is it the two males that He has forbidden, or the two females, or that which the wombs of the two females may contain? Tell me plainly if you are men of truth. And, likewise, a pair of camels and a pair of oxen. Say: Is it the two males that He has forbidden, or the two females, or that which the wombs of the two females may contain? Is it, perchance, that you were witnesses when God gave you these commandments? Who could be more wicked than one who, without any real knowledge, invents lies about God in order to lead people astray? God does not guide the wrongdoers.*" (Verses 143–4)

The cattle over which all this controversy is about, and which is certainly created for them by God, as stated in the previous verse, are eight types, made in four pairs. Thus we have a pair of sheep and a pair of goats. Which of them has God forbidden? Or has He made what is in their wombs forbidden? *"Tell me plainly if you are men of truth."* (Verse 143) There is no room in such matters for guesswork. No legislation may be put into effect concerning them without clear authority.

As for the other types, we have a male and a female camel, as well as a male and a female cow. Again the question is asked: which of the two has God forbidden? Or is it that He has forbidden what is in their wombs? Besides, what authority is there to support such a prohibition? *"Is it, perchance, that you were witnesses when God gave you these commandments?"* (Verse 144) Were you present to witness God's commandments? The fact is that there is no prohibition without a clear order by God. He alone has the authority to forbid anything. Clear evidence must be given in support of any prohibition.

Thus all legislation must come from the same source. Since they falsely claimed that their laws enjoyed the backing of God's authority, they are immediately given a very stern warning: *"Who could be more wicked than one who, without any real knowledge, invents lies about God in order to lead people astray? God does not guide the wrongdoers."* (Verse 144) There can be no one more unjust or wicked than a person who invents a law which is not sanctioned by God and then claims that it is God's law in order to lead people astray. Such a person has no real knowledge. He only relies on his own conjecture or desire. Such people can never receive God's guidance, because they have severed themselves from all means of guidance. They have attributed partners to God without His approval. God does not grant guidance to those who are wrongdoers.

Prohibitions by the Most Gracious

The Arabs' absurdity exposed, they are now made to realize that the false concepts they held before Islam have no foundation whatsoever. They are given an example to reflect upon in that God has brought into existence all their crops and cattle, yet they felt they had the right to determine how these were allocated, either by following their own whims or acting on the inspiration of evil ones. They did so knowing that those who were evil did not create the crops and cattle, but that these were of God's creation. Hence, it is He who determines what use is to be made of His creation given to His servants as sustenance or property.

In these verses God spells out clearly to them what He has actually forbidden, making His prohibition clear through revelations, not through guesswork and imagination. It goes without saying that God has the authority to legislate, and that what He forbids is totally forbidden and what He makes lawful is absolutely lawful. No human being can have any say in this, and He has no partners to make a similar decision or to add to or amend His prohibition. Within the same context, we have here an explanation of what God has forbidden the Jews in particular, although He has made it lawful to the Muslims. This prohibition was by way of punishment to the Jews for their wrongdoing and their deviation from God's law.

> *Say: In all that has been revealed to me, I do not find anything forbidden to eat, if one wishes to eat thereof, unless it be carrion, or blood poured forth, or the flesh of swine — for all that is unclean — or a sinful offering over which any name other than God's has been invoked. But if one is driven by necessity, neither intending disobedience nor exceeding his bare need, then know that your Lord is much-forgiving, merciful. To those who followed the Jewish faith did We forbid all animals that have claws; and We forbade them the fat of both oxen and sheep, except that which is in their backs and entrails and what is mixed with their bones. Thus did We requite them for their wrongdoing. We are certainly true to Our word. If they accuse you of lying, then say: "Limitless is your Lord in His grace; but His punishment shall not be warded off from evildoing folk."* (Verses 145–7)

Al-Ṭabarī, a leading early commentator on the Qur'ān, says:

God, limitless is He in His glory, gives here clear instructions to His Prophet Muḥammad (peace be upon him). He is to say to those who had assigned a portion of God's creation of crops and cattle to Him and another portion to the partners they associated with Him, who had made certain types of cattle and crops forbidden so that none may eat of them save those whom they permitted, who made some cattle forbidden to ride, or made what was in the wombs of their cattle forbidden to their women, lawful

345

to their men, who made unlawful what God provided for them as sustenance, falsely attributing such prohibitions to God; he should ask them all: "Has a messenger sent by God come to you with such prohibitions? If so, then tell us about that. Or is it that you yourselves have been present, witnessing the issuing of God's commandments of prohibition? Or could it be that you heard Him as He made the prohibition and you acted on that? If so, then you are liars inventing falsehood against God. Should you make any such claim, people will know that you are liars.

The Prophet is further instructed to make it clear to them that he does not find in what has been revealed to him of God's Book anything forbidden to eat, including all that they claimed to be unlawful, except for four types: "*carrion*", which refers to an animal dying by itself without being properly slaughtered, or "*blood poured forth, or the flesh of swine*". All three types are pronounced to be "*unclean*" which means that they are impure. The fourth forbidden type is "*a sinful offering*" which refers to an animal slaughtered by an idolater and consecrated to one of the idols they associated with God. Such an offering is forbidden to make and to eat by anyone who believes in God.

Thus God, limitless is He in His glory, tells those unbelievers who argued with the Prophet and his Companions concerning the prohibition of carrion that God has made forbidden the very thing they were arguing about. As such, it is unlawful. On the other hand, that which the idolaters claimed to be forbidden remains lawful, since God has made it so. They were lying when they claimed that their prohibition relied on God's authority.[5]

Al-Ṭabarī then explains the proviso made in the concluding part of the same verse, "*But if one is driven by necessity, neither intending disobedience nor exceeding his bare need, then know that your Lord is much-forgiving, merciful.*" (Verse 145)

This means that if a person finds himself in a position which drives him to eat something of what God has forbidden: either carrion, or blood, or pork, or a sinful offering, he may eat that. The condition is that he must not intend any enjoyment by his

---

5. Al-Ṭabarī, ibid., Vol. 8, p. 69.

eating or merely to satisfy an ordinary case of hunger, and he must not intend any transgression by eating what God has forbidden or eating more than what is absolutely necessary to save himself from starving to death. God tells us that He is much-forgiving, merciful. He forgives him what he has done, although He could punish him if He so willed. His mercy is manifested by the fact that He has allowed that person to eat something forbidden when he is driven to it by sheer necessity. Again, God could have made that forbidden even in these extreme cases.[6]

There are considerable differences among scholars with regard to the degree of necessity which allows a Muslim to eat forbidden food and the limits of what he may eat of that food. Some scholars say that what is permitted is simply an amount which ensures that one does not perish, and only when the fear of death is real. Other scholars say that a person in such a situation may eat a full meal, while others allow him to carry with him a further quantity to eat again, if he fears that he may still be without food for a long time. We do not wish to discuss these views in detail. This brief reference to them is sufficient for our purposes.

Other things were forbidden to the Jews such as animals that have undivided hoofs. These included camels, ostrich, geese and ducks. The fat of oxen and sheep was also forbidden, except for that in certain parts of their bodies. The entirety of this prohibition was a punishment for their transgression beyond the limits set by God: "*To those who followed the Jewish faith did We forbid all animals that have claws; and We forbade them the fat of both oxen and sheep, except that which is in their backs and entrails and what is mixed with their bones. Thus did We requite them for their wrongdoing. We are certainly true to Our word.*" (Verse 146)

Here the reason for this prohibition is made absolutely clear. It is a special case for the Jews only. It is emphasized here that this is the truth, not what is claimed by the Jews that their grandfather Jacob, who was also called Israel, had forbidden himself all this and that they followed in his footsteps. All this was perfectly permissible to Jacob. It was forbidden to them after they transgressed. They were simply forbidden to have such types of food which were wholesome.

---

6. Al-Ṭabarī, ibid., Vol. 8, p. 72.

"If they accuse you of lying, then say: 'Limitless is your Lord in His grace; but His punishment shall not be warded off from evildoing folk'." (Verse 147) Your Lord is most gracious, and His grace is bestowed on us and on every believer, as well as on other people. Indeed His grace is extended to those who are God-fearing and to evildoers. He does not inflict His punishment straightaway on those who deserve it, but leaves them for a while as a gesture of His grace. Some of them may repent and mend their ways. However, when He decides to inflict His punishment on those who deliberately do evil, they cannot ward it off in any way. If He delays it, He only does so until He inflicts it at the time He chooses. This should be enough to ensure people pray for God's grace because God's power is limitless. His punishment is so severe. If they fear the prospect of His punishment, then they should seek to avoid it through His grace. God, who has created people and who knows how we think, touches on both our hopes and fears so that we may consider, reflect and respond.

The Ultimate Argument in Defence of Falsehood

At this point in the passage, their last argument with which they tried to justify their erroneous beliefs and misguided practices comes under close scrutiny. They claim that they did not adopt those ill-founded beliefs by choice; rather, they were compelled to do so. Had God wished that they did not believe in these other gods and deities, He would have prevented them from doing so, since He is certainly able to accomplish whatever purpose He has in mind: *"Those who associate partners with God will say: 'Had God so willed, neither we nor our fathers would have associated any partners with Him; nor would we have declared anything as forbidden.' In like manner did those who have lived before them deny the truth, until they came to taste Our punishment. Say: Have you any certain knowledge which you can put before us? You follow nothing but conjecture, and you do nothing but guess. Say: With God alone rests the final evidence. Had He so willed, He would have guided you all aright."* (Verses 148–9)

The question of free-will, free choice or compulsion has been the subject of lengthy and intense argument in the history of Islamic thought. Different schools of thought and intellectual groups and sects were always ready to defend their points of view. Greek philosophy and logic and Christian schools of divinity provided further ammunition in this fierce argument, complicating it still more and making it totally alien to the Islamic standpoint. Had those people on all sides of the argument adopted the simple, uncomplicated, serious and direct method of the Qur'ān, their arguments would not have taken this complicated course. Instead, they would have been spared much of their futile effort.

For our part, we examine the unbelievers' argument and the Qur'ānic reply only to find that the whole question is clear, simple and precise: "*Those who associate partners with God will say: "Had God so willed, neither we nor our fathers would have associated any partners with Him; nor would we have declared anything as forbidden'.*" (Verse 148) In other words, they argue that their idolatrous beliefs, their unsanctioned prohibitions as well as their false assertions are all part of divine law, and they blame it all on God's will and what He has determined for them. Had He willed otherwise, they would not have associated any partners with Him and would not have made anything unlawful.

What is the Qur'ānic reply to this claim? The Qur'ān declares that they lie the same way as those who had gone before them lied and denied the truth. Those earlier people who persisted with their denial of the truth were made to suffer God's punishment and experience His might. The same fate awaits the new liars who follow in their footsteps: "*In like manner did those who have lived before them deny the truth, until they came to taste Our punishment.*" (Verse 148) This statement should shake and awaken people so that they reflect on the lessons that can be learned from the experience of earlier peoples.

The second point in the Qur'ānic reply aims at correcting the human method of reflection and deliberation. God has given people certain orders to fulfil and forbidden them certain things. They can have absolutely certain knowledge of all this. As for God's will, it belongs to the realm that lies beyond the reach of human thought or human perception. They have no way of knowing it for certain. If this is the case and they cannot know the dictates of God's will for certain, how is it, then, that they use this argument? "*Say: Have you any certain knowledge which you can put before us? You follow nothing but conjecture, and you do nothing but guess.*" (Verse 148) God's orders and prohibitions are known to all with certainty. Why, then, do these people ignore such truth, in order to indulge in guesswork and follow paths that can lead them nowhere?

This is all that can be said on this question. God does not require people to know what He has chosen to keep to Himself of His will and how it operates. He only wants them to know what commandments He has issued to them and what things He has forbidden them so that they conduct their lives in accordance with these orders and prohibitions. When they try to acquire this knowledge, God states that He will guide them to it and open their hearts to receive it so that they may declare their submission to God. This is all that human beings need, it is all so clear and simple, and free from all the ambiguity imparted by endless controversy.

God is able, should He so will, to create human beings with a nature that can only follow His guidance. He is certainly able to force them to follow His guidance or to put His guidance in their minds so that they follow it without compulsion. However, He has willed otherwise. It is His will that He tests us by giving us the ability to follow His guidance or to remain in error. He wants to extend His help to those who wish to follow His guidance and make it easy for them, and, on the other hand, He wants to let those who follow error continue in their misguided ways. His will is done and it is manifested in the situation that shapes human life.

"Say: With God alone rests the final evidence. Had He so willed, He would have guided you all aright." (Verse 149) The whole issue is very clear and expressed in a plain and simple statement to ensure that it is perfectly understood by all human beings. The endless debates and arguments about it are alien to the Islamic approach. Not a single school of philosophy or divinity has been able to arrive at a comfortable conclusion as a result of its treatment of this question. This is due to the fact that the methods adopted by these schools have always been unsuitable to the nature of the question.

It is the nature of any fact that determines the method of its treatment and how it should be expressed. When we deal with a material truism, we cannot adopt the laboratory approach. Similarly, a mathematical truth cannot be the subject of intellectual hypotheses. Hence, a truth that relates to the realm beyond human perception must be treated in a totally different way, relying, as we have already explained, on the practical manifestation and appreciation of this truth in its own field. It is most important that this question of choice and compulsion should be expressed in a way that is different from the type of intellectual approach that has given rise to all kinds of controversy in most communities and generations.

This religion of Islam has been revealed in order to establish a practical situation governed by clear commandments and prohibitions. To try to involve divine will, which cannot be perceived by our senses, is to try to traverse uncharted regions without guidance. It is a total waste of effort, which can be used more constructively elsewhere.

A Very Clear Course to Follow

Finally, God instructs His Messenger (peace be upon him) to confront the idolaters asking them to bring witnesses who can support them over the question of legislation, in the same way as He challenged them at the beginning of the *sūrah* to produce witnesses over the question of Godhead. Early in the *sūrah*, God says to His Messenger: "*Say: What is weightiest in testimony? Say: God is witness between me and you. This Qur'ān has been revealed to me that I may thereby warn you and all whom it may reach. Will you in truth bear witness that there are other deities beside God? Say: I bear no such witness. Say: He is but one God. I disown all that you associate with Him.*" (Verse 19) At this particular point, God gives him this instruction: "*Say: Bring forward your witnesses who will testify that God has forbidden this. If they so testify, do not you testify with them; and do not follow the wishes of those who deny Our revelations, and those who do not believe in the life to come and who consider others as equal to their Lord.*" (Verse 150)

This is a tremendous and decisive challenge, giving a clear idea of the nature of this religion of Islam which treats all forms of associating partners with God on the same level. Thus, the open and manifest form of claiming that certain beings are deities is equal to the implicit one represented by usurping the authority to legislate and enacting laws that are not sanctioned by God. Their claim that their legislation is God's law is totally discounted. The Qur'ān also denounces as liars those who make such an attempt to usurp God's sovereignty and His authority to legislate, who deny God's revelations, who do not believe in the life to come, and who consider others as equal to Him. The expression used here is the same as that used in the opening verse of this *sūrah* to describe the unbelievers: "*All praise is due to God, who has created the heavens and the earth, and brought into being darkness and light; yet those who disbelieve regard other beings as equal to their Lord."* (Verse 1)

This, then, is God's verdict concerning those who usurp His sovereignty and exercise His authority to legislate. The verdict is made without any consideration of those people's claims that their laws are part of God's law. When God has given His verdict, no one can voice any different opinion.

If we want to understand why God makes such a verdict, and why He considers them as liars denying His revelations, and as unbelievers denying the life to come, the door is open to us to deliberate on this. Indeed, such deliberation is required of Muslims.

Perhaps it should be explained first that the Arabic term used in this verse to mean God's 'revelations' is often used to refer to 'the signs' God has placed in the universe pointing to Him, or to refer to His 'revelations' vouchsafed to His Messenger. If we take the first meaning, and consider that God describes them as liars denying His signs in the universe, then the description is true, because all these signs give the same message and the same testimony that God alone is the Creator who has no partners and who gives sustenance to all His creation. Hence, He is the owner of the universe, which means that He alone has the power to conduct all the affairs of the universe as He wishes. Therefore, anyone who does not acknowledge that sovereignty belongs solely to God is an unbeliever in all these signs in the universe. On the other hand, if we take the verse to mean that they do not believe in the Qur'ānic revelations, the description is again true. All these revelations are clear and decisive. They require people to believe that all sovereignty and authority to legislate for human life belongs to God alone. It is His law that should be implemented, and we should submit to His authority and rule.

They are also denounced as unbelievers in the life to come. A person who believes in such a life and is certain that he will come face to face with his Lord on the Day of Judgement will never make an act of aggression against God and His most essential quality of Godhead. He will never claim for himself something that belongs to God alone, namely, the right to legislate.

They are finally denounced as people who consider other beings as equal to their Lord. In other words they are idolaters in the same way as those Arabs who worshipped idols were unbelievers. Had they believed in God's oneness, they would not have attributed sovereignty and the authority to legislate to anyone else. Nor would they have accepted any claim by anyone that he has such an authority.

This is what appears to me to be the reason for God's judgement of those people who usurp His authority to legislate and who enact laws not sanctioned by Him. As has already been explained, the verdict describes them in three ways: as liars, denying God's signs or revelations, as liars who do not believe in the life to come and as idolaters. No Muslim can argue with this verdict. It is the final word which needs no further comment. Let every Muslim take heed and speak in a becoming manner about the verdict of the Almighty, the Wise.

Detailed Commandments for Human Life

Having challenged the unbelievers to produce their witnesses and rejected their claims concerning what they considered as forbidden, the *sūrah* gives a detailed outline of what God has truly forbidden. Side by side with the list of prohibitions, we find some positive commandments that must be observed. Failure to act on these is also forbidden. The list begins with the most important prohibition of all, namely, associating partners with God. Indeed, the first article of faith which establishes the principle of God's oneness provides the foundation for all prohibitions.

Say: Come, let me tell you what your Lord has forbidden to you: Do not associate partners with Him; [do not offend against but, rather,] be kind to your parents; do not kill your children because of your poverty – We provide for you and for them; do not commit any shameful deed, whether open or secret; do not take any human being's life – which God has made sacred, except in the course of justice. This He has enjoined upon you so that you may use your reason. Do not touch the property of an orphan before he comes of age, except to improve it. Give just weight and full measure. We do not charge a soul with more than it can bear. When you speak, be just, even though it be against one of your close relatives. Be true to your covenant with God. This He has enjoined upon you so that you may bear it in mind. Know that this is the way leading to Me, a straight path. Follow it, then, and do not follow other ways, for they cause you to deviate from His way. All this He has enjoined upon you so that you may remain God-fearing. (Verses 151–3)

When we reflect on these commandments, we find that they provide an outline of our religion as a whole. They form the most essential element in the life of the human conscience as they establish the principle of God's oneness. They are also most essential for the life of the human family and human community since they ensure mutual security within society and make cleanliness an important quality of all social transactions. They are indeed pivotal for human life, since they guarantee the rights of every individual, linking them to the need to fulfil the covenant that exists between God and His servants. This keeps these commandments on the right course outlined by the starting principle of believing in God's oneness.

When we look at the comment made at the end of these commandments, we find that God, limitless is He in His glory, states that they constitute the right path leading to Him. All other routes and tracks are deviant, leading away from Him.

It is an especially important issue that these three verses tackle. They follow immediately after the discussion on what may appear to be only a side issue regarding the practices of *jāhiliyyah* society. But this issue relates, in fact, to the most fundamental question of faith. Hence why it is linked to this most important list of commandments.

"Say: Come, let me tell you what your Lord has forbidden to you." (Verse 151) The Prophet is here instructed to speak to people and tell them what their Lord has forbidden to them, not what they allege to have been forbidden. It is their Lord who has made the following items forbidden, because His alone is the position of Lordship which includes the aspects of fostering and directing, as well as issuing legislation. Hence, He is only exercising His authority, because He is the Lord. God alone is the one who enjoys all rights of Lordship.

"Do not associate partners with Him." (Verse 151) This is the foundation upon which the structure of faith is built. It is to this rule that all duties and obligations should refer and from which all rights and privileges are derived. It must be properly established before any discussion of commandments, prohibitions, obligations, systems and laws can take place. The first and most important requirement is that people should acknowledge that God is their Lord who governs their lives in the same way as they believe in His oneness. No partner can be associated with Him either as a deity or as a Lord. People must acknowledge that God alone controls the universe and conducts its affairs, as He indeed holds them accountable on the Day of Judgement

for what they have done in this life and rewards them accordingly. They must also acknowledge at the same time and in the same measure that He alone has the authority to provide the law which human beings must administer and enforce.

This guiding principle, then, purges human conscience of all traces of associating partners with God, purges the human mind from all traces of superstition, human society from the traditions of ignorance and purifies human life from people's submission to one another.

All forms of associating partners with God are included under the first and most important thing to be forbidden, because they lead to every objectionable thing. It is the practice which should be most forcefully denied so that people can acknowledge that God is their only God, Lord, King and Sovereign. Hence, they address all their acts of worship to Him alone. Believing in God's oneness is, thus, the most important rule which cannot be replaced by any type of worship, moral value, human quality or action. Hence, the list of commandments begins with it: "*Do not associate partners with Him.*" (Verse 151)

It is important that we should consider what this Qurʾānic passage tells us before it details these commandments. In other words, we should know exactly what is meant by associating partners with God, which is the first of all forbidden things. The whole drift of this *sūrah* focuses on a single issue, which is God's sovereignty and authority to legislate. The verse preceding these three verses challenges the unbelievers to produce their witnesses. It begins with this instruction to the Prophet: "*Say: Bring forward your witnesses who will testify that God has forbidden this. If they so testify, do not you testify with them; and do not follow the wishes of those who deny Our revelations, and those who do not believe in the life to come and who consider others as equal to their Lord.*" (Verse 150)

We need to remember this verse and what we said earlier in order to understand what is meant by associating partners with God. It is indeed the association of partners with respect to Godhead and to God's sovereignty.

We need this constant reminder because Satan and his disciples' strenuous efforts to split this faith from its most essential concept have unfortunately resulted in the separation of two intertwined questions, namely sovereignty and faith. This is the reason that makes some well-meaning people who are keen to serve Islam focus their efforts on establishing the proper form of a particular act of worship or denouncing a certain moral aspect or legal violation. They seldom speak about the concept of legislation and to whom it belongs or its central position in the Islamic faith. They give importance to malpractices of secondary importance, but little do they care about the most important violation of God's law which seeks to establish human life on a principle different from the one that assigns to God alone the whole authority to legislate.

Before giving man any order, God states His commandment that partners must not be associated with Him. He states this at a point in the *sūrah* which demonstrates precisely what is meant by such an association. This is the rule which provides enlightenment between human beings and God, and provides the life of the community with a standard to which it must refer in all situations. It imparts to human life its basic values, so that it is no longer subject to human whims or to traditions based on such whims.

"Be kind to your parents; do not kill your children because of your poverty – We provide for you and for them." (Verse 151) This highlights the family tie between human generations. God knows that He is more kind and compassionate to human beings than their parents or children. Hence, He enjoins upon children to be kind to their parents and on parents to be kind to their children. He links this commandment to the recognition of His absolute Godhead and the acknowledgement of His unique Lordship. He tells them that He alone provides for their sustenance. Hence, they must not impose any severe conditions on parents in their old age or on children in their tender years. They must not fear poverty, because God provides sustenance for parents and children alike.

Forbidden to People of Sound Mind

"Do not commit any shameful deed, whether open or secret." (Verse 151) Since God has urged His servants to take good care of their families, He has also impressed upon them the need to maintain the family foundation, which is also the basis of society. This equates with purity, decency and chastity. Hence, they are forbidden to commit all types of indecency, whether openly or secretly. This prohibition is then closely related to the commandment immediately preceding it and to the first commandment. No family can survive and no community can prosper if they sink into shameful indecency, whether open or secret. Purity, cleanliness and chastity are the basic essentials for the healthy living of

both the family and the community. Those who like to see indecency spread throughout the community are the ones who try to weaken the structure of the family and to bring about society's collapse.

The Arabic term translated here as 'shameful indecency' refers, from the linguistic point of view, to everything that goes beyond its proper limits. The term is also frequently used to denote a particular type of indecency, namely adultery and fornication. It is most probably in this sense that the term is used here. The present context is one of enumerating certain forbidden beliefs and practices. Adultery is the one particularly meant here. If we were to take the general meaning of the word, we should remember that, murder and the squandering of an orphan's property are both indecencies, but associating partners with God is the greatest indecency of all. Hence, giving the term 'indecency' the narrower sense of adultery in this context is perhaps more fitting to the general drift of the *sūrah*. It also explains why the plural form is used here. The crime of adultery is normally preceded by actions and circumstances that are also indecent. Clothing which is too revealing, wanton behaviour, uninhibited flirtation with the opposite sex, shameless behaviour, speech and laughter, deliberate temptation and inviting adornments are all indecencies, leading to the ultimate one of adultery. All these may be brought into the open or kept secret. Some may be entertained within oneself, while others are expressed in words and actions. They all work together to destroy the structure of the family and to weaken the community from within. In addition, they leave their stains on people's consciences and limit their concerns to what is petty and abject. Hence, this prohibition follows immediately upon the commandments concerned with the relationship between parents and children.

Because all these indecencies have their own attraction and temptation, the *sūrah* tells us not to go near them. Staying away from them is the best way to avoid the preliminaries and attractions which could weaken one's resolve. Hence, to cast a second, penetrative look at a woman, after the first casual one, is forbidden, while mixing between men and women is kept within the limits of what is necessary. Wearing too many adornments, even using perfumes when going out are forbidden for women. Tempting movements and loud laughter are also disallowed in a pure Islamic social life. Islam does not like people to expose themselves to attraction as it only makes resistance harder. Islam believes in taking protective measures before there is any need to inflict punishments. It protects consciences, feelings and senses.

God knows His creation best and He helps protect them, for He is compassionate and all-knowing.

Those who provide all types of temptation and attraction, trying to unleash wild desires, utilizing verbal expression, pictures, films, stories, mixed camps as well as other methods of communication have a certain objective in mind. We know the purpose of their schemes, and we know what they would love to do with this religion and what they try to do to the life of the family and the community.

"*Do not take any human being's life – which God has made sacred, except in the course of justice.*" (Verse 151) These three offences, associating partners with God, adultery and murder are frequently mentioned in the Qur'ān in quick succession as things to avoid. This is because they are, in a sense, crimes of murder. The first, associating partners with God, murders sound human nature, while the second, adultery, is a murder of the community, and the third is a murder of individuals. When human nature is not nurtured by belief in God's oneness, it becomes dead.[7] The community which allows adultery to spread is a dead community, heading straight for destruction. We need only to remember the examples of the Greek, Roman and Persian civilizations, which all provide historical evidence supporting this fact. We can also see the beginnings of collapse and the eventual demise of the modern Western civilization after it has allowed this plague to corrupt its very structure and social fabric. Again, a society in which killing and vengeance killing are tolerated is one which is threatened with destruction. Hence, Islam prescribes very severe punishments for all these crimes, because it wants to protect its community from destruction.

Killing children by reason of poverty has already been forbidden. This is now followed by a prohibition of killing any human being. The way this prohibition is phrased suggests that every individual crime of murder seeks to kill the human soul in general. This is supported by the verse in the preceding *sūrah* which states: "*If anyone slays a human being, for anything other than in punishment of murder or for spreading corruption on earth, it shall be as though he had slain all mankind; and if anyone saves a human life, it shall be as though he had saved all mankind.*" (5: 32) The aggression used in killing is

---

7. Reference may be made to the comments given on Verse 122, which states: "*Is he who was dead and whom We have raised to life, and for whom We set up a light to see his way among men, to be compared to one who is in deep darkness out of which he cannot emerge? Thus do their deeds seem goodly to the unbelievers.*" [Chapter 13, pp. 298–301].

against the right to life and against humanity in general. It is on the basis of this rule that God has guaranteed that human life shall always be considered sacred. In addition, the Muslim community feels safe and secure in the land of Islam. Every individual in that community feels secure as he works and contributes to the life of that community. He is exposed to no risk except by the dictates of justice. Such justice which allows a human being to be killed is clearly explained in God's law. This is not left to anyone's decision or interpretation. Furthermore, its detailed explanation only became law after the Muslim state was established and had acquired enough power to be able to implement its laws.

This last point tells us something about the nature of this religion and how it operates in practical life. These rules which are essential to society were only explained in the Qur'ān at the appropriate time.

Before continuing with the list of prohibitions and commandments, the *sūrah* separates what has already been mentioned from what is to come by highlighting God's directives and commandments: "*This He has enjoined upon you so that you may use your reason.*" (Verse 151)

This comment is given in accordance with the Qur'ānic method which makes it clear that every instruction and every prohibition is given by God. This serves to enhance the impression that the authority which bids and forbids in human life belongs to God alone. This adds much weight to the effectiveness of these instructions and prohibitions. There is also a reference here to using our reason. Indeed, it is only logical that this authority is the only one to whom people submit. We have already mentioned that this authority belongs to God, the Creator, who provides sustenance and who controls every aspect in human life and in the life of the universe.

One last word remains which is to point out that the first group of commandments are perfectly harmonious within themselves, while the second group also contains its own harmony. Hence, each group is outlined in a separate verse, but the two verses maintain a perfect rhythm.

Maintaining the Path Leading to God

"*Do not touch the property of an orphan before he comes of age, except to improve it.*" (Verse 152) Every orphan feels weak within the community because he has lost his father who is supposed to bring him up well and protect him. His weakness, then, imposes a duty on the Muslim community, on the basis of the principle of mutual social solidarity which is central to the Islamic social system. An orphan used to find himself in total loss in pre-Islamic Arabian society. The frequent and varied Qur'ānic directives concerning the care that should be taken of orphans, and the stern warning occasionally added to these directives give us an impression of how orphans used to be badly treated in society. This continued to be the case until God selected an honoured orphan from that community to entrust him with the most noble task of all. He made that orphan, Muḥammad (peace be upon him), the bearer of His final message to mankind. He also made taking proper care of orphans one of the practices encouraged by Islam which gives its followers this kind of directive: "*Do not touch the property of an orphan before he comes of age, except to improve it.*" (Verse 152)

Therefore, anyone who is looking after an orphan must not touch that orphan's property except in a way which is certain to bring a good return to the orphan. He must protect that property and try to improve it until the orphan comes of age and becomes physically and mentally able to receive his property and make good use of it. Thus, the community adds to its ranks a useful member who obtains his full rights.

Scholars have different views concerning the stage when a person comes of age. According to 'Abd al-Raḥmān ibn Zayd and Imām Mālik, it signifies the attaining of puberty. According to Imām Abū Ḥanīfah, a person comes of age when he is twenty-five, while al-Suddī raises that higher to the age of thirty. Scholars of Madinah set two criteria for that stage: attaining puberty and showing maturity. No particular age is specified.

"*Give just weight and full measure. We do not charge a soul with more than it can bear.*" (Verse 152) This clearly applies to commercial transactions and requires people to do their best to ensure that everyone gets what is due to them. The *sūrah* provides a direct link between these transactions and faith, because this is the Islamic attitude. It is God who gives this directive and who urges people to give just weight and full measure.

Commercial transactions thus have a very real link with the question of Godhead and servitude. They are mentioned here in a context which clarifies that faith has a direct relationship with all aspects of life. *Jāhiliyyah* societies, past and present, separate faith and worship on the one side and laws and human dealings and transactions on the other. An example of this separation is related in the Qur'ān as it tells us about the Prophet Shuʿayb's people who said to him: *"Shuʿayb, does your praying require you to demand of us that we give up all that our forefathers used to worship, or that we refrain from doing whatever we please with our property?"* (11: 87) Hence, the Qur'ān makes this link between the rules governing financial and commercial transactions on the one hand and faith on the other, in order to make it clear that Islam makes both faith and human dealings integral parts of it, firmly established within its constitution.

"When you speak, be just, even though it be against one of your close relatives." (Verse 152) Here the Qur'ān elevates the human conscience, already refined through a sense of watching God, to the even higher level of being guided by belief in God and the need to fulfil His commandments. Within the context of blood relations there lies a human weakness. People tend to think that family relations dictate mutual support in all situations. A human being knows that he himself is weak and lives only a limited period of time. With his relatives he finds strength. The wider his relations extend, the more firmly established is his existence. It is through his relations that his presence in this world is extended to future generations. For all this, a man is weak when it comes to testifying for or against his relatives or to making a judgement between them and other people. Hence, the Qur'ān provides the necessary support so that a Muslim's conscience prompts him to say words of truth and justice, thinking only of his relationship with God and watching Him alone. This gives him the strength which outweighs by far any support he may have from his relatives, as he places his obligation towards God above his duties to his relatives.

Again this particular instruction seeks to remind people of their covenant with God: *"Be true to your covenant with God."* (Verse 152) It is part of that covenant that people should speak the truth, even when it affects their relatives. This covenant also requires people to give just weight and full measure and that they do not come near the property of an orphan except to improve it, and to treat human life as sacred, killing no one except in the course of justice. But before all this, the covenant which exists between human beings and God dictates that they must associate no partners with Him. This is a pledge made by them and is strongly impressed on their nature by its very constitution. It is God who has made human nature firmly related to its Creator, feeling His presence through the laws that cover its own existence and the existence of the universe.

The Qur'ānic comment on all these directives is a most appropriate one: "*This He has enjoined upon you so that you may bear it in mind.*" (Verse 152) They must always remember this covenant with God in all its details and its binding duties.

These basic rules are made crystal clear. They also provide a summary of the Islamic faith and its social legislation. They start with God's oneness and they conclude with the mention of man's covenant with God. They were preceded by a long discourse on sovereignty and the fact that it belongs to God alone. These rules, then, outline the straight path leading to God. Any path that deviates from this one can only lead to complete loss: "*Know that this is the way leading to Me, a straight path. Follow it, then, and do not follow other ways, for they cause you to deviate from His way. All this He has enjoined upon you so that you may remain God-fearing.*" (Verse 153)

With this verse, a long part of the *sūrah* is concluded. It starts with the verse saying: "*Is he who was dead and whom We have raised to life, and for whom We set up a light to see his way among men, to be compared to one who is in deep darkness out of which he cannot emerge? Thus do their deeds seem goodly to the unbelievers.*" (Verse 122) The conclusion, as we can observe, is highly inspiring and leaves us with a general but profound effect. Between the outset and the conclusion the question of sovereignty and the authority to legislate is presented in full clarity. As its discussion concentrates on certain points of detail, such as those concerned with agricultural produce, cattle, slaughtered animals and offerings, it is closely linked to the central question of faith in order to make it clear that it is part of it. This is why the Qur'ān deals with this question of sovereignty at such length and relates it to all other aspects of the *sūrah* which discusses the whole question of faith and explains basic issues of Godhead and servitude to God in a most unequivocal way.

God's path is a single one leading to Him. This is the path of maintaining that Lordship belongs only to God and that people must submit to Him alone. People must realize fully that sovereignty belongs only to Him and they must translate this into practice by accepting only His legislation in their practical life. Any path that differs with this can only lead them astray.

"*All this He has enjoined upon you so that you may remain God-fearing.*" (Verse 153) It is being conscious of God and fearing Him that ensures purity of faith and action. It is through remaining conscious of God and fearing Him that people can strengthen their resolve to always turn to God alone.

16

The Law of Divine Retribution

Moreover, We gave Moses the Book in fulfilment [of Our favour] upon him who would do right, clearly spelling out everything, and providing guidance and grace, so that they might believe in the meeting with their Lord. (154)

ثُمَّ ءَاتَيْنَا مُوسَى ٱلْكِتَبَ تَمَامًا عَلَى ٱلَّذِىٓ أَحْسَنَ وَتَفْصِيلًا لِّكُلِّ شَىْءٍ وَهُدًى وَرَحْمَةً لَّعَلَّهُم بِلِقَآءِ رَبِّهِمْ يُؤْمِنُونَ ١٥٤

And this is a Book which We have bestowed from on high, a blessed one. Follow it, then, and be conscious of God, so that you might be graced with His mercy. (155)

وَهَذَا كِتَبٌ أَنزَلْنَهُ مُبَارَكٌ فَٱتَّبِعُوهُ وَٱتَّقُوا لَعَلَّكُمْ تُرْحَمُونَ ١٥٥

[It has been given to you] lest you say, "Only two groups of people before our time have received revelations from on high; and we were unaware of what they learned." (156)

أَن تَقُولُوٓا إِنَّمَآ أُنزِلَ ٱلْكِتَبُ عَلَى طَآئِفَتَيْنِ مِن قَبْلِنَا وَإِن كُنَّا عَن دِرَاسَتِهِمْ لَغَفِلِينَ ١٥٦

Or lest you say, "If a Book had been revealed to us, we would surely have followed its guidance better than they did." Now then a clear evidence of the truth has

أَوْ تَقُولُوا لَوْ أَنَّآ أُنزِلَ عَلَيْنَا ٱلْكِتَبَ لَكُنَّآ أَهْدَى مِنْهُمْ فَقَدْ جَآءَكُم بَيِّنَةٌ مِّن رَّبِّكُمْ وَهُدًى وَرَحْمَةٌ

come to you from your Lord, and guidance, and grace. Who could be more wicked than he who denies God's revelations and turns away from them in disdain? We shall punish those who turn away from Our revelations in disdain with grave suffering for so turning away. (157)

فَمَنْ أَظْلَمُ مِمَّن كَذَّبَ بِـَٔايَٰتِ ٱللَّهِ وَصَدَفَ عَنْهَا سَنَجْزِى ٱلَّذِينَ يَصْدِفُونَ عَنْ ءَايَٰتِنَا سُوٓءَ ٱلْعَذَابِ بِمَا كَانُوا۟ يَصْدِفُونَ ١٥٧

Are they waiting for the angels to come to them, or for your Lord [Himself], or certain of your Lord's signs to appear? On the day when certain of your Lord's signs do appear, believing will be of no avail to any human being who did not believe before, or who did not put its faith to good uses. Say: Wait if you will; we too are waiting. (158)

هَلْ يَنظُرُونَ إِلَّآ أَن تَأْتِيَهُمُ ٱلْمَلَٰٓئِكَةُ أَوْ يَأْتِىَ رَبُّكَ أَوْ يَأْتِىَ بَعْضُ ءَايَٰتِ رَبِّكَ يَوْمَ يَأْتِى بَعْضُ ءَايَٰتِ رَبِّكَ لَا يَنفَعُ نَفْسًا إِيمَٰنُهَا لَمْ تَكُنْ ءَامَنَتْ مِن قَبْلُ أَوْ كَسَبَتْ فِىٓ إِيمَٰنِهَا خَيْرًا قُلِ ٱنتَظِرُوٓا۟ إِنَّا مُنتَظِرُونَ ١٥٨

As for those who have broken the unity of their faith and have become sects, you certainly have nothing to do with them. Their case rests with God. In time He will tell them the truth of what they were doing. (159)

إِنَّ ٱلَّذِينَ فَرَّقُوا۟ دِينَهُمْ وَكَانُوا۟ شِيَعًا لَّسْتَ مِنْهُمْ فِى شَىْءٍ إِنَّمَآ أَمْرُهُمْ إِلَى ٱللَّهِ ثُمَّ يُنَبِّئُهُم بِمَا كَانُوا۟ يَفْعَلُونَ ١٥٩

Whoever does a good deed shall be credited with ten times as much; and whoever does an evil deed will be requited with no more than its like. None shall be wronged. (160)

مَن جَآءَ بِٱلْحَسَنَةِ فَلَهُۥ عَشْرُ أَمْثَالِهَا وَمَن جَآءَ بِٱلسَّيِّئَةِ فَلَا يُجْزَىٰٓ إِلَّا مِثْلَهَا وَهُمْ لَا يُظْلَمُونَ ١٦٠

Say: My Lord has guided me to a straight way, to an ever-true faith; the way of Abraham, who turned away from all that is false, and was not of those who associate partners with God. (161)

قُلْ إِنَّنِي هَدَىٰنِي رَبِّيٓ إِلَىٰ صِرَٰطٍ مُّسْتَقِيمٍ دِينًا قِيَمًا مِّلَّةَ إِبْرَٰهِيمَ حَنِيفًا وَمَا كَانَ مِنَ ٱلْمُشْرِكِينَ ١٦١

Say: My prayers, my worship, my living and my dying are for God alone, the Lord of all the worlds. (162)

قُلْ إِنَّ صَلَاتِي وَنُسُكِي وَمَحْيَايَ وَمَمَاتِي لِلَّهِ رَبِّ ٱلْعَٰلَمِينَ ١٦٢

He has no partner. Thus have I been commanded, and I shall be the first of those who surrender themselves to Him. (163)

لَا شَرِيكَ لَهُۥ وَبِذَٰلِكَ أُمِرْتُ وَأَنَا۠ أَوَّلُ ٱلْمُسْلِمِينَ ١٦٣

Say: Am I, then, to seek a lord other than God, when He is the Lord of all things? Whatever wrong any human being commits rests upon himself alone. No one shall be made to bear the burden of another. In time, to your Lord you all must return; and then He will tell you the truth of all that over which you were in dispute. (164)

قُلْ أَغَيْرَ ٱللَّهِ أَبْغِي رَبًّا وَهُوَ رَبُّ كُلِّ شَيْءٍ وَلَا تَكْسِبُ كُلُّ نَفْسٍ إِلَّا عَلَيْهَا وَلَا تَزِرُ وَازِرَةٌ وِزْرَ أُخْرَىٰ ثُمَّ إِلَىٰ رَبِّكُم مَّرْجِعُكُمْ فَيُنَبِّئُكُم بِمَا كُنتُمْ فِيهِ تَخْتَلِفُونَ ١٦٤

He it is who has made you inherit the earth and has raised some of you by degrees above others, so that He might try you by means of what He has bestowed upon you. For certain, your Lord is swift in retribution; yet, He is indeed much-forgiving, merciful. (165)

وَهُوَ ٱلَّذِي جَعَلَكُمْ خَلَٰئِفَ ٱلْأَرْضِ وَرَفَعَ بَعْضَكُمْ فَوْقَ بَعْضٍ دَرَجَٰتٍ لِّيَبْلُوَكُمْ فِي مَآ ءَاتَىٰكُمْ إِنَّ رَبَّكَ سَرِيعُ ٱلْعِقَابِ وَإِنَّهُۥ لَغَفُورٌ رَّحِيمٌ ١٦٥

Overview

The main theme in the last part of the *sūrah*, which concentrates on God's sovereignty, authority to legislate, and their inter-relation with faith, continues in this passage. It speaks of the main principles of faith with regard to sovereignty and legislation, while the first part of the *sūrah* dealt with these main principles as they relate to faith. In this way the *sūrah* makes it clear that the issues relevant to law and sovereignty are the same as those that are relevant to faith. The Qur'ān asserts this fact most emphatically. As we study the *sūrah*, we realize that the same inspirations, scenes and expressions used in the first part are employed again in the second part.

This means that this second part of the *sūrah*

- Refers to divine books, God's messengers, revelation and the miracles unbelievers demanded;
- Speaks of the destruction that follows denying the truth after miracles have been shown;
- Speaks of the life to come and the rules concerning accountability and reward and punishment there;
- Refers to the total separation between God's Messenger (peace be upon him) and his people who regard certain beings as equal to their Lord, acknowledge other deities besides Him and accept the laws these deities enact for them. It directs the Prophet to declare decisively the true nature of his faith, clear, free of all equivocation and ambiguity;
- Makes it clear that there is one Lord for all the worlds. No believer may acknowledge any other lordship whatsoever;
- States God's ownership and control of everything in the universe. He assigns the role He wants human beings to play. It makes it clear that God is able to remove any group or community as He wills.

These very issues were also employed earlier in the *sūrah* when dealing with the greater question of faith in its totality and the relationship between God and His servants. That they are employed in both parts of the *sūrah* is clearly significant and easily appreciated by anyone who studies how the Qur'ān addresses its concerns.

This last passage of the *sūrah* begins by speaking about the book revealed to Moses, i.e. the Torah. This continues the discussion of

God's straight way at the end of the last passage which concluded with the verse stating: "*Know that this is the way leading to Me, a straight path. Follow it, then, and do not follow other ways, for they cause you to deviate from His way.*" (Verse 153) This suggests that God's way stretches long in history, as was outlined in previous divine messages. The most recent code of law given in these messages prior to Islam was that of Moses. To him, God revealed a book in which He spelled out everything, providing guidance and bestowing grace, in the hope that his people would believe in the resurrection and the meeting with their Lord: "*Moreover, We gave Moses the Book in fulfilment [of Our favour] upon him who would do right, clearly spelling out everything, and providing guidance and grace, so that they might believe in the meeting with their Lord.*" (Verse 154)

The *sūrah* then moves on to mention the new blessed book, which is closely related to the one revealed to Moses. It gives full details of the faith and the law which people are required to accept and implement consciously. This will ensure that people receive God's grace in both this life and the life to come: "*And this is a Book which We have bestowed from on high, a blessed one. Follow it, then, and be conscious of God, so that you might be graced with His mercy.*" (Verse 155)

This new book, the Qur'ān, was revealed so as to refute any argument the Arabs would have had. Thus, they would not be able to claim that they had not received a book similar to those vouchsafed to the Jews and Christians, or that they would have done better than them had they received such revelations. Now that they have a book revealed by God, anyone who denies it deserves a painful punishment: "*[It has been given to you] lest you say, 'Only two groups of people before our time have received revelations from on high; and we were unaware of what they learned.' Or lest you say, 'If a Book had been revealed to us, we would surely have followed its guidance better than they did.' Now then a clear evidence of the truth has come to you from your Lord, and guidance, and grace. Who could be more wicked than he who denies God's revelations and turns away from them in disdain? We shall punish those who turn away from Our revelations in disdain with grave suffering for so turning away.*" (Verses 156–7)

All arguments are ended with the revelation of this new book, but they continued to assign partners to God and enact legislation which they claimed to be part of God's law. How can they do this when God's book is readily available, containing nothing of what they allege to be God's law? Moreover, they persist in demanding miracles so that they can believe in God's book. Had these miracles been given to them, they would have spelled their inevitable doom: *"Are they waiting for the angels to come to them, or for your Lord [Himself], or certain of your Lord's signs to appear? On the day when certain of your Lord's signs do appear, believing will be of no avail to any human being who did not believe before, or who did not put its faith to good uses. Say: Wait if you will; we too are waiting."* (Verse 158)

At this point, God demarcates the line between His Prophet and all religions that do not acknowledge God's oneness, in both faith and law. He makes it clear that they will all return to Him when He will hold them to account and will reward them in accordance with His justice and grace: *"As for those who have broken the unity of their faith and have become sects, you certainly have nothing to do with them. Their case rests with God. In time He will tell them the truth of what they were doing. Whoever does a good deed shall be credited with ten times as much; and whoever does an evil deed will be requited with no more than its like. None shall be wronged."* (Verses 159–60)

The remaining verses of the *sūrah* provide its final rhythm in a devotional but decisive glorification of God. It sums up the most profound truism of the Islamic faith: God's absolute oneness and man's total submission to Him. It reflects the seriousness of the hereafter and individual responsibility and accountability in this life. It describes God's sovereignty as the Supreme Lord of all, and His assignment of vicegerency to whom He pleases. This extended glorification of God also gives us a splendid image of how the truth of Godhead is viewed in the purest and most sincere human heart; the heart of Muḥammad, God's Messenger (peace be upon him). It is an image only the Qur'ān can describe: *"Say: My Lord has guided me to a straight way, to an ever-true faith; the way of Abraham, who turned away from all that is false, and was not of those who associate partners with God. Say: My prayers, my worship, my living and my dying are for God alone, the Lord of all the worlds. He has no partner. Thus have I been commanded, and I shall be the first of those who surrender themselves to Him. Say: Am I, then, to seek a lord other than God, when He is the Lord of all things? Whatever wrong any human being commits rests upon himself alone. No one shall be made to bear the burden of another. In time, to your Lord you all must return; and then He will tell you the truth of all that over which you were in dispute. He it is who has made you inherit the earth and has raised some of you by degrees above others, so that He might try you by means of what He has bestowed upon you. For certain, your Lord is swift in retribution; yet, He is indeed much-forgiving, merciful."* (Verses 161–5)

Let us now look at this passage in detail.

A Book to Bring Mercy to Mankind

"Moreover, We gave Moses the Book in fulfilment [of Our favour] upon him who would do right, clearly spelling out everything, and providing guidance and grace, so that they might believe in the meeting with their Lord." (Verse 154) This verse starts with the conjunction, 'moreover', while in Arabic the conjunction used signifies 'then', but there is no time gap in the text here. The conjunction relates the statement following it to what occurs before it. That is, the instruction to the Prophet: *"Say: Come, let me tell you what your Lord has forbidden to you."* (Verse 151) This is followed by the statement: *"Know that this is the way leading to Me, a straight path."* (Verse 153) The present statement starting with 'moreover' is added to the two earlier statements as part of what the Prophet is instructed to convey to people, detailing with what God has forbidden, outlining the path to follow and showing the continuity from earlier messages.

The interpretation of the next clause, *"in fulfilment [of Our favour] upon him who would do right"*, according to al-Ṭabarī, is as follows: "We have given the Torah to Moses so as to complete the favours We have bestowed on him. Thus We perfect the honour We have granted him in reward for his obedience to his Lord and implementation of his religion. It spells out every thing he and his people need to know in order to put their faith in practice."[1]

According to Qatādah, the phrase, *'clearly spelling out everything'*, means that it gives a detailed outline of what is permissible and what is forbidden. Moreover, the Torah revealed to Moses provides his people with guidance and ensures mercy to them so that they may believe that they will meet their Lord and receive His grace that wards off His punishment.

---

1. Al-Ṭabarī, *Jāmi' al-Bayān*, Dār al-Fikr, Beirut, 1984, Vol. 8, p. 92.

The same purpose applies to the Book addressed to you. With it you may have guidance in addition to God's mercy: *"And this is a Book which We have bestowed from on high, a blessed one. Follow it, then, and be conscious of God, so that you might be graced with His mercy."* (Verse 155)

The Qur'ān is indeed a blessed book, as we have explained in Chapter 11: *"This is a blessed book which We have revealed, confirming what came before it, that you may warn the Mother City and all who dwell around it. Those who believe in the life to come do believe in it, and they are ever-mindful of their prayers."* (Verse 92) This Book was mentioned there within the context of faith in general. It is mentioned here in a similar statement, but in the context of jurisprudence. People are ordered to follow it, because receiving God's grace is made conditional on such following.

The Arabs who were the first to be addressed by the Qur'ān are told that with the revelation of this blessed book spelling out everything most clearly, all arguments and excuses are useless. Now that you have the Qur'ān, you do not need to refer to anything else. It covers all aspects of life. Therefore, they do not need to legislate for any purpose without guidance: *"[It has been given to you] lest you say, 'Only two groups of people before our time have received revelations from on high; and we were unaware of what they learned.' Or lest you say, 'If a Book had been revealed to us, we would surely have followed its guidance better than they did.' Now then a clear evidence of the truth has come to you from your Lord, and guidance, and grace. Who could be more wicked than he who denies God's revelations and turns away from them in disdain? We shall punish those who turn away from Our revelations in disdain with grave suffering for so turning away."* (Verses 156–7)

It has been God's will that every messenger was sent to his people, speaking their language. When He willed to send His final message, He sent the last of all prophets, Muḥammad, to all mankind. As His final Messenger, it is only right that he should address all mankind equally.

God forestalls the Arabs' argument should they say that Moses and Jesus were sent to their own people, while they, i.e. the Arabs, were oblivious of what the Jews and the Christians studied in their Books. They might have argued that had they received a book in their own language, addressed to them and providing guidance and warnings, they would have been better guided than the Jews and the Christians. Now this Book has been revealed and given to them by a Messenger from among them, even though he is a Messenger to all mankind. The Book he brings is, in itself, a clear proof of its truth. It gives them some very clear, unambiguous and unequivocal information. It provides them with guidance out of the error in which they live, and ensures God's grace will be bestowed on them in this life as well as in the life to come.

Bearing all this in mind, who could be more in the wrong than one who denies God's revelations and turns his back on them when they show him the way to goodness and success? Who is more unjust to himself and to mankind by denying himself and others all these blessings, and by spreading corruption on earth through upholding ignorant concepts and laws? Those who turn away from the truth have a malignant nature, just like the disease that affects a camel's hoof, causing it to become lop-sided. They are lop-sided in the sense that they cannot maintain a straight path to the truth. Their attitude qualifies them for the worst punishment: "*We shall punish those who turn away from Our revelations in disdain with grave suffering for so turning away.*" (Verse 157)

The Qur'ān uses this particular expression, borrowed from a physical condition to describe a mental one, so that the original sense imparts an added connotation. This is frequently employed in the Qur'ān. It describes an arrogant person as one who 'turns his cheek away from people' (31: 18). This is borrowed from the image of a disease affecting camels and humans, giving them a stiff neck, so that they lift their cheeks and turn them away. It also describes the useless deeds of the unbelievers as swelling and coming to nothing, giving an image of a camel grazing in a poisoned area. Its belly swells then it dies. In all this, the physical image is used to describe a mental situation in a highly vivid and inspiring manner.

Further Warnings

More warnings are added to answer their demands for physical miracles in order to believe in God's revelations. Similar warnings were given earlier in the *sūrah* where it addressed their denial of the faith altogether. Here the warnings are in relation to their denial of God's law and the need to implement it in life. Earlier in the *sūrah* we read:

"*They say: 'Why has not an angel been sent down to him?' If We had sent down an angel, all would have been decided, and they would have been allowed no further respite.*" (Verse 8) Here, at the end of the *sūrah*, the matter is clearly explained: "*Are they waiting for the angels to come to them, or for your Lord [Himself], or certain of your Lord's signs to appear? On the day when certain of your Lord's signs do appear, believing will be of no avail to any human being who did not believe before, or who did not put its faith to good uses. Say: Wait if you will; we too are waiting.*" (Verse 158)

This is a very clear and decisive warning. It has always been God's law that should a miracle been given and the unbelievers continue to reject the truth, they will inevitably be destroyed. Here, God tells them in plain terms that if only some of the signs they ask for were shown to them, they would be destroyed thereafter should they continue to disbelieve. They are further told that when some of God's signs are shown, they spell the end that renders all subsequent actions futile. Accepting the faith should come before this, and should be translated into practical action. Good action is always associated with true faith, as it is, in the Islamic view, the practical translation of faith.

A number of reports suggest that what is meant by the phrase, '*when certain of your Lord's signs do appear*', (Verse 158), is certain signs of the Day of Judgement, the appearance of which renders the acceptance of the faith and doing good works of no avail. Some scholars even mention some particular signs of the Day of Judgement. However, it is better to interpret this verse according to God's law that operates in this life. A similar warning was given earlier in the *sūrah*: "*They say: 'Why has not an angel been sent down to him?' If We had sent down an angel, all would have been decided, and they would have been allowed no further respite.*" (Verse 8)

It should be noted that the *sūrah* repeats what it has said within the context of faith and belief when it speaks about God's sovereignty and law. This is clearly seen and intentionally used to emphasize a particular fact. Hence, it is better to interpret the statements that occur here at the end of the *sūrah* in the same light as those which occur at its beginning, reading them as referring to the laws of nature God has set in operation. This is sufficient to understand the Qur'ānic statements without having to resort to something that we cannot fathom because it is beyond the reach of our perception.

Only One of a Kind

At this point the *sūrah* addresses God's Messenger, Muḥammad (peace be upon him), singling him out with his faith, law, way of life and operational mode. His faith is different from all creeds and religions known to mankind, including the erring ways of the Arab idolaters: "*As for those who have broken the unity of their faith and have become sects, you certainly have nothing to do with them. Their case rests with God. In time He will tell them the truth of what they were doing.*" (Verse 159)

This is the parting point between God's Messenger and his faith on the one hand and all other doctrines and creeds on the other. In the latter group we may include the idolaters who were divided into groups, sects, tribes and clans on the basis of the myths, traditions and disputes of *jāhiliyyah*, the Christians and Jews with their unending disputes and rivalries which break them into quarrelling blocs and states, as well as other creeds, ideologies, theories, and regimes that may surface at any time until the Day of Judgement.

God's Messenger has nothing to do with any of these. His faith is Islam, his law is God's book and his way of life is unique and independent. The Islamic faith cannot mix with any sort of belief or ideology; its law and system cannot merge with other systems and theories. No legal system or regime can carry a dual status of being Islamic and something else at the same time. Islam is independent of all creeds and colours; its legal, social, political and economic systems are clearly Islamic and have no other description. The Prophet has nothing to do with any other situation or condition at any time.

When a Muslim is faced with any faith other than Islam, his attitude to it is that of outright rejection. The same applies to any regime or situation where sovereignty is not acknowledged to God alone; or, in other words, where Godhead and Lordship are not recognized as belonging only to God. A Muslim takes a clear stand at the outset, rejecting all these creeds before trying to identify any similarities or conflict between them and Islam. According to God's standard, true religion is that of self-surrender to Him alone. The Prophet has nothing to do with anything produced by those who differed over their faith and did not establish their attitudes on the principle of self-surrender to God.

In God's sight, religion incorporates a law and a way of life. And God's Messenger has nothing to do with anyone who adopts a law and a way of life other than those approved by God. The question is viewed in its totality, without pausing to look at different details.

As for those who have split into groups over their faith, and about whom God has declared that His Messenger will have nothing to do with them, they will be judged by God, and then they will have to account for all their deeds: "*Their case rests with God. In time He will tell them the truth of what they were doing.*" (Verse 159)

As accountability and reward are mentioned here, God states what mercy He has committed Himself to show to His servants. He will reward every good deed done by a believer ten times its value. It is a condition that such a good deed is done by a believer, because with rejection of faith no deed remains good. On the other hand, a person who does a bad deed is requited with its like only. God will never be unjust to anyone or stint his or her reward: "*Whoever does a good deed shall be credited with ten times as much; and whoever does an evil deed will be requited with no more than its like. None shall be wronged.*" (Verse 160)

A Heart-Felt Appeal

At the end of the *sūrah* with its long discourse on legislation and sovereignty we have a devotional glorification of God which carries with it a pleasant rhythm and a decisive verdict. The beat is repeated in each verse as it starts with the same word, '*Say*'. Each verse touches the heart, where the core of oneness lies: the oneness of the creed, goal, Lord and worship. It also provides a total look at the universe and its laws: "*Say: My Lord has guided me to a straight way, to an ever-true faith; the way of Abraham, who turned away from all that is false, and was not of those who associate partners with God. Say: My prayers, my worship, my living and my dying are for God alone, the Lord of all the worlds. He has no partner. Thus have I been commanded, and I shall be the first of those who surrender themselves to Him. Say: Am I, then, to seek a lord other than God, when He is the Lord of all things? Whatever wrong any human being commits rests upon himself alone. No one shall be made to bear the burden of another. In time, to your Lord you all must return; and then He will tell you the truth of all that over which you were in dispute. He it is who has made you inherit the earth and has raised some of you by degrees above others, so that He might try you by means of what He has bestowed upon you. For certain, your Lord is swift in retribution; yet, He is indeed much-forgiving, merciful.*" (Verses 161–5)

This long and final comment, together with the opening of the *sūrah,* plays a fascinating, perfectly harmonious tune. Yet it is a comment which concludes the discourse on animal slaughtering, offerings, agricultural produce and all the regulations alleged by the people of ignorance to be laid down by God. All that they say is a shameless lie. So, what do we make of this comment? In fact we do not need to make any further explanation after all that we have already said on the subject.

"*Say: My Lord has guided me to a straight way, to an ever-true faith; the way of Abraham, who turned away from all that is false, and was not of those who associate partners with God.*" (Verse 161) This declaration expresses gratitude and trust, and overflows with certainty. We see the certainty in both the verbal expression in worship and its mental effect. The trust is derived from the bond with the Lord who guides and takes care of His servants. The gratitude is felt for being guided to a straight way that is free of diversion and crookedness. This straight way is the 'ever true faith' of Abraham, the father of this community who submitted himself to God in total devotion: "*the way of Abraham, who turned away from all that is false, and was not of those who associate partners with God.*" (Verse 161)

"*Say: My prayers, my worship, my living and my dying are for God alone, the Lord of all the worlds. He has no partner. Thus have I been commanded, and I shall be the first of those who surrender themselves to Him.*" (Verses 162–3) This expresses complete dedication, with every pulse and every life movement. It is a form of glorification of God and submission to Him in the most absolute of terms: it combines obligatory and voluntary prayer, life and death. All is dedicated to God alone, the Lord of all the worlds, who controls and sustains them all and conducts and determines all their affairs. It is the sort of submission to God that leaves out nothing within oneself, one's conscience or in life, without dedicating it totally to God. "*Thus have I been commanded*", and I understood and obeyed, and "*I shall be the first of those who surrender themselves to Him.*" (Verse 163)

"*Say: Am I, then, to seek a lord other than God, when He is the Lord of all things? Whatever wrong any human being commits rests upon himself alone. No one shall be made to bear the burden of another. In time, to your Lord you all must return; and then He will tell you the truth of all that over which you were in dispute.*" (Verse 164) This is a word that encompasses all the heavens and earth as well as all that is in or on them, every creature known or unknown to man, everything to be done or to take place in public or private. It puts them all under the umbrella of God's Lordship of everything in the universe. They must all submit to God's absolute sovereignty in faith, worship and law.

This verse asks rhetorically and in amazement: "*Am I, then, to seek a lord other than God, when He is the Lord of all things?*" (Verse 164) Am I to seek a lord other than God to be my master who conducts my affairs and determines my course in life, when I am accountable to God for my intentions and actions, and will be rewarded for whatever obedience or disobedience to God I do? Am I to seek a lord other than God when this whole universe is in His hand, and both you and I are sustained by Him?

Am I to seek a lord other than God when everyone will be requited for his or her sins? No one shall bear responsibility for anyone else's actions. "*Whatever wrong any human being commits rests upon himself alone. No one shall be made to bear the burden of another.*" (Verse 164) Am I to seek a lord other than God when to Him you must all return and face His reckoning of all that over which you are in dispute?

Am I to seek a lord other than God when it is He who has placed human beings on earth to inherit it, and placed some of them above others in their mental and physical abilities and in the provisions they receive. He does all this to test them, so that they may prove whether they are grateful or ungrateful to Him.

Am I to seek a lord other than God when He is swift in retribution, and He is the One who grants grace and forgiveness to all those who repent of their misdeeds? Am I to seek a lord other than God so as to replace his law, orders and rulings for those of God, when I have all these indications, inspirations and evidence pointing to the truth of God being the only Lord of the universe?

As we have said, these verses are a devotional prayer and a glorification of God's oneness, reflecting the splendid image of pure faith as God's Messenger (peace be upon him) feels it in his heart. It is an image the splendour of which cannot be expressed in human terms. Only the Qur'ān, God's own word, can express it fully in its unique style.

And as we have said, this last beat in the *sūrah* addressing the question of sovereignty and legislation is in full harmony with the early part of the *sūrah* where the issue addressed was that of faith. We see this clearly in verses like these: "*Say: Am I to take for my master anyone but God, the Originator of the heavens and the earth, who gives nourishment to all and Himself needs none? Say: I am commanded to be the first of those who surrender themselves to God, and not to be among those who associate partners with Him. Say: Indeed I would dread, were I to disobey my Lord, the suffering of an awesome day. He who is spared that shall have received His grace. This will be a manifest triumph.*" (Verses 14–16)

A Final Word

We do not need to repeat here what we have said time and again about the significance of such pairs of thoughts, expressions and rhythms that occur in both the early and later parts of the *sūrah*. They are simply different facets of the same truth, reflected at one time as a belief and faith, and at another as a code of living.

Now that the *sūrah* is completed, if we look back at its great dimensions, the wide range it covers and the profound depths it goes into, we are overwhelmed. It all takes a small number of pages, 165 verses and a limited number of clauses and sentences. Had this space been used by a human being, it would not have covered one-hundredth of this great panorama of scenes, truths, inspirations and indications, let alone the sublime level it attains and the superb expression it uses.

The *sūrah* has taken us on a fascinating and breathtaking journey, to look at the great truths of existence. It is a journey that covers the major and fundamental Islamic concepts.

It portrays the truth of Godhead in all its awesome glory, majesty, splendour and beauty. It holds in front of our eyes the truths of the universe, life and what lies beyond life which we cannot perceive with our limited faculties. It shows us the truth of God's will and how it initiates and obliterates, gives life and causes death, and runs the universe and all living things. It reflects the truth of the human soul: its depths, apparent and hidden pathways, desires and leanings, the guidance it follows and the errors it commits, how it reacts to the whispers of evil humans and *jinn*, as well as how it is led along the right or wrong way.

It portrays scenes of the Day of Judgement, the gathering of all creatures, their moments of great distress and moments of hope and happiness. It gives us scenes of human history on earth, and shots of the history of life and the universe.

The panorama it shows us is vast and extensive. We cannot sum it up in words. It can only be seen through the *sūrah* itself, with its surpassing excellence and inimitable style of expression. No wonder it is part of this blessed book.

All praise is due to God, the Lord of all the worlds.

> *He it is who has made you inherit the earth and has raised some of you by degrees above others, so that He might try you by means of what He has bestowed upon you. For certain, your Lord is swift in retribution; yet, He is indeed much-forgiving, merciful."* (Verse 165)

Index

379